T0325629

Twenty Lectures on Algorithmic Game Theory

Computer science and economics have engaged in a lively interaction over the past 15 years, resulting in the new field of algorithmic game theory. Many problems central to modern computer science, ranging from resource allocation in large networks to online advertising, involve interactions between multiple self-interested parties. Economics and game theory offer a host of useful models and definitions to reason about such problems. The flow of ideas also travels in the other direction, and concepts from computer science are increasingly important in economics.

This book grew out of the author's Stanford course on algorithmic game theory, and aims to give students and other newcomers a quick and accessible introduction to many of the most important concepts in the field. The book also includes case studies on online advertising, wireless spectrum auctions, kidney exchange, and network management.

Tim Roughgarden is an Associate Professor of Computer Science at Stanford University. For his research in algorithmic game theory, he has been awarded the ACM Grace Murray Hopper Award, the Presidential Early Career Award for Scientists and Engineers (PECASE), the Kalai Prize in Game Theory and Computer Science, the Social Choice and Welfare Prize, the Mathematical Programming Society's Tucker Prize, and the EATCS-SIGACT Gödel Prize. He wrote the book *Selfish Routing and the Price of Anarchy* (2005) and coedited the book *Algorithmic Game Theory* (2007).

Twenty Lectures on Algorithmic Game Theory

Tim Roughgarden
Stanford University, California

CAMBRIDGE
UNIVERSITY PRESS

CAMBRIDGE
UNIVERSITY PRESS

University Printing House, Cambridge CB2 8BS, United Kingdom

One Liberty Plaza, 20th Floor, New York, NY 10006, USA

477 Williamstown Road, Port Melbourne, VIC 3207, Australia

4843/24, 2nd Floor, Ansari Road, Daryaganj, Delhi - 110002, India

79 Anson Road, #06-04/06, Singapore 079906

Cambridge University Press is part of the University of Cambridge.

It furthers the University's mission by disseminating knowledge in the pursuit of
education, learning and research at the highest international levels of excellence.

www.cambridge.org
Information on this title: www.cambridge.org/9781107172661
10.1017/9781316779309

© Tim Roughgarden 2016

This publication is in copyright. Subject to statutory exception
and to the provisions of relevant collective licensing agreements,
no reproduction of any part may take place without the written
permission of Cambridge University Press.

First published 2016

A catalogue record for this publication is available from the British Library

Library of Congress Cataloging in Publication data
Names: Roughgarden, Tim.
Title: Twenty lectures on algorithmic game theory / Tim Roughgarden,
Stanford University, California.
Description: Cambridge : Cambridge University Press, 2016. | Includes
bibliographical references and index.
Identifiers: LCCN 2016028351 | ISBN 9781107172661 (hardback : alk. paper)
Subjects: LCSH: Game theory. | Algorithms.
Classification: LCC QA269 .R68 2016 | DDC 519.3–dc23
LC record available at https://lccn.loc.gov/2016028351

ISBN 978-1-107-17266-1 Hardback
ISBN 978-1-316-62479-1 Paperback

Cambridge University Press has no responsibility for the persistence or
accuracy of URLs for external or third-party internet websites referred to in
this publication, and does not guarantee that any content on such websites is,
or will remain, accurate or appropriate.

To Emma

Contents

Preface

Computer science and economics have engaged in a lively interaction over the past 15 years, resulting in a new field called *algorithmic game theory* or alternatively *economics and computation*. Many problems central to modern computer science, ranging from resource allocation in large networks to online advertising, fundamentally involve interactions between multiple self-interested parties. Economics and game theory offer a host of useful models and definitions to reason about such problems. The flow of ideas also travels in the other direction, as recent research in computer science complements the traditional economic literature in several ways. For example, computer science offers a focus on and a language to discuss computational complexity; has popularized the widespread use of approximation bounds to reason about models where exact solutions are unrealistic or unknowable; and proposes several alternatives to Bayesian or average-case analysis that encourage robust solutions to economic design problems.

This book grew out of my lecture notes for my course "Algorithmic Game Theory," which I taught at Stanford five times between 2004 and 2013. The course aims to give students a quick and accessible introduction to many of the most important concepts in the field, with representative models and results chosen to illustrate broader themes. This book has the same goal, and I have stayed close to the structure and spirit of my classroom lectures. Brevity necessitates omitting several important topics, including Bayesian mechanism design, compact game representations, computational social choice, contest design, cooperative game theory, incentives in cryptocurrencies and networked systems, market equilibria, prediction markets, privacy, reputation systems, and social computing. Many of these areas are covered in the books by Brandt et al. (2016), Hartline (2016), Nisan et al. (2007), Parkes and Seuken (2016), Shoham and Leyton-Brown (2009), and Vojnović (2016).

Reading the first paragraph of every lecture provides a quick sense of the book's narrative, and the "top 10 list" on pages 299–300 summarizes the key results in the book. In addition, each lecture includes an "Upshot" section that highlights its main points. After the introductory lecture, the book is loosely organized into three parts. Lectures 2–10 cover several aspects of "mechanism design"—the science of rule-making—including case studies in online advertising, wireless spectrum auctions, and kidney exchange. Lectures 11–15 outline the theory of the "price of anarchy"—approximation guarantees for equilibria of games found "in the wild," such as large networks with competing users. Lectures 16–20 describe positive and negative results for the computation of equilibria, both by distributed learning algorithms and by computationally efficient centralized algorithms. The second and third parts can be read independently of the first part. The third part depends only on Lecture 13, with the exceptions that Sections 16.2–16.3 depend on Section 12.4 and Section 16.4 on Lecture 14. The starred sections are the more technical ones, and they can be omitted on a first reading.

I assume that the reader has a certain amount of mathematical maturity, and Lectures 4, 19, and 20 assume familiarity with polynomial-time algorithms and $\mathcal{NP}$-completeness. I assume no background in game theory or economics, nor can this book substitute for a traditional book on these subjects. At Stanford, the course is attended by advanced undergraduates, masters students, and first-year PhD students from many different fields, including computer science, economics, electrical engineering, operations research, and mathematics.

Every lecture concludes with brief bibliographic notes, exercises, and problems. Most of the exercises fill in or reinforce the lecture material. The problems are more difficult, and often take the reader step-by-step through recent research results. Hints to exercises and problems that are marked with an "*(H)*" appear at the end of the book.

Videos of my classroom lectures in the most recent (2013) offering of the course have been uploaded to YouTube and can be accessed through my home page (`www.timroughgarden.org`). Lecture notes and videos on several other topics in theoretical computer science are also available there.

I am grateful to all of the Stanford students who took my course, which has benefited from their many excellent questions and comments. I am especially indebted to my teaching assistants: Peerapong Dhangwatnotai, Kostas Kollias, Okke Schrijvers, Mukund Sundararajan, and Sergei Vassilvitskii. Kostas and Okke helped prepare several of the figures in this book. I thank Yannai Gonczarowski, Warut Suksompong, and Inbal Talgam-Cohen for particularly detailed feedback on an earlier draft of this book, and Lauren Cowles, Michal Feldman, Vasilis Gkatzelis, Weiwei Jiang, Yishay Mansour, Michael Ostrovsky, Shay Palachy, and Rakesh Vohra for many helpful comments. The cover art is by Max Greenleaf Miller. The writing of this book was supported in part by NSF awards CCF-1215965 and CCF-1524062.

I always appreciate suggestions and corrections from readers.

Stanford University   Tim Roughgarden
Stanford, California   June 2016

Lecture 1

Introduction and Examples

This book has three parts, each with its own overarching goal. Lectures 2–10 develop tools for designing systems with strategic participants that have good performance guarantees. The goal of Lectures 11–15 is to understand when selfish behavior is largely benign. Lectures 16–20 study if and how strategic players reach an equilibrium of a game. The three sections of this lecture offer motivating examples for the three parts of the book.

1.1 The Science of Rule-Making

We begin with a cautionary tale. In 2012, the Olympics were held in London. One of the biggest scandals of the event concerned, of all sports, women's badminton. The scandal did not involve any failed drug tests, but rather a failed tournament design that did not carefully consider *incentives*.

The tournament design used is familiar from World Cup soccer. There are four groups (A, B, C, D) of four teams each. The tournament has two phases. In the first "round-robin" phase, each team plays the other three teams in its group, and does not play teams in other groups. The top two teams from each group advance to the second phase, while the bottom two teams from each group are eliminated. In the second phase, the remaining eight teams play a standard "knockout" tournament. There are four quarterfinals, with the losers eliminated, followed by two semifinals, with the losers playing an extra match to decide the bronze medal. The winner of the final gets the gold medal, the loser the silver.

The incentives of participants and of the Olympic Committee and fans are not necessarily aligned in such a tournament. What does a team want? To get as prestigious a medal as possible. What does the Olympic Committee want? They didn't seem to think carefully

1

about this question, but in hindsight it is clear that they wanted every team to try their best to win every match. Why would a team ever want to lose a match? Indeed, in the knockout phase of the tournament, where losing leads to instant elimination, it is clear that winning is always better than losing.

To understand the incentive issues, we need to explain how the eight winners from the round-robin phase are paired up in the quarterfinals (Figure 1.1). The team with the best record from group A plays the second-best team from group C in the first quarterfinal, and similarly with the best team from group C and the second-best team from group A in the third quarterfinal. The top two teams from groups B and D are paired up analogously in the second and fourth quarterfinals. The dominoes started to fall when, on the last day of round-robin competition, there was a shocking upset: the Danish team of Pedersen and Juhl (PJ) beat the Chinese team of Tian and Zhao (TZ), and as a result PJ won group D with TZ coming in second. Both teams advanced to the knockout stage of the tournament.

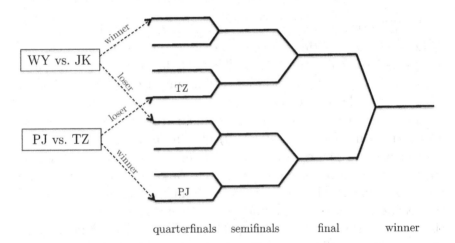

quarterfinals   semifinals   final   winner

Figure 1.1: The women's badminton tournament at the 2012 Olympics. Both WY and JK preferred to play TZ in as late a round as possible.

The first controversial match involved another team from China, Wang and Yu (WY), and the South Korean team of Jung and Kim (JK). Both teams had a 2-0 record in group A play. Thus, both were headed for the knockout stage, with the winner and loser of this match the top and second-best team from the group, respectively. Here was the issue: the group A winner would likely meet the fearsome TZ team in the semifinals of the knockout stage, where a loss means a bronze medal at best, while the second-best team in group A would not face TZ until the final, with a silver medal guaranteed. Both the WY and JK teams found the difference between these two scenarios significant enough to try to deliberately lose the match![1] This unappealing spectacle led to scandal, derision, and, ultimately, the disqualification of the WY and JK teams.[2] Two group C teams, one from Indonesia and a second team from South Korea, were disqualified for similar reasons.

The point is that, in systems with strategic participants, *the rules matter*. Poorly designed systems suffer from unexpected and undesirable results. The burden lies on the system designer to anticipate strategic behavior, not on the participants to behave against their own interests. We can't blame the badminton players for optimizing their own medal placement.

There is a well-developed science of rule-making, the field of *mechanism design*. The goal in this field is to design rules so that strategic behavior by participants leads to a desirable outcome. Killer applications of mechanism design that we discuss in detail include Internet search auctions, wireless spectrum auctions, the matching of medical residents to hospitals, and kidney exchanges.

Lectures 2–10 cover some of the basics of the traditional economic approach to mechanism design, along with several complementary contributions from computer science that focus on computational efficiency, approximate optimality, and robust guarantees.

1.2   When Is Selfish Behavior Near-Optimal?

1.2.1   Braess's Paradox

Sometimes you don't have the luxury of designing the rules of a game from scratch, and instead want to understand a game that occurs

---

[1] In hindsight, it seems justified that the teams feared the Chinese team TZ far more than the Danish team PJ: PJ were knocked out in the quarterfinals, while TZ won the gold medal.

[2] If you're having trouble imagining what a badminton match looks like when both teams are trying to lose, by all means track down the video on YouTube.

"in the wild." For a motivating example, consider *Braess's paradox* (Figure 1.2). There is an origin o, a destination d, and a fixed number of drivers commuting from o to d. For the moment, assume that there are two non-interfering routes from o to d, each comprising one long wide road and one short narrow road (Figure 1.2(a)). The travel time on a long wide road is one hour, no matter how much traffic uses it, while the travel time in hours on a short narrow road equals the fraction of traffic that uses it. This is indicated in Figure 1.2(a) by the edge labels "$c(x) = 1$" and "$c(x) = x$," respectively. The combined travel time in hours of the two edges in one of these routes is $1 + x$, where x is the fraction of the traffic that uses the route. Since the routes are identical, traffic should split evenly between them. In this case, all drivers arrive at d an hour and a half after their departure from o.

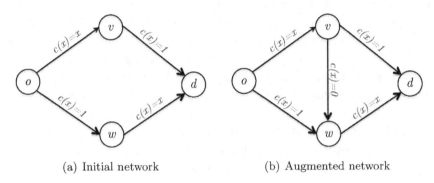

(a) Initial network   (b) Augmented network

Figure 1.2: Braess's paradox. Each edge is labeled with a function that describes the travel time as a function of the fraction of the traffic that uses the edge. After the addition of the (v, w) edge, the price of anarchy is $4/3$.

Suppose we try to improve commute times by installing a tele-portation device that allows drivers to travel instantly from v to w (Figure 1.2(b)). How will the drivers react?

We cannot expect the previous traffic pattern to persist in the new network. The travel time along the new route $o \to v \to w \to d$ is never worse than that along the two original paths, and it is strictly less whenever some traffic fails to use it. We therefore expect all drivers to deviate to the new route. Because of the ensuing heavy congestion on the edges (o, v) and (w, d), all of these drivers now experience *two* hours of travel time from o to d. Braess's paradox thus shows that the intuitively helpful action of adding a new superfast link can negatively impact all of the traffic!

Braess's paradox also demonstrates that selfish routing does not minimize the commute time of drivers—in the network with the teleportation device, an altruistic dictator could assign routes to traffic to improve everyone's commute time by 25%. We define the *price of anarchy (POA)* as the ratio between the system performance with strategic players and the best-possible system performance. For the network in Figure 1.2(b), the POA is $\frac{2}{3/2} = \frac{4}{3}$.

The POA is close to 1 under reasonable conditions in a remarkably wide range of application domains, including network routing, scheduling, resource allocation, and auctions. In such cases, selfish behavior leads to a near-optimal outcome. For example, Lecture 12 proves that modest over-provisioning of network capacity guarantees that the POA of selfish routing is close to 1.

1.2.2   Strings and Springs

Braess's paradox is not just about traffic networks. For example, it has an analog in mechanical networks of strings and springs. In the device pictured in Figure 1.3, one end of a spring is attached to a fixed support and the other end to a string. A second identical spring is hung from the free end of the string and carries a heavy weight. Finally, strings are connected, with a tiny bit of slack, from the support to the upper end of the second spring and from the lower end of the first spring to the weight. Assuming that the springs are ideally elastic, the stretched length of a spring is a linear function of the force applied to it. We can therefore view the network of strings and springs as a traffic network, where force corresponds to traffic and physical distance corresponds to travel time.

With a suitable choice of string and spring lengths and spring constants, the equilibrium position of this mechanical network is described by Figure 1.3(a). Perhaps unbelievably, severing the taut string causes the weight to *rise*, as shown in Figure 1.3(b)! To explain this curiosity, note that the two springs are initially connected in series, so each bears the full weight and is stretched out to a certain length. After cutting the taut string, the two springs carry the weight in parallel. Each spring now carries only half of the weight, and accordingly is stretched to only half of its previous length. The

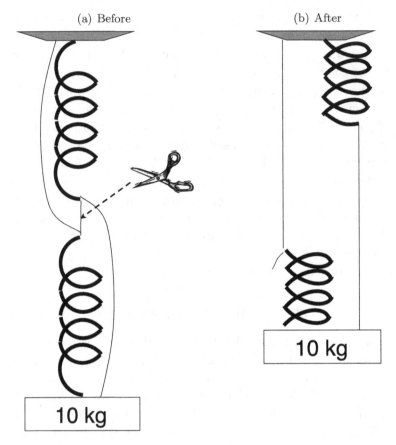

Figure 1.3: Strings and springs. Severing a taut string lifts a heavy weight.

rise in the weight is the same as the decrease in the commute time achieved by removing the teleporter from the network in Figure 1.2(b) to obtain the network in Figure 1.2(a).

1.3   Can Strategic Players Learn an Equilibrium?

Some games are easy to play. For example, in the second network of Braess's paradox (Figure 1.2(b)), using the teleporter is a no-brainer—it is the best route, no matter what other drivers do.

In most games, however, the best action to play depends on what the other players do. Rock-Paper-Scissors, rendered below in "bimatrix" form, is a canonical example.

	Rock	Paper	Scissors
Rock	0, 0	−1, 1	1, −1
Paper	1, −1	0, 0	−1, 1
Scissors	−1, 1	1, −1	0, 0

One player chooses a row and the other a column. The numbers in the corresponding matrix entry are the payoffs for the row and column player, respectively. More generally, a two-player game is specified by a finite strategy set for each player, and a payoff to each player for every pair of strategies that the players might choose.

Informally, an equilibrium is a steady state of a system where each participant, assuming everything else stays the same, wants to remain as is. There is certainly no "deterministic equilibrium" in the Rock-Paper-Scissors game: whatever the current state, at least one player can benefit from a unilateral deviation. For example, the outcome (Rock, Paper) cannot be an equilibrium, since the row player wants to switch and play Scissors.

When playing Rock-Paper-Scissors, it appears as if your opponent is randomizing over her three strategies. Such a probability distribution over strategies is called a *mixed* strategy. If both players randomize uniformly in Rock-Paper-Scissors, then neither player can increase her expected payoff via a unilateral deviation (all such deviations yield an expected payoff of zero). A pair of probability distributions with this property is a *(mixed-strategy) Nash equilibrium*.

Remarkably, allowing randomization, *every* game has at least one Nash equilibrium.

Theorem 1.1 (Nash's Theorem) *Every finite two-player game has a Nash equilibrium.*

Nash's theorem holds more generally in games with any finite number of players (Lecture 20).

Can a Nash equilibrium be computed efficiently, either by an algorithm or by strategic players themselves? In zero-sum games like Rock-Paper-Scissors, where the payoff pair in each entry sums to zero, this can be done via linear programming or, if a small amount of error can be tolerated, via simple iterative learning algorithms (Lecture 18). These algorithmic results give credence to the Nash equilibrium concept as a good prediction of behavior in zero-sum games.

In non-zero-sum two-player games, however, recent results indicate that there is no computationally efficient algorithm for computing a Nash equilibrium (Lecture 20). Interestingly, the standard argument for computational intractability, "$\mathcal{NP}$-hardness," does not seem to apply to the problem. In this sense, the problem of computing a Nash equilibrium of a two-player game is a rare example of a natural problem exhibiting intermediate computational difficulty.

Many interpretations of an equilibrium concept involve someone—the participants or a designer—determining an equilibrium. If all parties are boundedly rational, then an equilibrium can be interpreted as a credible prediction only if it can be computed with reasonable effort. Computational intractability thus casts doubt on the predictive power of an equilibrium concept. Intractability is certainly not the first stone to be thrown at the Nash equilibrium concept. For example, games can have multiple Nash equilibria, and this non-uniqueness diminishes the predictive power of the concept. Nonetheless, the intractability critique is an important one, and it is most naturally formalized using concepts from computer science. It also provides novel motivation for studying computationally tractable equilibrium concepts such as correlated and coarse correlated equilibria (Lectures 13, 17, and 18).

The Upshot

☆ The women's badminton scandal at the 2012 Olympics was caused by a misalignment of the goal of the teams and that of the Olympic Committee.

☆ The burden lies on the system designer to anticipate strategic behavior, not on the participants to behave against their own interests.

☆ Braess's paradox shows that adding a superfast link to a network can negatively impact all of the traffic. Analogously, cutting a taut string in a network of strings and springs can cause a heavy weight to rise.

☆ The price of anarchy (POA) is the ratio between the system performance with strategic players and the best-possible system performance. When the POA is close to 1, selfish behavior is largely benign.

☆ A game is specified by a set of players, a strategy set for each player, and a payoff to each player in each outcome.

☆ In a Nash equilibrium, no player can increase her expected payoff by a unilateral deviation. Nash's theorem states that every finite game has at least one Nash equilibrium in mixed (i.e., randomized) strategies.

☆ The problem of computing a Nash equilibrium of a two-player game is a rare example of a natural problem exhibiting intermediate computational difficulty.

Notes

Hartline and Kleinberg (2012) relate the 2012 Olympic women's badminton scandal to mechanism design. Braess's paradox is from Braess (1968), and the strings and springs interpretation is from Cohen and Horowitz (1991). There are several physical demonstrations of Braess's paradox on YouTube. See Roughgarden (2006) and the references therein for numerous generalizations of Braess's paradox. Koutsoupias and Papadimitriou (1999) define the price of anarchy. Theorem 1.1 is from Nash (1950). The idea that markets implicitly compute a solution to a significant computational problem goes back at least to Adam Smith's "invisible hand" (Smith, 1776). Rabin (1957) is an early discussion of the conflict between bounded rationality and certain game-theoretic equilibrium concepts.

Exercises

Exercise 1.1 Give at least two suggestions for how to modify the Olympic badminton tournament format to reduce or eliminate the incentive for a team to intentionally lose a match.

Exercise 1.2 Watch the scene from the movie *A Beautiful Mind* that purports to explain what a Nash equilibrium is. (It's easy to find on YouTube.) The scenario described is most easily modeled as a game with four players (the men), each with the same five actions (the women). Explain why the solution proposed by the John Nash character is not a Nash equilibrium.

Exercise 1.3 Prove that there is a unique (mixed-strategy) Nash equilibrium in the Rock-Paper-Scissors game.

Problems

Problem 1.1 Identify a real-world system in which the goals of some of the participants and the designer are fundamentally misaligned, leading to manipulative behavior by the participants. A "system" could be, for example, a Web site, a competition, or a political process. Propose how to improve the system to mitigate the incentive problems. Your answer should include:

(a) A description of the system, detailed enough that you can express clearly the incentive problems and your solutions for them.

(b) Anecdotal or demonstrated evidence that participants are gaming the system in undesirable ways.

(c) A convincing argument why your proposed changes would reduce or eliminate the strategic behavior that you identified.

Problem 1.2 Can you produce a better video demonstration of Braess's paradox than those currently on YouTube? Possible dimensions for improvement include the magnitude of the weight's rise, production values, and dramatic content.

Lecture 2

Mechanism Design Basics

With this lecture we begin our formal study of mechanism design, the science of rule-making. This lecture introduces an important and canonical example of a mechanism design problem, the design of single-item auctions, and develops some mechanism design basics in this relatively simple setting. Later lectures extend the lessons learned to more complex applications.

Section 2.1 defines a model of single-item auctions, including the quasilinear utility model for bidders. After quickly formalizing sealed-bid auctions in Section 2.2 and mentioning first-price auctions in Section 2.3, in Section 2.4 we introduce second-price (a.k.a. Vickrey) auctions and establish their basic properties. Section 2.5 formalizes what we want in an auction: strong incentive guarantees, strong performance guarantees, and computational efficiency. Section 2.6 presents a case study on sponsored search auctions for selling online advertising, a "killer application" of auction theory.

2.1 Single-Item Auctions

We start our discussion of mechanism design with *single-item auctions*. Recall our overarching goal in this part of the course.

Course Goal 1 Understand how to design systems with strategic participants that have good performance guarantees.

Consider a seller with a single item, such as a slightly antiquated smartphone. This is the setup in a typical eBay auction, for example. There is some number n of (strategic!) bidders who are potentially interested in buying the item.

We want to reason about bidder behavior in various auction formats. To do this, we need a model of what a bidder wants. The

11

first key assumption is that each bidder i has a nonnegative *valuation* v_i—her maximum willingness-to-pay for the item being sold. Thus bidder i wants to acquire the item as cheaply as possible, provided the selling price is at most v_i. Another important assumption is that this valuation is *private*, meaning it is unknown to the seller and to the other bidders.

Our bidder utility model, called the *quasilinear utility model*, is the following. If a bidder i loses an auction, her utility is 0. If the bidder wins at a price p, her utility is $v_i - p$. This is arguably the simplest natural utility model, and it is the one we focus on in these lectures.

2.2   Sealed-Bid Auctions

For the most part, we focus on a simple class of auction formats: *sealed-bid auctions*. Here's what happens:

> 1. Each bidder i privately communicates a bid b_i to the seller—in a sealed envelope, if you like.
>
> 2. The seller decides who gets the item (if anyone).
>
> 3. The seller decides on a selling price.

There is an obvious way to implement the second step—give the item to the highest bidder. This is the only selection rule that we consider in this lecture.[1]

There are multiple reasonable ways to implement the third step, and the choice of implementation significantly affects bidder behavior. For example, suppose we try to be altruistic and charge the winning bidder nothing. This idea backfires badly, with the auction devolving into a game of "who can name the highest number?"

2.3   First-Price Auctions

In a *first-price auction*, the winning bidder pays her bid. Such auctions are common in practice.

---

[1]When we study revenue maximization in Lectures 5 and 6, we'll see why other winner selection rules are important.

First-price auctions are hard to reason about. First, as a participant, it's hard to figure out how to bid. Second, as a seller or auction designer, it's hard to predict what will happen. To drive this point home, imagine participating in the following first-price auction. Your valuation (in dollars) for the item for sale is the number of your birth month plus the day of your birth. Thus, your valuation is somewhere between 2 (for January 1) and 43 (for December 31). Suppose there is exactly one other bidder (drawn at random from the world) whose valuation is determined in the same way. What bid would you submit to maximize your expected utility? Would it help to know your opponent's birthday? Would your answer change if you knew there were two other bidders in the auction rather than one?[2]

2.4   Second-Price Auctions and Dominant Strategies

We now focus on a different single-item auction, also common in practice, which is much easier to reason about. What happens when you win an eBay auction? If you bid $100 and win, do you pay $100? Not necessarily: eBay uses a "proxy bidder" that increases your bid on your behalf until your maximum bid is reached, or until you are the highest bidder, whichever comes first. For example, if the highest other bid is only $90, then you only pay $90 (plus a small increment) rather than your maximum bid of $100. *If you win an eBay auction, the sale price is essentially the highest other bid—the second highest overall.*

A *second-price* or *Vickrey* auction is a sealed-bid auction in which the highest bidder wins and pays a price equal to the second-highest bid. To state the most important property of second-price auctions, we define a *dominant strategy* as a strategy (i.e., a bid) that is guaranteed to maximize a bidder's utility, no matter what the other bidders do.

Proposition 2.1 (Incentives in Second-Price Auctions) *In a second-price auction, every bidder i has a dominant strategy: set the bid b_i equal to her private valuation v_i.*

Proposition 2.1 implies that second-price auctions are particularly easy to participate in. When selecting a bid, a bidder doesn't need

---

[2]For more on the theory of first-price auctions, see Problem 5.3.

to reason about the other bidders in any way—how many there are, what their valuations are, whether or not they bid truthfully, etc. This is completely different from a first-price auction, where it never makes sense to bid one's valuation—this guarantees zero utility—and the optimal amount to underbid depends on the bids of the other bidders.

Proof of Proposition 2.1: Fix an arbitrary bidder i, valuation v_i, and the bids $\mathbf{b}_{-i}$ of the other bidders. Here $\mathbf{b}_{-i}$ means the vector $\mathbf{b}$ of all bids, but with the ith component removed.[3] We need to show that bidder i's utility is maximized by setting $b_i = v_i$.

Let $B = \max_{j \neq i} b_j$ denote the highest bid by some other bidder. What's special about a second-price auction is that, even though there are an infinite number of bids that i could make, only two distinct outcomes can result. If $b_i < B$, then i loses and receives utility 0. If $b_i \geq B$, then i wins at price B and receives utility $v_i - B$.[4]

We conclude by considering two cases. First, if $v_i < B$, the maximum utility that bidder i can obtain is $\max\{0, v_i - B\} = 0$, and it achieves this by bidding truthfully (and losing). Second, if $v_i \geq B$, the maximum utility that bidder i can obtain is $\max\{0, v_i - B\} = v_i - B$, and it achieves this by bidding truthfully (and winning). ∎

Another important property is that a truthful bidder—meaning one that bids her true valuation—never regrets participating in a second-price auction.

Proposition 2.2 (Nonnegative Utility) *In a second-price auction, every truthful bidder is guaranteed nonnegative utility.*

Proof: Losers receive utility 0. If a bidder i is the winner, then her utility is $v_i - p$, where p is the second-highest bid. Since i is the winner (and hence the highest bidder) and bid her true valuation, $p \leq v_i$ and hence $v_i - p \geq 0$. ∎

Exercises 2.1–2.5 ask you to explore further properties of and variations on second-price auctions. For example, truthful bidding is the *unique* dominant strategy for a bidder in a second-price auction.

---

[3]This may be wonky notation, but it's good to get used to it.

[4]We're assuming here that ties are broken in favor of bidder i. You should check that Proposition 2.1 holds no matter how ties are broken.

2.5   Ideal Auctions

Second-price single-item auctions are "ideal" in that they enjoy three quite different and desirable properties. We formalize the first of these in the following definition.

Definition 2.3 (Dominant-Strategy Incentive Compatible)
An auction is *dominant-strategy incentive compatible (DSIC)* if truthful bidding is always a dominant strategy for every bidder and if truthful bidders always obtain nonnegative utility.[5]

Define the *social welfare* of an outcome of a single-item auction by

$$\sum_{i=1}^{n} v_i x_i,$$

where x_i is 1 if i wins and 0 if i loses. Because there is only one item, we have the feasibility constraint that $\sum_{i=1}^{n} x_i \leq 1$. Thus, the social welfare is just the valuation of the winner, or 0 if there is no winner.[6] An auction is *welfare maximizing* if, when bids are truthful, the auction outcome has the maximum possible social welfare. The next theorem follows from Proposition 2.1, Proposition 2.2, and the definition of second-price auctions.

Theorem 2.4 (Second-Price Auctions Are Ideal) *A second-price single-item auction satisfies the following:*

(1) [strong incentive guarantees] It is a DSIC auction.

(2) [strong performance guarantees] It is welfare maximizing.

(3) [computational efficiency] It can implemented in time polynomial (indeed, linear) in the size of the input, meaning the number of bits necessary to represent the numbers $v_1, \ldots, v_n$.

---

[5]The condition that truthful bidders obtain nonnegative utility is traditionally considered a separate requirement, called *individual rationality* or *voluntary participation*. To minimize terminology in these lectures, we fold this constraint into the DSIC condition, unless otherwise noted.

[6]The sale price does not appear in the definition of the social welfare of an outcome. We think of the seller as an agent whose utility is the revenue she earns; her utility then cancels out the utility lost by the auction winner from paying for the item.

All three properties are important. From a bidder's perspective, the DSIC property makes it particularly easy to choose a bid, and levels the playing field between sophisticated and unsophisticated bidders. From the perspective of the seller or auction designer, the DSIC property makes it much easier to reason about the auction's outcome. Note that *any* prediction of an auction's outcome has to be predicated on assumptions about how bidders behave. In a DSIC auction, the only assumption is that a bidder with an obvious dominant strategy will play it. Behavioral assumptions don't get much weaker than that.[7]

The DSIC property is great when you can get it, but we also want more. For example, an auction that gives the item away for free to a random bidder is DSIC, but it makes no effort to identify which bidders actually want the item. The welfare maximization property states something rather amazing: even though the bidder valuations are a priori unknown to the seller, the auction nevertheless identifies the bidder with the highest valuation! (Provided bids are truthful, a reasonable assumption in light of the DSIC property.) That is, a second-price auction solves the social welfare maximization problem as well as if all of the bidders' valuations were known in advance.

Computational efficiency is important because, to have potential practical utility, an auction should run in a reasonable amount of time. For example, auctions for online advertising, like those in Section 2.6, generally need to run in real time.

Section 2.6 and Lectures 3–4 strive for ideal auctions, in the sense of Theorem 2.4, for applications more complex than single-item auctions.

2.6   Case Study: Sponsored Search Auctions

2.6.1   Background

A Web search results page comprises a list of organic search results— deemed relevant to your query by an algorithm like PageRank—and a list of sponsored links, which have been paid for by advertisers. (Go do a Web search now to remind yourself, preferably on a valuable keyword like "mortgage" or "attorney.") Every time you type a

---

[7]Non-DSIC auctions are also important; see Section 4.3 for a detailed discussion.

search query into a search engine, an auction is run in real time to decide which advertisers' links are shown, how these links are arranged visually, and what the advertisers are charged. It is impossible to overstate how important such *sponsored search auctions* have been to the Internet economy. Here's one jaw-dropping statistic: around 2006, sponsored search auctions generated roughly 98% of Google's revenue. While online advertising is now sold in many different ways, sponsored search auctions continue to generate tens of billions of dollars of revenue every year.

2.6.2   The Basic Model of Sponsored Search Auctions

We discuss next a simplistic but useful and influential model of sponsored search auctions. The items for sale are k "slots" for sponsored links on a search results page. The bidders are the advertisers who have a standing bid on the keyword that was searched on. For example, Volvo and Subaru might be bidders on the keyword "station wagon," while Nikon and Canon might be bidders on the keyword "camera." Such auctions are more complex than single-item auctions in two ways. First, there are generally multiple items for sale (i.e., $k > 1$). Second, these items are not identical. For example, if ads are displayed as an ordered list, then higher slots in the list are more valuable than lower ones, since people generally scan the list from top to bottom.

We quantify the difference between different slots using *click-through rates (CTRs)*. The CTR α_j of a slot j represents the probability that the end user clicks on this slot. Ordering the slots from top to bottom, we make the reasonable assumption that $\alpha_1 \geq \alpha_2 \geq \cdots \geq \alpha_k$. For simplicity, we also make the unreasonable assumption that the CTR of a slot is independent of its occupant. Everything we'll say about sponsored search auctions extends to the more general and realistic model in which each advertiser i has a "quality score" β_i (the higher the better) and the CTR of advertiser i in slot j is the product $\beta_i \alpha_j$ (e.g., Exercise 3.4).

We assume that an advertiser is not interested in an impression (i.e., being displayed on a page) per se, but rather has a private valuation v_i for each *click* on her link. Hence, the expected value derived by advertiser i from slot j is $v_i \alpha_j$.

2.6.3   What We Want

Is there an ideal sponsored search auction? Our desiderata are:

(1) DSIC. That is, truthful bidding should be a dominant strategy, and never leads to negative utility.

(2) Social welfare maximization. That is, the assignment of bidders to slots should maximize $\sum_{i=1}^{n} v_i x_i$, where x_i now denotes the CTR of the slot to which i is assigned (or 0 if i is not assigned to a slot). Each slot can only be assigned to one bidder, and each bidder gets only one slot.

(3) Computational efficiency. The running time should be polynomial (or even near-linear) in the size of the input $v_1, \ldots, v_n$. Remember that zillions of these auctions need to be run every day!

2.6.4   Our Design Approach

What's hard about auction design problems is that we have to design jointly two things: the choice of who wins what, and the choice of who pays what. Even in single-item auctions, it is not enough to make the "correct" choice to the first design decision (e.g., giving the item to the highest bidder)—if the payments are not just right, then strategic participants will game the system.

Happily, in many applications including sponsored search auctions, we can tackle this two-prong design problem one step at a time.

> **Step 1:** Assume, without justification, that bidders bid truthfully. Then, how should we assign bidders to slots so that the above properties (2) and (3) hold?
>
> **Step 2:** Given our answer to Step 1, how should we set selling prices so that the above property (1) holds?

If we efficiently solve both of these problems, then we have constructed an ideal auction. Step 2 ensures the DSIC property, which means that bidders will bid truthfully (provided each bidder with an obvious dominant strategy plays it). The hypothesis in Step 1 is then satisfied, so the outcome of the auction is indeed welfare-maximizing (and computable in polynomial time).

We conclude this lecture by executing Step 1 for sponsored search auctions. Given truthful bids, how should we assign bidders to slots to maximize the social welfare? Exercise 2.8 asks you to prove that the natural greedy algorithm is optimal (and computationally efficient): for $i = 1, 2, \ldots, k$, assign the ith highest bidder to the ith best slot.

Can we implement Step 2? Is there an analog of the second-price rule—sale prices that render truthful bidding a dominant strategy for every bidder? The next lecture gives an affirmative answer via Myerson's lemma, a powerful tool in mechanism design.

The Upshot

☆ In a single-item auction there is one seller with one item and multiple bidders with private valuations. Single-item auction design is a simple but canonical example of mechanism design.

☆ An auction is DSIC if truthful bidding is a dominant strategy and if truthful bidders always obtain nonnegative utility.

☆ An auction is welfare maximizing if, assuming truthful bids, the auction outcome always has the maximum possible social welfare.

☆ Second-price auctions are "ideal" in that they are DSIC, welfare maximizing, and can be implemented in polynomial time.

☆ Sponsored search auctions are a huge component of the Internet economy. Such auctions are more complex than single-item auctions because there are multiple slots for sale, and these slots vary in quality.

☆ A general two-step approach to designing ideal auctions is to first assume truthful bids and understand how to allocate items to maximize the social welfare, and second to design selling prices that turn truthful bidding into a dominant strategy.

Notes

The concept of dominant-strategy incentive-compatibility is articulated in Hurwicz (1972). Theorem 2.4 is from Vickrey (1961), the paper that effectively founded the field of auction theory. The model of sponsored search presented in Section 2.6 is due independently to Edelman et al. (2007) and Varian (2007). The former paper contains the mentioned jaw-dropping statistic. Problem 2.1 is closely related to the secretary problem of Dynkin (1963); see also Hajiaghayi et al. (2004).

The 2007 Nobel Prize citation (Nobel Prize Committee, 2007) presents a historical overview of the development of mechanism design theory in the 1970s and 1980s. Modern introductions to the field include Börgers (2015), Diamantaras et al. (2009), and chapter 23 of Mas-Colell et al. (1995). Krishna (2010) is a good introduction to auction theory.

Exercises

Exercise 2.1 Consider a single-item auction with at least three bidders. Prove that awarding the item to the highest bidder, at a price equal to the third-highest bid, yields an auction that is *not* DSIC.

Exercise 2.2 Prove that for every false bid $b_i \neq v_i$ by a bidder in a second-price auction, there exist bids $\mathbf{b}_{-i}$ by the other bidders such that i's utility when bidding b_i is strictly less than when bidding v_i.

Exercise 2.3 Suppose there are k identical copies of an item and $n > k$ bidders. Suppose also that each bidder can receive at most one item. What is the analog of the second-price auction? Prove that your auction is DSIC.

Exercise 2.4 Consider a seller that incurs a cost of $c > 0$ for selling her item—either because she has a value of c for retaining the item or because she would need to produce the item at a cost of c. The social welfare is now defined as the valuation of the winning buyer (if any) minus the cost incurred by the seller (if any). How would you modify the second-price auction so that it remains DSIC and welfare maximizing? Argue that your auction is *budget-balanced*, meaning that whenever the seller sells the item, her revenue is at least her cost c.

Exercise 2.5 Suppose you want to hire a contractor to perform some task, like remodeling a house. Each contractor has a cost for performing the task, which a priori is known only to the contractor. Give an analog of a second-price auction in which contractors report their costs and the auction chooses a contractor and a payment. Truthful reporting should be a dominant strategy in your auction and, assuming truthful bids, your auction should select the contractor with the smallest cost. The payment to the winner should be at least her reported cost, and losers should be paid nothing.

[Auctions of this type are called *procurement* or *reverse* auctions.]

Exercise 2.6 Compare and contrast an eBay auction with a sealed-bid second-price auction. (Read up on eBay auctions if you don't already know how they work.) Should you bid differently in the two auctions? State explicitly your assumptions about how bidders behave.

Exercise 2.7 You've probably seen—in the movies, at least—the call-and-response format of *open ascending single-item auctions*, where an auctioneer asks for takers at successively higher prices. Such an auction ends when no one accepts the currently proposed price, the winner (if any) is the bidder who accepted the previously proposed price, and this previous price is the final sale price.

Compare and contrast open ascending auctions with sealed-bid second-price auctions. Do bidders have dominant strategies in open ascending auctions?

Exercise 2.8 Recall the sponsored search setting of Section 2.6, in which bidder i has a valuation v_i per click. There are k slots with click-through rates (CTRs) $\alpha_1 \geq \alpha_2 \geq \cdots \geq \alpha_k$. The social welfare of an assignment of bidders to slots is $\sum_{i=1}^{n} v_i x_i$, where x_i equals the CTR of the slot to which i is assigned (or 0 if bidder i is not assigned to any slot).

Prove that the social welfare is maximized by assigning the bidder with the ith highest valuation to the ith best slot for $i = 1, 2, \ldots, k$.

Problems

Problem 2.1 This problem considers *online* single-item auctions, where bidders arrive one-by-one. Assume that the number n of bidders is known, and that bidder i has a private valuation v_i. We consider auctions of the following form.

Online Single-Item Auction

For each bidder arrival $i = 1, 2, \ldots, n$:
    if the item has not been sold in a previous
    iteration, formulate a price p_i and then accept a
    bid b_i from bidder i
    if $p_i \leq b_i$, then the item is sold to bidder i at the
    price p_i; otherwise, bidder i departs and the
    item remains unsold

(a) Prove that an auction of this form is DSIC.

(b) Assume that bidders bid truthfully. Prove that if the valuations of the bidders and the order in which they arrive are arbitrary, then for every constant $c > 0$ independent of n, there is no deterministic online auction that always achieves social welfare at least c times the highest valuation.

(c) *(H)* Assume that bidders bid truthfully. Prove that there is a constant $c > 0$, independent of n, and a deterministic online auction with the following guarantee: for every unordered set of n bidder valuations, if the bidders arrive in a uniformly random order, then the expected welfare of the auction's outcome is at least c times the highest valuation.

Problem 2.2 Suppose a subset S of the bidders in a second-price single-item auction decide to collude, meaning that they submit their bids in a coordinated way to maximize the sum of their utilities. Assume that bidders outside of S bid truthfully. Prove necessary and sufficient conditions on the set S such that the bidders of S can increase their combined utility via non-truthful bidding.

Problem 2.3 We proved that second-price auctions are DSIC under the assumption that every bidder's utility function is quasilinear, with the utility of a bidder with valuation v_i winning the item at price p given by $v_i - p$. Identify significantly weaker assumptions on bidders' utility functions under which truthful bidding remains a dominant strategy for every bidder.

Lecture 3

Myerson's Lemma

Last lecture advocated a two-step approach to the design of auctions that are DSIC, welfare maximizing, and computationally efficient (Section 2.6.4). The first step assumes truthful bids and identifies how to allocate items to bidders to maximize the social welfare. For instance, in sponsored search auctions, this step is implemented by assigning the ith highest bidder to the ith best slot. The second step derives the appropriate selling prices, to render truthful bidding a dominant strategy. This lecture states and proves *Myerson's lemma*, a powerful and general tool for implementing this second step. This lemma applies to sponsored search auctions as a special case, and Lectures 4 and 5 provide further applications.

Section 3.1 introduces single-parameter environments, a convenient generalization of the mechanism design problems introduced in Lecture 2. Section 3.2 rephrases the three steps of sealed-bid auctions (Section 2.2) in terms of allocation and payment rules. Section 3.3 defines two properties of allocation rules, implementability and monotonicity, and states and interprets Myerson's lemma. Section 3.4 gives a proof sketch of Myerson's lemma; it can be skipped on a first reading. Myerson's lemma includes a formula for payments in DSIC mechanisms, and Section 3.5 applies this formula to sponsored search auctions.

3.1 Single-Parameter Environments

A good level of abstraction at which to state Myerson's lemma is *single-parameter environments*. Such an environment has some number n of agents. Each agent i has a private nonnegative valuation v_i, her value "per unit of stuff" that she acquires. Finally, there is a *feasible set* X. Each element of X is a nonnegative n-vector $(x_1, x_2, \ldots, x_n)$, where x_i denotes the "amount of stuff" given to agent i.

Example 3.1 (Single-Item Auction) In a single-item auction (Section 2.1), X is the set of 0-1 vectors that have at most one 1—that is, $\sum_{i=1}^{n} x_i \leq 1$.

Example 3.2 (k-Unit Auction) With k identical items and the constraint that each bidder gets at most one (Exercise 2.3), the feasible set is the set of 0-1 vectors that satisfy $\sum_{i=1}^{n} x_i \leq k$.

Example 3.3 (Sponsored Search Auction) In a sponsored search auction (Section 2.6), X is the set of n-vectors corresponding to assignments of bidders to slots, where each slot is assigned to at most one bidder and each bidder is assigned to at most one slot. If bidder i is assigned to slot j, then the component x_i equals the click-through rate α_j of her slot.

Example 3.4 (Public Project) Deciding whether or not to build a public project that can be used by all, such as a new bridge, can be modeled by the set $X = \{(0, 0, \ldots, 0), (1, 1, \ldots, 1)\}$.

Example 3.4 shows that single-parameter environments are general enough to capture applications different from auctions. At this level of generality, we refer to *agents* rather than bidders. We sometimes use the term *reports* instead of bids. A *mechanism* is a general procedure for making a decision when agents have private information (like valuations), whereas an *auction* is a mechanism specifically for the exchange of goods and money. See also Table 3.1.

auction	mechanism
bidder	agent
bid	report
valuation	valuation

Table 3.1: Correspondence of terms in auctions and mechanisms. An auction is the special case of a mechanism that is designed for the exchange of goods and money.

3.2   Allocation and Payment Rules

Recall that a sealed-bid auction has to make two choices: who wins
and who pays what. These two decisions are formalized via an *allocation rule* and a *payment rule*, respectively. Here are the three
steps:

---

1. Collect bids $\mathbf{b} = (b_1, \ldots, b_n)$ from all agents. The
   vector $\mathbf{b}$ is called the *bid vector* or *bid profile*.

2. [allocation rule] Choose a feasible allocation $\mathbf{x}(\mathbf{b}) \in$
   $X \subseteq \mathbb{R}^n$ as a function of the bids.

3. [payment rule] Choose payments $\mathbf{p}(\mathbf{b}) \in \mathbb{R}^n$ as a
   function of the bids.

Procedures of this type are called *direct-revelation mechanisms*, because in the first step agents are asked to reveal directly their private
valuations. An example of an indirect mechanism is an iterative ascending auction (cf., Exercise 2.7).

    With our quasilinear utility model, in a mechanism with alloca-
tion and payment rules $\mathbf{x}$ and $\mathbf{p}$, respectively, agent i receives utility

$$u_i(\mathbf{b}) = v_i \cdot x_i(\mathbf{b}) - p_i(\mathbf{b})$$

when the bid profile is $\mathbf{b}$.

    We focus on payment rules that satisfy

$$p_i(\mathbf{b}) \in [0, b_i \cdot x_i(\mathbf{b})] \tag{3.1}$$

for every agent i and bid profile $\mathbf{b}$. The constraint that $p_i(\mathbf{b}) \geq 0$
is equivalent to prohibiting the seller from paying the agents. The
constraint that $p_i(\mathbf{b}) \leq b_i \cdot x_i(\mathbf{b})$ ensures that a truthful agent receives
nonnegative utility (do you see why?).[1]

3.3   Statement of Myerson's Lemma

Next are two important definitions. Both articulate a property of
allocation rules.

---

[1]There are applications where it makes sense to relax one or both of these restrictions on payments, including those discussed in Exercise 2.5 and Problem 7.1.

Definition 3.5 (Implementable Allocation Rule) An   allocation rule **x** for a single-parameter environment is *implementable* if there is a payment rule **p** such that the direct-revelation mechanism $(\mathbf{x}, \mathbf{p})$ is DSIC.

That is, the implementable allocation rules are those that extend to DSIC mechanisms. Equivalently, the projection of DSIC mechanisms onto their allocation rules is the set of implementable rules. If our aim is to design a DSIC mechanism, we must confine ourselves to implementable allocation rules—they form our "design space." In this terminology, we can rephrase the cliffhanger from the end of Lecture 2 as: is the welfare-maximizing allocation rule for sponsored search auctions, which assigns the ith highest bidder to the ith best slot, implementable?

For instance, consider a single-item auction (Example 3.1). Is the allocation rule that awards the item to the highest bidder implementable? Sure—we've already constructed a payment rule, the second-price rule, that renders it DSIC. What about the allocation rule that awards the item to the *second-highest* bidder? Here, the answer is not clear: we haven't seen a payment rule that extends it to a DSIC mechanism, but it also seems tricky to argue that no payment rule could conceivably work.

Definition 3.6 (Monotone Allocation Rule) An allocation rule **x** for a single-parameter environment is *monotone* if for every agent i and bids $\mathbf{b}_{-i}$ by the other agents, the allocation $x_i(z, \mathbf{b}_{-i})$ to i is nondecreasing in her bid z.

That is, in a monotone allocation rule, bidding higher can only get you more stuff.

For example, the single-item auction allocation rule that awards the item to the highest bidder is monotone: if you're the winner and you raise your bid (keeping other bids fixed), you continue to win. By contrast, awarding the item to the second-highest bidder is a nonmonotone allocation rule: if you're the winner and you raise your bid high enough, you lose.

The welfare-maximizing allocation rule for sponsored search auctions (Example 3.3), with the ith highest bidder awarded the ith best slot, is monotone. When a bidder raises her bid, her position in the sorted order of bids can only increase, and this can only increase the click-through rate of her assigned slot.

We state Myerson's lemma in three parts; each is conceptually interesting and useful in later applications.

Theorem 3.7 (Myerson's Lemma) *Fix a single-parameter environment.*

(a) *An allocation rule* $\mathbf{x}$ *is implementable if and only if it is monotone.*

(b) *If* $\mathbf{x}$ *is monotone, then there is a unique payment rule for which the direct-revelation mechanism* $(\mathbf{x}, \mathbf{p})$ *is DSIC and* $p_i(\mathbf{b}) = 0$ *whenever* $b_i = 0$.

(c) *The payment rule in (b) is given by an explicit formula.*[2]

Myerson's lemma is the foundation on which we'll build most of our mechanism design theory. Part (a) states that Definitions 3.5 and 3.6 define exactly the same class of allocation rules. This equivalence is incredibly powerful: Definition 3.5 describes our design goal but is unwieldy to work with and verify, while Definition 3.6 is far more "operational." Usually, it's not difficult to check whether or not an allocation rule is monotone. Part (b) states that when an allocation rule is implementable, there is no ambiguity in how to assign payments to achieve the DSIC property—there is only one way to do it. Moreover, there is a relatively simple and explicit formula for this payment rule (part (c)), a property we apply to sponsored search auctions in Section 3.5 and to revenue-maximizing auction design in Lectures 5–6.

*3.4   Proof of Myerson's Lemma (Theorem 3.7)

Fix a single-parameter environment and consider an allocation rule $\mathbf{x}$, which may or may not be monotone. Suppose there is a payment rule $\mathbf{p}$ such that $(\mathbf{x}, \mathbf{p})$ is a DSIC mechanism—what could $\mathbf{p}$ look like? The plan of the proof is to use the stringent DSIC constraint to whittle the possibilities for $\mathbf{p}$ down to a single candidate. We establish all three parts of the theorem in one fell swoop.

---

[2]See formulas (3.5) and (3.6) for details and Section 3.5 for concrete examples.

Recall the DSIC condition: for every agent i, every possible private valuation v_i, every set of bids $\mathbf{b}_{-i}$ by the other agents, it must be that i's utility is maximized by bidding truthfully. For now, fix i and $\mathbf{b}_{-i}$ arbitrarily. As shorthand, write $x(z)$ and $p(z)$ for the allocation $x_i(z, \mathbf{b}_{-i})$ and payment $p_i(z, \mathbf{b}_{-i})$ of i when she bids z, respectively. Figure 3.1 gives two examples of a possible *allocation curve*, meaning the graph of such an x as a function of z.

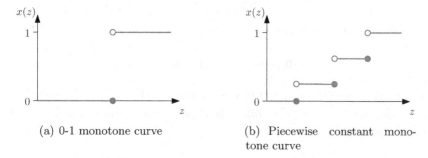

(a) 0-1 monotone curve

(b) Piecewise constant monotone curve

Figure 3.1: Examples of allocation curves $x(\cdot)$.

We invoke the DSIC constraint via a simple but clever swapping trick. Suppose $(\mathbf{x}, \mathbf{p})$ is DSIC, and consider any $0 \le y < z$. Because agent i might well have private valuation z and is free to submit the false bid y, DSIC demands that

$$\underbrace{z \cdot x(z) - p(z)}_{\text{utility of bidding } z} \ge \underbrace{z \cdot x(y) - p(y)}_{\text{utility of bidding } y}. \tag{3.2}$$

Similarly, since agent i might well have the private valuation y and could submit the false bid z, $(\mathbf{x}, \mathbf{p})$ must satisfy

$$\underbrace{y \cdot x(y) - p(y)}_{\text{utility of bidding } y} \ge \underbrace{y \cdot x(z) - p(z)}_{\text{utility of bidding } z}. \tag{3.3}$$

Myerson's lemma is, in effect, trying to solve for the payment rule $\mathbf{p}$ given the allocation rule $\mathbf{x}$. Rearranging inequalities (3.2) and (3.3) yields the following "payment difference sandwich," bounding $p(y) - p(z)$ from below and above:

$$z \cdot [x(y) - x(z)] \le p(y) - p(z) \le y \cdot [x(y) - x(z)]. \tag{3.4}$$

The payment difference sandwich already implies that every implementable allocation rule is monotone (Exercise 3.1). Thus, we can assume for the rest of the proof that $\mathbf{x}$ is monotone.

Next, consider the case where x is a piecewise constant function, as in Figure 3.1. The graph of x is flat except for a finite number of "jumps." In (3.4), fix z and let y tend to z from above. Taking the limit $y \downarrow z$ from above in (3.4), the left- and right-hand sides become 0 if there is no jump in x at z. If there is a jump of magnitude h at z, then the left- and right-hand sides both tend to $z \cdot h$. This implies the following constraint on p, for every z:

$$\text{jump in } p \text{ at } z = z \cdot [\text{jump in } x \text{ at } z].$$

Combining this with the initial condition $p(0) = 0$, we've derived the following *payment formula*, for every agent i, bids $\mathbf{b}_{-i}$ by other agents, and bid b_i by i:

$$p_i(b_i, \mathbf{b}_{-i}) = \sum_{j=1}^{\ell} z_j \cdot [\text{jump in } x_i(\cdot, \mathbf{b}_{-i}) \text{ at } z_j], \qquad (3.5)$$

where $z_1, \ldots, z_\ell$ are the breakpoints of the allocation function $x_i(\cdot, \mathbf{b}_{-i})$ in the range $[0, b_i]$.

A similar argument applies when x is a monotone function that is not piecewise constant. For instance, suppose that x is differentiable.[3] Dividing the payment difference sandwich (3.4) by $y - z$ and taking the limit as $y \downarrow z$ yields the constraint

$$p'(z) = z \cdot x'(z).$$

Combining this with the condition $p(0) = 0$ yields the payment formula

$$p_i(b_i, \mathbf{b}_{-i}) = \int_0^{b_i} z \cdot \tfrac{d}{dz} x_i(z, \mathbf{b}_{-i}) dz \qquad (3.6)$$

for every agent i, bid b_i, and bids $\mathbf{b}_{-i}$ by the other agents.

We reiterate that these payment formulas give the *only possible* payment rule that has a chance of extending the given allocation rule $\mathbf{x}$ into a DSIC mechanism. Thus, for every allocation rule $\mathbf{x}$,

---

[3]With some additional facts from calculus, the proof extends to general monotone functions. We omit the details.

there is at most one payment rule $\mathbf{p}$ such that $(\mathbf{x}, \mathbf{p})$ is DSIC (cf., part (b) of Theorem 3.7). But the proof is not complete: we still have to check that this payment rule works provided $\mathbf{x}$ is monotone! Indeed, we already know that even this payment rule cannot extend a non-monotone allocation rule to a DSIC mechanism.

We give a proof by picture that, if $\mathbf{x}$ is a monotone and piece-wise constant allocation rule and $\mathbf{p}$ is defined by (3.5), then $(\mathbf{x}, \mathbf{p})$ is a DSIC mechanism. The same argument works more generally for monotone allocation rules that are not piecewise constant, with payments defined as in (3.6). This will complete the proof of all three parts of Myerson's lemma.

Figures 3.2(a)–(i) depict the utility of an agent when she bids truthfully, overbids, and underbids, respectively. The allocation curve $x(z)$ and the private valuation v of the agent is the same in all three cases. Recall that the agent's utility when she bids b is $v \cdot x(b) - p(b)$. We depict the first term $v \cdot x(b)$ as a shaded rectangle of width v and height $x(b)$ (Figures 3.2(a)–(c)). Using the formula (3.5), we see that the payment $p(b)$ can be represented as the shaded area to the left of the allocation curve in the range $[0, b]$ (Figures 3.2(d)–(f)). The agent's utility is the difference between these two terms (Figures 3.2(g)–(i)). When the agent bids truthfully, her utility is precisely the area under the allocation curve in the range $[0, v]$ (Figure 3.2(g)). When the agent overbids, her utility is this same area, minus the area above the allocation curve in the range $[v, b]$ (Figure 3.2(h)). When the agent underbids, her utility is a subset of the area under the allocation curve in the range $[0, v]$ (Figure 3.2(i)). Since the agent's utility is the largest in the first case, the proof is complete.

3.5   Applying the Payment Formula

The explicit payment rule given by Myerson's lemma (Theorem 3.7(c)) is easy to understand and apply in many applications. For starters, consider a single-item auction (Example 3.1) with the allocation rule that allocates the item to the highest bidder. Fixing a bidder i and bids $\mathbf{b}_{-i}$ by the others, the function $x_i(z, \mathbf{b}_{-i})$ is 0 up to $B = \max_{j \neq i} b_j$ and 1 thereafter. Myerson's payment formula for such piecewise constant functions, derived in Section 3.4 as equation (3.5),

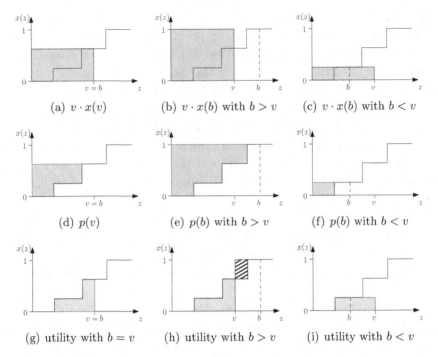

(a) $v \cdot x(v)$ (b) $v \cdot x(b)$ with $b > v$ (c) $v \cdot x(b)$ with $b < v$

(d) $p(v)$ (e) $p(b)$ with $b > v$ (f) $p(b)$ with $b < v$

(g) utility with $b = v$ (h) utility with $b > v$ (i) utility with $b < v$

Figure 3.2: Proof by picture that the payment rule in (3.5), coupled with the given monotone and piecewise constant allocation rule, yields a DSIC mechanism. The three columns consider the cases of truthful bidding, overbidding, and underbidding, respectively. The three rows show the welfare $v \cdot x(b)$, the payment $p(b)$, and the utility $v \cdot x(b) - p(b)$, respectively. In (h), the solid region represents positive utility and the lined region represents negative utility.

is

$$p_i(b_i, \mathbf{b}_{-i}) = \sum_{j=1}^{\ell} z_j \cdot [\text{jump in } x_i(\cdot, \mathbf{b}_{-i}) \text{ at } z_j],$$

where $z_1, \dots, z_\ell$ are the breakpoints of the allocation function $x_i(\cdot, \mathbf{b}_{-i})$ in the range $[0, b_i]$. For the highest-bidder single-item allocation rule, this is either 0 (if $b_i < B$) or, if $b_i > B$, there is a single breakpoint (a jump of 1 at B) and the payment is $p_i(b_i, \mathbf{b}_{-i}) = B$. Thus, Myerson's lemma regenerates the second-price payment rule as a special case.

Next, consider a sponsored search auction (Example 3.3), with

k slots with click-through rates $\alpha_1 \geq \alpha_2 \geq \cdots \geq \alpha_k$. Let $\mathbf{x}(\mathbf{b})$ be the allocation rule that assigns the ith highest bidder to the ith best slot, for $i = 1, 2, \ldots, k$. This rule is monotone and, assuming truthful bids, welfare maximizing (Exercise 2.8). Myerson's payment formula then gives the unique payment rule $\mathbf{p}$ such that $(\mathbf{x}, \mathbf{p})$ is DSIC. To describe it, consider a bid profile $\mathbf{b}$, and re-index the bidders so that $b_1 \geq b_2 \geq \cdots \geq b_n$. First focus on the highest bidder and imagine increasing her bid from 0 to b_1, holding the other bids fixed. The allocation $x_1(z, \mathbf{b}_{-1})$ increases from 0 to α_1 as z increases from 0 to b_1, with a jump of $\alpha_j - \alpha_{j+1}$ at the point where z becomes the jth highest bid in the profile $(z, \mathbf{b}_{-1})$, namely b_{j+1}. In general, Myerson's payment formula gives the payment

$$p_i(\mathbf{b}) = \sum_{j=i}^{k} b_{j+1}(\alpha_j - \alpha_{j+1}) \tag{3.7}$$

for the ith highest bidder (where $\alpha_{k+1} = 0$).

Our sponsored search model assumes that bidders don't care about impressions (i.e., having their link shown), except inasmuch as it leads to a click. This motivates charging bidders per click rather than per impression. The per-click payment for the bidder i in slot i is simply that in (3.7), scaled by $\frac{1}{\alpha_i}$:

$$p_i(\mathbf{b}) = \sum_{j=i}^{k} b_{j+1} \frac{\alpha_j - \alpha_{j+1}}{\alpha_i}. \tag{3.8}$$

Thus, when a bidder's link is clicked, she pays a suitable convex combination of the lower bids.

By historical accident, the sponsored search auctions used by search engines are based on the "generalized second-price (GSP)" auction, which is a simpler version of the DSIC auction above. The GSP allocation rule also assigns the ith highest bidder to the ith best slot, but its payment rule charges this bidder a per-click payment equal to the $(i + 1)$th highest bid. For a fixed set of bids, these per-click payments are generally higher than those in (3.8). Myerson's lemma asserts that the payment rule in (3.8) is the unique one that, when coupled with the GSP allocation rule, yields a DSIC mechanism. We can immediately conclude that the GSP auction is *not* DSIC. It still has a number of nice properties, however, and is equivalent to the

DSIC auction in certain senses. Problem 3.1 explores this point in detail.

The Upshot

☆ In a single-parameter environment, every agent has a private valuation per "unit of stuff," and a feasible set defines how much "stuff" can be jointly allocated to the agents. Examples include single-item auctions, sponsored search auctions, and public projects.

☆ The allocation rule of a direct-revelation mechanism specifies, as a function of agents' bids, who gets what. The payment rule of such a mechanism specifies, as a function of agents' bids, who pays what.

☆ An allocation rule is implementable if there exists a payment rule that extends it to a DSIC mechanism.

☆ An allocation rule is monotone if bidding higher can only increase the amount of stuff allocated to an agent, holding other agents' bids fixed.

☆ Myerson's lemma states that an allocation rule is implementable if and only if it is monotone. In this case, the corresponding payment rule is unique (assuming that bidding 0 results in paying 0).

☆ There is an explicit formula, given in (3.5) and (3.6), for the payment rule that extends a monotone allocation rule to a DSIC mechanism.

☆ Myerson's payment formula yields an elegant payment rule (3.8) for the payments-per-click in an ideal sponsored search auction.

Notes

Myerson's lemma is from Myerson (1981). The sponsored search payment formula (3.8) is noted in Aggarwal et al. (2006). Problem 3.1 is due independently to Edelman et al. (2007) and Varian (2007). Problem 3.2 is related to the "profit extractors" introduced by Goldberg et al. (2006) and the cost-sharing mechanisms studied by Moulin and Shenker (2001). Problem 3.3 is a special case of the theory developed by Moulin and Shenker (2001).

Exercises

Exercise 3.1 Use the "payment difference sandwich" in (3.4) to prove that if an allocation rule is not monotone, then it is not implementable.

Exercise 3.2 The proof of Myerson's lemma (Section 3.4) concludes with a "proof by picture" that coupling a monotone and piecewise constant allocation rule $\mathbf{x}$ with the payment rule defined by (3.5) yields a DSIC mechanism. Where does the proof-by-picture break down if the piecewise constant allocation rule $\mathbf{x}$ is not monotone?

Exercise 3.3 Give an algebraic proof that coupling a monotone and piecewise constant allocation rule $\mathbf{x}$ with the payment rule defined by (3.5) yields a DSIC mechanism.

Exercise 3.4 Consider the following extension of the sponsored search setting described in Section 2.6. Each bidder i now has a publicly known *quality* β_i, in addition to a private valuation v_i per click. As usual, each slot j has a CTR α_j, and $\alpha_1 \geq \alpha_2 \cdots \geq \alpha_k$. We assume that if bidder i is placed in slot j, then the probability of a click is $\beta_i \alpha_j$. Thus bidder i derives value $v_i \beta_i \alpha_j$ from the jth slot.

Describe the welfare-maximizing allocation rule in this generalized sponsored search setting. Prove that this rule is monotone. Give an explicit formula for the per-click payment of each bidder that extends this allocation rule to a DSIC mechanism.

Problems

Problem 3.1 Recall our model of sponsored search auctions (Section 2.6): there are k slots, the jth slot has a click-through rate

(CTR) of α_j (nonincreasing in j), and the utility of bidder i in slot j is $\alpha_j(v_i - p_j)$, where v_i is the (private) value-per-click of the bidder and p_j is the price charged per-click in slot j. The *Generalized Second-Price (GSP)* auction is defined as follows:

The Generalized Second Price (GSP) Auction

1. Rank advertisers from highest to lowest bid; assume without loss of generality that $b_1 \geq b_2 \geq \cdots \geq b_n$.

2. For $i = 1, 2, \ldots, k$, assign the ith bidder to the i slot.

3. For $i = 1, 2, \ldots, k$, charge the ith bidder a price of b_{i+1} per click.

The following subproblems show that the GSP auction always has a canonical equilibrium that is equivalent to the truthful outcome in the corresponding DSIC sponsored search auction.

(a) Prove that for every $k \geq 2$ and sequence $\alpha_1 \geq \cdots \geq \alpha_k > 0$ of CTRs, the GSP auction is not DSIC.

(b) *(H)* Fix CTRs for slots and values-per-click for bidders. We can assume that $k = n$ by adding dummy slots with zero CTR (if $k < n$) or dummy bidders with zero value-per-click (if $k > n$). A bid profile **b** is an *equilibrium* of GSP if no bidder can increase her utility by unilaterally changing her bid. Verify that this condition translates to the following inequalities, under our standing assumption that $b_1 \geq b_2 \geq \cdots \geq b_n$: for every i and higher slot $j < i$,

$$\alpha_i(v_i - b_{i+1}) \geq \alpha_j(v_i - b_j);$$

and for every lower slot $j > i$,

$$\alpha_i(v_i - b_{i+1}) \geq \alpha_j(v_i - b_{j+1}).$$

(c) A bid profile **b** with $b_1 \geq \cdots \geq b_n$ is *envy-free* if for every bidder i and slot $j \neq i$,

$$\alpha_i(v_i - b_{i+1}) \geq \alpha_j(v_i - b_{j+1}). \tag{3.9}$$

Verify that every envy-free bid profile is an equilibrium.[4]

(d) *(H)* A bid profile is *locally envy-free* if the inequality (3.9) holds for every pair of adjacent slots—for every i and $j \in \{i-1, i+1\}$. By definition, an envy-free bid profile is also locally envy-free. Prove that, for every set of strictly decreasing CTRs, every locally envy-free bid profile is also envy-free.

(e) *(H)* Prove that, for every set of values-per-click and strictly decreasing CTRs, there is an equilibrium of the GSP auction in which the assignments of bidders to slots and all payments-per-click equal those in the truthful outcome of the corresponding DSIC sponsored search auction.

(f) Prove that the equilibrium in (e) is the lowest-revenue envy-free bid profile.

Problem 3.2 This problem considers a k-unit auction (Example 3.2) in which the seller has a specific revenue target R. Consider the following algorithm that, given bids $\mathbf{b}$ as input, determines the winning bidders and their payments.

Revenue Target Auction

initialize a set S to the top k bidders
while there is a bidder $i \in S$ with $b_i < R/|S|$ **do**
    remove an arbitrary such bidder from S
allocate an item to each bidder of S (if any) at a
    price of $R/|S|$

(a) Give an explicit description of the allocation rule of the Revenue Target Auction, and prove that it is monotone.

(b) *(H)* Conclude from Myerson's lemma that the Revenue Target Auction is a DSIC mechanism.

---

[4]Why "envy-free?" Because if we write $p_j = b_{j+1}$ for the current price-per-click of slot j, then these inequalities translate to: "every bidder i is as happy getting her current slot at her current price as she would be getting any other slot and that slot's current price."

(c) Prove that whenever the DSIC and welfare-maximizing k-unit auction (Exercise 2.3) obtains revenue at least R, the Revenue Target Auction obtains revenue R.

(d) Prove that there exists a valuation profile for which the Revenue Target Auction obtains revenue R but the DSIC and welfare-maximizing auction earns revenue less than R.

Problem 3.3 This problem revisits the issue of collusion in auctions; see also Problem 2.2.

(a) Prove that the Revenue Target Auction in Problem 3.2 is *group-strategyproof*, meaning that no coordinated false bids by a subset of bidders can ever strictly increase the utility of one of its members without strictly decreasing the utility of some other member.

(b) Is the DSIC and welfare-maximizing k-unit auction group-strategyproof?

Lecture 4

Algorithmic Mechanism Design

This lecture pursues mechanisms that are DSIC, welfare maximizing, and computationally efficient for single-parameter environments that are more complex than those in Lectures 2 and 3. These environments are general enough that the welfare maximization problem is $\mathcal{NP}$-hard, so we consider allocation rules that only maximize the social welfare approximately. There are many techniques for designing such rules, but not all of them yield rules that are monotone in the sense required by Myerson's lemma. This lecture also discusses the revelation principle, the formal justification for our restriction to direct-revelation mechanisms.

Section 4.1 introduces knapsack auctions, which are conceptually simple single-parameter environments in which welfare maximization is a computationally intractable (i.e., $\mathcal{NP}$-hard) problem. Section 4.2 uses knapsack auctions to illustrate some representative results in algorithmic mechanism design, where the goal to design DSIC and polynomial-time mechanisms that guarantee near-optimal welfare. Section 4.3 presents the revelation principle.

4.1 Knapsack Auctions

4.1.1 Problem Definition

Knapsack auctions are another example of single-parameter environments (Section 3.1).

Example 4.1 (Knapsack Auction) In a knapsack auction, each bidder i has a publicly known *size* w_i and a private valuation. The seller has a capacity W. The feasible set X is defined as the 0-1 vectors $(x_1, \ldots, x_n)$ such that $\sum_{i=1}^{n} w_i x_i \leq W$. (As usual, $x_i = 1$ indicates that i is a winning bidder.)

39

Whenever there is a shared resource with limited capacity, you have a knapsack problem. For instance, each bidder's size could represent the duration of a company's television ad, the valuation its willingness-to-pay for its ad being shown during the Super Bowl, and the seller capacity the length of a commercial break. Other situations that can be modeled with knapsack auctions include bidders who want files stored on a shared server, data streams sent through a shared communication channel, or processes to be executed on a shared supercomputer. A k-unit auction (Example 3.2) corresponds to a knapsack auction with $w_i = 1$ for all i and $W = k$.

Let's try to design an ideal auction using our two-step design paradigm (Section 2.6.4). First, we assume without justification that we receive truthful bids and decide on our allocation rule. Then we pay the piper and devise a payment rule that extends the allocation rule to a DSIC mechanism.

4.1.2   Welfare-Maximizing DSIC Knapsack Auctions

Since ideal auctions are supposed to maximize welfare, the answer to the first step is clear: define the allocation rule by

$$\mathbf{x}(\mathbf{b}) = \operatorname{argmax}_X \sum_{i=1}^{n} b_i x_i. \tag{4.1}$$

That is, the allocation rule solves an instance of the knapsack problem[1] in which the item (i.e., bidder) values are the reported bids $b_1, \ldots, b_n$, and the item sizes are the a priori known sizes $w_1, \ldots, w_n$. By definition, when bidders bid truthfully, this allocation rule maximizes the social welfare. This allocation rule is also monotone in the sense of Definition 3.6; see Exercise 4.1.

4.1.3   Critical Bids

Myerson's lemma (Theorem 3.7, parts (a) and (b)) guarantees the existence of a payment rule $\mathbf{p}$ such that the mechanism $(\mathbf{x}, \mathbf{p})$ is DSIC. This payment rule is easy to understand. Fix a bidder i and

---

[1] An instance of the knapsack problem is defined by $2n + 1$ positive numbers: item values $v_1, \ldots, v_n$, item sizes $w_1, \ldots, w_n$, and a knapsack capacity W. The goal is to compute the subset of items of maximum total value that has total size at most W.

bids $\mathbf{b}_{-i}$ by the other bidders. Since the allocation rule is monotone and assigns 0 or 1 to every bidder, the allocation curve $x_i(\cdot, \mathbf{b}_{-i})$ is 0 until some breakpoint z, at which point it jumps to 1 (Figure 4.1). Recall the payment formula in (3.5):

$$p_i(b_i, \mathbf{b}_{-i}) = \sum_{j=1}^{\ell} z_j \cdot [\text{jump in } x_i(\cdot, \mathbf{b}_{-i}) \text{ at } z_j],$$

where $z_1, \ldots, z_\ell$ are the breakpoints of the allocation function $x_i(\cdot, \mathbf{b}_{-i})$ in the range $[0, b_i]$. Thus, if i bids less than z, she loses and pays 0. If i bids more than z, she pays $z \cdot (1 - 0) = z$. That is, when i wins, she pays her *critical bid*—the infimum of the bids she could make and continue to win (holding the other bids $\mathbf{b}_{-i}$ fixed). This is analogous to the familiar payment rule of a single-item second-price auction.

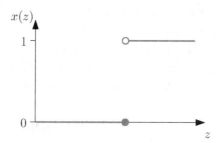

Figure 4.1: A monotone 0-1 allocation rule.

4.1.4   Intractability of Welfare Maximization

Is the mechanism proposed in Section 4.1.2 ideal in the sense of the second-price auction (Theorem 2.4)? Recall this means that the mechanism:

(1) is DSIC;

(2) is welfare maximizing, assuming truthful bids; and

(3) runs in time polynomial in the input size, which is the number of bits needed to represent all of the relevant numbers (bids, sizes, and the capacity).[2]

---

[2]More precisely, the running time of the mechanism on inputs of size s should be at most cs^d, where c and d are constants independent of s.

The answer is *no*. The reason is that the knapsack problem is $\mathcal{NP}$-hard. This means that there is no polynomial-time implementation of the allocation rule in (4.1), unless $\mathcal{P} = \mathcal{NP}$.[3] Thus, properties (2) and (3) are incompatible.

The fact that there is no ideal knapsack auction (assuming $\mathcal{P} \neq \mathcal{NP}$) motivates relaxing at least one of our three goals. But which one? First, note that relaxing the DSIC condition will not help at all, since it is the second and third properties that conflict.

One sensible approach, which won't get much airtime in this course, is to relax the third constraint. This is particularly attractive for knapsack auctions, since the allocation rule (4.1) can be implemented in pseudopolynomial time using dynamic programming.[4] More generally in mechanism design, if your instances are small or structured enough and you have enough time and computing power to implement optimal welfare maximization, by all means do it. The resulting allocation rule is monotone and can be extended to a DSIC mechanism (Exercise 4.1).[5]

For the rest of this lecture, we'll compromise on the second goal—begrudgingly accepting near-optimal welfare maximization in exchange for computational efficiency and without losing DSIC.

4.2   Algorithmic Mechanism Design

Algorithmic mechanism design is one of the first and most well-studied branches of algorithmic game theory, and this section presents a representative result from the field.

The dominant paradigm in algorithmic mechanism design is to relax the second requirement of ideal auctions (welfare maximization) as little as possible, subject to the first (DSIC) and third (polynomial-time) requirements. For single-parameter environments, Myerson's

---

[3]$\mathcal{P}$ and $\mathcal{NP}$ denote the sets of problems that can be solved in polynomial time and for which a correct solution can be verified in polynomial time, respectively. $\mathcal{NP}$ can only be larger than $\mathcal{P}$, and $\mathcal{P} \neq \mathcal{NP}$ is an unproven but widely-accepted hypothesis about computation.

[4]That is, if either the bids or the sizes require only a small number of bits to describe, then the problem can be solved efficiently. See any undergraduate algorithms textbook for details.

[5]Don't forget that the payments also need to be computed, and this generally requires solving n more welfare maximization problems (one per agent). See also Exercise 4.3.

lemma (Theorem 3.7) reduces this task to the design of a polynomial-time and monotone allocation rule that comes as close as possible to maximizing the social welfare.

4.2.1   The Best-Case Scenario: DSIC for Free

One reason there has been so much progress in algorithmic mechanism design over the past 15 years is its strong resemblance to the mature field of *approximation algorithms*. The primary goal in approximation algorithms is to design polynomial-time algorithms for $\mathcal{NP}$-hard optimization problems that are as close to optimal as possible. Algorithmic mechanism design has exactly the same goal, except that the algorithms must additionally obey a monotonicity constraint. The incentive constraints of the mechanism design goal are neatly compiled into a relatively intuitive extra constraint on the allocation rule, and so algorithmic mechanism design reduces to algorithm design in an oddly restricted "computational model."

The design space of polynomial-time DSIC mechanisms is only smaller than that of polynomial-time approximation algorithms. The best-case scenario is that the extra DSIC (equivalently, monotonicity) constraint causes no additional welfare loss, beyond the loss we already have to suffer from the polynomial-time requirement. We've been spoiled so far, since exact welfare maximization automatically yields a monotone allocation rule (see Exercise 4.1). Does an analogous fact hold for *approximate* welfare maximization?

4.2.2   Knapsack Auctions Revisited

To explore the preceding question in a concrete setting, let's return to knapsack auctions. There are several heuristics for the knapsack problem that have good worst-case performance guarantees. For example, consider the following allocation rule, which given bids **b** chooses a feasible set—a set S of winners with total size $\sum_{i \in S} w_i$ at most the capacity W—via a simple greedy algorithm. Since it's harmless to remove bidders i with $w_i > W$, we can assume that $w_i \leq W$ for every i.

A Greedy Knapsack Heuristic

1. Sort and re-index the bidders so that

$$\frac{b_1}{w_1} \geq \frac{b_2}{w_2} \geq \cdots \geq \frac{b_n}{w_n}.^6$$

2. Pick winners in this order until one doesn't fit, and then halt.[7]

3. Return either the solution from the previous step or the highest bidder, whichever has larger social welfare.[8]

This greedy algorithm is a $\frac{1}{2}$-approximation algorithm for the knapsack problem, meaning that for every instance of the knapsack problem, the algorithm returns a feasible solution with total value at least $\frac{1}{2}$ times the maximum possible. This fact implies the following guarantee.

Theorem 4.2 (Knapsack Approximation Guarantee)
Assuming truthful bids, the social welfare achieved by the greedy allocation rule is at least 50% of the maximum social welfare.

Proof (sketch):   Consider truthful bids $v_1, \ldots, v_n$, known sizes w_1, $\ldots, w_n$, and a capacity W. Suppose, as a thought experiment, we make the problem easier by allowing bidders to be chosen *fractionally*, with the value prorated accordingly. For example, if 70% of a bidder with value 10 is chosen, then it contributes 7 to the welfare. Here is a greedy algorithm for this "fractional knapsack problem:" sort the bidders as in step (1) above, and pick winners in this order until the entire capacity is fully used (picking the final winner fractionally,

---

[6]Intuitively, what makes a bidder attractive is a high bid and a small size. This heuristic trades these two properties off by ordering bidders by "bang-per-buck"—the value contributed per unit of capacity used.

[7]Alternatively, continue to follow the sorted order, packing any further bidders that fit. This modified heuristic is only better than the original.

[8]The motivation for this step is that the solution produced by the second step can be highly suboptimal if there is a very valuable and very large bidder. In lieu of considering only the highest bidder, this step can also sort the bidders in nondecreasing bid order and pack them greedily. This modification can only improve the heuristic.

as needed). A straightforward exchange argument proves that this algorithm maximizes the welfare over all feasible solutions to the fractional knapsack problem (Exercise 4.4).

In the optimal fractional solution, suppose that the first k bidders in the sorted order win and that the $(k+1)$th bidder fractionally wins. The welfare achieved by steps (1) and (2) in the greedy allocation rule is exactly the total value of the first k bidders. The welfare of the solution consisting only the highest bidder is at least the fractional value of the $(k+1)$th bidder. The better of these two solutions is at least half of the welfare of the optimal fractional solution, and thus at least half the welfare of an optimal (non-fractional) solution to the original problem. ∎

The greedy allocation rule above is also monotone (Exercise 4.5). Using Myerson's lemma (Theorem 3.7), we can extend it to a DSIC mechanism that runs in polynomial time and, assuming truthful bids, achieves social welfare at least 50% of the maximum possible.[9]

You may have been lulled into complacency, thinking that every reasonable allocation rule is monotone. The only non-monotone rule that we've seen is the "second-highest bidder wins" rule for single-item auctions (Section 3.3), which we don't care about anyways. Consider yourself warned.

> **Warning**
>
> Natural allocation rules are not always monotone.

For example, for every $\epsilon > 0$, there is a $(1 - \epsilon)$-approximation algorithm for the knapsack problem that runs in time polynomial in the input and $\frac{1}{\epsilon}$—a "fully polynomial-time approximation scheme (FPTAS)" (see Problem 4.2). The rule induced by the standard implementation of this algorithm is *not* monotone, although it can be tweaked to restore monotonicity without degrading the approximation guarantee (again, see Problem 4.2). This is characteristic of work in algorithmic mechanism design: for an $\mathcal{NP}$-hard optimization problem of interest, check if the state-of-the-art approximation

---

[9]The greedy allocation rule is even better under additional assumptions. For example, if $w_i \le \alpha W$ for every bidder i, with $\alpha \in (0, \frac{1}{2}]$, then the approximation guarantee improves to $1 - \alpha$, even if the third step of the algorithm is omitted.

algorithm directly leads to a DSIC mechanism. If not, tweak it or design a new approximation algorithm that does, hopefully without degrading the approximation guarantee.

4.3   The Revelation Principle

4.3.1   DSIC Revisited

To this point, our mechanism design theory has studied only DSIC mechanisms. We reiterate that there are good reasons to strive for a DSIC guarantee. First, it is easy for a participant to figure out what to do in a DSIC mechanism: just play the obvious dominant strategy and truthfully reveal one's private information. Second, the designer can predict the mechanism's outcome assuming only that participants play their dominant strategies, a relatively weak behavioral assumption. Nevertheless, non-DSIC mechanisms like first-price auctions (Section 2.3) are also important in practice.

Can non-DSIC mechanisms accomplish things that DSIC mechanisms cannot? To answer this question, we need to tease apart two different conditions that are conflated in our DSIC definition (Definition 2.3).[10]

The DSIC Condition

(1) For every valuation profile, the mechanism has a *dominant-strategy equilibrium*—an outcome that results from every participant playing a dominant strategy.

(2) In this dominant-strategy equilibrium, every participant truthfully reports her private information to the mechanism.

There are mechanisms that satisfy (1) but not (2). To give a silly example, imagine a single-item auction in which the seller, given bids **b**, runs a Vickrey auction on the bids 2**b**. Every bidder's dominant strategy is then to bid half her value.

---

[10]We'll ignore the "individual rationality" condition in Definition 2.3, which does not matter for the main points of this section.

4.3.2   Justifying Direct Revelation

The revelation principle states that, given requirement (1) in Section 4.3.1, requirement (2) comes for free.

Theorem 4.3 (Revelation Principle for DSIC Mechanisms)
For every mechanism M in which every participant always has a dominant strategy, there is an equivalent direct-revelation DSIC mechanism M'.

"Equivalence" in Theorem 4.3 means that, for every valuation profile, the outcome (e.g., winners of an auction and selling prices) of M' under direct revelation is identical to that of M when agents play their dominant strategies.

Proof: The proof uses a simulation argument; see Figure 4.2. By assumption, for every participant i and private information v_i that i might have, i has a dominant strategy $s_i(v_i)$ in the given mechanism M.

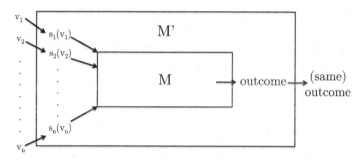

Figure 4.2: Proof of the revelation principle. Construction of the direct-revelation mechanism M', given a mechanism M with dominant strategies.

We next construct a mechanism M', to which participants delegate the responsibility of playing the appropriate dominant strategy. Precisely, the (direct-revelation) mechanism M' accepts bids $b_1, \ldots, b_n$ from the agents. It submits the bids $s_1(b_1), \ldots, s_n(b_n)$ to the mechanism M and chooses the same outcome that M does.

Mechanism M' is DSIC: If a participant i has private information v_i, then submitting a bid other than v_i can only result in M' playing a strategy other than $s_i(v_i)$ in M, which can only decrease i's utility. ∎

The point of Theorem 4.3 is that, at least in principle, if you want to design a mechanism with dominant strategies, then you might as well design one in which direct revelation (in auctions, truthful bidding) is a dominant strategy. Thus *truthfulness per se is not important*; what makes DSIC mechanism design difficult is the requirement that a desired outcome is a dominant-strategy equilibrium.

4.3.3   Beyond Dominant-Strategy Equilibria

Can we obtain better mechanisms by relaxing condition (1) from Section 4.3.1? An immediate issue with this idea is that, when agents do not have dominant strategies, we require stronger behavioral assumptions to predict what participants will do and what the mechanism's outcome will be. For example, we can consider a Bayes-Nash equilibrium with respect to a common prior distribution over the private information of the participants (see Problem 5.3) or a Nash equilibrium in a full-information model (similar to Problem 3.1). If we're willing to make such assumptions, can we do better than with DSIC mechanisms?

The answer is "sometimes, yes." For this reason, and because non-DSIC mechanisms are common in practice, it is important to develop mechanism design theory beyond DSIC mechanisms. Remark 5.5 and Problem 5.3 offer a brief glimpse of this theory. A rough rule of thumb is that, for sufficiently simple problems like those we've studied up until now, DSIC mechanisms can do everything that non-DSIC mechanisms can. In more complex problems, however, weakening the DSIC constraint often allows the designer to achieve performance guarantees that are provably impossible for DSIC mechanisms. DSIC and non-DSIC mechanisms are incomparable in such settings—the former enjoy stronger incentive guarantees, the latter better performance guarantees. Which of these is more important depends on the details of the application.

The Upshot

☆ Knapsack auctions model the allocation of a shared resource with limited capacity. Bidders have private valuations and publicly known sizes. In a feasible outcome, the total size of the winning bidders is at most the resource capacity.

☆ The problem of computing the outcome of a knapsack auction that maximizes social welfare is $\mathcal{NP}$-hard. Thus, if $\mathcal{P} \neq \mathcal{NP}$, there are no ideal knapsack auctions.

☆ The goal in algorithmic mechanism design is to relax the second requirement of ideal auctions (welfare maximization) as little as possible, subject to the first (DSIC) and third (polynomial-time) requirements. In the best-case scenario, there is a polynomial-time DSIC mechanism with an approximate welfare guarantee matching that of state-of-the-art polynomial-time approximation algorithms.

☆ State-of-the-art approximation algorithms for the welfare maximization problem may or may not induce monotone allocation rules.

☆ The revelation principle states that, for every mechanism with a dominant-strategy equilibrium, there is an equivalent mechanism in which direct revelation is a dominant-strategy equilibrium.

☆ In many complex mechanism design problems, non-DSIC mechanisms can achieve performance guarantees that are provably impossible for DSIC mechanisms.

Notes

The origins of algorithmic mechanism design are in Nisan and Ronen (2001) and Lehmann et al. (2002); see Nisan (2015) for a recent survey. Single-parameter environments are studied by Archer and Tardos (2001). Knapsack auctions are introduced in

Mu'Alem and Nisan (2008). The first formulation of the revelation principle appears in Gibbard (1973). Garey and Johnson (1979) give a good exposition of $\mathcal{NP}$-completeness and how to interpret it.

Problem 4.1 is related to Chekuri and Gamzu (2009). The classical FPTAS for the knapsack problem (Problem 4.2) is due to Ibarra and Kim (1975); see the books by Vazirani (2001) and Williamson and Shmoys (2010) for detailed coverage of this and dozens of other state-of-the-art polynomial-time approximation algorithms. The rest of Problem 4.2 is from Briest et al. (2005). Problem 4.3 is from Lehmann et al. (2002).

Exercises

Exercise 4.1 Consider an arbitrary single-parameter environment, with feasible set X. Prove that the welfare-maximizing allocation rule

$$\mathbf{x}(\mathbf{b}) = \mathrm{argmax}_{(x_1,\ldots,x_n) \in X} \sum_{i=1}^{n} b_i x_i \qquad (4.2)$$

is monotone in the sense of Definition 3.6.

[Assume that ties are broken in a deterministic and consistent way, such as lexicographically.]

Exercise 4.2 Continuing the previous exercise, restrict now to feasible sets X that contain only 0-1 vectors—that is, each bidder either wins or loses. We can identify each feasible outcome with a "feasible set" of bidders (the winners). Assume that for every bidder i, there is an outcome in which i does not win. Myerson's payment formula (3.5) dictates that a winning bidder pays her "critical bid"—the infimum of the bids at which she would continue to win.

Prove that, when S^* is the set of winning bidders under the allocation rule (4.2) and $i \in S^*$, i's critical bid equals the difference between (1) the maximum social welfare of a feasible set that excludes i; and (2) the social welfare $\sum_{j \in S^* \setminus \{i\}} v_j$ of the bidders other than i in the chosen outcome S^*.

[In this sense, each winning bidder pays her "externality"—the welfare loss she imposes on others.]

Exercise 4.3 Continuing the previous exercise, consider a 0-1 single-parameter environment. Suppose you are given a subroutine that, given bids **b**, computes the outcome of the welfare-maximizing allocation rule (4.2).

(a) Explain how to implement a welfare-maximizing DSIC mechanism by invoking this subroutine $n + 1$ times, where n is the number of participants.

(b) Conclude that mechanisms that are ideal in the sense of Theorem 2.4 exist for precisely the families of single-parameter environments in which the welfare-maximization problem (given **b** as input, compute (4.2)) can be solved in polynomial time.

Exercise 4.4 Prove that the greedy algorithm in the proof of Theorem 4.2 always computes an optimal fractional knapsack solution.

Exercise 4.5 Prove that the three-step greedy knapsack auction allocation rule in Section 4.2.2 is monotone. Does it remain monotone with the two optimizations discussed in the footnotes?

Exercise 4.6 Consider a variant of a knapsack auction in which we have two knapsacks, with known capacities W_1 and W_2. Feasible sets of this single-parameter environment now correspond to subsets S of bidders that can be partitioned into sets S_1 and S_2 satisfying $\sum_{i \in S_j} w_i \leq W_j$ for $j = 1, 2$.

Consider the allocation rule that first uses the single-knapsack greedy allocation rule of Section 4.2.2 to pack the first knapsack, and then uses it again on the remaining bidders to pack the second knapsack. Does this algorithm define a monotone allocation rule? Give either a proof of this fact or an explicit counterexample.

Exercise 4.7 *(H)* The revelation principle (Theorem 4.3) states that (direct-revelation) DSIC mechanisms can simulate all other mechanisms with dominant-strategy equilibria. Critique the revelation principle from a practical perspective. Name a specific situation where you might prefer a non-direct-revelation mechanism with a dominant-strategy equilibrium to the corresponding DSIC mechanism, and explain your reasoning.

Problems

Problem 4.1 Consider a variant of a knapsack auction in which both the valuation v_i and the size w_i of each bidder i are private. A mechanism now receives both bids $\mathbf{b}$ and reported sizes $\mathbf{a}$ from the bidders. An allocation rule $\mathbf{x}(\mathbf{b}, \mathbf{a})$ now specifies the amount of capacity allocated to each bidder, as a function of the bids and reported sizes. Feasibility dictates that $\sum_{i=1}^{n} x_i(\mathbf{b}, \mathbf{a}) \leq W$ for every $\mathbf{b}$ and $\mathbf{a}$, where W is the total capacity of the shared resource. We define the utility of a bidder i as $v_i - p_i(\mathbf{b}, \mathbf{a})$ if she gets her required capacity (i.e., $x_i(\mathbf{b}, \mathbf{a}) \geq w_i$) and as $-p_i(\mathbf{b}, \mathbf{a})$ otherwise. This is not a single-parameter environment.

Consider the following mechanism. Given bids $\mathbf{b}$ and reported sizes $\mathbf{a}$, the mechanism runs the greedy knapsack auction of Section 4.2.2, taking the reported sizes $\mathbf{a}$ at face value, to obtain a subset of winning bidders and prices $\mathbf{p}$. The mechanism concludes by awarding each winning bidder capacity equal to her reported size a_i, at a price of p_i; losing bidders receive and pay nothing. Is this mechanism DSIC? Prove it or give an explicit counterexample.

Problem 4.2 Section 4.2.2 gives an allocation rule for knapsack auctions that is monotone, guarantees at least 50% of the maximum social welfare, and runs in polynomial time. Can we do better?

We first describe a classical fully polynomial-time approximation scheme (FPTAS) for the knapsack problem. The input to the problem is item values $v_1, \ldots, v_n$, item sizes $w_1, \ldots, w_n$, and a knapsack capacity W. For a user-supplied parameter $\epsilon > 0$, we consider the following algorithm $\mathcal{A}_\epsilon$; m is a parameter that will be chosen shortly.

- Round each v_i up to the nearest multiple of m, call it v_i'.

- Divide the v_i''s through by m to obtain integers $\tilde{v}_1, \ldots, \tilde{v}_n$.

- For item values $\tilde{v}_1, \ldots, \tilde{v}_n$, compute the optimal solution using a pseudopolynomial-time algorithm.

  [You can assume that there exists such an algorithm with running time polynomial in n and $\max_{i=1}^{n} \tilde{v}_i$.]

(a) Prove that if we run algorithm $\mathcal{A}_\epsilon$ with the parameter m set to $\epsilon(\max_{i=1}^{n} v_i)/n$, then the running time of the algorithm is polynomial in n and $\frac{1}{\epsilon}$ (independent of the v_i's).

(b) *(H)* Prove that if we run algorithm $\mathcal{A}_\epsilon$ with the parameter m set to $\epsilon(\max_{i=1}^n v_i)/n$, then the algorithm outputs a solution with total value at least $1 - \epsilon$ times the maximum possible.

(c) Prove that if we run algorithm $\mathcal{A}_\epsilon$ with the parameter m set to a fixed constant, independent of the v_i's, then the algorithm yields a monotone allocation rule.

(d) Prove that if we run algorithm $\mathcal{A}_\epsilon$ with the parameter m set as in (a) and (b), then the algorithm need *not* yield a monotone allocation rule.

(e) *(H)* Give a DSIC mechanism for knapsack auctions that, for a user-specified parameter ϵ and assuming truthful bids, outputs an outcome with social welfare at least $1 - \epsilon$ times the maximum possible, in time polynomial in n and $\frac{1}{\epsilon}$.

Problem 4.3 Consider a set M of distinct items. There are n bidders, and each bidder i has a publicly known subset $T_i \subseteq M$ of items that it wants, and a private valuation v_i for getting them. If bidder i is awarded a set S_i of items at a total price of p, then her utility is $v_i x_i - p$, where x_i is 1 if $S_i \supseteq T_i$ and 0 otherwise. This is a single-parameter environment. Since each item can only be awarded to one bidder, a subset W of bidders can all receive their desired subsets simultaneously if and only if if $T_i \cap T_j = \emptyset$ for each distinct $i, j \in W$.

(a) *(H)* Prove that the problem of computing a welfare-maximizing feasible outcome, given the v_i's and T_i's as input, is $\mathcal{NP}$-hard.

(b) Here is a greedy algorithm for the social welfare maximization problem, given bids $\mathbf{b}$ from the bidders.

```
initialize W = ∅ and X = M
sort and re-index the bidders so that
b₁ ≥ b₂ ≥ ··· ≥ bₙ
for i = 1, 2, 3, ..., n do
    if Tᵢ ⊆ X then
        remove Tᵢ from X and add i to W
return winning bidders W
```

Does this algorithm define a monotone allocation rule? Prove it or give an explicit counterexample.

(c) *(H)* Prove that if all bidders report truthfully and have sets T_i of cardinality at most d, then the outcome of the allocation rule in (b) has social welfare at least $\frac{1}{d}$ times that of the maximum possible.

Lecture 5

Revenue-Maximizing Auctions

Lectures 2–4 focused on the design of mechanisms that maximize, exactly or approximately, the social welfare of the outcome. Revenue is generated in such mechanisms only as a side effect, a necessary evil to incentivize agents to report truthfully their private information. This lecture studies mechanisms that are designed to raise as much revenue as possible, and characterizes the expected revenue-maximizing mechanism with respect to a prior distribution over agents' valuations.

Section 5.1 explains why reasoning about revenue maximization is harder than welfare maximization, and introduces Bayesian environments. Section 5.2 is the heart of this lecture, and it characterizes expected revenue-maximizing mechanisms as "virtual welfare maximizers." Section 5.3 describes how this theory was used to boost sponsored search revenue at Yahoo. Section 5.4 proves a technical lemma needed for the characterization in Section 5.2.

5.1 The Challenge of Revenue Maximization

5.1.1 Spoiled by Social Welfare Maximization

There are several reasons to begin the study of mechanism design with the objective of maximizing social welfare. The first reason is that this objective is relevant to many real-world scenarios. For instance, in government auctions (e.g., to sell wireless spectrum; see Lecture 8), the primary objective is welfare maximization. Revenue is also a consideration in such auctions, but it is usually not the first-order objective. Also, in competitive markets, a rule of thumb is that a seller should focus on welfare maximization, since otherwise a competitor will (thereby stealing their customers).

The second reason to start with social welfare maximization is pedagogical: social welfare is special. In every single-parameter environment, there is a DSIC mechanism that, for every profile of private valuations, assuming truthful bids, computes the welfare-maximizing outcome (cf., Exercise 4.1).[1] Such a mechanism optimizes the social welfare as effectively as if all of the private information was known in advance—the DSIC constraint is satisfied for free. This amazingly strong performance guarantee, called an "ex post" guarantee, cannot generally be achieved for other objective functions.

5.1.2 One Bidder and One Item

The following trivial example is illuminating. Suppose there is one item and only one bidder, with a private valuation v. With only one bidder, the space of direct-revelation DSIC auctions is small: they are precisely the *posted prices*, meaning take-it-or-leave-it offers.[2] With a posted price of $r \geq 0$, the auction's revenue is either r (if $v \geq r$) or 0 (if $v < r$).

Maximizing social welfare in this setting is trivial: just set $r = 0$, so that the auction always awards the item to the bidder for free. This optimal posted price is *independent of v*.

Suppose we wanted to maximize revenue. How should we set r? If we telepathically knew v, we would set $r = v$. But with v private to the bidder, what should we do? It is not clear how to reason about this question.

The fundamental issue is that the revenue-maximizing auction varies with the private valuations. With a single item and bidder, a posted price of 20 will do very well on inputs where v is 20 or a little larger, and terribly when v is less than 20 (while smaller posted prices will do better). Welfare maximization, for which there is an input-independent optimal DSIC mechanism, is special indeed.

5.1.3 Bayesian Analysis

To compare the revenue of two different auctions, we require a model to compare trade-offs across different inputs. The classical approach is to use *average-case* or *Bayesian* analysis. We consider a model comprising the following ingredients:

---

[1]This holds even more generally; see Lecture 7.

[2]These are the deterministic DSIC auctions. An auction can also randomize over posted prices, but the point of this example remains the same.

- A single-parameter environment (Section 3.1). We assume that there is a constant M such that $x_i \leq M$ for every i and feasible solution $(x_1, \ldots, x_n) \in X$.

- Independent distributions $F_1, \ldots, F_n$ with positive and continuous density functions $f_1, \ldots, f_n$. We assume that the private valuation v_i of participant i is drawn from the distribution F_i.[3] We also assume that the support of every distribution F_i belongs to $[0, v_{\max}]$ for some $v_{\max} < \infty$.[4]

A key assumption is that the mechanism designer knows the distributions $F_1, \ldots, F_n$.[5] The realizations $v_1, \ldots, v_n$ of agents' valuations are private, as usual. Since we focus on DSIC auctions, where agents have dominant strategies, the agents do not need to know the distributions $F_1, \ldots, F_n$.[6]

In a Bayesian environment, it is clear how to define the "optimal" mechanism—it is the one that, among all DSIC mechanisms, has the highest expected revenue (assuming truthful bids). The expectation is with respect to the given distribution $F_1 \times F_2 \times \cdots \times F_n$ over valuation profiles.

5.1.4   One Bidder and One Item, Revisited

With our Bayesian model, single-bidder single-item auctions are easy to reason about. The expected revenue of a posted price r is simply

$$\underbrace{r}_{\text{revenue of a sale}} \cdot \underbrace{(1 - F(r))}_{\text{probability of a sale}} .$$

Given a distribution F, it is usually a simple matter to solve for the best posted price r. An optimal posted price is called a *monopoly*

---

[3]The distribution function $F_i(z)$ denotes the probability that a random variable with distribution F_i has value at most z.

[4]The results of this lecture hold more generally if every distribution F_i has finite expectation.

[5]In practice, these distributions are typically derived from data, such as bids in past auctions.

[6]In mechanisms without dominant strategies, such as first-price single-item auctions, the standard approach is to consider "Bayes-Nash equilibria"; see Problem 5.3 for details. Bayes-Nash equilibrium analysis assumes a "common prior," meaning that all of the agents know the distributions $F_1, \ldots, F_n$.

price of the distribution F. Since DSIC mechanisms are posted prices (and distributions thereof), posting a monopoly price is a revenue-maximizing auction. For instance, if F is the uniform distribution on $[0, 1]$, so that $F(x) = x$ on $[0, 1]$, then the monopoly price is $\frac{1}{2}$, achieving an expected revenue of $\frac{1}{4}$.

5.1.5 Multiple Bidders

The plot thickens already with two bidders, where the space of DSIC auctions is more complicated than the space of posted prices. For example, consider a single-item auction with two bidders with valuations drawn independently from the uniform distribution on $[0, 1]$. We could of course run a second-price auction (Section 2.4); its expected revenue is the expected value of the smaller bid, which is $\frac{1}{3}$ (Exercise 5.1(a)).

We can also supplement a second-price auction with a *reserve price*, analogous to the opening bid in an eBay auction. In a second-price auction with reserve r, the allocation rule awards the item to the highest bidder, unless all bids are less than r, in which case no one gets the item. The corresponding payment rule charges the winner (if any) the second-highest bid or r, whichever is larger. From a revenue standpoint, adding a reserve price r is both good and bad: you lose revenue when all bids are less than r, but when exactly one bid is above r the reserve price boosts the revenue. With two bidders with valuations drawn independently from the uniform distribution on $[0, 1]$, adding a reserve price of $\frac{1}{2}$ raises the expected revenue of a second-price auction from $\frac{1}{3}$ to $\frac{5}{12}$ (Exercise 5.1(b)). Can we do better? Either by using a different reserve price, or with a entirely different auction format?

5.2 Characterization of Optimal DSIC Mechanisms

The primary goal of this lecture is to give an explicit description of an optimal (i.e., expected revenue-maximizing) DSIC mechanism for every single-parameter environment and distributions $F_1, \ldots, F_n$.

5.2.1   Preliminaries

We can simplify the problem by applying the revelation principle from last lecture (Theorem 4.3). Since every DSIC mechanism is equivalent to—and hence has the same expected revenue as—a direct-revelation DSIC mechanism $(\mathbf{x}, \mathbf{p})$, we can restrict our attention to such mechanisms. We correspondingly assume truthful bids (i.e., $\mathbf{b} = \mathbf{v}$) for the rest of the lecture.

The expected revenue of a DSIC mechanism $(\mathbf{x}, \mathbf{p})$ is, by definition,

$$\mathbf{E}_{\mathbf{v} \sim \mathbf{F}} \left[\sum_{i=1}^{n} p_i(\mathbf{v}) \right], \tag{5.1}$$

where the expectation is with respect to the distribution $\mathbf{F} = F_1 \times \cdots \times F_n$ over agents' valuations. It is not clear how to directly maximize the expression (5.1) over the space of DSIC mechanisms. We next work toward a *second* formula for the expected revenue of a mechanism. This alternative formula only references the allocation rule of a mechanism, and not its payment rule, and for this reason is far easier to maximize.

5.2.2   Virtual Valuations

The second formula for expected revenue uses the important concept of virtual valuations. For an agent i with valuation distribution F_i and valuation v_i, her *virtual valuation* is defined as

$$\varphi_i(v_i) = v_i - \frac{1 - F_i(v_i)}{f_i(v_i)}. \tag{5.2}$$

The virtual valuation of an agent depends on her own valuation and distribution, and not on those of the other agents. For example, if F_i is the uniform distribution on $[0, 1]$, with $F_i(z) = z$ for $z \in [0, 1]$, then $f_i(z) = 1$, and $\varphi_i(z) = z - \frac{1-z}{1} = 2z - 1$ on $[0, 1]$. A virtual valuation is always at most the corresponding valuation, and it can be negative. See Exercise 5.2 for more examples.

Virtual valuations play a central role in the design of expected revenue-maximizing auctions. But what do they mean? One way to interpret the formula

$$\varphi_i(v_i) = \underbrace{v_i}_{\text{what you'd like to charge}} - \underbrace{\frac{1 - F_i(v_i)}{f_i(v_i)}}_{\text{information rent earned by agent}}$$

is to think of v_i as the maximum revenue obtainable from agent i, and the second term as the inevitable revenue loss caused by not knowing v_i in advance, known as the *information rent*. A second interpretation of $\varphi_i(v_i)$ is as the slope of a "revenue curve" at v_i, where the revenue curve plots the expected revenue obtained from an agent with valuation drawn from F_i as a function of the probability of a sale. Problem 5.1 elaborates on this interpretation.

5.2.3   Expected Revenue Equals Expected Virtual Welfare

The following lemma is the workhorse of our characterization of optimal auctions. We give the proof, which is really just some calculus, in Section 5.4.

Lemma 5.1 *For every single-parameter environment with valuation distributions $F_1, \ldots, F_n$, every DSIC mechanism $(\mathbf{x}, \mathbf{p})$, every agent i, and every value $\mathbf{v}_{-i}$ of the valuations of the other agents,*

$$\mathbf{E}_{v_i \sim F_i}[p_i(\mathbf{v})] = \mathbf{E}_{v_i \sim F_i}[\varphi_i(v_i) \cdot x_i(\mathbf{v})] . \tag{5.3}$$

That is, the expected payment of an agent equals the expected virtual value earned by the agent. This identity holds only in expectation over v_i, and not pointwise.[7]

Taking Lemma 5.1 as given, we have the following important result.

Theorem 5.2 (Exp. Revenue Equals Exp. Virtual Welfare)
For every single-parameter environment with valuation distributions $F_1, \ldots, F_n$ and every DSIC mechanism $(\mathbf{x}, \mathbf{p})$,

$$\underbrace{\mathbf{E}_{\mathbf{v} \sim \mathbf{F}}\left[\sum_{i=1}^{n} p_i(\mathbf{v})\right]}_{\text{expected revenue}} = \underbrace{\mathbf{E}_{\mathbf{v} \sim \mathbf{F}}\left[\sum_{i=1}^{n} \varphi_i(v_i) \cdot x_i(\mathbf{v})\right]}_{\text{expected virtual welfare}} . \tag{5.4}$$

---

[7]For example, virtual valuations can be negative while payments are always nonnegative.

Proof: Taking the expectation, with respect to $\mathbf{v}_{-i} \sim \mathbf{F}_{-i}$, of both sides of (5.3) we obtain

$$\mathbf{E}_{\mathbf{v} \sim \mathbf{F}}[p_i(\mathbf{v})] = \mathbf{E}_{\mathbf{v} \sim \mathbf{F}}[\varphi_i(v_i) \cdot x_i(\mathbf{v})].$$

Applying the linearity of expectation (twice) then gives

$$\mathbf{E}_{\mathbf{v} \sim \mathbf{F}}\left[\sum_{i=1}^{n} p_i(\mathbf{v})\right] = \sum_{i=1}^{n} \mathbf{E}_{\mathbf{v} \sim \mathbf{F}}[p_i(\mathbf{v})]$$

$$= \sum_{i=1}^{n} \mathbf{E}_{\mathbf{v} \sim \mathbf{F}}[\varphi_i(v_i) \cdot x_i(\mathbf{v})]$$

$$= \mathbf{E}_{\mathbf{v} \sim \mathbf{F}}\left[\sum_{i=1}^{n} \varphi_i(v_i) \cdot x_i(\mathbf{v})\right],$$

as desired. ∎

The second term in (5.4) is our second formula for the expected revenue of a mechanism, and we should be pleased with its simplicity. If we replaced the $\varphi_i(v_i)$'s by v_i's, then we would be left with an old friend: the expected *welfare* of the mechanism. For this reason, we refer to $\sum_{i=1}^{n} \varphi_i(v_i) \cdot x_i(\mathbf{v})$ as the *virtual welfare* of a mechanism on the valuation profile $\mathbf{v}$. Theorem 5.2 implies that maximizing expected revenue over the space of DSIC mechanisms reduces to maximizing expected virtual welfare over the same space.

5.2.4   Maximizing Expected Virtual Welfare

It is shocking that a formula as simple as (5.4) holds. It says that even though we only care about payments, we can focus on an optimization problem that concerns only the mechanism's allocation rule. This second form is far more operational, and we proceed to determine the mechanisms that maximize it.

How should we choose the allocation rule $\mathbf{x}$ to maximize the expected virtual welfare

$$\mathbf{E}_{\mathbf{v} \sim \mathbf{F}}\left[\sum_{i=1}^{n} \varphi_i(v_i) x_i(\mathbf{v})\right]? \tag{5.5}$$

We have the freedom of choosing $\mathbf{x}(\mathbf{v})$ for each valuation profile $\mathbf{v}$, and have no control over the input distribution $\mathbf{F}$ or the virtual values $\varphi_i(v_i)$. Thus, the obvious approach is to *maximize pointwise*: separately for each $\mathbf{v}$, we choose $\mathbf{x}(\mathbf{v})$ to maximize the virtual welfare $\sum_{i=1}^{n} \varphi_i(v_i)x_i(\mathbf{v})$ obtained on the input $\mathbf{v}$, subject to feasibility of the allocation. We call this the *virtual welfare-maximizing allocation rule*. This is the same as the welfare-maximizing allocation rule of (4.1) and (4.2), except with agents' valuations replaced by their virtual valuations (5.2).

For example, in a single-item auction, where the feasibility constraint is $\sum_{i=1}^{n} x_i(\mathbf{v}) \leq 1$ for every $\mathbf{v}$, the virtual welfare-maximizing rule just awards the item to the bidder with the highest virtual valuation. Well, not quite: recall that virtual valuations can be negative— for instance, $\varphi_i(v_i) = 2v_i - 1$ when v_i is uniformly distributed between 0 and 1—and if every bidder has a negative virtual valuation, then the virtual welfare is maximized by not awarding the item to anyone.[8]

The virtual welfare-maximizing allocation rule maximizes the expected virtual welfare (5.5) over *all* allocation rules, monotone or not. The key question is: *Is the virtual welfare-maximizing rule monotone?* If so, then by Myerson's lemma (Theorem 3.7) it can be extended to a DSIC mechanism, and by Theorem 5.2 this mechanism has the maximum possible expected revenue.

5.2.5 Regular Distributions

Monotonicity of the virtual welfare-maximizing allocation rule depends on the valuation distributions. The next definition identifies a sufficient condition for monotonicity.

Definition 5.3 (Regular Distribution) A distribution F is *regular* if the corresponding virtual valuation function $v - \frac{1-F(v)}{f(v)}$ is nondecreasing.

If every agent's valuation is drawn from a regular distribution, then with consistent tie-breaking, the virtual welfare-maximizing allocation rule is monotone (Exercise 5.5).

---

[8]Recall from the single-bidder example in Section 5.1 that maximizing expected revenue entails not always selling the item.

For example, the uniform distribution on $[0, 1]$ is regular because the corresponding virtual valuation function is $2v - 1$. Many other common distributions are also regular (Exercise 5.3). Irregular distributions include many multi-modal distributions and distributions with extremely heavy tails.

With regular valuation distributions, we can extend the (monotone) virtual welfare-maximizing allocation rule to a DSIC mechanism using Myerson's lemma (Theorem 3.7). This is an expected revenue-maximizing DSIC mechanism.[9]

Virtual Welfare Maximizer

Assumption: the valuation distribution F_i of every agent is regular (Definition 5.3).

1. Transform the (truthfully reported) valuation v_i of agent i into the corresponding virtual valuation $\varphi_i(v_i)$ according to (5.2).

2. Choose the feasible allocation $(x_1, \ldots, x_n)$ that maximizes the virtual welfare $\sum_{i=1}^{n} \varphi_i(v_i) x_i$.[10]

3. Charge payments according to Myerson's payment formula (see (3.5) and (3.6)).[11]

We call this mechanism the *virtual welfare maximizer* for the given single-parameter environment and valuation distributions.

Theorem 5.4 (Virtual Welfare Maximizers Are Optimal)
For every single-parameter environment and regular distributions $F_1, \ldots, F_n$, the corresponding virtual welfare maximizer is a DSIC mechanism with the maximum-possible expected revenue.

A stunning implication of Theorem 5.4 is that revenue-maximizing mechanisms are almost the same as welfare-maximizing

---

[9]With additional work, the results of this lecture can be extended to irregular valuation distributions. See the Notes for details.

[10]The simplest way to break ties is lexicographically with respect to some fixed total ordering over the feasible outcomes.

[11]If every x_i can only be 0 or 1, then these payments are particularly simple: every winner pays the infimum of the bids at which she would continue to win, holding others' bids fixed.

mechanisms, and differ only in using virtual valuations in place of valuations. In this sense, revenue maximization reduces to welfare maximization.

Remark 5.5 (Bayesian Incentive Compatible Mechanisms)
Generalizing the derivations in Section 3.4 and this section yields a substantially stronger version of Theorem 5.4: the mechanism identified in the theorem maximizes expected revenue not only over all DSIC mechanisms but more generally over all "Bayesian incentive compatible (BIC)" mechanisms. A BIC mechanism for valuation distributions $F_1, \ldots, F_n$ is one in which truthful revelation forms a Bayes-Nash equilibrium (see Problem 5.3 for a definition). Every DSIC mechanism is BIC with respect to every choice of $F_1, \ldots, F_n$. Since optimizing expected revenue over all BIC mechanisms yields a DSIC mechanism, the DSIC property comes for free. The revelation principle (Theorem 4.3) can be adapted to BIC mechanisms (Problem 5.4), implying that, under the assumptions of Theorem 5.4, no Bayes-Nash equilibrium of any mechanism (e.g., first-price auctions) results in expected revenue larger than that earned by the optimal DSIC mechanism.

5.2.6   Optimal Single-Item Auctions

Theorem 5.4 gives a satisfying solution to the problem of expected revenue-maximizing mechanism design, in the form of a relatively explicit and easy-to-implement optimal mechanism. However, these mechanisms are not easy to interpret. Do they ever simplify to familiar mechanisms?

Let's return to single-item auctions. Assume that bidders are *i.i.d.*, meaning that they have a common valuation distribution F and hence a common virtual valuation function φ. Assume also that F is *strictly regular*, meaning that φ is a strictly increasing function. The virtual-welfare-maximizing mechanism awards the item to the bidder with the highest nonnegative virtual valuation, if any. Since all bidders share the same increasing virtual valuation function, the bidder with the highest virtual valuation is also the bidder with the highest valuation. This allocation rule is the same as that of a second-price auction with a reserve price of $\varphi^{-1}(0)$. By Theorem 3.7(b), the payment rules also coincide. Thus, for any number of i.i.d. bidders and a strictly regular valuation distribution, eBay (with a suitable opening bid) is the optimal auction format! Returning to the setting described at the end of Section 5.1, with all valuations distributed uniformly on $[0,1]$, the second-price auction with reserve $\frac{1}{2} = \varphi^{-1}(0)$ is optimal. Given the richness of the DSIC auction design space, it is astonishing that such a simple and practical auction pops out as the theoretically optimal one.

5.3   Case Study: Reserve Prices in Sponsored Search

So how does all this optimal mechanism design theory get used, anyway? This section discusses a 2008 field experiment that explored whether or not the lessons of optimal auction theory could be used to increase sponsored search revenue at Yahoo.

Recall from Section 2.6 our model of sponsored search auctions. Which such auction maximizes the expected revenue, at least in theory? If we assume that bidders' valuations-per-click are drawn i.i.d. from a regular distribution F with virtual valuation function φ, then the optimal auction considers only bidders who bid at least the reserve price $\varphi^{-1}(0)$, and ranks these bidders by bid (from the best slot to the worst). See Exercise 5.8.

What had Yahoo been doing, up to 2008? First, they were using relatively low reserve prices—initially \$.01, later \$.05, and then \$.10. Perhaps more naively, they were using the same reserve price of \$.10 across all keywords, even though some keywords surely warranted higher reserve prices than did others (e.g., "divorce lawyer" versus "pizza"). How would Yahoo's revenue change if reserve prices were updated, independently for each keyword, to the theoretically optimal ones?

In the first step of the field experiment, a lognormal valuation distribution was fitted to past bidding data for approximately 500,000 different keywords.[12] The qualitative conclusions of the experiment appear to be independent of the details of this step, such as the particular family of valuation distributions chosen.

---

[12]Since Yahoo, like other search engines, uses a non-DSIC auction based on the GSP auction (Problem 3.1), one cannot expect the bids to be truthful. In this field experiment, valuations were reversed engineered from bids under the assumption that bidders are playing the equilibrium that is outcome-equivalent to the dominant-strategy outcome of the revenue-maximizing DSIC sponsored search auction (Exercise 5.8).

In the second step, theoretically optimal reserve prices were computed for each keyword, assuming that valuations were distributed according to the fitted distributions. As expected, the optimal reserve price varied significantly across keywords. There were plenty of keywords with a theoretically optimal reserve price of $.30 or $.40. Yahoo's uniform reserve price was much too low, relative to the advice provided by optimal auction theory, on these keywords.

The obvious experiment is to try out the theoretically optimal (and generally higher) reserve prices to see how they do. Yahoo's top brass wanted to be a little more conservative, though, and set the new reserve prices to be the average of the old ones ($.10) and the theoretically optimal ones.[13] And the change worked: auction revenues went up several percent (of a very large number). The new reserve prices were especially effective in markets that are valuable but "thin," meaning not very competitive (less than six bidders). Better reserve prices were credited by Yahoo's president as the biggest reason for higher search revenue in Yahoo's third-quarter report in 2008.

*5.4   Proof of Lemma 5.1

This section sketches a proof of Lemma 5.1, that the expected (over $v_i \sim F_i$) revenue obtained from an agent i equals the expected virtual value that she earns. As a starting point, recall Myerson's payment formula (3.6)

$$p_i(v_i, \mathbf{v}_{-i}) = \int_0^{v_i} z \cdot x_i'(z, \mathbf{v}_{-i}) dz$$

for the payment made by agent i in a DSIC mechanism with allocation rule $\mathbf{x}$ on the valuation profile $\mathbf{v}$. We derived this equation assuming that the allocation function $x_i(z, \mathbf{v}_{-i})$ is differentiable. By standard advanced calculus, the same formula holds more generally for an arbitrary monotone function $x_i(z, \mathbf{v}_{-i})$, including piecewise constant functions, for a suitable interpretation of the derivative $x_i'(z, \mathbf{v}_{-i})$ and the corresponding integral. Similarly, all of the following proof

---

[13]Both in theory and empirically, this more conservative change accounts for most of the revenue increase. There are usually diminishing returns to revenue as the reserve price approaches the theoretical optimum, providing flexibility near the optimal price. The intuition for this principle is that the derivative of the expected revenue with respect to the reserve price is 0 at the optimal point.

steps, which make use of calculus maneuvers like integration by parts, can be made fully rigorous for arbitrary bounded monotone functions without significant difficulty. We leave the details to the interested reader.[14]

Equation (3.6) states that payments are fully dictated by the allocation rule. Thus, at least in principle, we can express the expected revenue of an auction purely in terms of its allocation rule, with no explicit reference to its payment rule. Will the resulting revenue formula be easier to maximize than the original one? It's hard to know without actually doing it, so let's do it.

Step 1: Fix an agent i. By Myerson's payment formula, we can write the expected (over $v_i \sim F_i$) payment by i for a given value of $\mathbf{v}_{-i}$ as

$$
\mathbf{E}_{v_i \sim F_i}[p_i(\mathbf{v})] = \int_0^{v_{\max}} p_i(\mathbf{v}) f_i(v_i) dv_i
$$
$$
= \int_0^{v_{\max}} \left[\int_0^{v_i} z \cdot x_i'(z, \mathbf{v}_{-i}) dz \right] f_i(v_i) dv_i.
$$

The first equality exploits the independence of agents' valuations—the fixed value of $\mathbf{v}_{-i}$ has no bearing on the distribution F_i from which v_i is drawn.

This step is exactly what we knew was possible in principle—rewriting the expected payment in terms of the allocation rule. For this to be useful, we need some simplifications.

Step 2: Whenever you have a double integral (or double sum) that you don't know how to interpret, it's worth reversing the integration order. Reversing the order of integration in

$$
\int_0^{v_{\max}} \left[\int_0^{v_i} z \cdot x_i'(z, \mathbf{v}_{-i}) dz \right] f_i(v_i) dv_i
$$

yields

$$
\int_0^{v_{\max}} \left[\int_z^{v_{\max}} f_i(v_i) dv_i \right] z \cdot x_i'(z, \mathbf{v}_{-i}) dz,
$$

which simplifies to

$$
\int_0^{v_{\max}} (1 - F_i(z)) \cdot z \cdot x_i'(z, \mathbf{v}_{-i}) dz,
$$

---

[14]For example, every bounded monotone function is integrable, and is differentiable except at a countable set of points.

suggesting that we're on the right track.

Step 3: Integration by parts is also worth trying when massaging an integral into a more interpretable form, especially if there's an obvious derivative hiding in the integrand. We again get some encouraging simplifications:

$$
\int_0^{v_{\max}} \underbrace{(1 - F_i(z)) \cdot z}_{g(z)} \cdot \underbrace{x_i'(z, \mathbf{v}_{-i})}_{h'(z)} \, dz
$$

$$
= \underbrace{(1 - F_i(z)) \cdot z \cdot x_i(z, \mathbf{v}_{-i})|_0^{v_{\max}}}_{=0-0}
$$

$$
\quad - \int_0^{v_{\max}} x_i(z, \mathbf{v}_{-i}) \cdot (1 - F_i(z) - z f_i(z)) dz
$$

$$
= \int_0^{v_{\max}} \underbrace{\left(z - \frac{1 - F_i(z)}{f_i(z)} \right)}_{=\varphi_i(z)} x_i(z, \mathbf{v}_{-i}) f_i(z) dz. \qquad (5.6)
$$

Step 4: We can interpret (5.6) as an expected value, with z drawn from the distribution F_i. Recalling the definition (5.2) of virtual valuations, this expectation is $\mathbf{E}_{v_i \sim F_i}[\varphi_i(v_i) \cdot x_i(\mathbf{v})]$. Summarizing, we have

$$
\mathbf{E}_{v_i \sim F_i}[p_i(\mathbf{v})] = \mathbf{E}_{v_i \sim F_i}[\varphi_i(v_i) \cdot x_i(\mathbf{v})],
$$

as desired.

The Upshot

☆ Unlike welfare-maximizing mechanisms, the revenue-maximizing mechanism for an environment varies with the (private) valuations.

☆ In the average-case or Bayesian approach to comparing different mechanisms, each agent's valuation is drawn independently from a distribution known to the mechanism designer. The optimal mechanism is the one with the highest expected revenue with respect to these distributions.

☆ The expected revenue of a DSIC mechanism can be expressed purely in terms of its allocation rule, using the important concept of virtual valuations (5.2).

☆ A distribution is regular if the corresponding virtual valuation function is nondecreasing. Many common distributions are regular.

☆ With regular valuation distributions, the optimal mechanism is a virtual welfare maximizer, which for each valuation profile chooses an outcome with maximum virtual welfare.

☆ In a single-item auction with bidders' valuations drawn i.i.d. from a regular distribution, the optimal auction is a second-price auction with a reserve price.

☆ The lessons learned from the theory of optimal mechanism design were used in 2008 to increase Yahoo's sponsored search revenue by several percent.

Notes

The model and main results of this lecture are due to Myerson (1981), as are the mentioned extensions to irregular valuation distributions and to Bayesian incentive compatible mechanisms (Remark 5.5). Myerson (1981) also notes the crucial importance of the independence assumption on agents' valuations, an observation that is developed further by Crémer and McLean (1985). With irregular distributions, the virtual welfare-maximizing allocation rule is not monotone, and it is necessary to solve for the monotone allocation rule with the maximum expected virtual welfare. This can be done by "ironing" virtual valuation functions to make them monotone, while at the same time preserving the virtual welfare of the mechanisms that matter. See Hartline (2016) for a textbook treatment of these extensions.

The field experiment with reserve prices in Yahoo sponsored search auctions (Section 5.3) is reported by Ostrovsky and Schwarz (2009). The revenue curve interpretation of virtual valuations in Problem 5.1 is due to Bulow and Roberts (1989). Problem 5.2 is from Azar et al. (2013). Problem 5.3 is closely related to the property of "revenue equivalence," identified already in Vickrey (1961); see Krishna (2010) for an excellent exposition.

Exercises

Exercise 5.1 Consider a single-item auction with two bidders with valuations drawn independently from the uniform distribution on $[0, 1]$.

(a) Prove that the expected revenue obtained by a second-price auction (with no reserve) is $\frac{1}{3}$.

(b) Prove that the expected revenue obtained by a second-price auction with reserve $\frac{1}{2}$ is $\frac{5}{12}$.

Exercise 5.2 Compute the virtual valuation function of the following distributions.

(a) The uniform distribution on $[0, a]$ with $a > 0$.

(b) The exponential distribution with rate $\lambda > 0$ (on $[0, \infty)$).

(c) The distribution given by $F(v) = 1 - \frac{1}{(v+1)^c}$ on $[0, \infty)$, where $c > 0$ is some constant.

Exercise 5.3 Which of the distributions in Exercise 5.2 are regular (Definition 5.3)?

Exercise 5.4 A valuation distribution meets the *monotone hazard rate (MHR)* condition if its *hazard rate* $\frac{f_i(v_i)}{1-F_i(v_i)}$ is nondecreasing in v_i.[15]

---

[15]For intuition behind the MHR condition, consider waiting for a light bulb to burn out. Given that the bulb hasn't burned out yet, the probability that it burns out right now is increasing in the amount of time that has elapsed.

(a) Prove that every distribution meeting the MHR condition is regular.

(b) Which of the distributions in Exercise 5.2 satisfy the MHR condition?

Exercise 5.5 Prove that for every single-parameter environment and regular valuation distributions $F_1, \ldots, F_n$, the virtual-welfare-maximizing allocation rule is monotone in the sense of Definition 3.6. Assume that ties are broken lexicographically with respect to some fixed total ordering over the feasible outcomes.

Exercise 5.6 *(H)* For the valuation distribution in Exercise 5.2(c), with $c = 1$, argue that the expected revenue of an auction does *not* necessarily equal its expected virtual welfare. How do you reconcile this observation with Theorem 5.2?

Exercise 5.7 Consider a k-unit auction (Example 3.2) in which bidders' valuations are drawn i.i.d. from a regular distribution F. Describe an optimal auction. Which of the following does the reserve price depend on: k, n, or F?

Exercise 5.8 Repeat the previous exercise for sponsored search auctions (Example 3.3).

Exercise 5.9 Consider a single-parameter environment and regular valuation distributions $F_1, \ldots, F_n$. For $\alpha \in [0, 1]$, call a DSIC mechanism an α-*approximate virtual welfare maximizer* if it always selects a feasible allocation with virtual welfare at least α times the maximum possible. Prove that the expected revenue of an α-approximate virtual welfare maximizer is at least α times that of an optimal mechanism.

Exercise 5.10 In the sponsored search auction case study in Section 5.3, raising reserve prices was particularly effective for valuable keywords (typical valuations-per-click well above the old reserve price of \$.10) that had few bidders (6 or less). Give at least two examples of keywords that you think might have these properties, and explain your reasoning.

Problems

Problem 5.1 This problem derives an interesting interpretation of a virtual valuation $\varphi(v) = v - \frac{1-F(v)}{f(v)}$ and the regularity condition. Consider a strictly increasing distribution function F with a strictly positive density function f on the interval $[0, v_{\max}]$, with $v_{\max} < +\infty$.

For a single bidder with valuation drawn from F, for $q \in [0, 1]$, define $V(q) = F^{-1}(1 - q)$ as the (unique) posted price that yields a probability q of a sale. Define $R(q) = q \cdot V(q)$ as the expected revenue obtained from a single bidder when the probability of a sale is q. The function $R(q)$, for $q \in [0, 1]$, is the *revenue curve* of F. Note that $R(0) = R(1) = 0$.

(a) What is the revenue curve for the uniform distribution on $[0, 1]$?

(b) Prove that the slope of the revenue curve at q (i.e., $R'(q)$) is precisely $\varphi(V(q))$, where φ is the virtual valuation function for F.

(c) Prove that a distribution is regular if and only if its revenue curve is concave.

Problem 5.2 *(H)* Consider a single bidder with valuation drawn from a regular distribution F that satisfies the assumptions of Problem 5.1. Let p be the *median* of F, meaning the value for which $F(p) = \frac{1}{2}$. Prove that the price p earns at least 50% of the expected revenue of the optimal posted price for F.

Problem 5.3 This problem introduces the Bayes-Nash equilibrium concept and compares the expected revenue earned by first- and second-price single-item auctions.

First-price auctions have no dominant strategies, and we require a new concept to reason about them. For this problem, assume that bidders' valuations are drawn i.i.d. from a commonly known distribution F. A *strategy* of a bidder i in a first-price auction is a predetermined plan for bidding—a function $b_i(\cdot)$ that maps her valuation v_i to a bid $b_i(v_i)$. The semantics are: "when my valuation is v_i, I will bid $b_i(v_i)$." We assume that bidders' strategies are common knowledge, with bidders' valuations (and hence induced bids) private as usual.

A strategy profile $b_1(\cdot), \cdots, b_n(\cdot)$ is a *Bayes-Nash equilibrium* if every bidder always bids optimally given her information—if for every bidder i and every valuation v_i, the bid $b_i(v_i)$ maximizes i's expected utility, where the expectation is with respect to the distribution over others bids induced by F and $\mathbf{b}_{-i}$.

(a) Suppose F is the uniform distribution on $[0, 1]$. Verify that setting $b_i(v_i) = v_i(n-1)/n$ for every i and v_i yields a Bayes-Nash equilibrium.

(b) Prove that the expected revenue of the seller (over $\mathbf{v}$) at this equilibrium of the first-price auction is exactly the expected revenue of the seller in the truthful outcome of a second-price auction.

(c) *(H)* Extend the conclusion in (b) to every continuous and strictly increasing distribution function F on $[0, 1]$.

Problem 5.4 This problem uses first-price auctions to illustrate the extension of the revelation principle (Theorem 4.3) to Bayesian incentive compatible mechanisms (Remark 5.5).

(a) Let $F_1, \ldots, F_n$ be valuation distributions and $b_1, \ldots, b_n$ a Bayes-Nash equilibrium of a first-price auction, as defined in Problem 5.3. Prove that there exists a single-item auction M' such that truthful bidding is a Bayes-Nash equilibrium and, for every valuation profile $\mathbf{v}$, the truthful outcome of M' is identical to the equilibrium outcome of the first-price auction.

(b) A first-price auction is "prior-independent" in that its description makes no reference to bidders' valuation distributions. (See also Section 6.4.) Is the auction M' in part (a) prior-independent in this sense?

Lecture 6

Simple Near-Optimal Auctions

The preceding lecture identified the expected-revenue-maximizing auction for a wide range of Bayesian single-parameter environments. When agents' valuations are not identically distributed, the optimal mechanism is relatively complex, requires detailed information about the valuation distributions, and does not resemble the auction formats used in practice. This lecture pursues approximately optimal mechanisms that are simpler, more practical, and more robust than the theoretically optimal mechanism.

Section 6.1 motivates the pursuit of simple near-optimal auctions. Section 6.2 covers a fun result from optimal stopping theory, the "prophet inequality," and Section 6.3 uses it to design a simple and provably near-optimal single-item auction. Section 6.4 introduces prior-independent mechanisms, which are mechanisms whose description makes no reference to any valuation distributions, and proves the Bulow-Klemperer theorem, which explains why competition is more valuable than information.

6.1 Optimal Auctions Can Be Complex

Theorem 5.4 states that, for every single-parameter environment in which agents' valuations are drawn independently from regular distributions, the corresponding virtual welfare maximizer maximizes the expected revenue over all DSIC mechanisms. The allocation rule of this mechanism sets

$$\mathbf{x}(\mathbf{v}) = \mathrm{argmax}_X \sum_{i=1}^{n} \varphi_i(v_i) x_i(\mathbf{v})$$

for each valuation profile $\mathbf{v}$, where

$$\varphi_i(v_i) = v_i - \frac{1 - F_i(v_i)}{f_i(v_i)}$$

74

is the virtual valuation corresponding to the distribution F_i.[1]

Section 5.2.6 noted that the optimal single-item auction with i.i.d. bidders and a regular distribution is shockingly simple: it is simply a second-price auction, augmented with the reserve price $\varphi^{-1}(0)$. This is a true "killer application" of auction theory—it gives crisp and practically useful guidance to auction design.

The plot thickens if the problem is a bit more complex. Consider again a single-item auction, but with bidders' valuations drawn independently from *different* regular distributions. The optimal auction can get weird, and it does not generally resemble any auctions used in practice (Exercise 6.1). Someone other than the highest bidder might win, and the payment made by the winner seems impossible to explain without referencing virtual valuations. This weirdness is inevitable if you really want every last cent of the maximum-possible expected revenue, with respect to the exact valuation distributions $F_1, \ldots, F_n$.

Are there simpler and more practical single-item auction formats that are at least *approximately* optimal?[2]

6.2   The Prophet Inequality

Consider the following game with n stages. In stage i, you are offered a nonnegative prize π_i, drawn from a distribution G_i. You are told the distributions $G_1, \ldots, G_n$ in advance, and these distributions are independent. You are told the realization π_i only at stage i. After seeing π_i, you can either accept the prize and end the game or discard the prize and proceed to the next stage. The decision's difficulty stems from the trade-off between the risk of accepting a reasonable prize early, and then missing out later on a great one, and the risk of having to settle for a lousy prize in one of the final stages.

The amazing "prophet inequality" offers a simple strategy that performs almost as well as a fully clairvoyant prophet.

---

[1]Since we only consider DSIC mechanisms, we assume truthful reports (i.e., $\mathbf{b} = \mathbf{v}$) throughout the lecture.

[2]This lecture leaves terms like "simple," "practical," and "robust" largely undefined. This contrasts with our use of approximation in algorithmic mechanism design (Lecture 4) to escape a different kind of complexity imposed by full optimality; there, we identified "practical" with "runs in polynomial time."

Theorem 6.1 (Prophet Inequality) *For every sequence* $G_1, \ldots,$ G_n *of independent distributions, there is a strategy that guarantees expected reward at least* $\frac{1}{2}\mathbf{E}_{\pi \sim \mathbf{G}}[\max_i \pi_i]$. *Moreover, there is such a threshold strategy, which accepts prize i if and only if π_i is at least some threshold t.*

Proof: Let z^+ denote $\max\{z, 0\}$. Consider a threshold strategy with threshold t. It is difficult to compare directly the expected payoff of this strategy with the expected payoff of a prophet. Instead, we derive lower and upper bounds, respectively, on these two quantities that are easy to compare.

Let $q(t)$ denote the probability that the threshold strategy accepts no prize at all.[3] As t increases, the risk $q(t)$ increases but the expected value of an accepted prize goes up.

What payoff does the t-threshold strategy obtain? With probability $q(t)$, zero, and with probability $1 - q(t)$, at least t. Let's improve our lower bound in the second case. If exactly one prize i satisfies $\pi_i \geq t$, then we should get "extra credit" of $\pi_i - t$ above and beyond our baseline payoff of t. If at least two prizes exceed the threshold, say i and j, then things are more complicated: our "extra credit" is either $\pi_i - t$ or $\pi_j - t$, according to which corresponds to the earlier stage. We'll be lazy and punt on this complication: when two or more prizes exceed the threshold, we'll only credit the baseline t to the strategy's payoff.

Formally, we can bound

$$\mathbf{E}_{\pi \sim \mathbf{G}}[\text{payoff of the } t\text{-threshold strategy}]$$

from below by

$$(1 - q(t))t +$$

$$\sum_{i=1}^{n} \mathbf{E}_{\pi}[\pi_i - t \mid \pi_i \geq t, \pi_j < t \; \forall j \neq i] \, \mathbf{Pr}[\pi_i \geq t] \, \mathbf{Pr}[\pi_j < t \; \forall j \neq i]$$

$$= (1 - q(t))t + \sum_{i=1}^{n} \underbrace{\mathbf{E}_{\pi}[\pi_i - t \mid \pi_i \geq t] \, \mathbf{Pr}[\pi_i \geq t]}_{=\mathbf{E}[(\pi_i - t)^+]} \underbrace{\mathbf{Pr}[\pi_j < t \; \forall j \neq i]}_{\geq q(t)}$$

$$\geq (1 - q(t))t + q(t) \sum_{i=1}^{n} \mathbf{E}_{\pi}\left[(\pi_i - t)^+\right], \tag{6.1}$$

---

[3] Note that discarding the final stage's prize is clearly suboptimal!

where we use the independence of the G_i's to factor the two probability terms and drop the conditioning on the event that $\pi_j < t$ for every $j \neq i$. In (6.1), we use that $q(t) = \mathbf{Pr}[\pi_j < t \ \forall j] \leq \mathbf{Pr}[\pi_j < t \ \forall j \neq i]$.

Now we produce an upper bound on the prophet's expected payoff $\mathbf{E}_\pi[\max_i \pi_i]$ that is easy to compare to (6.1). The expression $\mathbf{E}_\pi[\max_i \pi_i]$ doesn't reference the strategy's threshold t, so we add and subtract it to derive

$$
\mathbf{E}_\pi\left[\max_{i=1}^{n} \pi_i\right] = \mathbf{E}_\pi\left[t + \max_{i=1}^{n}(\pi_i - t)\right]
$$

$$
\leq t + \mathbf{E}_\pi\left[\max_{i=1}^{n}(\pi_i - t)^+\right]
$$

$$
\leq t + \sum_{i=1}^{n} \mathbf{E}_\pi\left[(\pi_i - t)^+\right]. \qquad (6.2)
$$

Comparing (6.1) and (6.2), we can set t so that $q(t) = \frac{1}{2}$, with a 50/50 chance of accepting a prize, and complete the proof.[4] ∎

Remark 6.2 (Guarantee with Adversarial Tie-Breaking)
The proof of Theorem 6.1 implies a stronger statement that is useful in the next section. Our lower bound (6.1) on the revenue of the t-threshold strategy only credits t units of value when two or more prizes exceed the threshold t. Only the realizations in which exactly one prize exceeds the threshold contribute to the second, "extra credit" term in (6.1). For this reason, the guarantee of $\frac{1}{2}\mathbf{E}_\pi[\max_i \pi_i]$ holds for the strategy even if, whenever there are multiple prizes above the threshold, it somehow always picks the smallest of these.

6.3   Simple Single-Item Auctions

We now return to our motivating example of a single-item auction with n bidders with valuations drawn independently from regular distributions $F_1, \ldots, F_n$ that need not be identical. We use the prophet inequality (Theorem 6.1) to design a relatively simple and near-optimal auction.

---

[4]If there is no such t because of point masses in the G_i's, then a minor extension of the argument yields the same result (Exercise 6.2).

The key idea is to define the ith prize as the positive part $\varphi_i(v_i)^+$ of bidder i's virtual valuation. G_i is then the corresponding distribution induced by F_i; since the F_i's are independent, so are the G_i's. To see an initial connection to the prophet inequality, we can use Theorem 5.2 to note that the expected revenue of the optimal auction is

$$\mathbf{E}_{\mathbf{v} \sim \mathbf{F}}\left[\sum_{i=1}^{n} \varphi_i(v_i) x_i(\mathbf{v})\right] = \mathbf{E}_{\mathbf{v} \sim \mathbf{F}}\left[\max_{i=1}^{n} \varphi_i(v_i)^+\right],$$

precisely the expected value obtained by a prophet with prizes $\varphi_1(v_1)^+, \ldots, \varphi_n(v_n)^+$.

Now consider any allocation rule that has the following form.

Virtual Threshold Allocation Rule

1. Choose t such that $\mathbf{Pr}[\max_i \varphi_i(v_i)^+ \geq t] = \frac{1}{2}$.[5]

2. Give the item to a bidder i with $\varphi_i(v_i) \geq t$, if any, breaking ties among multiple candidate winners arbitrarily.

The prophet inequality, strengthened as in Remark 6.2, immediately implies the following guarantee for such allocation rules.

Corollary 6.3 (Virtual Threshold Rules Are Near-Optimal)
If $\mathbf{x}$ *is a virtual threshold allocation rule, then*

$$\mathbf{E}_{\mathbf{v}}\left[\sum_{i=1}^{n} \varphi_i(v_i)^+ x_i(\mathbf{v})\right] \geq \frac{1}{2}\mathbf{E}_{\mathbf{v}}\left[\max_{i=1}^{n} \varphi_i(v_i)^+\right]. \tag{6.3}$$

Because a virtual threshold allocation rule never awards the item to a bidder with negative virtual valuation, the left-hand side of (6.3) also equals $\mathbf{E}_{\mathbf{v}}[\sum_i \varphi_i(v_i) x_i(\mathbf{v})]$.

Here is a specific virtual threshold allocation rule.

Second-Price with Bidder-Specific Reserves

1. Set a reserve price $r_i = \varphi_i^{-1}(t)$ for each bidder i, with t defined as for virtual threshold allocation rules.

---

[5]See Exercise 6.2 for the case where no such t exists.

> 2. Give the item to the highest bidder that meets her reserve, if any.

This auction first filters bidders using bidder-specific reserve prices, and then awards the item to the highest bidder remaining. With regular valuation distributions, this allocation rule is monotone (Exercise 6.3) and hence can be extended to a DSIC auction using Myerson's lemma. The winner's payment is then the maximum of her reserve price and the highest bid by another bidder that meets her reserve price. By Theorem 5.2 and Corollary 6.3, this auction approximately maximizes the expected revenue over all DSIC auctions.

Theorem 6.4 (Simple Versus Optimal Auctions) *For all $n \geq 1$ and regular distributions $F_1, \ldots, F_n$, the expected revenue of a second-price auction with suitable reserve prices is at least 50% of that of the optimal auction.*

The guarantee of 50% can be improved for many distributions, but it is tight in the worst case, even with only two bidders (see Problem 6.1).

The second-price auction with bidder-specific reserve prices is simpler than the optimal auction in two senses. First, virtual valuation functions are only used to set reserve prices. Second, the highest bidder wins, as long as she clears her reserve price.

An even simpler auction would use a common, or "anonymous," reserve price for all bidders. For example, the opening bid in eBay is anonymous.[6] See the Notes for approximation guarantees for single-item auctions with anonymous reserve prices.

6.4   Prior-Independent Mechanisms

This section explores a different critique of the theory of optimal mechanisms developed in Lecture 5: the valuation distributions $F_1, \ldots, F_n$ were assumed to be known to the mechanism designer in advance. In some applications, where there is lots of data and

---

[6]Some real-world auctions do use bidder-specific reserve prices. For example, in some sponsored search auctions, "higher-quality" advertisers (as estimated by the search company) face lower reserve prices than "lower-quality" advertisers.

bidders' preferences are not changing too rapidly, this is a reasonable assumption. But what if the mechanism designer does not know, or is not confident about, the valuation distributions? This problem is especially relevant in thin markets where there is not much data, including sponsored search auctions for rarely used but potentially valuable keywords (as in Exercise 5.10).

Removing advance knowledge of the valuation distributions might seem to return us to the single-bidder single-item quandary that motivated the Bayesian approach (Section 5.1.2). The difference is that we continue to assume that bidders' valuations are drawn from distributions; it's just that these distributions are unknown to the mechanism designer. That is, we continue to use distributions in the *analysis* of mechanisms, but not in their *design*. The goal is to design a good *prior-independent* mechanism, meaning one whose description makes no reference to a valuation distribution. Examples of prior-independent mechanisms include second-price single-item auctions, and more generally welfare-maximizing DSIC mechanisms (as in Exercise 4.1). Non-examples include monopoly prices, which are a function of the underlying distribution, and more generally virtual welfare maximizers.

Next is a beautiful result from auction theory: the expected revenue of an optimal single-item auction is at most that of a second-price auction (with no reserve price) with one extra bidder.

Theorem 6.5 (Bulow-Klemperer Theorem) *Let F be a regular distribution and n a positive integer. Let $\mathbf{p}$ and $\mathbf{p}^*$ denote the payment rules of the second-price auction with $n + 1$ bidders and the optimal auction (for F) with n bidders, respectively.[7] Then*

$$\mathbf{E}_{\mathbf{v} \sim F^{n+1}} \left[\sum_{i=1}^{n+1} p_i(\mathbf{v}) \right] \geq \mathbf{E}_{\mathbf{v} \sim F^n} \left[\sum_{i=1}^{n} p_i^*(\mathbf{v}) \right]. \tag{6.4}$$

The usual interpretation of the Bulow-Klemperer theorem, which also has anecdotal support in practice, is that extra competition is more important than getting the auction format just right. It is better to invest your resources to recruit more serious participants

---

[7]The latter auction is a second-price auction with reserve price $\varphi^{-1}(0)$, where φ is the virtual valuation function of F (Section 5.2.6).

than to sharpen your knowledge of their preferences. (Of course, do both if you can!)

The Bulow-Klemperer theorem gives a sense in which the (prior-independent) second-price auction is simultaneously competitive with an infinite number of different optimal auctions, ranging over all single-item environments with bidders' valuations drawn i.i.d. from a regular distribution. Exercise 6.4 shows another consequence of the theorem: for every such environment and $n \geq 2$, the expected revenue of the second-price auction with n bidders is at least $\frac{n-1}{n}$ times that of an optimal auction (again with n bidders). Problem 6.4 outlines some further extensions and variations of the Bulow-Klemperer theorem.

Proof of Theorem 6.5: The two sides of (6.4) are tricky to compare directly, so for the analysis we define a fictitious auction $\mathcal{A}$ to facilitate the comparison. This $(n + 1)$-bidder single-item DSIC auction works as follows.

The Fictitious Auction $\mathcal{A}$

1. Simulate an optimal n-bidder auction for F on the first n bidders $1, 2, \ldots, n$.

2. If the item was not awarded in the first step, then give the item to bidder $n + 1$ for free.

We defined $\mathcal{A}$ to possess two properties useful for the analysis. First, its expected revenue equals that of an optimal auction with n bidders, the right-hand side of (6.4). Second, it always allocates the item.

We can finish the proof by arguing that the expected revenue of a second-price auction (with $n + 1$ bidders) is at least that of $\mathcal{A}$. We show the stronger statement that, when bidders' valuations are drawn i.i.d. from a regular distribution, the second-price auction maximizes the expected revenue over all DSIC auctions that always allocate the item.

We can identify the optimal such auction using the tools developed in Section 5.2. By the equivalence of expected revenue and expected virtual welfare (Theorem 5.2), it suffices to maximize the latter. The allocation rule with maximum possible expected virtual welfare subject to always allocating the item always awards the item to a bidder with the highest virtual valuation, even if this is negative.

A second-price auction always awards the item to a bidder with the highest valuation. Since bidders' valuations are drawn i.i.d. from a regular distribution, all bidders share the same nondecreasing virtual valuation function φ. Thus, a bidder with the highest valuation also has the highest virtual valuation. We conclude that the second-price auction maximizes expected revenue subject to always awarding the item, and the proof is complete. ∎

The Upshot

☆ When bidders' valuations are drawn from different distributions, the optimal single-item auction is complex, requires detailed information about the distributions, and does not resemble the auction formats used in practice.

☆ The prophet inequality states that, given a sequence of prizes drawn from known and independent distributions, there is a threshold strategy with expected value at least 50% of the expected value of the biggest prize.

☆ The prophet inequality implies that a second-price auction with suitably chosen bidder-specific reserve prices has expected revenue at least 50% of the maximum possible.

☆ A prior-independent mechanism is one whose description makes no reference to any valuation distributions. Welfare-maximizing mechanisms are prior-independent; virtual welfare-maximizing mechanisms are not.

☆ The Bulow-Klemperer theorem states that the expected revenue of an optimal single-item auction is at most that of a second-price auction with one extra bidder.

Notes

The prophet inequality (Theorem 6.1) is due to Samuel-Cahn (1984). Theorem 6.4 is from Chawla et al. (2007). Approximation guarantees for second-price auctions with anonymous reserve prices are considered by Hartline and Roughgarden (2009), and a recent result of Alaei et al. (2015) shows that such an auction can always extract at least a $1/e \approx 37\%$ fraction of the optimal expected revenue. Problem 6.2 also appears in Hartline and Roughgarden (2009). The result in Problem 6.3 is due to Chawla et al. (2010).

The Bulow-Klemperer theorem (Theorem 6.5) and its extension in Problem 6.4(a) are from Bulow and Klemperer (1996). Our proof follows Kirkegaard (2006). The consequent approximation guarantee (Exercise 6.4) is observed in Roughgarden and Sundararajan (2007). The general agenda of designing good prior-independent mechanisms is articulated in Dhangwatnotai et al. (2015), and Problem 6.4(b) is a special case of their "single sample" mechanism. Prior-independent mechanism design can be considered a relaxation of "prior-free" mechanism design, as developed by Goldberg et al. (2006).

In contrast to the classical optimal auction theory developed in Lecture 5, the theories of simple near-optimal and prior-independent mechanisms emerged only over the past 10 years, primarily in the computer science literature. See Hartline (2016) for a survey of the latest developments.

Exercises

Exercise 6.1 Consider an n-bidder single-item auction, with bidders' valuations drawn independently from regular distributions $F_1, \ldots, F_n$.

(a) Give a formula for the winner's payment in an optimal auction, in terms of the bidders' virtual valuation functions.

(b) *(H)* Show by example that, in an optimal auction, the highest bidder need not win, even if it has a positive virtual valuation.

(c) Give an intuitive explanation of why the property in (b) might be beneficial to the expected revenue of an auction.

Exercise 6.2 *(H)* Extend the prophet inequality (Theorem 6.1) to the case where there is no threshold t with $q(t) = \frac{1}{2}$, where $q(t)$ is the probability that no prize meets the threshold.

Exercise 6.3 Prove that with regular valuation distributions $F_1, \dots,$ F_n, the allocation rule of a second-price auction with bidder-specific reserve prices (Section 6.3) is monotone.

Exercise 6.4 *(H)* Consider an n-bidder single-item auction, with bidders' valuations drawn i.i.d. from a regular distribution F. Prove that the expected revenue of a second-price auction (with no reserve price) is at least $\frac{n-1}{n}$ times that of an optimal auction.

Problems

Problem 6.1 This problem investigates improvements to the prophet inequality (Theorem 6.1) and its consequences for simple near-optimal auctions (Theorem 6.4).

(a) *(H)* Show that the factor of $\frac{1}{2}$ in the prophet inequality cannot be improved: for every constant $c > \frac{1}{2}$, there are distributions $G_1, \dots, G_n$ such that *every* strategy, threshold or otherwise, has expected value less than $c \cdot \mathbf{E}_{\pi \sim \mathbf{G}}[\max_i \pi_i]$.

(b) Prove that Theorem 6.4 does not hold with 50% replaced by any larger constant factor.

(c) Can the factor of $\frac{1}{2}$ in the prophet inequality be improved for the special case of i.i.d. distributions, with $G_1 = G_2 = \cdots = G_n$?

Problem 6.2 This problem steps through a reasonably general result about simple and near-optimal mechanisms. Consider a single-parameter environment in which every feasible outcome is a 0-1 vector, indicating the winning agents (cf., Exercise 4.2). Assume that the feasible set is *downward-closed*, meaning that if S is a feasible set of winning agents and $T \subseteq S$, then T is also a feasible set of winning agents. Finally, assume that the valuation distribution F_i

of every agent i satisfies the monotone hazard rate (MHR) condition (Exercise 5.4), meaning that $\frac{f_i(v_i)}{1 - F_i(v_i)}$ is nondecreasing in v_i.

Let $\mathcal{M}^*$ denote the expected revenue-maximizing DSIC mechanism. Our protagonist is the following DSIC mechanism $\mathcal{M}$.

Welfare Maximization with Monopoly Reserves

1. Let r_i be a monopoly price (i.e., in $\mathrm{argmax}_{r \geq 0}\{r \cdot (1 - F_i(r))\}$) for the distribution F_i.

2. Let S denote the agents i that satisfy $v_i \geq r_i$.

3. Choose winners $W \subseteq S$ to maximize the social welfare:
$$W = \underset{T \subseteq S \,:\, T \text{ feasible}}{\mathrm{argmax}} \sum_{i \in T} v_i.$$

4. Define payments according to Myerson's payment formula (3.5).

(a) Let φ_i denote the virtual valuation function of F_i. Use the MHR condition to prove that, for every $v_i \geq r_i$, $r_i + \varphi_i(v_i) \geq v_i$.

(b) *(H)* Prove that the expected social welfare of $\mathcal{M}$ is at least that of $\mathcal{M}^*$.

(c) *(H)* Prove that the expected revenue of $\mathcal{M}$ is at least half of its expected social welfare.

(d) Conclude that the expected revenue of $\mathcal{M}$ is at least half the expected revenue of the optimal mechanism $\mathcal{M}^*$.

Problem 6.3 Consider a single consumer who is interested in purchasing at most one of n non-identical items. Assume that the consumer's private valuations $v_1, \ldots, v_n$ for the n items are drawn from known independent regular distributions $F_1, \ldots, F_n$. The design space is the set of *posted prices*, with one price per item. Faced with prices $p_1, \ldots, p_n$, the consumer selects no item if $p_j > v_j$ for every item j. Otherwise, she selects the item that maximizes $v_j - p_j$, breaking ties arbitrarily, providing revenue p_j to the seller.

(a) Explain why this setting does not correspond to a single-parameter environment.

(b) *(H)* Prove that for every $F_1, \ldots, F_n$, the maximum expected revenue achievable by posted prices is at most that of an optimal single-item auction with n bidders with valuations drawn independently from the distributions $F_1, \ldots, F_n$.

(c) *(H)* Prove that, for every $F_1, \ldots, F_n$, there are posted prices that achieve expected revenue at least half that of the upper bound identified in (b).

Problem 6.4 This problem considers some variations of the Bulow-Klemperer theorem (Theorem 6.5). Consider an n-bidder k-unit auction (Example 3.2) with $n \geq k \geq 1$ and with bidders' valuations drawn i.i.d. from a regular distribution F.

(a) Prove that the expected revenue of the optimal auction for F (Exercise 5.7) is at most that of the DSIC welfare-maximizing auction (Exercise 2.3) with k extra bidders.

(b) *(H)* Assume that $n \geq k + 1$. Prove that the following randomized auction is DSIC and has expected revenue at least $\frac{n-1}{2n}$ times that of the optimal auction.[8]

A Prior-Independent Auction

1. Choose one bidder j uniformly at random.

2. Let S denote the k highest bidders other than j, and ℓ the next-highest such bidder. (If $n = k = 1$, interpret v_ℓ as 0.)

3. Award an item to every bidder i of S with $v_i \geq v_j$, at a price of $\max\{v_j, v_\ell\}$.

---

[8] A randomized mechanism is DSIC if for every agent i and reports $\mathbf{v}_{-i}$ by the others, truthful reporting maximizes the expected utility of i. The expectation is over the coin flips of the mechanism.

Lecture 7

Multi-Parameter Mechanism Design

Lectures 2–6 considered only single-parameter mechanism design problems, where the only private parameter of an agent is her valuation per unit of stuff. Mechanism design is much more difficult for *multi-parameter* problems, where each agent has multiple private parameters. The Vickrey-Clarke-Groves (VCG) mechanisms provide a sweeping positive result: DSIC welfare maximization is possible in principle in every multi-parameter environment.

Section 7.1 formally defines general mechanism design environments. Section 7.2 derives the VCG mechanisms and proves that they are DSIC. Section 7.3 discusses the challenges of implementing VCG mechanisms in practice.

7.1 General Mechanism Design Environments

A general multi-parameter mechanism design environment comprises the following ingredients:

- n strategic participants, or "agents";

- a finite set Ω of outcomes;

- each agent i has a private nonnegative valuation $v_i(\omega)$ for each outcome $\omega \in \Omega$.

The outcome set Ω is abstract and could be very large. The *social welfare* of an outcome $\omega \in \Omega$ is defined as $\sum_{i=1}^{n} v_i(\omega)$.

Example 7.1 (Single-Item Auction Revisited) In a single-item auction, Ω has only $n + 1$ elements, corresponding to the winner of the item (if any). In the standard single-parameter model of a single-item auction, we assume that the valuation of a bidder is 0 in all of the n outcomes in which she doesn't win, leaving only one unknown

87

parameter per bidder. In the more general multi-parameter frame-work, a bidder can have a different valuation for each possible winner of the auction. For example, in a bidding war over a hot startup, if a bidder loses, she might prefer that the startup be bought by a company in a different market, rather than by a direct competitor.

Example 7.2 (Combinatorial Auctions) In a combinatorial auction, there are multiple indivisible items for sale, and bidders can have complex preferences between different subsets of items (called *bundles*). With n bidders and a set M of m items, the outcomes of Ω correspond to n-vectors $(S_1, \ldots, S_n)$, with $S_i \subseteq M$ denoting the bundle allocated to bidder i, and with no item allocated twice. There are $(n + 1)^m$ different outcomes. Each bidder i has a private valuation $v_i(S)$ for each bundle $S \subseteq M$ of items she might get. Thus, each bidder has 2^m private parameters.

Combinatorial auctions are important in practice. For example, dozens of government spectrum auctions around the world have raised hundreds of billions of dollars of revenue. In such auctions, typical bidders are telecommunication companies like Verizon or AT&T, and each item is a license awarding the right to broadcast on a certain frequency in a given geographic area. Combinatorial auctions have also been used for other applications such as allocating takeoff and landing slots at airports.

7.2 The VCG Mechanism

Our next result is a cornerstone of mechanism design theory, and one of the most sweeping positive results in the field: *every* multi-parameter environment admits a DSIC welfare-maximizing mechanism.

Theorem 7.3 (Multi-Parameter Welfare Maximization)
In every general mechanism design environment, there is a DSIC welfare-maximizing mechanism.

Recall the three properties of ideal mechanisms that we singled out in Theorem 2.4, in the context of second-price auctions. Theorem 7.3 asserts the first two properties (DSIC and welfare maximization) but not the third (computational efficiency). We already know from Section 4.1.4 that, even in single-parameter environments, we can't always have the second and third properties (unless $\mathcal{P} = \mathcal{NP}$). We'll see that the mechanism identified in Theorem 7.3 is highly non-ideal in many important applications.

We discuss the main ideas behind Theorem 7.3 before proving it formally. Designing a (direct-revelation) DSIC mechanism is tricky because the allocation and payment rules need to be coupled carefully.[1] We apply the same two-step approach that served us so well in single-parameter environments (Section 2.6.4).

The first step is to assume, without justification, that agents truthfully report their private information, and then figure out which outcome to pick. Since Theorem 7.3 demands welfare maximization, the only solution is to pick a welfare-maximizing outcome, using bids as proxies for the unknown valuations. That is, given reports $\mathbf{b}_1, \ldots, \mathbf{b}_n$, where each report $\mathbf{b}_i$ is now a vector indexed by Ω, we define the allocation rule $\mathbf{x}$ by

$$\mathbf{x}(\mathbf{b}) = \mathrm{argmax}_{\omega \in \Omega} \sum_{i=1}^{n} b_i(\omega). \tag{7.1}$$

The second step is to define a payment rule that, when coupled with this allocation rule, yields a DSIC mechanism. Last time we faced this problem (Section 3.3), for single-parameter environments, we formulated and proved Myerson's lemma (Theorem 3.7), which is a general solution to this second step for all such environments. Myerson's lemma does not hold beyond single-parameter environments— with each agent submitting a multidimensional report, it's not even clear how to define "monotonicity" of an allocation rule (cf., Definition 3.6).[2] Similarly, the "critical bid" characterization of DSIC

---

[1] The statement and proof of the revelation principle (Theorem 4.3) extend immediately to general mechanism design environments, so we can restrict attention to direct-revelation mechanisms without loss of generality.

[2] There is an analogous characterization of the implementable multi-parameter allocation rules in terms of "cycle monotonicity"; see the Notes. This is an elegant result, analogous to the fact that a network with real-valued lengths on its edges admits well-defined shortest paths if and only if it possesses no negative cycle. Cycle monotonicity is far more unwieldy than single-parameter monotonicity, however. Because it is so brutal to verify, cycle monotonicity is rarely used to argue implementability or to derive DSIC payment rules in concrete settings.

payments for 0-1 single-parameter problems (Section 4.1.3) does not have an obvious analog in multi-parameter problems.

The key idea is to generalize an alternative characterization of an agent i's payment in a DSIC welfare-maximizing mechanism, as the "externality" caused by i— the welfare loss inflicted on the other $n-1$ agents by i's presence (cf., Exercise 4.2). For example, in a single-item auction, the winning bidder inflicts a welfare loss on the others equal to the second-highest bid (assuming truthful bids), and this is precisely the payment rule of a second-price auction. "Charging an agent her externality" remains well defined in general mechanism design environments, and corresponds to the payment rule

$$p_i(\mathbf{b}) = \underbrace{\left(\max_{\omega \in \Omega} \sum_{j \neq i} b_j(\omega) \right)}_{\text{without } i} - \underbrace{\sum_{j \neq i} b_j(\omega^*)}_{\text{with } i}, \qquad (7.2)$$

where $\omega^* = \mathbf{x}(\mathbf{b})$ is the outcome chosen in (7.1). Intuitively, these payments force the agents to "internalize" their externalities, thereby aligning their incentives with those of a welfare-maximizing decision maker. The payment $p_i(\mathbf{b})$ is always at least 0 (Exercise 7.1).

Definition 7.4 (VCG Mechanism) A mechanism $(\mathbf{x}, \mathbf{p})$ with allocation and payment rules as in (7.1) and (7.2), respectively, is a *Vickrey-Clarke-Groves* or *VCG* mechanism.

For an alternative interpretation of the payments in a VCG mechanism, rewrite the expression in (7.2) as

$$p_i(\mathbf{b}) = \underbrace{b_i(\omega^*)}_{\text{bid}} - \underbrace{\left[\sum_{j=1}^{n} b_j(\omega^*) - \max_{\omega \in \Omega} \sum_{j \neq i} b_j(\omega) \right]}_{\text{rebate}}. \qquad (7.3)$$

We can therefore think of agent i's payment as her bid minus a "rebate," equal to the increase in welfare attributable to i's presence. For example, in a second-price auction, the highest bidder pays her bid b_1 minus a rebate of $b_1 - b_2$ (where b_2 is the second-highest bid), the increase in welfare that the bidder brings to the table. With nonnegative reports, the rebate in (7.3) is nonnegative (Exercise 7.1).

This implies that $p_i(\mathbf{b}) \leq b_i(\omega^*)$ and hence truthful reporting always guarantees nonnegative utility.

Proof of Theorem 7.3: Fix an arbitrary general mechanism design environment and let $(\mathbf{x}, \mathbf{p})$ denote the corresponding VCG mechanism. By definition, the mechanism maximizes the social welfare whenever all reports are truthful. To verify the DSIC condition (Definition 2.3), we need to show that for every agent i and every set $\mathbf{b}_{-i}$ of reports by the other agents, agent i maximizes her quasilinear utility $v_i(\mathbf{x}(\mathbf{b})) - p_i(\mathbf{b})$ by setting $\mathbf{b}_i = \mathbf{v}_i$.

Fix i and $\mathbf{b}_{-i}$. When the chosen outcome $\mathbf{x}(\mathbf{b})$ is ω^*, we can use (7.2) to write i's utility as

$$
v_i(\omega^*) - p_i(\mathbf{b}) = \underbrace{\left[v_i(\omega^*) + \sum_{j \neq i} b_j(\omega^*) \right]}_{(A)} - \underbrace{\left[\max_{\omega \in \Omega} \sum_{j \neq i} b_j(\omega) \right]}_{(B)}.
$$

The term (B) is a constant, independent of i's report $\mathbf{b}_i$. Thus, the problem of maximizing agent i's utility reduces to the problem of maximizing the first term (A). As a thought experiment, suppose agent i has the power to choose the outcome ω^* directly, rather than merely influencing the chosen outcome indirectly via her choice of bid $\mathbf{b}_i$. Agent i would, of course, use this extra power to choose an outcome that maximizes the term (A). If agent i sets $\mathbf{b}_i = \mathbf{v}_i$, then the function (7.1) that the mechanism maximizes becomes identical to the term (A) that the agent wants maximized. Thus, truthful reporting coaxes the mechanism to choose an outcome that maximizes agent i's utility; no other report can be better. ∎

7.3 Practical Considerations

Theorem 7.3 shows that, in general multi-parameter environments, DSIC welfare maximization is always possible in principle. However, there are several major obstacles to implementing the VCG mechanism in most multi-parameter environments.[3]

---

[3] The VCG mechanism can still serve as a useful benchmark for other, more practical solutions (cf., Lecture 6).

The first challenge of implementing the VCG mechanism is *preference elicitation*, meaning getting the reports $\mathbf{b}_1, \ldots, \mathbf{b}_n$ from the agents. For example, in a combinatorial auction with m items (Example 7.2), each bidder has 2^m private parameters, which is roughly a thousand when $m = 10$ and a million when $m = 20$. No bidder in her right mind would want to figure out or write down so many numbers, and no seller would want to read them. This critique applies to every direct-revelation mechanism, not just to the VCG mechanism, for an environment with a large outcome space.

The second challenge is familiar from algorithmic mechanism design (Lecture 4). Even when the first challenge is not an issue and preference elicitation is easy, as in single-parameter environments, welfare maximization can be a computationally intractable problem. This is already the case in (single-parameter) knapsack auctions (Section 4.1.4), and in more complex settings even approximate welfare maximization can be computationally intractable.

The third challenge is that, even in applications where the first two challenges are not relevant, VCG mechanisms can have bad revenue and incentive properties (despite being DSIC). For instance, consider a combinatorial auction with two bidders and two items, A and B. The first bidder only wants both items, so $v_1(AB) = 1$ and is 0 otherwise. The second bidder only wants item A, so $v_2(AB) = v_2(A) = 1$ and is 0 otherwise. The revenue of the VCG mechanism is 1 in this example (Exercise 7.2). Now suppose we add a third bidder who only wants item B, so $v_3(AB) = v_3(B) = 1$. The maximum welfare jumps to 2, but the VCG revenue drops to 0 (Exercise 7.2)! The fact that the VCG mechanism has zero revenue in seemingly competitive environments is a dealbreaker in practice. The revenue non-monotonicity in this example also leads to numerous incentive problems, including vulnerability to collusion and false-name bids (Exercises 7.3 and 7.4).

The next lecture discusses how practitioners cope with these challenges in real-world combinatorial auctions.

The Upshot

☆ In a general mechanism design environment, each agent has a private valuation for each possible outcome. Combinatorial auctions are an important example in both theory and practice.

☆ In the VCG mechanism for an environment, the allocation rule selects an outcome that maximizes the social welfare with respect to agents' reports. The payment rule charges each agent her externality—the welfare loss inflicted on the other agents by her presence.

☆ Every VCG mechanism is DSIC.

☆ There are several obstacles to implementing VCG mechanisms in practice, including the difficulty of eliciting a large number of private parameters, the computational intractability of computing a welfare-maximizing outcome, and their bad revenue and incentive properties.

Notes

Our definition of VCG mechanisms follows Clarke (1971), generalizing the second-price single-item auction of Vickrey (1961). Groves (1973) gives a still more general class of mechanisms, where a bid-independent "pivot term" $h_i(\mathbf{b}_{-i})$ is added to each agent's payment, as in Problem 7.1. The equivalence of multi-parameter implementability and "cycle monotonicity" is due to Rochet (1987); see Vohra (2011) for a lucid exposition and some applications. Rothkopf et al. (1990) and Ausubel and Milgrom (2006) detail the many challenges of implementing VCG mechanisms in practice. Problem 7.1 is due to Holmstrom (1977). Problem 7.3 is from Dobzinski et al. (2010); see Blumrosen and Nisan (2007) for a survey of further results of this type.

Exercises

Exercise 7.1 Prove that the payment $p_i(\mathbf{b})$ charged to an agent i in the VCG mechanism is at least 0 and at most $b_i(\omega^*)$, where ω^* is the outcome chosen by the mechanism.

Exercise 7.2 Consider a combinatorial auction (Example 7.2) with two items, A and B, and three bidders. The first bidder has valuation 1 for receiving both items (i.e., $v_1(AB) = 1$) and 0 otherwise. The second bidder has valuation 1 for item A (i.e., $v_2(AB) = v_2(A) = 1$) and 0 otherwise. The third bidder has valuation 1 for B and 0 otherwise.

(a) Compute the outcome of the VCG mechanism when only the first two bidders are present and when all three bidders are present. What can you conclude?

(b) Can adding an extra bidder ever decrease the revenue of a second-price single-item auction?

Exercise 7.3 Exhibit a combinatorial auction and bidder valuations such that the VCG mechanism has the following property: there are two bidders who receive no items when all bidders bid truthfully, but can both achieve positive utility by submitting suitable false bids (assuming others bid truthfully). Why doesn't this example contradict Theorem 7.3?

Exercise 7.4 Consider a combinatorial auction in which bidders can submit multiple bids under different names, unbeknownst to the mechanism. The allocation and payment of a bidder is the union and sum of the allocations and payments, respectively, assigned to all of her pseudonyms.

(a) Exhibit a combinatorial auction and bidder valuations such that, in the VCG mechanism, there is a bidder who can earn higher utility by submitting multiple bids than by bidding truthfully as a single agent (assuming others bid truthfully).

(b) Can this ever happen in a second-price single-item auction?

Exercise 7.5 *(H)* A bidder i in a combinatorial auction has a *unit-demand* valuation if there exist parameters $v_{i1}, \ldots, v_{im}$, one per item, such that $v_i(S) = \max_{j \in S} v_{ij}$ for every bundle S of items (and $v_i(\emptyset) = 0$). A bidder with a unit-demand valuation only wants one item—for instance, a hotel room for a given night—and only retains her favorite item from a bundle.

Give an implementation of the VCG mechanism in combinatorial auctions with unit-demand bidder valuations that runs in time polynomial in the number of bidders and the number of items.

Problems

Problem 7.1 Consider a general mechanism design environment, with outcome set Ω and n agents. In this problem, we use the term DSIC to refer to the first condition of Definition 2.3 (truthful reporting is a dominant strategy) and do not consider the individual rationality condition (truthful bidders receive nonnegative utility).

(a) Suppose we modify the payments (7.2) of the VCG mechanism by adding a *pivot term* $h_i(\mathbf{b}_{-i})$ to each agent i's payment, where $h_i(\cdot)$ is an arbitrary function of the other agents' reports. These pivot terms can be positive or negative, and can result in payments from the mechanism to the agents. Prove that for every choice of pivot terms, the resulting mechanism is DSIC.

(b) *(H)* Suppose agents' valuations are restricted to lie in the set $\mathcal{V} \subseteq \mathbb{R}^\Omega$. We say that the pivot terms $\{h_i(\cdot)\}_{i=1}^n$ *budget-balance the VCG mechanism* if, for all possible reports $b_1(\cdot), \ldots, b_n(\cdot) \in \mathcal{V}$, the corresponding VCG payments (including the h_i's) sum to 0.

Prove that there exist pivot terms that budget-balance the VCG mechanism if and only if the maximum social welfare can be represented as the sum of bid-independent functions—if and only if we can write

$$\max_{\omega \in \Omega} \sum_{i=1}^n b_i(\omega) = \sum_{i=1}^n g_i(\mathbf{b}_{-i}) \tag{7.4}$$

for every $b_1(\cdot), \ldots, b_n(\cdot) \in \mathcal{V}$, where each g_i is a function that does not depend on b_i.

(c) Either directly or using part (b), prove that there are no pivot terms that budget-balance a second-price single-item auction.

Conclude that there is no DSIC single-item auction that maximizes social welfare and is budget-balanced.

Problem 7.2 Consider a general mechanism design environment, with outcome set Ω and n agents. Suppose the function $f : \Omega \to \mathbb{R}$ has the form

$$f(\omega) = c(\omega) + \sum_{i=1}^{n} w_i v_i(\omega),$$

where c is a publicly known function of the outcome, and where each w_i is a nonnegative, public, agent-specific weight. Such a function is called an *affine maximizer*.

Show that for every affine maximizer f and every subset $\Omega' \subseteq \Omega$ of the outcomes, there is a DSIC mechanism that maximizes f over Ω'.

Problem 7.3 Consider a combinatorial auction (Example 7.2) with a set M of m items, where the valuation function $v_i : 2^M \to \mathbb{R}^+$ of each bidder i satisfies: (i) $v_i(\emptyset) = 0$; (ii) $v_i(S) \leq v_i(T)$ whenever $S \subseteq T \subseteq M$; and (iii) $v_i(S \cup T) \leq v_i(S) + v_i(T)$ for all bundles $S, T \subseteq M$. Such functions are called *subadditive*.

(a) Call a profile **v** of subadditive valuations *lopsided* if there is a social welfare-maximizing allocation in which at least 50% of the social welfare is contributed by bidders who are each allocated at least $\sqrt{m}$ items. Prove that if **v** is lopsided, then there is an allocation that gives all of the items to a single bidder and has social welfare at least $\frac{1}{2\sqrt{m}}$ times the maximum possible.

(b) *(H)* Prove that if **v** is not lopsided, then there is an allocation that gives at most one item to each bidder and has social welfare at least $\frac{1}{2\sqrt{m}}$ times the maximum possible.

(c) *(H)* Give a mechanism with the following properties: (1) for some collection $\mathcal{S}$ of bundles, with $|\mathcal{S}|$ polynomial in m, each bidder i submits a bid $b_i(S)$ only on the bundles $S \in \mathcal{S}$; (2) for every bidder i and bids by the others, it is a dominant strategy to set $b_i(S) = v_i(S)$ for all $S \in \mathcal{S}$; (3) assuming truthful bids, the outcome of the mechanism has social welfare at least $\frac{1}{2\sqrt{m}}$ times the maximum possible; (4) the running time of the mechanism is polynomial in m and the number n of bidders.

Lecture 8

Spectrum Auctions

This lecture is a case study on the practical implementation of combinatorial auctions for wireless spectrum, an important and challenging multi-parameter mechanism design problem. While our sponsored search case studies (Sections 2.6 and 5.3) involve billions of small-stakes auctions, spectrum auction design concerns a single auction with billions of dollars of potential revenue.

Section 8.1 explains the practical benefits of indirect mechanisms. Section 8.2 discusses the prospects for selling multiple items via separate single-item auctions. Section 8.3 describes simultaneous ascending auctions, the primary workhorse in wireless spectrum auctions, while Section 8.4 weighs the pros and cons of packing bidding. Section 8.5 outlines the cutting edge of spectrum auction design, the 2016 FCC Incentive Auction.

8.1 Indirect Mechanisms

In a combinatorial auction (Example 7.2) there are n bidders, m items, and each bidder i's valuation specifies her value $v_i(S)$ for each bundle S of items that she might receive. In principle, the VCG mechanism provides a DSIC and welfare-maximizing combinatorial auction (Theorem 7.3). This mechanism is potentially practical if bidders' valuations are sufficiently simple (Exercise 7.5), but not otherwise (Section 7.3). For example, the number of parameters that each bidder reports in the VCG mechanism, or any other direct-revelation mechanism, grows exponentially with the number of items m.

The utter absurdity of direct-revelation combinatorial auctions motivates *indirect* mechanisms, which learn information about bidders' preferences only on a "need-to-know" basis. The canonical indirect auction is the ascending English auction; see also Exercise 2.7. This auction format is familiar from the movies: an auctioneer keeps

track of the current price and tentative winner, and the auction stops
when only one interested bidder remains.[1] Each bidder has a dominant strategy, which is to stay in the auction as long as the current
price is below her valuation (the bidder might win for positive utility)
and to drop out once the current price reaches her valuation (after
which winning can only lead to negative utility). If all bidders play
these strategies, then the outcome of the English auction is the same
as that of a second-price (sealed-bid) auction. The second-price auction is the result of applying the revelation principle (Theorem 4.3)
to the English auction.

Indirect mechanisms that elicit only a modest amount of information about bidders' valuations are unavoidable for all but the simplest
combinatorial auction design problems.[2] This entails giving up on
both the DSIC guarantee and full welfare maximization; we will miss
these properties, but have no alternative.

8.2   Selling Items Separately

What's a natural indirect auction format for combinatorial auctions
that avoids eliciting valuations for every possible bundle from each
bidder? The simplest mechanisms to try are those that sell the items
separately, using some type of single-item auction for each. Such
a mechanism requires only one bid per bidder per item, and this
is arguably the minimum number imaginable. Before pinning down
the precise single-item auction format, we consider a basic question:

---

[1]There are a few variants. The movies, and auction houses like Christie's and
Sotheby's, use an "open outcry" auction in which bidders can drop out and return,
and can make "jump bids" to aggressively raise the current price. When doing
mathematical analysis, the "Japanese" variant is usually more convenient: the
auction begins at some opening price, which is publicly displayed and increases
at a steady rate. Each bidder either chooses "in" or "out" at the current price,
and once a bidder drops out, she cannot return. The winner is the last bidder in,
and the sale price is the price at which the second-to-last bidder dropped out.

[2]Indirect mechanisms can also be useful in single-parameter settings like
single-item auctions. Empirical studies show that bidders are more likely to play
their dominant strategy in an English auction than in a sealed-bid second-price
auction, where some bidders inexplicably overbid. Second, ascending auctions
leak less valuation information to the seller. In a second-price auction, the seller
learns the highest bid; in an English auction, the seller only learns a lower bound
on the highest bid, namely the final selling price.

could selling items separately conceivably lead to allocations with high social welfare, even in principle?

There is a fundamental dichotomy between combinatorial auctions in which items are *substitutes* and those in which items can also be *complements*. The former are far easier than the latter, in both theory and practice. Roughly speaking, items are substitutes if they provide diminishing returns—having one item only makes others less valuable. For two items A and B, for example, the substitutes condition means that $v(AB) \leq v(A) + v(B)$. In a spectrum auction context, two licenses for the same area with equal-sized frequency ranges are usually substitute items. Theory indicates that selling items separately can work well when items are (mostly) substitutes. For starters, welfare maximization is a computationally tractable problem when items are substitutes and the true valuations are known. Also, the undesirable incentive and revenue properties of the VCG mechanism (Section 7.3 and Exercises 7.3 and 7.4) evaporate when items are substitutes, generalizing the reassuring properties of second-price single-item auctions. But even though substitute items constitute the "easy" case, we'll see that it is easy to screw up when trying to sell them separately.

Items are complements if there are synergies between them, so that possessing one makes others more valuable. With two items A and B, this translates to the property $v(AB) > v(A) + v(B)$. Complements arise naturally in wireless spectrum auctions, as some bidders want a collection of licenses that are adjacent, either in their geographic areas or in their frequency ranges. When items can be complements, welfare maximization is a computationally intractable problem, even without incentive constraints (Problem 4.3). We cannot expect a simple auction format like separate single-item auctions to perform well in these cases.

The items in spectrum auctions, and most real-world combinatorial auctions, are a mixture of substitutes and complements. If the problem is "mostly substitutes," then separate single-item auctions can perform well, if properly implemented. If not, then more complex auction formats are needed to achieve allocations with high social welfare (see Section 8.4).

8.3   Case Study: Simultaneous Ascending Auctions

8.3.1   Two Rookie Mistakes

There are numerous ways to organize separate single-item auctions. This section discusses two design decisions that seem to matter a lot in practice.

Rookie Mistake #1

Hold the single-item auctions sequentially, one at a time.

To see why holding auctions sequentially can be a bad idea, consider the especially easy case of k-unit auctions (Example 3.2), where the items are identical and each bidder only wants one of them. There is a simple DSIC and welfare-maximizing auction in this case (Exercise 2.3). Suppose we instead hold a sequence of single-item auctions—say, two identical items, sold via back-to-back second-price auctions. Now imagine that you are a bidder with a very high valuation—you expect to win any auction that you participate in. What should you do? First, suppose that every other bidder participates and bids her true valuation (until she wins an item). If you participate in the first auction, you would win and pay the second-highest valuation. If you skip it, the bidder with the second-highest valuation would win the first auction and disappear, leaving you to win the second auction at a price equal to the third-highest original valuation. Thus, straightforward bidding is not a dominant strategy in a sequence of second-price auctions. Intelligent bidding requires reasoning about the likely selling price of future auctions, and this in turn makes the auctions' outcomes unpredictable, with the possibility of low social welfare and revenue.

In March 2000, Switzerland auctioned off three blocks of spectrum via a sequence of second-price auctions. The first two auctions were for identical items, 28 MHz blocks, and sold for 121 million and 134 million Swiss francs, respectively. This is already more price variation than one would like for identical items. But the kicker was that in the third auction, where a larger 56 MHz block was being sold, the selling price was only 55 million francs! Some of the bids must have been far from optimal, and both the welfare and revenue achieved by this auction are suspect.[3]

The discussion and history lessons above suggest holding single-item auctions for multiple items *simultaneously* rather than sequentially. What single-item auction format should we choose?

Rookie Mistake #2

Use sealed-bid single-item auctions.

In 1990, the New Zealand government auctioned off essentially identical licenses for television broadcasting using simultaneous (sealed-bid) second-price auctions. It is again difficult for bidders to figure out how to bid in such an auction. Imagine that there are 10 licenses and you want only one of them. How should you bid? One legitimate strategy is to pick one of the licenses—at random, say—and go for it. Another strategy is to bid less aggressively on multiple licenses, hoping that you get one at a bargain price, and that you don't inadvertently win extra licenses that you don't want. The difficulty is trading off the risk of winning too many licenses with the risk of winning too few.

The challenge of bidding intelligently in simultaneous sealed-bid auctions makes the auction format prone to outcomes with low welfare and revenue. For example, suppose there are three bidders and two identical items, and each bidder wants only one. With simultaneous second-price auctions, if each bidder targets only one license, one of the licenses is likely to have only one bidder and will be given away for free (or sold at the reserve price).

The revenue in the 1990 New Zealand auction was only $36 million, a paltry fraction of the projected $250 million. On one license, the high bid was $100,000 while the second-highest bid (and selling price) was $6! On another, the high bid was $7 million and the second-highest was $5,000. To add insult to injury, the winning bids were made available to the public, who could then see just how much money was left on the table!

---

[3]In addition to the questionable auction format, there were some strategic mergers of potential bidders before the auction, leading to less competition than expected.

8.3.2   The Merits of Simultaneous Ascending Auctions

Simultaneous ascending auctions (SAAs) form the basis of most spectrum auctions run over the last 20 years. Conceptually, SAAs are like a bunch of single-item English auctions being run in parallel in the same room, with one auctioneer per item. More precisely, in each round, each bidder can place a new bid on any subset of items that it wants, subject to an *activity rule*. The activity rule forces all bidders to participate in the auction from the beginning and contribute to the discovery of appropriate prices. For example, such a rule makes it impossible for bidders to "snipe," meaning to enter the auction at last second and place a winning bid. The details of an activity rule can be complex, but the gist is to require that the number of items on which a bidder bids only decreases over time as prices rise. The high bids and bidders are usually visible to all, even though this can encourage signaling and retaliatory bids (Section 8.3.4). The first round with no new bids ends the auction.

The primary reason that SAAs work better than sequential or sealed-bid auctions is *price discovery*. As a bidder acquires better information about the likely selling prices of licenses, she can implement mid-course corrections: abandoning licenses for which competition is fiercer than anticipated, snapping up unexpected bargains, and rethinking which packages of licenses to assemble. The format typically resolves the miscoordination problems that plague simultaneous sealed-bid auctions. For instance, suppose there are two identical items and three bidders. Every round, some bidder will be losing both auctions. When she jumps back in, it makes sense to bid for the currently cheaper item, and this keeps the prices of the two items roughly the same.

Another bonus of the SAA format is that bidders only need to determine their valuations on a need-to-know basis. We've been assuming that valuations are known to bidders at the beginning of the auction, but in practice, determining the valuation for a bundle of items can be costly, involving research and expert advice. In sharp contrast to direct-revelation mechanisms, a bidder can often navigate an SAA with only coarse estimates for most valuations and precise estimates for the bundles that matter.

SAAs are thought to have achieved high social welfare and revenue in numerous spectrum auctions. This belief is not easy to test, since valuations remain unknown after an auction and bids are incomplete and potentially non-truthful. There are a number of sanity checks that can be used to argue good auction performance. First, there should be little or no resale of items after the auction, and any reselling should take place at a price comparable to the auction's selling price. This indicates that speculators did not play a significant role in the auction. Second, similar items should sell for similar prices (cf., the Swiss and New Zealand auctions). Third, revenue should meet or exceed projections. Fourth, there should be evidence of price discovery. For example, prices and provisional winners at the mid-point of the auction should be highly correlated with the final selling prices and winners. Finally, the packages assembled by bidders should be sensible, such as groups of licenses that are adjacent geographically or in frequency range.

8.3.3   Demand Reduction and the Exposure Problem

SAAs have two big vulnerabilities. The first problem is *demand reduction*, and this is relevant even when items are substitutes. Demand reduction occurs when a bidder asks for fewer items than it really wants, to lower competition and therefore the prices paid for the items that it gets.

To illustrate, suppose there are two identical items and two bidders. The first bidder has valuation 10 for one of the items and valuation 20 for both. The second bidder has valuation 8 for one of the items and does not want both (i.e., her valuation remains 8 for both). Giving both items to the first bidder maximizes the welfare, at 20. The VCG mechanism would earn revenue 8 in this example. Now consider how things play out in an SAA. The second bidder would be happy to have either item at any price less than 8. Thus, the second bidder drops out only when both items have price at least 8. If the first bidder stubbornly insists on winning both items, her utility is $20 - 16 = 4$. If, on the other hand, the first bidder targets just one item, then each of the bidders gets one of the items at a near-zero price. The first bidder's utility is then close to 10. In this example, demand reduction leads to a loss of welfare and revenue, relative to the VCG mechanism's outcome. There is ample evidence of demand reduction in many spectrum auctions.

The second big problem with SAAs is relevant when items can be complements, as in many spectrum auctions, and is called the *exposure problem*. As an example, consider two bidders and two non-identical items. The first bidder only wants both items—they are complementary items for the bidder—and her valuation is 100 for them (and 0 otherwise). The second bidder is willing to pay 75 for either item but only wants one item. The VCG mechanism would give both items to bidder 1, for a welfare of 100, and would generate revenue 75. In an SAA, the second bidder will not drop out until the price of both items reaches 75. The first bidder is in a no-win situation: to get both items it would have to pay 150, more than her value. The scenario of winning only one item for a nontrivial price could be even worse. On the other hand, if the second bidder's value for each item is only 40, then the first bidder should just go for it and outlast the second bidder. But how can the first bidder know which scenario is closer to the truth? The exposure problem makes bidding in an SAA difficult for a bidder for whom items are complements, and it leads to economically inefficient allocations for two reasons. First, an overly aggressive bidder might acquire unwanted items. Second, an overly tentative bidder might fail to acquire items for which it has the highest valuation.

8.3.4   Bid Signaling

Iterative auctions like SAAs offer opportunities for strategic behavior that do not exist in direct-revelation mechanisms. In early and relatively uncompetitive spectrum auctions, bidders sometimes used the low-order digits of their bids to effectively send messages to other bidders. In one example, USWest and McLeod were battling it out for license #378 in Rochester, Minnesota, with each repeatedly outbidding the other. Apparently, USWest tired of this bidding war and switched to a retaliatory strategy, bidding on licenses in other geographical areas on which McLeod was the standing high bidder and USWest had shown no interest in previous rounds. McLeod ultimately won back all of these licenses, but had to pay a higher price due to USWest's bids. To make sure its message came through loud and clear, all of USWest's retaliatory bids were a multiple of 1,000 *plus 378*—presumably warning McLeod to get the hell out of the market for Rochester, or else. While this particular type of signaling can be largely eliminated by forcing all bids to be multiples of a suitably large number, it seems impossible to design away all opportunities for undesirable strategic behavior.

8.4   Package Bidding

The exposure problem motivates supplementing the basic SAA format with *package bidding*, meaning bids on sets of items in addition to individual items. Package bidding allows a bidder to bid aggressively on a bundle of items without fear of receiving only a subset of them. There are also scenarios where package bids can remove the incentive for demand reduction.

There has been much discussion about how to implement package bidding, if at all, in wireless spectrum auctions. The conservative viewpoint, which dominated practice until relatively recently, is that package bids add complexity to a quite functional auction format and might lead to unpredictable outcomes. Limited forms of package bidding have been incorporated into spectrum auction designs only over the past 10 years or so, and only outside of the United States.

One design approach is to tack on one extra round after the SAA where bidders can submit package bids on any subsets of items that they want, subject to an activity rule. These package bids compete with each other as well as the winning bids on individual items from the SAA phase of the auction. The final allocation is determined by a welfare maximization computation, treating bids as true valuations. The biggest issue with this approach is that computing the final prices is tricky. The VCG payment rule is not used because of its poor revenue and incentive properties (Section 7.3 and Exercises 7.2–7.4). A more aggressive payment rule, which yields an auction that is not DSIC but does have other good incentive properties, is used instead.

A second approach is to predefine a limited set of allowable package bids rather than allowing bidders to propose their own. Ideally, the predefined package bids should be well aligned with what bidders want, yet structured enough to permit reasonably simple allocation and payment rules. Hierarchical packages have emerged as a sweet spot for this design approach. For example, an auction could allow bids on individual licenses, on regional bundles of licenses, and on nationwide bundles of licenses. The biggest issue with predefined

package bids is that they can do more harm than good when they
are poorly matched with bidders' goals. For example, imagine a bidder who wants the items $\{A, B, C, D\}$, but the available packages are
$\{A, B, E, F\}$ and $\{C, D, H, I\}$. What should her bidding strategy be?

8.5   Case Study: The 2016 FCC Incentive Auction

Wireless spectrum doesn't grow on trees. At this point, in the United
States, giving someone a new allocation of spectrum generally requires taking it away from someone else. The U.S. Federal Communications Commission (FCC) is doing precisely this, using a reverse
auction (cf., Exercise 2.5) to free up spectrum by buying out television (TV) broadcasters and a forward auction to resell the spectrum
to companies that can put it to more valuable use.[4]

The format of the forward auction is similar to past designs (Sections 8.3 and 8.4). The reverse auction is completely new.

After the reverse auction, the FCC will repack the remaining
broadcasters so that the newly available spectrum is contiguous. For
example, they might buy out a number of TV broadcasters across
the nation who were using a UHF channel between 38 and 51, and
reassign all of the other broadcasters using the channels to lower channels. This would leave the 84 MHz block of spectrum corresponding
to channels 38–51 free to be sold in the forward auction for new uses.

In a very cool development, the reverse auction format can be
thought of as a greedy allocation rule, not unlike the knapsack auction
allocation rules described in Section 4.2. To describe it, we adopt the
following model. Each bidder i (a TV broadcaster) has a private
valuation v_i for its broadcasting license. If bidder i loses (that is, is
not bought out), then her utility is 0. If bidder i wins (is bought out)
at a price of p, then her utility is $p - v_i$. Thus v_i is the "minimum
acceptable offer" for buying out i.[5] Letting N denote the set of
bidders, a set $W \subseteq N$ of winning bidders—where "winning" means
being bought out—is feasible if the remaining bidders $N \setminus W$ can

---

[4]The auction commenced on March 29, 2016 and is ongoing as of this writing.

[5]This single-parameter model assumes that each TV station is owned by a
different strategic agent. This assumption is not entirely true in practice, but it
makes the model much easier to reason about.

be repacked in the target range (e.g., the channels below 38).[6] For instance, if $W = N$, then all bidders are bought out and the entire spectrum is freed up, so W is certainly feasible. When $W = \emptyset$, no spectrum is reclaimed, an infeasible outcome. Two TV stations with overlapping geographic areas cannot be assigned the same or adjacent channels, and checking whether or not a given set W is feasible is a medium-size $\mathcal{NP}$-hard problem, closely related to graph coloring (Figure 8.1). State-of-the-art algorithms, building on satisfiability ("SAT") solvers, are used to perform each of these feasibility checks in seconds or less.

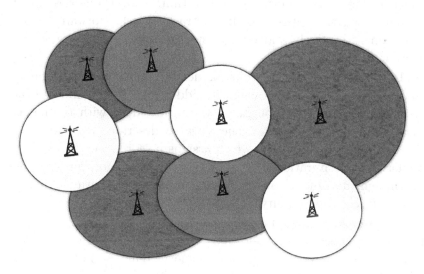

Figure 8.1: Different TV stations with overlapping broadcasting areas must be assigned different channels (indicated by shades of gray). Checking whether or not a given subset of stations can be assigned to a given number of channels without interference is an $\mathcal{NP}$-hard problem.

We next describe the form of the reverse auction allocation rule, which is a *deferred allocation rule*.[7]

---

[6]One interesting question is how to set this target. The bigger the target, the bigger the expenses per unit of spectrum in the reverse auction and the smaller the revenues per unit of spectrum in the forward auction. The goal is to set the target as large as possible, subject to a lower bound on the net revenue obtained.

[7]This terminology is inspired by the "deferred acceptance" algorithm for computing a stable matching (see Section 10.2).

Deferred Allocation Rule

initialize $W = N$ // initially feasible
while there is an $i \in W$ with $W \setminus \{i\}$ feasible **do**
   remove one such i from W // i not bought out
halt with winning bidders W

The allocation rule starts with the trivial feasible set (all bidders), and then iteratively removes bidders until a minimal feasible set is reached. This is a "reverse greedy algorithm," since it removes bidders starting from the entire set. In contrast, typical (forward) greedy algorithms iteratively add bidders starting from the empty set (cf., Section 4.2.2).

How should we choose which bidder to remove at each iteration? Natural ideas include removing the bidder with the highest bid (i.e., the least willing to be bought out), or the bidder with the highest ratio of bid to market size. A general way to describe such heuristics is through a *scoring function*, which assigns a score to each remaining bidder at each iteration of the auction. The algorithm can then be implemented by removing the remaining bidder with the highest score, subject to feasibility.[8]

One simple scoring function is the identity. The corresponding allocation rule performs a single pass over the bidders (from the highest to the lowest), removing a bidder whenever doing so preserves feasibility. For example, for the problem of hiring at least one contractor, this allocation rule just chooses the lowest bidder.

If the scoring function is increasing in a bidder's bid and independent of the bids of the other remaining bidders, then the corresponding deferred allocation rule is monotone; in the current context of a reverse auction, this means that bidding lower can only cause a bidder to win (Exercise 8.3). By Myerson's lemma (Theorem 3.7), paying each winner her critical bid—the largest bid at which she would have been bought out—yields a DSIC auction.[9] In the simple case of hiring

---

[8]The choice of the scoring function in the 2016 FCC Incentive Auction was guided by several factors, including the welfare achieved by different rules on synthetic data, and by constraints on how much price discrimination between bidders was politically feasible.

[9]For ease of participation, the actual FCC auction is iterative, not direct-

at least one contractor and the identity scoring function, this auction is identical to that in Exercise 2.5.

Remarkably, deferred allocation rules lead to mechanisms that have a number of good incentive properties above and beyond DSIC, and which are not shared by their forward-greedy cousins (Problem 8.1).

The Upshot

☆ Direct-revelation mechanisms are out of the question for all but the smallest combinatorial auctions.

☆ Indirect mechanisms learn information about bidders' preferences only on a need-to-know basis.

☆ Selling multiple items separately has the potential to work well when items are substitutes. When items can be complements, selling items separately can produce outcomes with low social welfare.

☆ The preferred method in practice of selling items separately is simultaneous ascending auctions (SAAs).

☆ SAAs are vulnerable to demand reduction, where a bidder reduces the number of items requested to depress the final selling prices.

☆ When items can be complements, SAAs also suffer from the exposure problem, where a bidder that desires a bundle of items runs the risk of acquiring only a useless subset of them.

revelation, and uses descending, bidder-specific prices. In each round, each bidder only has to decide whether to stay in at her current offer, or to drop out and retain her license. The offers at the beginning of the auction are high enough that everyone is happy to participate. For example, for WCBS-TV in New York, the opening offer is $900 million.

> ☆ Package bidding can mitigate the exposure
> problem but is tricky to implement.
>
> ☆ The 2016 FCC Incentive Auction is the first
> to include a reverse auction, where the govern-
> ment buys back licenses from TV broadcasters
> to reclaim spectrum.
>
> ☆ Deferred allocation rules are a rich family of
> reverse auction allocation rules with good in-
> centive properties.

Notes

The history and practice of wireless spectrum auctions are discussed in detail by Cramton (2006) and Milgrom (2004). See
also Cramton et al. (2006) and Klemperer (2004) for much more
on the theory and implementation of combinatorial auctions, and
Rassenti et al. (1982) for an early application of combinatorial auctions to the allocation of airport time slots.

Harstad (2000) demonstrates that bidders are more likely to play
their dominant strategies in an English auction than a sealed-bid
second-price auction. Cramton and Schwartz (2000) detail collusion
and bid signaling in early spectrum auctions. Ausubel and Milgrom
(2002) propose using a proxy round to implement package bids,
while Goeree and Holt (2010) advocate predefined hierarchical packages. The details of the FCC Incentive Auction design are described in a public notice (Federal Communications Commission,
2015). Milgrom and Segal (2015a,b) discuss the high-level design
decisions in the reverse auction, and also define deferred allocation rules. Exercise 8.3 and Problems 8.1 and 8.2 are from
Milgrom and Segal (2015a). The algorithms used to implement feasibility checks are described by Fréchette et al. (2016). Problem 8.3
is from Shapley and Shubik (1971).

Exercises

Exercise 8.1 *(H)* The ideal outcome of an SAA (Section 8.3) with
item set $M = \{1, 2, \ldots, m\}$ is a *Walrasian equilibrium*, meaning an

allocation $S_1, \ldots, S_n \subseteq M$ of bundles to the n bidders and item selling prices $p_1, \ldots, p_m$ that meet the following conditions.

Walrasian Equilibrium

1. Every bidder i gets her preferred bundle, given the prices $\mathbf{p}$:

$$S_i \in \operatorname*{argmax}_{S \subseteq M} \left(v_i(S) - \sum_{j \in S} p_j \right).$$

2. Supply equals demand: every item j appears in at most one bundle S_i, and goes unsold only if $p_j = 0$.

Prove that if an allocation $(S_1, \ldots, S_n)$ and prices $\mathbf{p}$ form a Walrasian equilibrium, then the allocation has the maximum possible social welfare. (This is a form of the "first welfare theorem.")

Exercise 8.2 *(H)* Prove that, even in combinatorial auctions with only two bidders and two items, there need not exist a Walrasian equilibrium.

Exercise 8.3 Consider a deferred allocation rule (Section 8.5) in which bidders are removed according to a scoring function. A scoring function assigns a score to every remaining bidder in the auction, and in each iteration the allocation rule removes, among all bidders whose removal does not destroy feasibility, the bidder with the highest score.

Consider a scoring function that satisfies two properties. First, the score of a bidder i is independent of the bids of the other remaining bidders. (The score can depend on i, on i's bid, on the bids of bidders that have already dropped out, and on the set of remaining bidders.) Second, holding other bids fixed, the score of a bidder is increasing in her bid. Prove that the corresponding deferred allocation rule is monotone: for every bidder i and bids $\mathbf{b}_{-i}$ by the other bidders, if i wins when bidding b_i and $b_i' < b_i$, then i also wins when bidding b_i'.

Problems

Problem 8.1 A direct-revelation mechanism is *weakly group-strategyproof* if for every colluding subset C of bidders, every profile $\mathbf{b}_{-C}$ of bids of the bidders outside C, and every profile $\mathbf{v}_C$ of valuations for C, there is no profile $\mathbf{b}_C$ of bids that results in every bidder of C receiving strictly higher utility than with truthful bids $\mathbf{v}_C$.

(a) In the same setting and with the same assumptions as in Exercise 8.3, prove that the corresponding DSIC mechanism is weakly group-strategyproof.

(b) Prove that the "forward greedy" DSIC mechanism defined in Problem 4.3 is not weakly group-strategyproof in general.

Problem 8.2 In the same setting and with the same assumptions as in Exercise 8.3, give an ascending implementation of the corresponding DSIC mechanism. Your ascending implementation should *not* accept explicit bids. It should proceed in rounds, and at each round, one of the remaining bidders should be given a take-it-or-leave-it offer for dropping out. Prove that straightforward bidding—continuing to the next round if and only if the current offer exceeds her private valuation—is a dominant strategy for every bidder. Prove that the final outcome, assuming straightforward bidding, is the same as the truthful outcome in the direct-revelation DSIC mechanism. For convenience, you can restrict attention to the case where all valuations and scores are positive integers bounded above by a known value $v_{\max}$.

Problem 8.3 *(H)* Prove that in every combinatorial auction in which every bidder has a unit-demand valuation (Exercise 7.5), there exists a Walrasian equilibrium.

Lecture 9

Mechanism Design with Payment Constraints

Lecture 2 introduced the quasilinear utility model, where each agent acts to maximize her valuation of the chosen outcome, less the payment she makes. We placed no restrictions on payments other than the modest conditions that they are nonnegative and guarantee nonnegative utility to truthful bidders. This lecture is the first to consider mechanism design problems with *payment constraints*, in addition to the usual incentive and feasibility constraints.

Section 9.1 extends the quasilinear utility model to accommodate budget constraints. Section 9.2 studies multi-unit auctions where bidders have budgets, and proposes an elegant if non-DSIC solution: the uniform-price auction. The clinching auction, described in Section 9.3, is a more complex auction for the same problem that is DSIC. Section 9.4 considers mechanism design with no payments whatsoever, introduces the canonical house allocation problem, and studies the properties of the Top Trading Cycle algorithm.

9.1 Budget Constraints

In many applications, there are constraints on the payments charged by a mechanism. Exhibit A is *budget constraints*, which limit the amount of money that an agent can pay. Budgets are especially relevant in auctions where an agent might buy a large number of items. For example, in the sponsored search auctions (Section 2.6) used in practice, every bidder is asked for her bid-per-click and her daily budget. Per-item values and overall budgets model well how many people make decisions in auctions with lots of items, especially when the items are identical.

The simplest way to incorporate budgets into our utility model is to redefine the utility of agent i with budget B_i for outcome ω and

113

payment p_i as
$$v_i(\omega) - p_i \quad \text{if } p_i \le B_i;$$
$$-\infty \quad \text{if } p_i > B_i.$$

A natural generalization, which we won't discuss, is to have a cost function that is increasing in the budget violation.

We need new auction formats to accommodate budget constraints. For example, consider the simple case of a single-item auction, where every bidder has a known budget of 1 and a private valuation. A second-price auction charges the winner the second-highest bid, which might well be more than her budget. More generally, no DSIC single-item auction with nonnegative payments maximizes the social welfare while respecting bidders' budgets (Problem 9.1).

9.2   The Uniform-Price Multi-Unit Auction

9.2.1   Multi-Unit Auctions

In a *multi-unit auction*, there are m identical items, and each bidder has a private valuation v_i for each item that she gets. Unlike the k-unit auctions of Example 3.2, we assume that each bidder wants as many units as possible. Thus bidder i obtains value $k \cdot v_i$ from k items. Such multi-unit auctions are single-parameter environments (Section 3.1). Finally, each bidder i has a budget B_i that we assume is *public*, meaning known to the seller in advance.[1]

9.2.2   The Uniform-Price Auction

The first multi-unit auction that we consider sells items at the "market-clearing price," where "supply equals demand." The supply is m, the number of items. The demand of a bidder depends on the selling price, with higher prices resulting in smaller demands. Formally, we define the *demand of bidder i at price p* as:

$$D_i(p) = \begin{cases} \min\left\{ \left\lfloor \frac{B_i}{p} \right\rfloor, m \right\} & \text{if } p < v_i; \\ 0 & \text{if } p > v_i. \end{cases} \tag{9.1}$$

---

[1]We'd love to assume that budgets are private and thus also subject to misreporting, but private budgets make the mechanism design problem more difficult, even impossible in some senses (see also Exercise 9.3). Also, the special case of public budgets guides us to some elegant and potentially useful auction formats, which is the whole point of the endeavor.

To explain, recall that bidder i has value v_i for every item that she gets. If the price is above v_i, then she doesn't want any (i.e., $D_i(p) = 0$), while if the price is below v_i, she wants as many as she can afford (i.e., $D_i(p) = \min\{\lfloor \frac{B_i}{p} \rfloor, m\}$). When $v_i = p$, the bidder does not care how many items she gets, as long as her budget is respected. The auction can break ties arbitrarily and take $D_i(v_i)$ to be any convenient integer between 0 and $\min\{\lfloor \frac{B_i}{p} \rfloor, m\}$, inclusive.

As the price p increases, the demand $D_i(p)$ decreases, from $D_i(0) = m$ to $D_i(\infty) = 0$. A drop in demand can have two different forms: from an arbitrary positive integer to 0 (when p exceeds v_i), or by a single unit (when $\lfloor B_i/p \rfloor$ becomes one smaller).

For a price p different from all bidders' valuations, we define the *aggregate demand* by $A(p) = \sum_{i=1}^{n} D_i(p)$. In general, we define $A^-(p) = \lim_{q \uparrow p} \sum_{i=1}^{n} D_i(q)$ and $A^+(p) = \lim_{q \downarrow p} \sum_{i=1}^{n} D_i(q)$ as the limits of $A(p)$ from below and above, respectively.

The uniform-price auction picks the price p that equalizes supply and aggregate demand, and gives every bidder her demanded number of items at a price of p each.

The Uniform-Price Auction

1. Let p equalize supply and aggregate demand, meaning $A^-(p) \geq m \geq A^+(p)$.

2. Award $D_i(p)$ items to each bidder i, each at the price p. Define demands $D_i(p)$ for bidders i with $v_i = p$ so that all m items are allocated.

While we describe the uniform-price auction as a direct-revelation auction, it is straightforward to give an ascending implementation.

9.2.3   The Uniform-Price Auction Is Not DSIC

The good news is that, by the definition (9.1) of the demand $D_i(p)$, the uniform-price auction respects bidders' budgets. The bad news is that it is not DSIC. Similarly to simultaneous ascending auctions, it is vulnerable to demand reduction (Section 8.3.3).

Example 9.1 (Demand Reduction) Suppose there are two items and two bidders, with $B_1 = +\infty$, $v_1 = 6$, and $B_2 = v_2 = 5$. If both bidders bid truthfully, then the aggregate demand $A(p)$ is at least 3 until the price hits 5, at which point $D_1(5) = 2$ and $D_2(5) = 0$. The uniform-price auction thus allocates both items to the first bidder at a price of 5 each, for a utility of 2. If the first bidder falsely bids 3, she does better. The reason is that the second bidder's demand then drops to 1 at the price $\frac{5}{2}$ (she can no longer afford both), and the auction stops at the price 3, at which point $D_1(3)$ is defined as 1. The first bidder only gets one item, but the price is only 3, so her utility is 3, more than with truthful bidding.

Can we modify the uniform-price auction to restore the DSIC guarantee? Because the auction has a monotone allocation rule, we can replace the uniform price with the payments dictated by Myerson's lemma (Theorem 3.7). To obtain a DSIC multi-unit auction format with still better properties, the next section modifies both the allocation and payment rules of the uniform-price auction.

*9.3   The Clinching Auction

The *clinching auction* is a DSIC multi-unit auction for bidders with public budgets.[2] The idea is to sell items piecemeal, at increasing prices. In addition to the current price p, the auction keeps track of the current supply s (initially m) and the residual budget $\hat{B}_i$ (initially B_i) of each bidder i. The residual demand $\hat{D}_i(p)$ of bidder i at price $p \neq v_i$ is defined with respect to the residual budget and supply, analogous to (9.1):

$$\hat{D}_i(p) = \begin{cases} \min\left\{\left\lfloor \frac{\hat{B}_i}{p} \right\rfloor, s\right\} & \text{if } p < v_i \\ 0 & \text{if } p > v_i. \end{cases} \tag{9.2}$$

Define $\hat{D}_i^+(p) = \lim_{q \downarrow p} \hat{D}_i(q)$.

The clinching auction iteratively raises the current price p, and a bidder i "clinches" some items at the price p whenever they are uncontested, meaning the sum of others' residual demands is strictly less than the current supply s. Different items are sold in different iterations, at different prices. The auction continues until all of the items have been allocated.

---

[2] Again, we give a direct-revelation description, but there is also a natural ascending implementation.

The Clinching Auction

initialize $p = 0$, $s = m$, and $\hat{B}_i = B_i$ for every i
while $s > 0$ **do**
    increase p to the next-highest value of v_i or $\hat{B}_i/k$
    for a positive integer k
    let i denote the bidder with the largest residual
    demand $\hat{D}_i^+(p)$, breaking ties arbitrarily
    while $\sum_{j \neq i} \hat{D}_j^+(p) < s$ **do**
        if $\sum_{j=1}^n \hat{D}_j^+(p) > s$ **then**
            award one item to bidder i at the price p
            `// this item is "clinched"`
            decrease $\hat{B}_i$ by p and s by 1
            recompute the bidder i with the largest
            residual demand at the price p, breaking
            ties arbitrarily
        else if $\sum_{j=1}^n \hat{D}_j^+(p) \leq s$ **then**
            award $\hat{D}_j^+(p)$ items to each bidder j at
            price p
            award any remaining items to the bidder ℓ
            that satisfies $v_\ell = p$, at a price of p per
            item
            decrease s to 0

The only relevant prices are those at which the residual demand of some bidder drops. Every such price p satisfies either $p = v_i$ or $p = \hat{B}_i/k$ for some bidder i and positive integer k. For simplicity, assume that all expressions of the form v_i and $\hat{B}_i/k$ for integers k that arise in the auction are distinct.

In the inner while loop, there are two cases. In the first case, the aggregate residual demand exceeds the residual supply, but the aggregate demand of bidders other than i is less than the supply. In this case, bidder i "clinches" an item at the current price p, and her budget is updated accordingly. Both the residual supply and i's residual demand decrease by 1 unit.

The second case can only occur when the aggregate demand

$\sum_{j=1}^{n} \hat{D}_j^+(p)$ drops by two or more at the price p. Assuming that all expressions of the form $\hat{B}_i/k$ for integers k are distinct, this can only happen if p equals the valuation v_ℓ of some bidder ℓ. In this case, when ℓ's demand drops to zero, there is no longer any competition for the remaining s items, so the residual demands of all of the bidders can be met simultaneously. There may be items remaining after satisfying all residual demands, in which case they are allocated to the indifferent bidder ℓ (at price $p = v_\ell$).

Example 9.2 (No Demand Reduction) Let's revisit Example 9.1: two items and two bidders, with $B_1 = +\infty$, $v_1 = 6$, and $B_2 = v_2 = 5$. Suppose both bidders bid truthfully. In the uniform-price auction (Example 9.1), the first bidder is awarded both items at a price of 5. In the clinching auction, because the demand $D_2(p)$ of the second bidder drops to 1 once $p = \frac{5}{2}$, the first bidder clinches one item at a price of $\frac{5}{2}$. The second item is sold to the first bidder at a price of 5, as before. The first bidder has utility $\frac{9}{2}$ when she bids truthfully in the clinching auction, and no false bid can be better (Theorem 9.4).

Exercise 9.1 asks you to prove the following proposition.

Proposition 9.3 (Clinching Auction Is Feasible) *The clinching auction always stops, allocates exactly m items, and charges payments that are at most bidders' budgets.*

We now turn to the clinching auction's incentive guarantee.

Theorem 9.4 (Clinching Auction Is DSIC) *The clinching auction for bidders with public budgets is DSIC.*

Proof: We could verify that the auction's allocation rule is monotone and that the payments conform to Myerson's payment formula (3.5), but it's easier to just verify the DSIC condition directly. So, fix a bidder i and bids $\mathbf{b}_{-i}$ by the others. Since bidder i's budget is public, she cannot affect the term $\lfloor \hat{B}_i/p \rfloor$ of her residual demand $\hat{D}_i^+(p)$. She can only affect the time at which she is kicked out of the auction, meaning $\hat{D}_i^+(p) = 0$ forevermore. Every item clinched by bidder i when $p < v_i$ contributes positively to her utility, while every item clinched when $p > v_i$ contributes negatively. Truthful bidding guarantees nonnegative utility.

First, compare the utility earned by a bid $b_i < v_i$ to that earned by a truthful bid. Imagine running the clinching auction twice in parallel, once when i bids b_i and once when i bids v_i. By induction on the number of iterations, the execution of the clinching auction is identical in the two scenarios as the price ascends from 0 to b_i. Thus, by bidding b_i, the bidder can only lose out on items that she otherwise would have clinched (for nonnegative utility) in the price interval $[b_i, v_i]$.

Similarly, if i bids $b_i > v_i$ instead of v_i, the only change is that she might acquire some additional items for nonpositive utility in the price interval $[v_i, b_i]$. Thus, no false bid nets i more utility than a truthful one does. ∎

If budgets are private and the clinching auction is run with reported budgets, then it is no longer DSIC (Exercise 9.3).

Is the allocation computed by the clinching auction "good" in some sense? (If only the DSIC condition mattered, then we could give away all the items for free to a random bidder.) There are several ways to formulate this question; see the Notes for details.

9.4   Mechanism Design without Money

There are a number of important applications where incentives matter and the use of money is infeasible or illegal. In these settings, all agents effectively have a budget of zero. Mechanism design without money is relevant for designing and understanding methods for voting, organ donation, and school choice. The designer's hands are tied without money, even tighter than with budget constraints. Despite this and strong impossibility results in general settings, some of mechanism design's greatest hits are for applications without money.

A representative example is the *house allocation problem*. There are n agents, and each initially owns one house. Each agent's preferences are represented by a total ordering over the n houses rather than by numerical valuations. An agent need not prefer her own house over the others. How can we sensibly reallocate the houses to make the agents better off? One answer is given by the *Top Trading Cycle (TTC) algorithm*.

Top Trading Cycle (TTC) Algorithm

initialize N to the set of all agents
while $N \neq \emptyset$ **do**
     form the directed graph G with vertex set N and
     edge set $\{(i, \ell) :$
     i's favorite house within N is owned by $\ell\}$
     compute the directed cycles $C_1, \ldots, C_h$ of G^3
     `// self-loops count as directed cycles`
     `// cycles are disjoint`
     for each edge (i, ℓ) of each cycle $C_1, \ldots, C_h$ **do**
         reallocate ℓ's house to agent i
     remove the agents of $C_1, \ldots, C_h$ from N

The following lemma, which follows immediately from the description of the TTC algorithm, is crucial for understanding the algorithm's properties.

Lemma 9.5 *Let N_k denote the set of agents removed in the kth iteration of the TTC algorithm. Every agent of N_k receives her favorite house outside of those owned by $N_1 \cup \cdots \cup N_{k-1}$, and the original owner of this house is in N_k.*

Example 9.6 (The TTC Algorithm) Suppose $N = \{1, 2, 3, 4\}$, that every agent prefers agent 1's house to the other three, and that the second-favorite houses of agents 2, 3, and 4 are those owned by agents 3, 4, and 2, respectively. (The rest of the agents' preferences do not matter for the example.) Figure 9.1(a) depicts the graph G in the first iteration of the TTC algorithm. There is only one cycle, the self-loop with agent 1. In the notation of Lemma 9.5, $N_1 = \{1\}$. Figure 9.1(b) shows the graph G in the second iteration of the TTC algorithm, after agent 1 and her house have been removed. All agents now participate in a single cycle, and each gets her favorite house among those owned by the agents in $N_2 = \{2, 3, 4\}$.

---

[3]G has at least one directed cycle, since traversing a sequence of outgoing edges must eventually repeat a vertex. Because all out-degrees are 1, these cycles are disjoint.

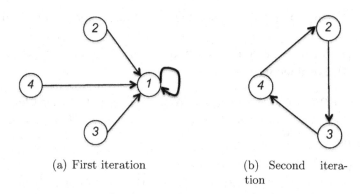

(a) First iteration   (b) Second itera-
                                       tion

Figure 9.1: The Top Trading Cycle algorithm (Example 9.6).

When agents' total orderings are private, we can consider the direct-revelation mechanism that accepts reported total orderings from the agents and then applies the TTC algorithm. There is no incentive for agents to misreport their preferences to this mechanism.

Theorem 9.7 (TTC Is DSIC) *The TTC algorithm induces a DSIC mechanism.*

Proof: Fix an agent i and reports by the others. Define the sets N_k as in Lemma 9.5, assuming that i reports truthfully. Suppose that $i \in N_j$. The key point is that no misreport can net agent i a house originally owned by an agent of $N_1 \cup \cdots \cup N_{j-1}$. For in each iteration $k = 1, 2, \ldots, j-1$, no agent $\ell \in N_k$ points to i's house—otherwise, i would belong to the same directed cycle as ℓ, and hence to N_k instead of N_j. No agent of N_k points to i's house in an iteration prior to k, either—if she did, she would still point to i's house in iteration k. Thus, whatever agent i reports, she cannot join any cycle involving the agents of $N_1 \cup \cdots \cup N_{j-1}$. Lemma 9.5 then implies that she has no incentive to misreport. ∎

Theorem 9.7 by itself is not impressive. For example, the mechanism that never reallocates anything is also DSIC. Our next result gives a sense in which the TTC algorithm is "optimal."

Consider an assignment of one distinct house to each agent. A subset of agents forms a *blocking coalition* for this assignment if they can internally reallocate their original houses to make some member better off while making no member worse off. For example, in an assignment where an agent i receives a house worse than her initial house, $\{i\}$ forms a blocking coalition. A *core allocation* is an assignment with no blocking coalitions.

Theorem 9.8 (TTC and Core Allocations) *For every house allocation problem, the allocation computed by the TTC algorithm is the unique core allocation.*

Proof: We first prove that the only possible core allocation is the one computed by the TTC algorithm. Define the sets N_k as in Lemma 9.5. In the TTC allocation, every agent of N_1 receives her first choice. Thus N_1 forms a blocking coalition for every allocation that differs from the TTC allocation on an agent of N_1. Similarly, in the TTC allocation, all agents of N_2 receive their first choice outside of the houses owned by N_1 (Lemma 9.5). Given that every core allocation agrees with the TTC allocation on the agents of N_1, such allocations must also agree on the agents of N_2—otherwise, N_2 forms a blocking coalition. Continuing inductively, we conclude that every allocation that differs from the TTC allocation is not a core allocation.

To verify that the TTC allocation is a core allocation, consider an arbitrary subset S of agents and an internal reallocation of the houses owned by S. This reallocation partitions S into directed cycles. If some such cycle contains agents from two different N_k's, then the reallocation gives at least one agent i from a set N_j a house originally owned by an agent from a set N_ℓ with $\ell > j$, leaving i worse off than in the TTC allocation (Lemma 9.5). Similarly, for a cycle contained in N_k, any agent that doesn't receive her favorite house from N_k is worse off than in the TTC allocation. We conclude that if the internal reallocation of the houses of S differs from the allocation computed by the TTC algorithm, then some agent of S is worse off. Since S is arbitrary, the TTC allocation has no blocking coalitions and is a core allocation. ∎

The Upshot

☆ In many important mechanism design problems, payments are restricted or forbidden. Payment constraints make mechanism design significantly harder.

☆ With multiple identical items and bidders with budgets, the uniform-price auction sells all of the items at a common price that equalizes supply and demand.

☆ The clinching auction is a more complex auction that sells items piecemeal at increasing prices. Unlike the uniform-price auction, the clinching auction is DSIC.

☆ The Top Trading Cycle (TTC) algorithm is a method for reallocating objects owned by agents (one per agent) to make the agents as well off as possible.

☆ The TTC algorithm leads to a DSIC mechanism and it computes the unique core allocation.

Notes

The original clinching auction, due to Ausubel (2004), is an ascending implementation of the VCG mechanism in multi-unit auctions with downward-sloping valuations and no budgets (see Problem 9.2). The version in this lecture, with constant valuations-per-item and public budgets, is from Dobzinski et al. (2012).

There are several ways to argue that the clinching auction is in some sense near-optimal. The first way is to follow the development of revenue-maximizing mechanisms (Lecture 5), by positing a distribution over bidders' valuations and solving for the DSIC mechanism that maximizes expected social welfare subject to the given budget constraints. Common budgets are better understood than general budgets are, and in this case the clinching auction is provably near-optimal (Devanur et al., 2013). A second approach, explored in Exercise 9.4, is to modify the social welfare objective function to take budgets into account, replacing $\sum_i v_i x_i$ by $\sum_i \min\{B_i, v_i x_i\}$. The clinching auction is provably near-optimal with respect to this objective function (Dobzinski and Paes Leme, 2014). The third way is to study Pareto optimality rather than an objective function.[4] Dobzinski et al. (2012) prove that the clinching auction is the unique deterministic DSIC auction that always computes a Pareto-optimal allocation. One caveat is that some desirable mechanisms, such as the Bayesian-optimal mechanisms produced by the first approach, need not be Pareto optimal.

Shapley and Scarf (1974) define the house allocation problem, and credit the TTC algorithm to D. Gale. Theorems 9.7 and 9.8 are from Roth (1982b) and Roth and Postlewaite (1977), respectively. Single-peaked preferences (Problem 9.3) are studied by Moulin (1980).

Exercises

Exercise 9.1 Prove Proposition 9.3.

Exercise 9.2 Extend the clinching auction and its analysis to the general case, where the valuations v_i and expressions of the form $\hat{B}_i/k$ for positive integers k need not be distinct.

Exercise 9.3 *(H)* Consider a multi-unit auction where bidders have private valuations per unit *and* private budgets. Prove that the clinching auction, executed with reported valuations and reported budgets, is not DSIC.

Exercise 9.4 Consider a single-parameter environment (Section 3.1) in which each bidder i has a publicly known budget B_i. Consider the allocation rule that, given bids $\mathbf{b}$, chooses the feasible outcome that maximizes the "truncated welfare" $\sum_{i=1}^n \min\{b_i x_i, B_i\}$. Ties between outcomes with equal truncated welfare are broken arbitrarily but consistently.

(a) Prove that this allocation rule is monotone, and that the corresponding DSIC mechanism, with payments given by Myerson's

---

[4]An allocation is *Pareto optimal* if there's no way to reassign items and payments to make some agent (a bidder or the seller) better off without making another worse off, where the seller's utility is her revenue.

payment formula (3.5), never charges a bidder more than her budget.

(b) Consider a single-item environment. Argue informally that the auction in (a) generally results in a "reasonable" outcome.

(c) *(H)* Consider a multi-unit auction with m identical items, where each bidder i has a private valuation v_i per item. Explain why the truncated welfare objective function might assign the same value to almost all of the feasible allocations, and therefore the auction in (a) can easily lead to "unreasonable" outcomes.

Exercise 9.5 Another mechanism for the house allocation problem, familiar from the assignment of dorm rooms to college students, is the *random serial dictatorship*.[5]

Random Serial Dictatorship

initialize H to the set of all houses
randomly order the agents
for $i = 1, 2, 3, \ldots, n$ **do**
    assign the ith agent her favorite house h from
    among those in H
    delete h from H

(a) Does an analog of Theorem 9.7 hold for the random serial dictatorship, no matter which random ordering is chosen by the mechanism?

(b) Does an analog of Theorem 9.8 hold for the random serial dictatorship, no matter which random ordering is chosen by the mechanism?

Problems

Problem 9.1 Consider single-item auctions with n bidders with known bidder budgets.

---

[5]Some prefer the less hostile term *random priority mechanism*.

(a) Give a DSIC auction, possibly randomized, that always uses nonnegative payments and respects bidders' budgets and achieves (expected) welfare at least $\frac{1}{n}$ times the highest valuation.

(b) *(H)* Prove that there is a constant $c > 0$ such that, for arbitrarily large n and suitable choices of bidders' budgets, for every DSIC single-item auction (possibly randomized) with nonnegative payments that always respects bidders' budgets, there is a valuation profile on which its expected welfare is at most c/n times the highest valuation.[6]

Problem 9.2 In this problem we modify the multi-unit auction setting studied in lecture in two ways. First, we make the mechanism design problem easier by assuming that bidders have no budgets. Along a different axis, we make the problem more general: rather than having a common value v_i for every item that she gets, a bidder i has a private marginal valuation v_{ij} for her jth item, given that she already has $j - 1$ items. Thus, if i receives k items at a combined price of p, her utility is $(\sum_{j=1}^{k} v_{ij}) - p$. We assume that every bidder i has a *downward-sloping* valuation, meaning that successive items offer diminishing returns: $v_{i1} \geq v_{i2} \geq v_{i3} \geq \cdots \geq v_{im}$. For simplicity, assume that all of the bidders' marginal valuations are distinct.

(a) Give a simple greedy algorithm for implementing the allocation rule of the VCG mechanism. Does your algorithm still work if bidders' valuations are not downward-sloping?

(b) Give a simple description of the payment of a bidder in the VCG mechanism, as a sum of marginal valuations reported by the other bidders.

(c) Adapt the clinching auction of Section 9.3 to the present setting by redefining bidders' demand functions appropriately. Prove that the allocation and payment rules of your auction are the same as in the VCG mechanism.

---

[6]Randomized DSIC mechanisms are defined in Problem 6.4.

Problem 9.3 Consider a mechanism design problem where the set of outcomes is the unit interval $[0, 1]$ and each agent i has *single-peaked preferences*, meaning that there is an agent-specific "peak" $x_i \in [0, 1]$ such that i strictly prefers y to z whenever $z < y \leq x$ or $x \geq y > z$. Thus an agent with single-peaked preferences wants the chosen outcome to be as close to her peak as possible.[7]

(a) Is the mechanism that accepts a reported peak from each agent and outputs the average DSIC?

(b) Is the mechanism that accepts a reported peak from each agent and outputs the median DSIC? Feel free to assume that the number of agents is odd.

(c) *(H)* The two mechanisms above are *anonymous*, meaning that the outcome depends only on the unordered set of reported peaks and not on the identity of who reported which peak. They are also *onto*, meaning that for every $x \in [0, 1]$ there is a profile of reported preferences such that x is the outcome of the mechanism. For n agents, can you find more than n different direct-revelation mechanisms that are deterministic, DSIC, anonymous, and onto?

---

[7]One natural interpretation of $[0, 1]$ is as the political spectrum, spanning the gamut from radical to reactionary.

Kidney Exchange and Stable Matching

This lecture is our last on mechanism design, and it covers some of the greatest hits of mechanism design without money. Kidney exchanges, the case study covered in Section 10.1, have been deeply influenced by ideas from mechanism design over the past ten years. These exchanges enable thousands of successful kidney transplants every year. Stable matching and the remarkable deferred acceptance algorithm (Section 10.2) form the basis of modern algorithms for many assignment problems, including medical residents to hospitals and students to elementary schools. This algorithm also enjoys some beautiful mathematical properties and incentive guarantees (Section 10.3).

10.1 Case Study: Kidney Exchange

10.1.1 Background

Many people suffer from kidney failure and need a kidney transplant. In the United States, more than 100,000 people are on the waiting list for such transplants. An old idea, used also for other organs, is deceased donors; when someone dies and is a registered organ donor, their organs can be transplanted into others. One special feature of kidneys is that a healthy person has two of them and can survive just fine with only one of them. This creates the possibility of *living* organ donors, such as a family member of the patient in need.

Unfortunately, having a living kidney donor is not always enough; sometimes a patient-donor pair is *incompatible*, meaning that the donor's kidney is unlikely to function well in the patient. Blood and tissue types are the primary culprits for incompatibilities. For example, a patient with O blood type can only receive a kidney from a donor with the same blood type, and similarly an AB donor can only donate to an AB patient.

Suppose patient P1 is incompatible with her donor D1 because they have blood types A and B, respectively. Suppose P2 and D2 are in the opposite boat, with blood types B and A, respectively (Figure 10.1). Even though (P1, D1) and (P2, D2) have probably never met, exchanging donors seems like a pretty good idea, with P1 receiving her kidney from D2 and P2 from D1. This is called a *kidney exchange*.

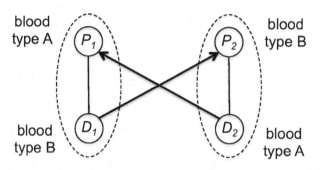

Figure 10.1: A kidney exchange. (P1, D1) and (P2, D2) form incompatible donor pairs. P1 receives her kidney from D2 and P2 from D1.

A few kidney exchanges were done, on an ad hoc basis, around the beginning of this century. These isolated successes made clear the need for a nationwide kidney exchange, where incompatible patient-donor pairs can register and be matched with others. How should such an exchange be designed? The goal is to enable as many matches as possible.

Currently, compensation for organ donation is illegal in the United States, and in every country except for Iran.[1] Kidney exchange is legal, and is naturally modeled as a mechanism design problem without money.

10.1.2   Applying the TTC Algorithm

Can we model kidney exchange as a house allocation problem (Section 9.4)? The idea is to treat each patient-donor pair as an agent, with the incompatible living donor acting as a house. A patient's

---

[1] It is no coincidence that Iran also does not have a waiting list for kidneys. Will other countries eventually follow suit and permit a monetary market for kidneys?

total ordering over the donors can be defined according to the estimated probability of a successful kidney transplant, based on the blood type, the tissue type, and other factors.

The hope is that the TTC algorithm finds cycles like that in Figure 10.2, where with patient-donor pairs as in Figure 10.1, each patient points to the other's donor as her favorite. Reallocating donors according to this cycle corresponds to the kidney exchange in Figure 10.1. More generally, the reallocation of donors to patients suggested by the TTC algorithm can only improve every patient's probability of a successful transplant (Theorem 9.8).

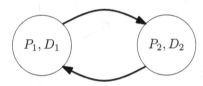

Figure 10.2: A good case for the TTC algorithm. Each circle represents an incompatible patient-donor pair, and each arrow represents a kidney transplant from the donor in the first pair to the patient in the second pair.

The dealbreaker is that the TTC algorithm may suggest reallocations that use long cycles, as in Figure 10.3. Why are long cycles a problem? A cycle of length two (Figure 10.2) already corresponds to four surgeries—two to extract donors' kidneys, and two to implant them in the patients. Moreover, these four surgeries *must happen simultaneously*. Incentives are the reason: in the example in Figure 10.1, if the surgeries for P1 and D2 happen first, then there is a risk that D1 will renege on her offer to donate her kidney to P2.[2] One problem is that P1 unfairly got a kidney for free. The much more serious problem is that P2 is as sick as before and, since her donor D2 donated her kidney, P2 can no longer participate in a kidney exchange. Because of this risk, non-simultaneous surgeries are almost never used in kidney exchange.[3] The constraint of simultaneous surg-

---

[2] Just as it is illegal to sell a kidney for money in most countries, it is also illegal to write a binding contract for a kidney donation.

[3] Sequential surgeries are used in a slightly different situation. There are a handful of altruistic living donors who want to donate a kidney even though they don't personally know anyone who needs one. An altruistic living donor can be the start of a chain of reallocations. Chains as long as 30 have been implemented,

eries, with each surgery needing its own operating room and surgical team, motivates keeping reallocation cycles as short as possible.

Figure 10.3: A bad case for the TTC algorithm.

Another critique of the TTC approach is that modeling a patient's preferences as a total ordering over donors is overkill. Patients don't really care which kidney they get as long as it is compatible. Binary preferences over donors are therefore more appropriate.

10.1.3   Applying a Matching Algorithm

The twin goals of binary preferences and short reallocation cycles suggest using graph matching. A *matching* of an undirected graph is a subset of edges that share no endpoints. The relevant graph for kidney exchange has a vertex set V corresponding to incompatible patient-donor pairs (one vertex per pair), and an undirected edge between vertices $(P1, D1)$ and $(P2, D2)$ if and only if P1 and D2 are compatible and P2 and D1 are compatible. Thus, the example in Figure 10.1 corresponds to the undirected graph in Figure 10.4. A matching in this graph corresponds to a collection of pairwise kidney exchanges, each involving four simultaneous surgeries. Maximizing the number of compatible kidney transplants corresponds to maximizing the size of a matching.

How do incentives come into play? We assume that each patient has a set E_i of compatible donors belonging to other patient-donor pairs, and can report any subset $F_i \subseteq E_i$ to a mechanism. Proposed kidney exchanges can be refused by a patient for any reason, so one way to implement a misreport is to refuse exchanges in $E_i \setminus F_i$. A patient cannot credibly misreport extra donors with whom she is incompatible. We assume that every patient has binary preferences, preferring every outcome where she is matched to every outcome where she is not.

---

and at this scale surgeries have to be sequential.   With a chain initiated by an altruistic living donor, there is no risk of a patient losing her living donor before receiving a kidney.

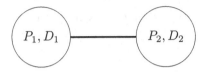

Figure 10.4: Applying a matching algorithm. Each circle represents an incompatible patient-donor pair, and each edge represents a pairwise kidney exchange, meaning transplants from each donor to the patient in the other pair.

The mechanism design goal is to maximize the number of kidney transplants. Direct-revelation solutions have the following form.

A Mechanism for Pairwise Kidney Exchange

1. Collect a report F_i from each agent i.

2. Form the graph $G = (V, E)$, where V corresponds to agent-donor pairs and $(i, j) \in E$ if and only if the patients corresponding to i and j report as compatible the donors corresponding to j and i, respectively.

3. Return a maximum-cardinality matching of the graph G.

Is this mechanism DSIC, in the sense that truthful reporting of the full set E_i is a dominant strategy for each patient i?[4] The answer depends on how ties are broken between different maximum matchings in the third step. There are two senses in which the maximum matching of a graph can fail to be unique. First, different sets of edges can be used to match the same set of vertices (see Figure 10.5). Since a patient does not care whom she is matched to, as long as she is matched, there is no reason to distinguish between different matchings that match the same set of vertices. More significantly, different maximum matchings can match different subsets of vertices. For example, in Figure 10.6, the first vertex is in every maximum matching, but only one of the other vertices can be included. How should we choose?

---

[4]With no payments, every agent is automatically guaranteed nonnegative utility.

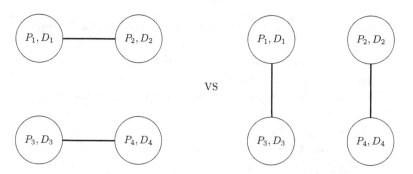

Figure 10.5: Different matchings can match the same set of vertices.

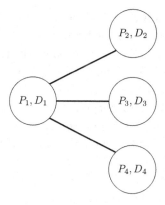

Figure 10.6: Different maximum matchings can match different subsets of vertices.

One solution is to prioritize the agent-donor pairs before the mechanism begins. Most hospitals already rely on priority schemes to manage their patients. The priority of a patient on a waiting list is determined by the length of time she has been on it, the difficulty of finding a compatible kidney, and other factors.

Precisely, we implement the third step of the mechanism as follows, assuming that the vertices $V = \{1, 2, \ldots, n\}$ of G are ordered from highest to lowest priority.

Priority Mechanism for Pairwise Kidney Exchange

initialize M_0 to the set of maximum matchings of G
for $i = 1, 2, \ldots, n$ **do**
    let Z_i denote the matchings in M_{i-1} that match
    vertex i
    if $Z_i \neq \emptyset$ **then**
        set $M_i = Z_i$
    else if $Z_i = \emptyset$ **then**
        set $M_i = M_{i-1}$
return an arbitrary matching of M_n

That is, in each iteration i, we ask if there is a maximum matching that respects previous commitments and also matches vertex i. If so, then we additionally commit to matching i in the final matching. If previous commitments preclude matching i in a maximum matching, then we skip i and move on to the next vertex. By induction on i, M_i is a nonempty subset of the maximum matchings of G. Every matching of M_n matches the same set of vertices—the vertices i for which Z_i is nonempty—so the choice of the matching in the final step is irrelevant.

Exercise 10.1 asks you to prove that the priority mechanism for pairwise kidney exchange is DSIC.

Theorem 10.1 (Priority Mechanism Is DSIC) *In the priority mechanism for pairwise kidney exchange, for every agent i and reports by the other agents, no false report $F_i \subset E_i$ yields a better outcome for i than the truthful report E_i.*

10.1.4 Incentives for Hospitals

Many patient-donor pairs are reported to national kidney exchanges by hospitals, rather than by the pairs themselves. The objective of a hospital, to match as many of its patients as possible, is not perfectly aligned with the societal objective of matching as many patients overall as possible. The key incentive issues are best explained through examples.

Example 10.2 (Benefits of Full Reporting) Suppose there are two hospitals, H_1 and H_2, each with three patient-donor pairs (Figure 10.7). Edges connect patient-donor pairs that are mutually compatible, as in Section 10.1.3. Each hospital has a pair of patient-donor pairs that it could match internally, without bothering to report them to a national exchange. We don't want the hospitals to execute these internal matches. If H_1 matches 1 and 2 internally and only reports 3 to the exchange, and H_2 matches 5 and 6 internally and only reports 4 to the exchange, then the exchange can't match 3 and 4 and no further matches are gained. If H_1 and H_2 both report their full sets of three patient-donor pairs to the national exchange, then 1, 2, and 3 can be matched with 4, 5, and 6, respectively, and all of the patients receive new kidneys. In general, the goal is to incentivize hospitals to report all of their patient-donor pairs to the exchange, to save as many lives as possible.

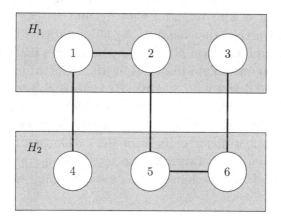

Figure 10.7: Example 10.2. Full reporting by hospitals leads to more matches.

Example 10.3 (No DSIC Maximum Matching Mechanism)
Consider again two hospitals, now with seven patients (Figure 10.8). Suppose the exchange always computes a maximum-cardinality matching of the patient-donor pairs that it knows about. With an odd number of vertices, every matching leaves at least one patient unmatched. If H_1 hides patients 2 and 3 from the exchange while H_2 reports truthfully, then H_1 guarantees that all of its patients

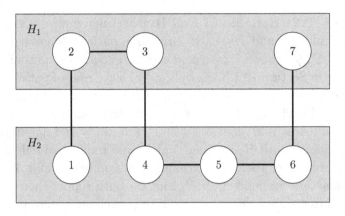

Figure 10.8: Example 10.3. Hospitals can have an incentive to hide patient-donor pairs.

are matched. The unique maximum matching in the reported graph matches patient 6 with 7 (and 4 with 5), and H_1 can match 2 and 3 internally. On the other hand, if H_2 hides patients 5 and 6 while H_1 reports truthfully, then all of H_2's patients are matched. In this case, the unique maximum matching in the reported graph matches patient 1 with 2 and 4 with 3, while H_2 can match patients 5 and 6 internally. We conclude that, no matter which maximum matching the exchange chooses, at least one of the hospitals has an incentive to withhold patient-donor pairs from the exchange. Thus, there is irreconcilable tension between the societal and hospital objectives, and there is no DSIC mechanism that always computes a maximum matching.

Duly warned by Example 10.3, current research on mechanism design for hospital reporting considers relaxed incentive constraints and approximate optimality.

10.2 Stable Matching

Stable matching is the canonical example of mechanism design without money. Killer applications of stable matching include assigning medical school graduates to hospital residencies and students to elementary schools. The following model and algorithm are directly useful for these and other applications with amazingly few modifications.

10.2.1   The Model

We consider two finite sets V and W of vertices—the "applicants" and the "hospitals"—with equal cardinality. Each vertex has a total ordering over the vertices of the other set. For example, in Figure 10.9, the applicants have a common ranking of the hospitals, while the hospitals have very different opinions about the applicants.

Let M be a perfect matching of V and W, assigning each vertex to one vertex from the other set. Vertices $v \in V$ and $w \in W$ form a *blocking pair for* M if they are not matched in M, v prefers w to her match in M, and w prefers v to its match in M. A blocking pair spells trouble, because the two vertices are tempted to secede from the process and match with each other. A perfect matching is *stable* if it has no blocking pairs.

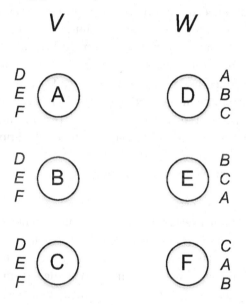

Figure 10.9: An instance of stable matching. Each vertex is annotated with its total ordering over the vertices of the opposite side, with the most preferred vertex on top.

10.2.2   The Deferred Acceptance Algorithm

We next discuss the elegant deferred acceptance algorithm for computing a stable matching.

Deferred Acceptance Algorithm

while there is an unmatched applicant $v \in V$ **do**
   v attempts to match with her favorite hospital w
   who has not rejected her yet
   if w is unmatched **then**
      v and w are tentatively matched
   else if w is tentatively matched to v' **then**
      w rejects whomever of v, v' it likes less and is
      tentatively matched to the other one
all tentative matches are made final

Example 10.4 (The Deferred Acceptance Algorithm)
Consider the instance in Figure 10.9. Suppose in the first iteration
we choose the applicant C, who tries to match with her first choice, D.
The hospital D accepts because it currently has no other offers. If
we pick the applicant B in the next iteration, she also proposes to
the hospital D. Since hospital D prefers B to C, it rejects C in favor
of B. If we pick applicant A next, the result is similar: D rejects B
in favor of A. A possible trajectory for the rest of the algorithm is:
applicant C now proposes to her second choice, E; applicant B then
also proposes to E, causing E to reject C in favor of B; and finally, C
proposes to her last choice F, who accepts.

We note several properties of the deferred acceptance algorithm.
First, each applicant systematically goes through her preference list,
from top to bottom. Second, because a hospital only rejects an applicant in favor of a better one, the applicants to whom it is tentatively
matched only improve over the course of the algorithm. Third, at all
times, each applicant is matched to at most one hospital and each
hospital is matched to at most one applicant.

Stable matchings and the deferred acceptance algorithm have an
astonishing number of remarkable properties. Here are the most basic
ones.

Theorem 10.5 (Fast Computation of a Stable Matching)
*The deferred acceptance algorithm completes with a stable matching
after at most n^2 iterations, where n is the number of vertices on each
side.*

Corollary 10.6 (Existence of a Stable Matching) *For   every collection of preference lists for the applicants and hospitals, there exists at least one stable matching.*

Corollary 10.6 is not obvious a priori. For example, there are some simple variants of the stable matching problem for which a solution is not guaranteed.

Proof of Theorem 10.5: The bound on the number of iterations is easy to prove. Each applicant works her way down her preference list, never trying to match to the same hospital twice, resulting in at most n attempted matches per applicant and n^2 overall.

Next, we claim that the deferred acceptance algorithm always completes with every applicant matched to some hospital (and vice versa). For if not, some applicant must have been rejected by all n hospitals. An applicant is only rejected by a hospital in favor of being matched to a better applicant, and once a hospital is matched to an applicant, it remains matched to some applicant for the remainder of the algorithm. Thus, all n hospitals must be matched at the end of the algorithm. But then all n applicants are also matched at the end of the algorithm, a contradiction.

To prove the stability of the final matching, consider an applicant v and hospital w that are not matched to each other. This can occur for two different reasons. In the first case, v never attempted to match to w. Since v worked her way down her preference list starting from the top, she ends up matched to a hospital she prefers to w. If v did attempt to match to w at some point in the algorithm, it must be that w rejected v in favor of an applicant it preferred (either at the time that v attempted to match to w, or subsequently). Since the sequence of applicants to whom w is matched only improves over the course of the algorithm, it ends up matched to an applicant it prefers to v. ∎

*10.3   Further Properties

The deferred acceptance algorithm is underdetermined, leaving open how the unmatched applicant is chosen in each iteration. Do all possible choices lead to the same stable matching? In Figure 10.9 there is only one stable matching, so in that example the answer is yes. In general, however, there can be more than one stable matching. In Figure 10.10, the applicants and the hospitals both disagree on the ranking of the others. In the matching computed by the deferred acceptance algorithm, both applicants get their first choice, with A and B matched to C and D, respectively. Giving the hospitals their first choices yields a different stable matching.

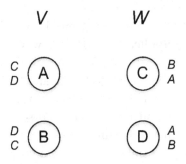

Figure 10.10: There can be multiple stable matchings.

Our next result implies, in particular, that the outcome of the deferred acceptance algorithm is independent of how the unmatched applicant is chosen in each iteration. For an applicant v, let $h(v)$ denote the highest-ranked hospital (in v's preference list) to which v is matched in *any* stable matching.

Theorem 10.7 (Applicant-Optimality) *The stable matching computed by the deferred acceptance algorithm matches every applicant $v \in V$ to $h(v)$.*

Theorem 10.7 implies the existence of an "applicant-optimal" stable matching, where every applicant simultaneously attains her best-case scenario. A priori, there is no reason to expect the $h(v)$'s to be distinct and therefore form a matching.

Proof of Theorem 10.7: Consider a run of the deferred acceptance algorithm, and let R denote the set of pairs (v, w) such that w rejected v at some point. Since each applicant systematically works her way down her preference list, if v is matched to w at the conclusion of the algorithm, then $(v, w') \in R$ for every w' that v prefers to w. Thus, the following claim would imply the theorem: for every $(v, w) \in R$, no stable matching pairs up v and w.

Let R_i denote the pairs (v, w) such that w rejected v at some point in the first i iterations. We prove by induction on i that no pair in R_i is matched in any stable matching. Initially, $R_0 = \emptyset$ and there is nothing to prove. For the inductive step, suppose that in the ith iteration of the deferred acceptance algorithm, w rejects v in favor of v'. This means that one of v, v' attempted to match to w in this iteration.

Since v' systematically worked her way down her preference list, for every w' that v' prefers to w, $(v', w') \in R_{i-1}$. By the inductive hypothesis, no stable matching pairs up v' with a hospital she prefers to w—in every stable matching, v' is paired with w or a less preferred hospital. Since w prefers v' to v, and v' prefers w to any other hospital she might be matched to in a stable matching, there is no stable matching that pairs v with w (otherwise v', w form a blocking pair). ∎

Also, the deferred acceptance algorithm outputs the worst-possible stable matching from the perspective of a hospital (Exercise 10.6).[5]

Suppose the preference lists of the applicants and hospitals are private. Can we obtain a DSIC mechanism by asking all vertices to report their preference lists and running the deferred acceptance algorithm? As Theorem 10.7 might suggest, the deferred acceptance algorithm is DSIC for the applicants but not for the hospitals (see Problem 10.1 and Exercise 10.7).

Theorem 10.8 (Incentive Properties) *Consider the mechanism that runs the deferred acceptance algorithm on reported preferences by the applicants and hospitals.*

(a) For every applicant v and reported preferences by the other applicants and hospitals, v is never strictly better off reporting falsely than truthfully.

(b) There exists preferences for a hospital w and reports for the other applicants and hospitals such that w is strictly better off reporting falsely than truthfully.

---

[5]Modifying the algorithm so that the hospitals initiate matches and the applicants reject reverses both of these properties.

The Upshot

☆ Kidney exchange enables two or more patients with incompatible living donors to receive kidney transplants from each other's donors.

☆ The TTC algorithm can be applied to the kidney exchange problem to exchange donors to improve everyone's compatibility, but the algorithm can result in infeasibly long cycles of exchanges.

☆ Matching algorithms can be used to restrict to pairwise kidney exchanges and incentivize patients to accept any donor with whom she is compatible.

☆ Hospitals can have an incentive to match incompatible patient-donor pairs internally rather than reporting them to a national exchange.

☆ A stable matching pairs applicants and hospitals so that no applicant and hospital would both be better off by matching to each other.

☆ The deferred acceptance algorithm computes an applicant-optimal stable matching.

☆ The deferred acceptance algorithm leads to a mechanism that is DSIC for the applicants but not for the hospitals.

Notes

The application of the TTC algorithm to kidney exchange is due to Roth et al. (2004). Building on the work of Abdulkadiroğlu and Sönmez (1999) on assigning students to college dorm rooms, Roth et al. (2004) also extend the TTC algorithm and its incentive guarantee to accommodate both deceased donors (houses without owners) and patients without a living donor (agents without houses). The application of graph matching to pairwise kidney exchange is from Roth et al. (2005). Roth et al. (2007) consider three-way kidney exchanges, with simultaneous surgeries on three donors and three patients. Three-way exchanges can significantly increase the number of matched patients, and for this reason are becoming common. Allowing four-way and larger exchanges does not seem to lead to significant further improvements. Sack (2012) describes a chain of 30 kidney transplants, triggered by an altruistic living donor. Incentives for hospitals are studied by Ashlagi et al. (2015).

Gale and Shapley (1962) formalize the stable matching problem, present the deferred acceptance algorithm, and prove Theorems 10.5 and 10.7. The variant of the algorithm described here, with the unmatched applicants attempting to match one-by-one rather than simultaneously, follows Dubins and Freedman (1981). Incredibly, it was later discovered that essentially the same algorithm had been used, since the 1950s, to assign medical residents to hospitals (Roth, 1984)![6] Theorem 10.8 is due to Dubins and Freedman (1981) and Roth (1982a). Exercise 10.6 is observed by McVitie and Wilson (1971), and Problem 10.2 is discussed in Gale and Sotomayor (1985).

Exercises

Exercise 10.1 *(H)* Prove Theorem 10.1.

Exercise 10.2 Exhibit a tie-breaking rule between maximum-cardinality matchings such that the corresponding pairwise kidney exchange mechanism is not DSIC.

Exercise 10.3 Extend Example 10.3 to show that there is no DSIC matching mechanism that always matches more than half of the maximum-possible number of patient-donor pairs.

Exercise 10.4 Prove that there exists a constant $c > 0$ such that, for arbitrarily large n, the deferred acceptance algorithm can require at least cn^2 iterations to complete.

---

[6]The original implementation was the hospital-optimal version of the deferred acceptance algorithm, but it was changed to favor the applicants in the 1990s (Roth and Peranson, 1999).

Exercise 10.5 Suppose each applicant and hospital has a total ordering over the vertices of the opposite side and also an "outside option." In other words, vertices can prefer to go unmatched over some of their potential matches.

(a) Extend the definition of a stable matching to accommodate outside options.

(b) Extend the deferred acceptance algorithm and Theorem 10.5 to compute a stable matching in the presence of outside options.

Exercise 10.6 *(H)* For a hospital w, let $l(w)$ denote the lowest-ranked applicant (in w's preference list) to whom w is matched in any stable matching. Prove that, in the stable matching computed by the deferred acceptance algorithm, each hospital $w \in W$ is matched to $l(w)$.

Exercise 10.7 Exhibit an example that proves Theorem 10.8(b).

Problems

Problem 10.1 *(H)* Prove Theorem 10.8(a).

Problem 10.2 Consider a hospital in the deferred acceptance algorithm. We say that one preference list *strictly dominates* another if the former always leads to at least as good an outcome as the latter for the hospital (holding the reports of other applicants and hospitals fixed), and in at least one case leads to a strictly better outcome. Prove that, for every hospital, every preference list with a misreported first choice is strictly dominated by a preference list with a truthfully reported first choice.

Lecture 11

Selfish Routing and the Price of Anarchy

This lecture commences the second part of the course. In many settings, there is no option to design a game from scratch. Unlike all of our carefully crafted DSIC mechanisms, games "in the wild" generally have no dominant strategies. Predicting the outcome of such a game requires a notion of "equilibrium." As the outcome of self-interested behavior, there is no reason to expect equilibria to be socially desirable outcomes. Happily, in many interesting models, equilibria are near-optimal under relatively weak assumptions. This lecture and the next consider "selfish routing," a canonical such model.

Section 11.1 uses three examples to provide a gentle introduction to selfish routing. Sections 11.2 and 11.3 state and interpret the main result of this lecture, that the worst-case price of anarchy of selfish routing is always realized in extremely simple networks, and consequently equilibria are near-optimal in networks without "highly nonlinear" cost functions. After Section 11.4 formally defines equilibrium flows and explains some of their properties, Section 11.5 proves the main result.

11.1 Selfish Routing: Examples

Before formally defining our model of selfish routing, we develop intuition and motivate the main results through a sequence of examples.

11.1.1 Braess's Paradox

Lecture 1 introduced Braess's paradox (Section 1.2). To recap, one unit of traffic, perhaps representing rush-hour drivers, leaves an origin o for a destination d. In the network in Figure 11.1(a), by symmetry, at equilibrium half of the traffic uses each route and the common travel time is $\frac{3}{2}$. After installing a teleportation device that allows drivers to travel instantly from v to w (Figure 11.1(b)), the new route

$o \to v \to w \to d$ is a dominant strategy for every driver. The common travel time in this new equilibrium is 2. The minimum-possible travel time in the new network is $\frac{3}{2}$, as there is no profitable way to use the teleporter. The *price of anarchy (POA)* of this selfish routing network, defined as the ratio between the travel time in an equilibrium and the minimum-possible average travel time, is $2/\frac{3}{2} = \frac{4}{3}$.[1]

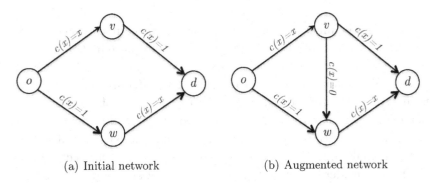

(a) Initial network   (b) Augmented network

Figure 11.1: Braess's paradox revisited. Edges are labeled with their cost functions, which describe the travel time of an edge as a function of the amount x of traffic that uses it. In (b), the price of anarchy is 4/3.

11.1.2 Pigou's Example

Pigou's example, shown in Figure 11.2(a), is an even simpler selfish routing network in which the POA is $\frac{4}{3}$. Even when the lower edge of this network carries all of the traffic, it is no worse than the alternative. Thus, the lower edge is a dominant strategy for every driver, and in equilibrium all drivers use it and experience travel time 1. An altruistic dictator would minimize the average travel time by splitting the traffic equally between the two edges. This results in an average travel time of $\frac{3}{4}$, showing that the POA in Pigou's example is $1/\frac{3}{4} = \frac{4}{3}$.

---

[1]This definition makes sense because the selfish routing networks considered in this lecture always have at least one equilibrium, and because the average travel time is the same in every equilibrium (see Lecture 13). Lecture 12 extends the definition of the POA to games with multiple equilibria.

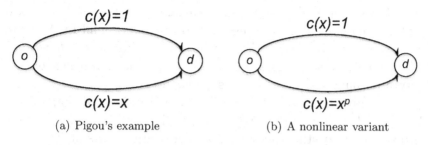

(a) Pigou's example   (b) A nonlinear variant

Figure 11.2: Pigou's example and a nonlinear variant.

11.1.3   Pigou's Example: A Nonlinear Variant

The POA is $\frac{4}{3}$ in both Braess's paradox and Pigou's example, which is quite reasonable for completely unregulated behavior. The story is not so rosy in all networks, however. In the nonlinear variant of Pigou's example (Figure 11.2(b)), the cost function of the lower edge is $c(x) = x^p$ rather than $c(x) = x$, where p is large. The lower edge remains a dominant strategy, and the equilibrium travel time remains 1. The optimal solution, meanwhile, is now much better. If the traffic is again equally split between the two edges, then the average travel time tends to $\frac{1}{2}$ as $p \to \infty$, with the traffic on the bottom edge arriving at d nearly instantaneously. Even better is to assign a $1 - \epsilon$ fraction of the traffic to the bottom edge, where ϵ tends to 0 as p tends to infinity. Then, almost all of the traffic gets to d with travel time $(1 - \epsilon)^p$, which is close to 0 when p is sufficiently large, and the ϵ fraction of martyrs on the upper edge contribute little to the average travel time. We conclude that the POA in the nonlinear variant of Pigou's example is unbounded as $p \to \infty$.

11.2   Main Result: Informal Statement

The POA of selfish routing can be large (Section 11.1.3) or small (Sections 11.1.1 and 11.1.2). The goal of this lecture is to provide a thorough understanding of when the POA of selfish routing is close to 1. Looking at our three examples, we see that "highly nonlinear" cost functions can prevent a selfish routing network from having a POA close to 1, while our two examples with linear cost functions have a small POA. The coolest statement that might be true is that highly nonlinear cost functions are the *only* obstacle to a small POA—that every selfish routing network with not-too-nonlinear cost functions, no matter how complex, has POA close to 1. The main result of this lecture formulates and proves this conjecture.

We study the following model. There is a directed graph $G = (V, E)$, with vertex set V and directed edge set E, with an origin vertex o and a destination vertex d. There are r units of traffic (or *flow*) destined for d from o.[2] We treat G as a flow network, in the sense of the classical maximum- and minimum-cost flow problems. Each edge e of the network has a *cost function*, describing the travel time (per unit of traffic) as a function of the amount of traffic using the edge. Edges do not have explicit capacities. In this lecture and the next, we always assume that every cost function is nonnegative, continuous, and nondecreasing. These are very mild assumptions in most relevant applications, like road or communication networks.

We first state an informal version of this lecture's main result and explain how to interpret and use it. We give a formal statement in Section 11.3 and a proof in Sections 11.4 and 11.5. Importantly, the theorem is parameterized by a set $\mathcal{C}$ of permissible cost functions. This reflects our intuition that the POA of selfish routing seems to depend on the "degree of nonlinearity" of the network's cost functions. The result is already interesting for simple classes $\mathcal{C}$ of cost functions, such as the set $\{c(x) = ax + b : a, b \geq 0\}$ of affine functions with nonnegative coefficients.

Theorem 11.1 (Tight POA Bounds for Selfish Routing)
Among all networks with cost functions in a set $\mathcal{C}$, the largest POA is achieved in a Pigou-like network.

Section 11.3 makes the term "Pigou-like networks" precise. The point of Theorem 11.1 is that worst-case examples are always simple. The principal culprit for inefficiency in selfish routing is nonlinear cost functions, not complex network structure.

For a particular cost function class $\mathcal{C}$ of interest, Theorem 11.1 reduces the problem of computing the worst-case POA to a back-of-

---

[2]To minimize notation, we state and prove the main result only for "single-commodity networks," where there is one origin and one destination. The main result and its proof extend to networks with multiple origins and destinations (Exercise 11.5).

the-envelope calculation. Without Theorem 11.1, one would effectively have to search through all networks with cost functions in $\mathcal{C}$ to find the one with the largest POA. Theorem 11.1 guarantees that the much simpler search through Pigou-like networks is sufficient.

For example, when $\mathcal{C}$ is the set of affine cost functions with nonnegative coefficients, Theorem 11.1 implies that Pigou's example (Section 11.1.2) maximizes the POA. Thus, the POA is always at most $\frac{4}{3}$ in selfish routing networks with such cost functions. When $\mathcal{C}$ is the set of polynomials with nonnegative coefficients and degree at most p, Theorem 11.1 implies that the worst example is the nonlinear variant of Pigou's example (Section 11.1.3). Computing the POA of this worst-case example yields an upper bound on the POA of every selfish routing network with such cost functions. See Table 11.1 for several examples, which demonstrate the point that the POA of selfish routing is large only in networks with "highly nonlinear" cost functions. For example, quartic functions have been proposed as a reasonable model of road traffic in some situations, and the worst-case POA with respect to such functions is slightly larger than 2. Lecture 12 discusses cost functions germane to communication networks.

Table 11.1: The worst-case POA in selfish routing networks with cost functions that are polynomials with nonnegative coefficients and degree at most p.

Description	Typical Representative	Price of Anarchy
Linear	$ax + b$	$4/3$
Quadratic	$ax^2 + bx + c$	$\frac{3\sqrt{3}}{3\sqrt{3}-2} \approx 1.6$
Cubic	$ax^3 + bx^2 + cx + d$	$\frac{4\sqrt[3]{4}}{4\sqrt[3]{4}-3} \approx 1.9$
Quartic	$ax^4 + bx^3 + cx^2 + dx + e$	$\frac{5\sqrt[4]{5}}{5\sqrt[4]{5}-4} \approx 2.2$
Degree $\leq p$	$\sum_{i=0}^{p} a_i x^i$	$\frac{(p+1)\sqrt[p]{p+1}}{(p+1)\sqrt[p]{p+1}-p} \approx \frac{p}{\ln p}$

11.3   Main Result: Formal Statement

To formalize the statement of Theorem 11.1, we need to define the "Pigou-like networks" for a class $\mathcal{C}$ of cost functions. We then formulate a lower bound on the POA based solely on these trivial instances.

Theorem 11.2 states a matching upper bound on the POA of every
selfish routing network with cost functions in $\mathcal{C}$.

Ingredients of a Pigou-Like Network

1. Two vertices, o and d.

2. Two edges from o to d, an "upper" edge and a "lower"
   edge.

3. A nonnegative traffic rate r.

4. A cost function $c(\cdot)$ on the lower edge.

5. The cost function everywhere equal to $c(r)$ on the
   upper edge.

See also Figure 11.3. There are two free parameters in the description
of a Pigou-like network, the traffic rate r and the cost function $c(\cdot)$
of the lower edge.

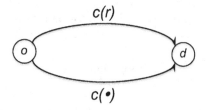

Figure 11.3: A Pigou-like network.

The POA of a Pigou-like network is easy to compute. By construction, the lower edge is a dominant strategy for all traffic—it is
no less attractive than the alternative (with constant cost $c(r)$), even
when it is fully congested. Thus, in the equilibrium all traffic travels
on the lower edge, and the total travel time is $r \cdot c(r)$—the amount of
traffic times the common per-unit travel time experienced by all of
the traffic. We can write the minimum-possible total travel time as

$$\inf_{0 \le x \le r} \{x \cdot c(x) + (r - x) \cdot c(r)\}, \tag{11.1}$$

where x is the amount of traffic routed on the lower edge.[3]   For later convenience, we allow x to range over all nonnegative reals, not just over $[0, r]$. Since cost functions are nondecreasing, this larger range does not change the quantity in (11.1)—there is always an optimal choice of x in $[0, r]$. We conclude that the POA in a Pigou-like network with traffic rate $r > 0$ and lower edge cost function $c(\cdot)$ is

$$\sup_{x \geq 0} \left\{ \frac{r \cdot c(r)}{x \cdot c(x) + (r - x) \cdot c(r)} \right\}.$$

Let $\mathcal{C}$ be an arbitrary set of nonnegative, continuous, and nondecreasing cost functions. Define the *Pigou bound* $\alpha(\mathcal{C})$ as the largest POA in a Pigou-like network in which the lower edge's cost function belongs to $\mathcal{C}$. Formally,

$$\alpha(\mathcal{C}) = \sup_{c \in \mathcal{C}} \sup_{r \geq 0} \sup_{x \geq 0} \left\{ \frac{r \cdot c(r)}{x \cdot c(x) + (r - x) \cdot c(r)} \right\}. \tag{11.2}$$

The first two suprema search over all choices of the two free parameters $c \in \mathcal{C}$ and $r \geq 0$ in a Pigou-like network; the third computes the best-possible outcome in the chosen Pigou-like network.[4]

The Pigou bound can be evaluated explicitly for many sets $\mathcal{C}$ of interest. For example, if $\mathcal{C}$ is the set of affine (or even concave) nonnegative and nondecreasing functions, then $\alpha(\mathcal{C}) = \frac{4}{3}$ (Exercises 11.1 and 11.2). The expressions in Table 11.1 are precisely the Pigou bounds for sets of polynomials with nonnegative coefficients and bounded degree (Exercise 11.3). The Pigou bound is achieved for these sets of cost functions by the nonlinear variant of Pigou's example (Section 11.1.3).

Suppose a set $\mathcal{C}$ contains all of the constant functions. Then the Pigou-like networks that define $\alpha(\mathcal{C})$ use only functions from $\mathcal{C}$, and $\alpha(\mathcal{C})$ is a lower bound on the worst-case POA of selfish routing networks with cost functions in $\mathcal{C}$.[5]

---

[3]Continuity of the cost function c implies that this infimum is attained, but we won't need this fact.

[4]Whenever the ratio reads $\frac{0}{0}$, we interpret it as 1.

[5]As long as $\mathcal{C}$ contains at least one function c with $c(0) > 0$, the Pigou bound is a lower bound on the POA of selfish routing networks with cost functions in $\mathcal{C}$. The reason is that, under this weaker assumption, Pigou-like networks can be simulated by slightly more complex networks with cost functions only in $\mathcal{C}$ (Exercise 11.4).

The formal version of Theorem 11.1 is that the Pigou bound $\alpha(\mathcal{C})$ is an upper bound on the POA of *every* selfish routing network with cost functions in $\mathcal{C}$, whether Pigou-like or not.

Theorem 11.2 (Tight POA Bounds for Selfish Routing)
For every set $\mathcal{C}$ of cost functions and every selfish routing network with cost functions in $\mathcal{C}$, the POA is at most $\alpha(\mathcal{C})$.

11.4 Technical Preliminaries

Before proving Theorem 11.2, we review some flow network preliminaries. While notions like flow and equilibria are easy to define in Pigou-like networks, defining them in general networks requires a little care.

Let $G = (V, E)$ be a selfish routing network, with r units of traffic traveling from o to d. Let $\mathcal{P}$ denote the set of o-d paths of G, which we assume is nonempty. A *flow* describes how traffic is split over the o-d paths, and is a nonnegative vector $\{f_P\}_{P \in \mathcal{P}}$ with $\sum_{P \in \mathcal{P}} f_P = r$. For example, in Figure 11.4, half of the traffic takes the zig-zag path $o \to v \to w \to d$, while the other half is split equally between the two two-hop paths.

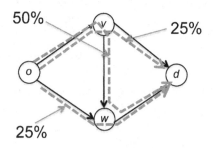

Figure 11.4: Example of a flow, with 25% of the traffic routed on each of the paths $o \to v \to t$ and $o \to w \to t$, and the remaining 50% on the path $o \to v \to w \to d$.

For an edge $e \in E$ and a flow f, we write $f_e = \sum_{P \in \mathcal{P}: e \in P} f_P$ for the amount of traffic that uses a path that includes e. For example, in Figure 11.4, $f_{(o,v)} = f_{(w,d)} = \frac{3}{4}$, $f_{(o,w)} = f_{(v,d)} = \frac{1}{4}$, and $f_{(v,w)} = \frac{1}{2}$.

In an equilibrium flow, traffic travels only on the shortest o-d paths, where "shortest" is defined using the travel times induced by the flow.

Definition 11.3 (Equilibrium Flow) A flow f is an *equilibrium* if $f_{\widehat{P}} > 0$ only when

$$\widehat{P} \in \operatorname{argmin}_{P \in \mathcal{P}} \left\{ \sum_{e \in P} c_e(f_e) \right\}.$$

For example, with cost functions as in Braess's paradox (Figure 11.1(b)), the flow in Figure 11.4 is not an equilibrium because the only shortest path is the zig-zag path, and some of the traffic doesn't use it.

We denote our objective function, the total travel time incurred by traffic in a flow f, by $C(f)$. We sometimes call the total travel time the *cost* of a flow. This objective function can be computed in two different ways, and both ways are useful. First, we can define

$$c_P(f) = \sum_{e \in E} c_e(f_e)$$

as the travel time along a path and tally the total travel time path-by-path:

$$C(f) = \sum_{P \in \mathcal{P}} f_P \cdot c_P(f). \tag{11.3}$$

Alternatively, we can tally it edge-by-edge:

$$C(f) = \sum_{e \in E} f_e \cdot c_e(f_e). \tag{11.4}$$

Recalling that $f_e = \sum_{P \in \mathcal{P} : e \in P} f_P$, a simple reversal of sums verifies the equivalence of (11.3) and (11.4).

*11.5   Proof of Theorem 11.2

We now prove Theorem 11.2. Fix a selfish routing network $G = (V, E)$ with cost functions in $\mathcal{C}$ and traffic rate r. Let f and f^* denote equilibrium and minimum-cost flows in the network, respectively. The proof has two parts.

The first part of the proof shows that after "freezing" the cost of every edge e at its equilibrium value $c_e(f_e)$, the equilibrium flow f is optimal. This makes sense, since an equilibrium flow routes all traffic on shortest paths with respect to the edge costs it induces.

Formally, since f is an equilibrium flow, if $f_{\hat{P}} > 0$, then $c_{\hat{P}}(f) \le c_P(f)$ for all $P \in \mathcal{P}$ (Definition 11.3). In particular, all paths $\hat{P}$ used by the equilibrium flow have a common cost $c_{\hat{P}}(f)$, call it L, and $c_P(f) \ge L$ for every path $P \in \mathcal{P}$. Thus,

$$\sum_{P \in \mathcal{P}} \underbrace{f_P}_{\text{sums to } r} \cdot \underbrace{c_P(f)}_{= L \text{ if } f_P > 0} = r \cdot L \tag{11.5}$$

while

$$\sum_{P \in \mathcal{P}} \underbrace{f_P^*}_{\text{sums to } r} \cdot \underbrace{c_P(f)}_{\ge L} \ge r \cdot L. \tag{11.6}$$

Expanding $c_P(f) = \sum_{e \in E} c_e(f_e)$ and reversing the order of summation as in (11.3)–(11.4), we can write the left-hand sides of (11.5) and (11.6) as sums over edges and derive

$$\sum_{e \in E} f_e \cdot c_e(f_e) = r \cdot L \tag{11.7}$$

and

$$\sum_{e \in E} f_e^* \cdot c_e(f_e) \ge r \cdot L. \tag{11.8}$$

Subtracting (11.7) from (11.8) yields

$$\sum_{e \in E} (f_e^* - f_e) c_e(f_e) \ge 0. \tag{11.9}$$

The inequality (11.9) is stating something very intuitive: since the equilibrium flow f routes all traffic on shortest paths, no other flow f^* can be better if we keep all edge costs fixed at $\{c_e(f_e)\}_{e \in E}$.

The second part of the proof quantifies the extent to which the optimal flow f^* can be better than f. The rough idea is to show that, edge by edge, the gap in costs between f and f^* is no worse than the Pigou bound. This statement only holds up to an error term for each edge, but we can control the sum of the error terms using the inequality (11.9) from the first part of the proof.

Formally, for each edge $e \in E$, instantiate the right-hand side of the Pigou bound (11.2) using c_e for c, f_e for r, and f_e^* for x. Since $\alpha(\mathcal{C})$ is the supremum over all possible choices of c, r, and x, we have

$$\alpha(\mathcal{C}) \geq \frac{f_e \cdot c_e(f_e)}{f_e^* \cdot c_e(f_e^*) + (f_e - f_e^*)c_e(f_e)}.$$

The definition of the Pigou bound accommodates both the cases $f_e^* < f_e$ and $f_e^* \geq f_e$. Rearranging,

$$f_e^* \cdot c_e(f_e^*) \geq \frac{1}{\alpha(\mathcal{C})} \cdot f_e \cdot c_e(f_e) + (f_e^* - f_e)c_e(f_e). \tag{11.10}$$

Summing (11.10) over all edges $e \in E$ gives

$$C(f^*) \geq \frac{1}{\alpha(\mathcal{C})} \cdot C(f) + \underbrace{\sum_{e \in E}(f_e^* - f_e)c_e(f_e)}_{\geq\, 0 \text{ by } (11.9)} \geq \frac{C(f)}{\alpha(\mathcal{C})}.$$

Thus the POA $C(f)/C(f^*)$ is at most $\alpha(\mathcal{C})$, and the proof of Theorem 11.2 is complete.

The Upshot

☆ In an equilibrium flow of a selfish routing network, all traffic travels from the origin to the destination on shortest paths.

☆ The price of anarchy (POA) of a selfish routing network is the ratio between the total travel time in an equilibrium flow and the minimum-possible total travel time.

☆ The POA is $\frac{4}{3}$ in Braess's paradox and Pigou's example, and is unbounded in the nonlinear variant of Pigou's example.

☆ The POA of a selfish routing network is large only if it has "highly nonlinear" cost functions.

☆ The Pigou bound for a set $\mathcal{C}$ of edge cost functions is the largest POA arising in a two-vertex, two-edge network with one cost function in $\mathcal{C}$ and one constant cost function.

☆ The Pigou bound for $\mathcal{C}$ is an upper bound on the POA of every selfish routing network with cost functions in $\mathcal{C}$.

Notes

Additional background on flow networks is in, for example, Cook et al. (1998). Pigou's example is described qualitatively by Pigou (1920). Selfish routing in general networks is proposed and studied in Wardrop (1952) and Beckmann et al. (1956). Braess's paradox is from Braess (1968). The price of anarchy of selfish routing is first considered in Roughgarden and Tardos (2002), who also proved that the POA is at most $\frac{4}{3}$ in every (multicommodity) network with affine cost functions. Theorem 11.2 is due to Roughgarden (2003) and Correa et al. (2004). Sheffi (1985) discusses the use of quartic cost functions for modeling road traffic. Problem 11.3 is from Roughgarden (2006). Roughgarden (2005) contains much more material on the price of anarchy of selfish routing.

Exercises

Exercise 11.1 *(H)* Prove that if $\mathcal{C}$ is the set of cost functions of the form $c(x) = ax + b$ with $a, b \geq 0$, then the Pigou bound $\alpha(\mathcal{C})$ is $\frac{4}{3}$.

Exercise 11.2 *(H)* Prove that if $\mathcal{C}$ is the set of nonnegative, nondecreasing, and concave cost functions, then $\alpha(\mathcal{C}) = \frac{4}{3}$.

Exercise 11.3 For a positive integer p, let $\mathcal{C}_p$ denote the set of polynomials with nonnegative coefficients and degree at most p: $\mathcal{C}_p = \{\sum_{i=0}^{p} a_i x^i : a_0, \ldots, a_p \geq 0\}$.

(a) Prove that the Pigou bound of the singleton set $\{x^p\}$ is increasing in p.

(b) Prove that the Pigou bound of the set $\{ax^i : a \geq 0, i \in \{0, 1, 2 \ldots, p\}\}$ is the same as that of the set $\{x^p\}$.

(c) *(H)* Prove that Pigou bound of $\mathcal{C}_p$ is the same as that of the set $\{x^p\}$.

Exercise 11.4 Let $\mathcal{C}$ be a set of nonnegative, continuous, and non-decreasing cost functions.

(a) *(H)* Prove that if $\mathcal{C}$ includes functions c with $c(0) = \beta$ for all $\beta > 0$, then there are selfish routing networks with cost functions in $\mathcal{C}$ and POA arbitrarily close to the Pigou bound $\alpha(\mathcal{C})$.

(b) *(H)* Prove that if $\mathcal{C}$ includes a function c with $c(0) > 0$, then there are selfish routing networks with cost functions in $\mathcal{C}$ and POA arbitrarily close to the Pigou bound $\alpha(\mathcal{C})$.

Exercise 11.5 Consider a *multicommodity* network $G = (V, E)$, where for each $i = 1, 2, \ldots, k$, r_i units of traffic travel from an origin $o_i \in V$ to a destination $d_i \in V$.

(a) Extend the definitions of a flow and of an equilibrium flow (Definition 11.3) to multicommodity networks.

(b) Extend the two expressions (11.3) and (11.4) for the total travel time to multicommodity networks.

(c) Prove that Theorem 11.2 continues to hold for multicommodity networks.

Problems

Problem 11.1 In Pigou's example (Section 11.1.2), the optimal flow routes some traffic on a path with cost twice that of a shortest path. Prove that, in every selfish routing network with affine cost functions, an optimal flow f^* routes all traffic on paths with cost at most twice that of a shortest path (according to the travel times induced by f^*).

Problem 11.2 In this problem we consider an alternative objective function, that of minimizing the *maximum* travel time

$$\max_{P \in \mathcal{P} : f_P > 0} \sum_{e \in P} c_e(f_e)$$

of a flow f. The price of anarchy (POA) with respect to this objective is then defined as the ratio between the maximum cost of an equilibrium flow and that of a flow with minimum-possible maximum cost.[6]

We assume throughout this problem that there is one origin, one destination, one unit of traffic, and affine cost functions (of the form $c_e(x) = a_e x + b_e$ for $a_e, b_e \geq 0$).

(a) Prove that in networks with only two vertices o and d, and any number of parallel edges, the POA with respect to the maximum cost objective is 1.

(b) *(H)* Prove that the POA with respect to the maximum cost objective can be as large as $4/3$.

(c) *(H)* Prove that the POA with respect to the maximum cost objective is never larger than $4/3$.

Problem 11.3 This problem considers Braess's paradox in selfish routing networks with nonlinear cost functions.

(a) Modify Braess's paradox (Section 11.1.1) to show that adding an edge to a network with nonlinear cost functions can double the travel time of traffic in an equilibrium flow.

(b) *(H)* Show that adding edges to a network with nonlinear cost functions can increase the equilibrium travel time by strictly more than a factor of 2.

---

[6]For an equilibrium flow, the maximum cost is just the common cost incurred by all of the traffic.

Lecture 12

Over-Provisioning and Atomic Selfish Routing

Last lecture proved generic tight bounds on the price of anarchy (POA) of selfish routing, parameterized by the edge cost functions. One particular instantiation of these bounds gives a rigorous justification for the common strategy of over-provisioning a communication network to achieve good performance (Section 12.1). A different result in the same vein states that a modest technology upgrade improves network performance more than implementing dictatorial control (Sections 12.2–12.3). Applications in which network users control a non-negligible fraction of the traffic are best modeled via an "atomic" variant of selfish routing (Section 12.4). The POA of atomic selfish routing is larger than in the "nonatomic" model, but remains bounded provided the network cost functions are affine (Sections 12.4–12.5), or more generally "not too nonlinear."

12.1 Case Study: Network Over-Provisioning

12.1.1 Motivation

The study of selfish routing provides insight into many different kinds of networks, including transportation, communication, and electrical networks. One big advantage in communication networks is that it is often relatively cheap to add additional capacity to a network. Because of this, a popular strategy to communication network management is to install more capacity than is needed, meaning that the network will generally not be close to fully utilized. One motivation for such network over-provisioning is to anticipate future growth in demand. Over-provisioning is also used for performance reasons, as it has been observed empirically that networks tend to suffer fewer packet drops and delays when they have extra capacity.

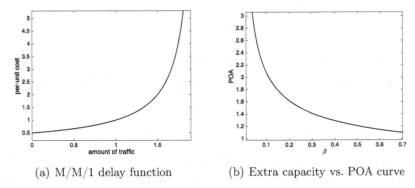

(a) M/M/1 delay function   (b) Extra capacity vs. POA curve

Figure 12.1: Modest over-provisioning guarantees near-optimal routing. The first figure displays the per-unit cost $c(x) = 1/(u - x)$ as a function of the amount of traffic x for an edge with capacity $u = 2$. The second figure shows the worst-case POA as a function of the fraction of unused network capacity.

12.1.2   POA Bounds for Over-Provisioned Networks

The POA bounds for selfish routing developed in Lecture 11 are parameterized by the class of permissible network cost functions. In this section, we consider networks in which every cost function $c_e(x)$ has the form

$$c_e(x) = \begin{cases} \frac{1}{u_e - x} & \text{if } x < u_e \\ +\infty & \text{if } x \geq u_e. \end{cases} \qquad (12.1)$$

The parameter u_e represents the capacity of edge e. A cost function of the form (12.1) is the expected per-unit delay in an M/M/1 queue, meaning a queue where jobs arrive according to a Poisson process with rate x and have independent and exponentially distributed services times with mean $1/u_e$. Such a function stays very flat until the amount of traffic nears the capacity, at which point the cost rapidly tends to $+\infty$ (Figure 12.1(a)). This is the simplest cost function used to model delays in communication networks.

For a parameter $\beta \in (0, 1)$, call a selfish routing network with cost functions of the form (12.1) β-over-provisioned if $f_e \leq (1 - \beta)u_e$ for every edge e, where f is some equilibrium flow. That is, at equilibrium, the maximum edge utilization in the network is at most $(1 - \beta) \cdot 100\%$.

Figure 12.1(a) suggests the following intuition: when β is not too close to 0, the equilibrium flow is not too close to the capacity on any edge, and in this range the edges' cost functions behave like low-degree polynomials with nonnegative coefficients. Theorem 11.2 implies that the POA is small in networks with such cost functions.

More formally, Theorem 11.2 reduces computing the worst-case POA in arbitrary β-over-provisioned selfish routing networks to computing the worst-case POA merely in β-over-provisioned Pigou-like examples. A computation (Exercise 12.2) then shows that the worst-case POA in β-over-provisioned networks is

$$\frac{1}{2}\left(1 + \sqrt{\frac{1}{\beta}}\right), \tag{12.2}$$

an expression graphed in Figure 12.1(b).

Unsurprisingly, the bound in (12.2) tends to 1 as β tends to 1 and to $+\infty$ as β tends to 0. These are the cases where the cost functions effectively act like constant functions and like very high-degree polynomials, respectively. Interestingly, even relatively small values of β imply good POA bounds. For example, if $\beta = .1$, corresponding to a maximum edge utilization of 90%, then the POA is always at most 2.1. Thus a little over-provisioning is sufficient for near-optimal selfish routing, corroborating empirical observations.

12.2   A Resource Augmentation Bound

This section proves a guarantee for selfish routing in arbitrary networks, with no assumptions on the cost functions. What could such a guarantee look like? Recall that the nonlinear variant of Pigou's example (Section 11.1.3) shows that the POA in such networks is unbounded.

The key idea is to compare the performance of selfish routing to a handicapped minimum-cost solution that is forced to route extra traffic. For example, in Figure 11.2(b) with p large, with one unit of traffic, the equilibrium flow has cost 1 while the optimal flow has near-zero cost. If the optimal flow has to route *two* units of traffic, then there is nowhere to hide: it again routes $(1 - \epsilon)$ units of traffic on the lower edge, with the remaining $(1+\epsilon)$ units of traffic routed on the upper edge. The cost of this flow exceeds that of the equilibrium flow with one unit of traffic.

This comparison between two flows at different traffic rates has an equivalent and easier-to-interpret formulation as a comparison between two flows with the same traffic rate but in networks with different cost functions. Intuitively, instead of forcing the optimal flow to route additional traffic, we allow the equilibrium flow to use a "faster" network, with each original cost function $c_e(x)$ replaced by the function $c_e(\frac{x}{2})/2$ (Exercise 12.3).

This transformation is particularly meaningful for cost functions of the form (12.1). If $c_e(x) = 1/(u_e - x)$, then the "faster" function is $1/(2u_e - x)$, corresponding to an edge with double the capacity. The next result, after this reformulation, gives a second justification for network over-provisioning: a modest technology upgrade improves performance more than implementing dictatorial control.

Theorem 12.1 (Resource Augmentation Bound) *For   every selfish routing network and $r > 0$, the cost of an equilibrium flow with traffic rate r is at most the cost of an optimal flow with traffic rate $2r$.*

Theorem 12.1 also applies to selfish routing networks with multiple origins and destinations (Exercise 12.1).

*12.3 Proof of Theorem 12.1

Fix a network G with nonnegative, nondecreasing, and continuous cost functions, and a traffic rate r. Let f and f^* denote equilibrium and minimum-cost flows at the traffic rates r and $2r$, respectively.

The first part of the proof reuses the trick from the proof of Theorem 11.2 (Section 11.5) of employing fictitious cost functions, frozen at the equilibrium costs, to get a handle on the cost of the optimal flow f^*. Recall that since f is an equilibrium flow (Definition (11.3)), all paths P used by f have a common cost $c_P(f)$, call it L. Moreover, $c_P(f) \geq L$ for every path $P \in \mathcal{P}$. Analogously to (11.5)–(11.8), we have

$$\sum_{e \in E} f_e \cdot c_e(f_e) = \sum_{P \in \mathcal{P}} \underbrace{f_P}_{\text{sums to } r} \cdot \underbrace{c_P(f)}_{= L \text{ if } f_P > 0} = r \cdot L$$

and

$$\sum_{e \in E} f_e^* \cdot c_e(f_e) = \sum_{P \in \mathcal{P}} \underbrace{f_P^*}_{\text{sums to } 2r} \cdot \underbrace{c_P(f)}_{\geq L} \geq 2r \cdot L.$$

With respect to the fictitious frozen costs, we get an excellent lower bound on the cost of f^*, of twice the cost of the equilibrium flow f. The second step of the proof shows that using the fictitious costs instead of the accurate ones overestimates the cost of f^* by at most the cost of f. Specifically, we complete the proof by showing that

$$\underbrace{\sum_{e \in E} f_e^* \cdot c_e(f_e^*)}_{\text{cost of } f^*} \geq \underbrace{\sum_{e \in E} f_e^* \cdot c_e(f_e)}_{\geq 2rL} - \underbrace{\sum_{e \in E} f_e \cdot c_e(f_e)}_{=rL}. \qquad (12.3)$$

We prove that (12.3) holds term-by-term, with

$$f_e^* \cdot [c_e(f_e) - c_e(f_e^*)] \leq f_e \cdot c_e(f_e) \qquad (12.4)$$

for every edge $e \in E$. When $f_e^* \geq f_e$, since the cost function c_e is nondecreasing and nonnegative, the left-hand side of (12.4) is nonpositive and there is nothing to show. Nonnegativity of c_e also implies that inequality (12.4) holds when $f_e^* < f_e$. This completes the proof of Theorem 12.1.

12.4   Atomic Selfish Routing

So far we've studied a *nonatomic* model of selfish routing, meaning that all agents have negligible size. This is a good model for cars on a highway or small users of a communication network. This section introduces *atomic* selfish routing networks, the more appropriate model for applications where each agent controls a significant fraction of the overall traffic. For example, an agent could represent an Internet service provider responsible for routing the data of a large number of end users.

An atomic selfish routing network consists of a directed graph $G = (V, E)$ with nonnegative and nondecreasing edge cost functions and a finite number k of agents. Agent i has an origin vertex o_i and a destination vertex d_i. Each agent routes 1 unit of traffic on a single o_i-d_i path, and seeks to minimize her cost.[1] Let $\mathcal{P}_i$ denote the o_i-d_i

---

[1] Two natural variants of the model allow agents to control different amounts of traffic or to split traffic over multiple paths. Tight worst-case POA bounds for both variants follow from ideas closely related to those of this and the next section. See the Notes for details.

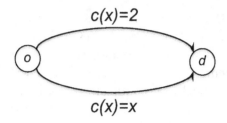

Figure 12.2: A Pigou-like network for atomic selfish routing.

paths of G. A *flow* can now be represented as a vector $(P_1, \ldots, P_k)$, with $P_i \in \mathcal{P}_i$ the path on which agent i routes her traffic. The *cost* of a flow is defined as in the nonatomic model, as (11.3) or (11.4). An *equilibrium* flow is one in which no agent can decrease her cost via a unilateral deviation.

Definition 12.2 (Equilibrium Flow (Atomic)) A flow $(P_1, \ldots, P_k)$ is an *equilibrium* if, for every agent i and path $\hat{P}_i \in \mathcal{P}_i$,

$$\underbrace{\sum_{e \in P_i} c_e(f_e)}_{\text{before deviating}} \leq \underbrace{\sum_{e \in \hat{P}_i \cap P_i} c_e(f_e) + \sum_{e \in \hat{P}_i \setminus P_i} c_e(f_e + 1)}_{\text{after deviating}}.$$

Definition 12.2 differs from Definition 11.3 because a deviation by an agent with non-negligible size increases the cost of the newly used edges.

To get a feel for the atomic model, consider the variant of Pigou's example shown in Figure 12.2. Suppose there are two agents, each controlling one unit of traffic. The optimal solution routes one agent on each edge, for a total cost of $1 + 2 = 3$. This is also an equilibrium flow, since neither agent can decrease her cost via a unilateral deviation. The agent on the lower edge does not want to switch, since her cost would jump from 1 to 2. More interestingly, the agent on the upper edge (with cost 2) has no incentive to switch to the lower edge, where her sudden appearance would drive the cost up to 2.

There is a second equilibrium flow in the network: if both agents take the lower edge, then both have a cost of 2 and neither can decrease her cost by switching to the upper edge. This equilibrium has cost 4. This example illustrates an important difference between nonatomic and atomic selfish routing: while different equilibria always have the same cost in the nonatomic model (see Lecture 13), they can have different costs in the atomic model.

Our definition of the POA in Lecture 11 assumes that all equilibria have the same cost. We next extend the definition to games with multiple equilibria using a worst-case approach.[2]   Formally, the *price of anarchy (POA)* of an atomic selfish routing network is the ratio

$$\frac{\text{cost of worst equilibrium flow}}{\text{cost of optimal flow}}.$$

For example, in the network in Figure 12.2, the POA is $\frac{4}{3}$.[3]

A second difference between nonatomic and atomic selfish routing is that the POA can be larger in the latter model. To see this, consider the four-agent bidirected triangle network shown in Figure 12.3. Each agent has two options, a one-hop path and a two-hop path. In the optimal flow, every agent routes her traffic on her one-hop path. These one-hop paths are precisely the four edges with the cost function $c(x) = x$, so the cost of this flow is 4. This flow is also an equilibrium flow. On the other hand, if every agent routes her traffic on her two-hop path, then we obtain a second equilibrium flow (Exercise 12.5). Since the first two agents each incur three units of cost and the last two agents each incur two units of cost, the cost of this flow is 10. The POA of this network is $10/4 = 2.5$.

No atomic selfish routing network with affine cost functions has a larger POA.

Theorem 12.3 (POA Bound for Atomic Selfish Routing)
In every atomic selfish routing network with affine cost functions, the POA is at most $\frac{5}{2}$.

Theorem 12.3 and its proof can be generalized to give tight POA bounds for arbitrary sets of cost functions; see the Notes.

*12.5   Proof of Theorem 12.3

The proof of Theorem 12.3 is a "canonical POA proof," in a sense made precise in Lecture 14. To begin, let's just follow our nose. We

---

[2]See Lecture 15 for some alternatives.

[3]The POA is well defined in every atomic selfish routing network, as every such network has at least one equilibrium flow (see Theorem 13.6).

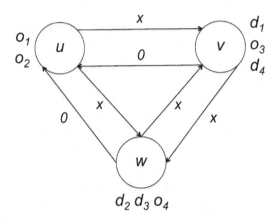

Figure 12.3: In atomic selfish routing networks with affine cost functions, the POA can be as large as $5/2$.

need to bound from above the cost of every equilibrium flow; fix one f arbitrarily. Let f^* denote a minimum-cost flow. Write f_e and f_e^* for the number of agents in f and f^*, respectively, that pick a path that includes the edge e. Write each affine cost function as $c_e(x) = a_e x + b_e$ for $a_e, b_e \geq 0$.

The first step of the proof identifies a useful way of applying our hypothesis that f is an equilibrium flow. If we consider any agent i, using the path P_i in f, and any unilateral deviation to a different path $\hat{P}_i$, then we can conclude that i's equilibrium cost using P_i is at most what her cost would be if she switched to $\hat{P}_i$ (Definition 12.2). This looks promising: we want an upper bound on the cost of the equilibrium flow f, and hypothetical deviations give us upper bounds on the equilibrium costs of individual agents. Which hypothetical deviations should we single out for the proof? Given that f^* is the only other object referenced in the theorem statement, a natural idea is to use the optimal flow f^* to suggest deviations.

Formally, suppose agent i uses path P_i in f and path P_i^* in f^*. By Definition 12.2,

$$\sum_{e \in P_i} c_e(f_e) \leq \sum_{e \in P_i^* \cap P_i} c_e(f_e) + \sum_{e \in P_i^* \setminus P_i} c_e(f_e + 1). \qquad (12.5)$$

This completes the first step, in which we apply the equilibrium hypothesis to generate an upper bound (12.5) on the equilibrium cost of each agent.

The second step of the proof sums the upper bound (12.5) on individual equilibrium costs over all agents to obtain a bound on the total equilibrium cost:

$$\underbrace{\sum_{i=1}^{k} \sum_{e \in P_i} c_e(f_e)}_{\text{cost of } f} \leq \sum_{i=1}^{k} \left(\sum_{e \in P_i^* \cap P_i} c_e(f_e) + \sum_{e \in P_i^* \backslash P_i} c_e(f_e + 1) \right) \quad (12.6)$$

$$\leq \sum_{i=1}^{k} \sum_{e \in P_i^*} c_e(f_e + 1) \quad (12.7)$$

$$= \sum_{e \in E} f_e^* \cdot c_e(f_e + 1) \quad (12.8)$$

$$= \sum_{e \in E} [a_e f_e^*(f_e + 1) + b_e f_e^*], \quad (12.9)$$

where inequality (12.6) follows from (12.5), inequality (12.7) from the assumption that cost functions are nondecreasing, equation (12.8) from the fact that the term $c_e(f_e + 1)$ is contributed once by each agent i for which $e \in P_i^*$ (f_e^* times in all), and equation (12.9) from the assumption that cost functions are affine. This completes the second step of the proof.

The previous step gives an upper bound on a quantity that we care about—the cost of the equilibrium flow f—in terms of a quantity that we don't care about, the "entangled" version of f and f^* on the right-hand side of (12.9). The third and most technically challenging step of the proof is to "disentangle" the right-hand side of (12.9) and relate it to the only quantities that we care about for a POA bound, the costs of f and f^*.

We use the following inequality, which is easily checked (Exercise 12.6).

Lemma 12.4 *For every* $y, z \in \{0, 1, 2, 3, \dots\}$,

$$y(z + 1) \leq \frac{5}{3}y^2 + \frac{1}{3}z^2.$$

We now apply Lemma 12.4 once per edge in the right-hand side of (12.9), with $y = f_e^*$ and $z = f_e$. Using the definition (11.4) of the cost $C(\cdot)$ of a flow, this yields

$$
\begin{aligned}
C(f) &\leq \sum_{e \in E} \left[a_e \left(\frac{5}{3}(f_e^*)^2 + \frac{1}{3}f_e^2 \right) + b_e f_e^* \right] \\
&\leq \frac{5}{3} \left[\sum_{e \in E} f_e^*(a_e f_e^* + b_e) \right] + \frac{1}{3} \sum_{e \in E} a_e f_e^2 \\
&\leq \frac{5}{3} \cdot C(f^*) + \frac{1}{3} \cdot C(f).
\end{aligned}
\tag{12.10}
$$

Subtracting $\frac{1}{3}C(f)$ from both sides and multiplying through by $\frac{3}{2}$ gives

$$
C(f) \leq \frac{5}{3} \cdot \frac{3}{2} \cdot C(f^*) = \frac{5}{2} \cdot C(f^*),
$$

which completes the proof of Theorem 12.3.

The Upshot

☆ A selfish routing network with cost functions of the form $c_e(x) = 1/(u_e - x)$ is β-over-provisioned if the amount of equilibrium flow on each edge e is at most $(1 - \beta)u_e$.

☆ The POA is small in β-over-provisioned networks even with fairly small β, corroborating empirical observations that a little over-provisioning yields good network performance.

☆ The cost of an equilibrium flow is at most that of an optimal flow that routes twice as much traffic. Equivalently, a modest technology upgrade improves performance more than implementing dictatorial control.

☆ In atomic selfish routing, where each agent controls a non-negligible fraction of the network traffic, different equilibrium flows can have different costs.

☆ The POA is the ratio between the objective function value of the worst equilibrium and that of an optimal outcome.

☆ The worst-case POA of atomic selfish routing
with affine cost functions is exactly 2.5. The
proof is "canonical" is a price sense.

Notes

Bertsekas and Gallager (1987) is a good reference for models
of communication networks, and Olifer and Olifer (2005) for
communication network management strategies such as over-
provisioning. POA bounds for β-over-provisioned networks are
discussed by Roughgarden (2010a). Theorem 12.1 is due to
Roughgarden and Tardos (2002). Atomic selfish routing networks first appear in Rosenthal (1973), and the POA of
such networks is first studied in Awerbuch et al. (2013) and
Christodoulou and Koutsoupias (2005b). Our proof of Theorem 12.3 follows Christodoulou and Koutsoupias (2005a). Defining the POA via the worst-case equilibrium is the original pro-
posal of Koutsoupias and Papadimitriou (1999). See Aland et al.
(2011) for tight POA bounds for atomic selfish routing networks
with polynomial cost functions, and Roughgarden (2015) for general cost functions. Tight POA bounds for agents controlling
different amounts of traffic are given by Awerbuch et al. (2013),
Christodoulou and Koutsoupias (2005b), Aland et al. (2011), and
Bhawalkar et al. (2014). For agents who can split traffic over multiple paths, POA bounds appear in Cominetti et al. (2009) and
Harks (2011), and tight bounds in Roughgarden and Schoppmann
(2015). In all of these atomic models, when edges' cost functions
are polynomials with nonnegative coefficients and degree at most p,
the POA is bounded by a constant that depends on p. The dependence on p is exponential, in contrast to the sublinear dependence in nonatomic selfish routing networks. Problems 12.1–12.4 are
from Chakrabarty (2004), Christodoulou and Koutsoupias (2005b),
Koutsoupias and Papadimitriou (1999), and Awerbuch et al. (2006),
respectively.

Exercises

Exercise 12.1 Multicommodity selfish routing networks are defined in Exercise 11.5. Generalize Theorem 12.1 to such networks.

Exercise 12.2 This exercise outlines the proof that the worst-case POA in β-over-provisioned networks is at most the expression in (12.2).

(a) Prove that, in a Pigou-like network (Section 11.3) with traffic rate r and cost function $1/(u-x)$ with $u > r$ on the lower edge, the POA is the expression in (12.2), where $\beta = 1 - \frac{r}{u}$.

(b) Adapt the Pigou bound (11.2) to β-over-provisioned networks by defining

$$\alpha_\beta = \sup_{u>0} \sup_{r \in [0, (1-\beta)u]} \sup_{x \geq 0} \left\{ \frac{r \cdot c_u(r)}{x \cdot c_u(x) + (r-x) \cdot c_u(r)} \right\},$$

where c_u denotes the cost function $1/(u - x)$. Prove that, for every $\beta \in (0, 1)$, α_β equals the expression in (12.2).

(c) *(H)* Prove that the POA of every β-over-provisioned network is at most the expression in (12.2).

Exercise 12.3 Prove that the following statement is equivalent to Theorem 12.1: If f^* is a minimum-cost flow in a selfish routing network with cost functions c and f is an equilibrium flow in the same network with cost functions $\tilde{c}$, where $\tilde{c}_e(x)$ is defined as $c_e(x/2)/2$, then

$$\widetilde{C}(f) \leq C(f^*).$$

The notation $\widetilde{C}$ and C refers to the cost of a flow (11.3) with the cost functions $\tilde{c}$ and c, respectively.

Exercise 12.4 Prove the following generalization of Theorem 12.1: for every selfish routing network and $r, \delta > 0$, the cost of an equilibrium flow with traffic rate r is at most $\frac{1}{\delta}$ times the cost of an optimal flow with traffic rate $(1 + \delta)r$.

Exercise 12.5 Verify that if each agent routes her traffic on her two-hop path in the network in Figure 12.3, then the result is an equilibrium flow.

Exercise 12.6 *(H)* Prove Lemma 12.4.

Problems

Problem 12.1 *(H)* For selfish routing networks with affine cost functions, prove the following stronger version of Theorem 12.1: for every such network and $r > 0$, the cost of an equilibrium flow with traffic rate r is at most that of an optimal flow with traffic rate $\frac{5}{4}r$.

Problem 12.2 Recall the four-agent atomic selfish routing network in Figure 12.3, where the POA is 2.5.

(a) Using a different network, show that the POA of atomic selfish routing with affine cost functions can be 2.5 even when there are only three agents.

(b) How large can the POA be with affine cost functions and only two agents?

Problem 12.3 This problem studies a scenario with k agents, where agent i has a positive weight w_i. There are m identical machines. Each agent chooses a machine, and wants to minimize the *load* of her machine, defined as the sum of the weights of the agents who choose it. This problem considers the objective of minimizing the *makespan*, defined as the maximum load of a machine. A *pure Nash equilibrium* is an assignment of agents to machines so that no agent can unilaterally switch machines and decrease the load she experiences.

(a) *(H)* Prove that the makespan of a pure Nash equilibrium is at most twice that of the minimum possible.

(b) Prove that, as k and m tend to infinity, pure Nash equilibria can have makespan arbitrarily close to twice the minimum possible.

Problem 12.4 This problem modifies the model in Problem 12.3 in two ways. First, every agent has unit weight. Second, each agent i must choose from a restricted subset S_i of the m machines.

(a) Prove that, for every constant $a \geq 1$, with sufficiently many agents and machines, the makespan of a pure Nash equilibrium can be more than a times the minimum makespan of a feasible schedule (assigning each agent i to a machine in her set S_i).

(b) Prove that there is a constant $a > 0$ such that the makespan of every pure Nash equilibrium is at most $a \ln m$ times the minimum possible. Can you obtain an even tighter dependence on the number m of machines?

Lecture 13

Equilibria: Definitions, Examples, and Existence

Equilibrium flows in atomic selfish routing networks (Definition 12.2) are a form of "pure" Nash equilibria, in that the agents do not randomize over paths. The Rock-Paper-Scissors game (Section 1.3) shows that some games have no pure Nash equilibria. When are pure Nash equilibria guaranteed to exist? How do we analyze games without any pure Nash equilibria?

Section 13.1 introduces three relaxations of pure Nash equilibria, each more permissive and computationally tractable than the previous one. All three of these relaxed equilibrium concepts are guaranteed to exist in all finite games. Section 13.2 proves that every routing game has at least one pure Nash equilibrium. Section 13.3 generalizes the argument and defines the class of potential games.

13.1 A Hierarchy of Equilibrium Concepts

Many games have no pure Nash equilibria. In addition to Rock-Paper-Scissors, another example is the generalization of atomic selfish routing networks to agents with different sizes (Exercise 13.5). For a meaningful equilibrium analysis of such games, such as a price-of-anarchy analysis, we need to enlarge the set of equilibria to recover guaranteed existence. Figure 13.1 illustrates the hierarchy of equilibrium concepts defined in this section. Lecture 14 proves worst-case performance guarantees for all of these equilibrium concepts in several games of interest.

13.1.1 Cost-Minimization Games

A *cost-minimization game* has the following ingredients:

- a finite number k of agents;

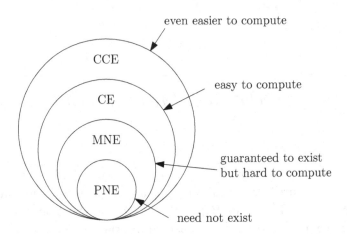

Figure 13.1: A hierarchy of equilibrium concepts: pure Nash equilibria (PNE), mixed Nash equilibria (MNE), correlated equilibria (CE), and coarse correlated equilibria (CCE).

- a finite set S_i of *pure strategies*, or simply *strategies*, for each agent i;

- a nonnegative cost function $C_i(\mathbf{s})$ for each agent i, where $\mathbf{s} \in S_1 \times \cdots \times S_k$ denotes a *strategy profile* or *outcome*.

For example, every atomic selfish routing network corresponds to a cost-minimization game, with $C_i(\mathbf{s})$ denoting i's travel time on her chosen path, given the paths chosen by the other agents.

Remark 13.1 (Payoff-Maximization Games) In a *payoff-maximization game*, the cost function C_i of each agent i is replaced by a payoff function π_i. This is the more conventional way to define games, as in the Rock-Paper-Scissors game in Section 1.3. The following equilibrium concepts are defined analogously in payoff-maximization games, except with all of the inequalities reversed. The formalisms of cost-minimization and payoff-maximization games are equivalent, but in most applications one is more natural than the other.

13.1.2   Pure Nash Equilibria (PNE)

A pure Nash equilibrium is an outcome in which a unilateral deviation by an agent can only increase the agent's cost.

Definition 13.2 (Pure Nash Equilibrium (PNE)) A strategy profile s of a cost-minimization game is a *pure Nash equilibrium (PNE)* if for every agent $i \in \{1, 2, \ldots, k\}$ and every unilateral deviation $s_i' \in S_i$,

$$C_i(\mathbf{s}) \leq C_i(s_i', \mathbf{s}_{-i}). \tag{13.1}$$

By $\mathbf{s}_{-i}$ we mean the vector s of all strategies, with the ith component removed. Equivalently, in a PNE s, every agent i's strategy s_i is a *best response* to $\mathbf{s}_{-i}$, meaning that it minimizes $C_i(s_i', \mathbf{s}_{-i})$ over $s_i' \in S_i$. PNE are easy to interpret but, as discussed above, do not exist in many games of interest.

13.1.3 Mixed Nash Equilibria (MNE)

Lecture 1 introduced the idea of an agent randomizing over her strategies via a *mixed strategy*. In a mixed Nash equilibrium, agents randomize independently and unilateral deviations can only increase an agent's expected cost.

Definition 13.3 (Mixed Nash Equilibrium (MNE))
Distributions $\sigma_1, \ldots, \sigma_k$ over strategy sets $S_1, \ldots, S_k$ of a cost-minimization game constitute a *mixed Nash equilibrium (MNE)* if for every agent $i \in \{1, 2, \ldots, k\}$ and every unilateral deviation $s_i' \in S_i$,

$$\mathbf{E}_{\mathbf{s} \sim \sigma}[C_i(\mathbf{s})] \leq \mathbf{E}_{\mathbf{s} \sim \sigma}\left[C_i(s_i', \mathbf{s}_{-i})\right], \tag{13.2}$$

where σ denotes the product distribution $\sigma_1 \times \cdots \times \sigma_k$.

Definition 13.3 considers only unilateral deviations to pure strategies, but allowing deviations to mixed strategies does not change the definition (Exercise 13.1).

Every PNE is a MNE in which every agent plays deterministically. The Rock-Paper-Scissors game shows that a game can have MNE that are not PNE.

Two facts discussed at length in Lecture 20 are relevant here. First, every cost-minimization game has at least one MNE. We can therefore define the *POA of MNE* of a cost-minimization game, with respect to an objective function defined on the game's outcomes, as the ratio

$$\frac{\text{expected objective function value of worst MNE}}{\text{objective function value of best outcome}}. \tag{13.3}$$

Second, computing a MNE appears to be a computationally intractable problem, even when there are only two agents.[1] This raises the concern that POA bounds for MNE need not be meaningful. In games where we don't expect the agents to quickly reach an equilibrium, why should we care about performance guarantees for equilibria? This objection motivates the search for more permissive and computationally tractable equilibrium concepts.

13.1.4   Correlated Equilibria (CE)

Our next equilibrium notion takes some getting used to. We define it, then explain the standard semantics, and then offer an example.

Definition 13.4 (Correlated Equilibrium (CE)) A distribution σ on the set $S_1 \times \cdots \times S_k$ of outcomes of a cost-minimization game is a *correlated equilibrium (CE)* if for every agent $i \in \{1, 2, \ldots, k\}$, strategy $s_i \in S_i$, and deviation $s_i' \in S_i$,

$$\mathbf{E}_{\mathbf{s} \sim \sigma}[C_i(\mathbf{s}) \mid s_i] \leq \mathbf{E}_{\mathbf{s} \sim \sigma}\left[C_i(s_i', \mathbf{s}_{-i}) \mid s_i\right]. \tag{13.4}$$

Importantly, the distribution σ in Definition 13.4 need not be a product distribution; in this sense, the strategies chosen by the agents are correlated. The MNE of a game correspond to the CE that are product distributions (Exercise 13.2). Since MNE are guaranteed to exist, so are CE. CE also have a useful equivalent definition in terms of "swapping functions" (Exercise 13.3).

The usual interpretation of a correlated equilibrium involves a trusted third party. The distribution σ over outcomes is publicly known. The trusted third party samples an outcome $\mathbf{s}$ according to σ. For each agent $i = 1, 2, \ldots, k$, the trusted third party privately suggests the strategy s_i to i. The agent i can follow the suggestion s_i, or not. At the time of decision making, an agent i knows the distribution σ and one component s_i of the realization $\mathbf{s}$, and accordingly has a posterior distribution on others' suggested strategies $\mathbf{s}_{-i}$. With these semantics, the correlated equilibrium condition (13.4) requires that every agent minimizes her expected cost by playing the suggested

---

[1] The precise statement uses an analog of $\mathcal{NP}$-completeness suitable for equilibrium computation problems (see Lecture 20).

strategy s_i. The expectation is conditioned on i's information—σ and s_i—and assumes that other agents play their recommended strategies $\mathbf{s}_{-i}$.

Believe it or not, a traffic light is a perfect example of a CE that is not a MNE. Consider the following two-agent game, with each matrix entry listing the costs of the row and column agents in the corresponding outcome:

	Stop	Go
Stop	1,1	1,0
Go	0,1	5,5

There is a modest cost (1) for waiting and a large cost (5) for getting into an accident. This game has two PNE, the outcomes (Stop, Go) and (Go, Stop). Define σ by randomizing uniformly between these two PNE. This is not a product distribution over the game's four outcomes, so it cannot correspond to a MNE of the game. It is, however, a CE. For example, consider the row agent. If the trusted third party (i.e., the stoplight) recommends the strategy "Go" (i.e., is green), then the row agent knows that the column agent was recommended "Stop" (i.e., has a red light). Assuming the column agent plays her recommended strategy and stops at the red light, the best strategy for the row agent is to follow her recommendation and to go. Similarly, when the row agent is told to stop, she assumes that the column agent will go, and under this assumption stopping is the best strategy.

Lecture 18 proves that, unlike MNE, CE are computationally tractable. There are even distributed learning algorithms that quickly guide the history of joint play to the set of CE. Thus bounding the POA of CE, defined as the ratio (13.3) with "MNE" replaced by "CE," provides a meaningful equilibrium performance guarantee.

13.1.5   Coarse Correlated Equilibria (CCE)

We should already be quite pleased with positive results, such as good POA bounds, that apply to the computationally tractable set of CE. But if we can get away with it, we'd be happy to enlarge the set of equilibria even further, to an "even more tractable" concept.

Definition 13.5 (Coarse Correlated Equilibrium (CCE))

A distribution σ on the set $S_1 \times \cdots \times S_k$ of outcomes of a cost-minimization game is a *coarse correlated equilibrium (CCE)* if for every agent $i \in \{1, 2, \ldots, k\}$ and every unilateral deviation $s_i' \in S_i$,

$$\mathbf{E}_{\mathbf{s} \sim \sigma}[C_i(\mathbf{s})] \leq \mathbf{E}_{\mathbf{s} \sim \sigma}\left[C_i(s_i', \mathbf{s}_{-i})\right]. \tag{13.5}$$

The condition (13.5) is the same as that for MNE (13.2), except without the restriction that σ is a product distribution. In this condition, when an agent i contemplates a deviation s_i', she knows only the distribution σ and *not* the component s_i of the realization. Put differently, a CCE only protects against unconditional unilateral deviations, as opposed to the unilateral deviations conditioned on s_i that are addressed in Definition 13.4. It follows that every CE is a CCE, and so CCE are guaranteed to exist and are computationally tractable. Lecture 17 demonstrates that the distributed learning algorithms that quickly guide the history of joint play to the set of CCE are even simpler and more natural than those for the set of CE.

13.1.6   An Example

We next increase intuition for the four equilibrium concepts in Figure 13.1 with a concrete example. Consider an atomic selfish routing network (Section 12.4) with four agents. The network is simply a common origin vertex o, a common destination vertex d, and an edge set $E = \{0, 1, 2, 3, 4, 5\}$ consisting of 6 parallel o-d edges. Each edge has the cost function $c(x) = x$.

The pure Nash equilibria are the outcomes in which each agent chooses a distinct edge. Every agent suffers only one unit of cost in such an equilibrium. One mixed Nash equilibrium that is obviously not pure has each agent independently choosing an edge uniformly at random. Every agent suffers expected cost $\frac{3}{2}$ in this equilibrium. The uniform distribution over all outcomes in which there is one edge with two agents and two edges with one agent each is a (non-product) correlated equilibrium, since both sides of (13.4) read $\frac{3}{2}$ for every i, s_i, and s_i'. The uniform distribution over the subset of these outcomes in which the set of chosen edges is either $\{0, 2, 4\}$ or $\{1, 3, 5\}$ is a coarse correlated equilibrium, since both sides of (13.5) read $\frac{3}{2}$ for every i and s_i'. It is not a correlated equilibrium, since an agent i that is recommended the edge s_i can reduce her conditional expected cost to 1 by choosing the deviation s_i' to the successive edge (modulo 6).

13.2   Existence of Pure Nash Equilibria

This section proves that equilibrium flows exist in atomic selfish routing networks (Section 13.2.1) and are also essentially unique in nonatomic selfish routing networks (Section 13.2.2), and introduces the class of congestion games (Section 13.2.3).

13.2.1   Existence of Equilibrium Flows

Section 12.4 asserts that atomic selfish routing networks are special games, in that a (pure) equilibrium flow always exists. We now prove this fact.

Theorem 13.6 (Existence of PNE in Routing Games) *Every atomic selfish routing network has at least one equilibrium flow.*

Proof: Define a function on the flows of an atomic selfish routing network by

$$\Phi(f) = \sum_{e \in E} \sum_{i=1}^{f_e} c_e(i), \qquad (13.6)$$

where f_e is the number of agents that choose a path in f that includes the edge e. The inner sum in (13.6) is the "area under the curve" of the cost function c_e; see Figure 13.2. By contrast, the corresponding term $f_e \cdot c_e(f_e)$ of the cost objective function (11.4) corresponds to the shaded bounding box in Figure 13.2.[2]

Consider a flow f, an agent i using the o_i-d_i path P_i in f, and a deviation to some other o_i-d_i path $\hat{P}_i$. Let $\hat{f}$ denote the flow after i's deviation from P_i to $\hat{P}_i$. We claim that

$$\Phi(\hat{f}) - \Phi(f) = \sum_{e \in \hat{P}_i} c_e(\hat{f}_e) - \sum_{e \in P_i} c_e(f_e). \qquad (13.7)$$

In words, the change in Φ under a unilateral deviation is exactly the same as the change in the deviator's individual cost. Thus, the single

---

[2]This similarity between the function Φ and the cost objective function is useful; see Lecture 15.

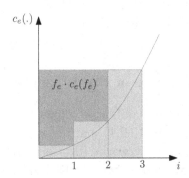

Figure 13.2: Edge e's contribution to the potential function Φ and to the cost objective function.

function Φ simultaneously tracks the effect of deviations by each of the agents.

To prove this claim, consider how Φ changes when i switches her path from P_i to $\hat{P}_i$. The inner sum of the potential function corresponding to edge e picks up an extra term $c_e(f_e + 1)$ whenever e is in $\hat{P}_i$ but not P_i, and sheds its final term $c_e(f_e)$ whenever e is in P_i but not $\hat{P}_i$. Thus, the left-hand side of (13.7) is

$$\sum_{e \in \hat{P}_i \setminus P_i} c_e(f_e + 1) - \sum_{e \in P_i \setminus \hat{P}_i} c_e(f_e),$$

which is exactly the same as the right-hand side of (13.7).

To complete the proof of the theorem, consider a flow f that minimizes Φ. There are only finitely many flows, so such a flow exists. No unilateral deviation by any agent can decrease Φ. By (13.7), no agent can decrease her cost by a unilateral deviation, and f is an equilibrium flow. ∎

13.2.2   Uniqueness of Nonatomic Equilibrium Flows

This section sketches the analog of Theorem 13.6 for the nonatomic selfish routing networks introduced in Lecture 11. Since agents have negligible size in such networks, we replace the inner sum in (13.6) by an integral:

$$\Phi(f) = \sum_{e \in E} \int_0^{f_e} c_e(x)dx, \qquad (13.8)$$

where f_e is the amount of traffic routed on edge e by the flow f. Because edge cost functions are continuous and nondecreasing, the function Φ is continuously differentiable and convex. The first-order optimality conditions of Φ are precisely the equilibrium flow conditions (Definition 11.3), and so the local minima of Φ correspond to equilibrium flows. Since Φ is continuous and the space of all flows is compact, Φ has a global minimum, and this flow is an equilibrium. Moreover, the convexity of Φ implies that its only local minima are its global minima. When Φ is strictly convex, there is only one global minimum and hence only one equilibrium flow. When Φ has multiple global minima, these correspond to equilibrium flows that all have the same cost.

13.2.3   Congestion Games

The proof of Theorem 13.6 never uses the network structure of an atomic selfish routing game. The argument remains valid for *congestion games*, where there is an abstract set E of resources (previously, the edges), each with a cost function, and each agent i has an arbitrary collection $S_i \subseteq 2^E$ of strategies (previously, the o_i-d_i paths), each a subset of resources. Congestion games play an important role in Lecture 19.

The proof of Theorem 13.6 also does not use the assumption that edge cost functions are nondecreasing. The generalization of Theorem 13.6 to networks with decreasing cost functions is useful in Lecture 15.

13.3   Potential Games

A *potential game* is one for which there exists a *potential function* Φ with the property that, for every unilateral deviation by some agent, the change in the potential function value equals the change in the deviator's cost. Formally,

$$\Phi(s_i', \mathbf{s}_{-i}) - \Phi(\mathbf{s}) = C_i(s_i', \mathbf{s}_{-i}) - C_i(\mathbf{s}) \qquad (13.9)$$

for every outcome $\mathbf{s}$, agent i, and unilateral deviation $s_i' \in S_i$. Intuitively, the agents of a potential game are inadvertently and collectively striving to optimize Φ. We consider only finite potential games in these lectures.

The identity (13.7) in the proof of Theorem 13.6 shows that every atomic selfish routing game, and more generally every congestion game, is a potential game. Lectures 14 and 15 furnish additional examples.

The final paragraph of the proof of Theorem 13.6 implies the following result.

Theorem 13.7 (Existence of PNE in Potential Games)
Every potential game has at least one PNE.

Potential functions are one of the only general tools for proving the existence of PNE.

The Upshot

☆ Pure Nash equilibria (PNE) do not exist in many games, motivating relaxations of the equilibrium concept.

☆ Mixed Nash equilibria (MNE), where each agent randomizes independently over her strategies, are guaranteed to exist in all finite games.

☆ In a correlated equilibrium (CE), a trusted third party chooses an outcome **s** from a public distribution σ, and every agent i, knowing σ and s_i, prefers strategy s_i to every unilateral deviation s_i'.

☆ Unlike MNE, CE are computationally tractable.

☆ A coarse correlated equilibrium (CCE) is a relaxation of a correlated equilibrium in which an agent's unilateral deviation must be independent of s_i.

☆ CCE are even easier to learn than CE.

☆ A potential game is one with a potential function such that, for every unilateral deviation by some agent, the change in the potential function value equals the change in the deviator's cost.

☆ Every potential game has at least one PNE.

☆ Every atomic selfish routing game is a potential game.

Notes

Nash (1950) proves that every finite game has at least one mixed Nash equilibrium. The correlated equilibrium concept is due to Aumann (1974). Coarse correlated equilibria are implicit in Hannan (1957) and explicit in Moulin and Vial (1978). The existence and uniqueness of equilibrium flows in nonatomic selfish routing networks (Section 13.2.2) is proved in Beckmann et al. (1956). Theorem 13.6 and the definition of congestion games are from Rosenthal (1973). Theorem 13.7 and the definition of potential games are from Monderer and Shapley (1996).

The example in Exercise 13.5 is from Goemans et al. (2005), while Exercise 13.6 is due to Fotakis et al. (2005). Problem 13.1 is discussed by Koutsoupias and Papadimitriou (1999). The results in Problems 13.2 and 13.4 are due to Monderer and Shapley (1996), although the suggested proof of the latter follows Voorneveld et al. (1999). Problem 13.3 is from Facchini et al. (1997).

Exercises

Exercise 13.1 Prove that the mixed Nash equilibria of a cost-minimization game are precisely the mixed strategy profiles $\sigma_1, \ldots, \sigma_k$ that satisfy

$$\mathbf{E}_{\mathbf{s} \sim \sigma}[C_i(\mathbf{s})] \leq \mathbf{E}_{s_i' \sim \sigma_i', \mathbf{s}_{-i} \sim \sigma_{-i}}\left[C_i(s_i', \mathbf{s}_{-i})\right]$$

for every agent i and mixed strategy σ_i' of i.

Exercise 13.2 Consider a cost-minimization game and a product distribution $\sigma = \sigma_1 \times \cdots \times \sigma_k$ over the game's outcomes, where σ_i is a mixed strategy for agent i. Prove that σ is a correlated equilibrium of the game if and only if $\sigma_1, \ldots, \sigma_k$ form a mixed Nash equilibrium of the game.

Exercise 13.3 Prove that a distribution σ over the outcomes $S_1 \times \cdots \times S_k$ of a cost-minimization game is a correlated equilibrium if and only if it has the following property: for every agent i and swapping function $\delta : S_i \to S_i$,

$$\mathbf{E}_{\mathbf{s} \sim \sigma}[C_i(\mathbf{s})] \le \mathbf{E}_{\mathbf{s} \sim \sigma}[C_i(\delta(s_i), \mathbf{s}_{-i})] \,.$$

Exercise 13.4 *(H)* Consider an atomic selfish routing network where each edge e has an affine cost function $c_e(x) = a_e x + b_e$ with $a_e, b_e \ge 0$. Let $C(f)$ denote the cost (11.4) of a flow f and $\Phi(f)$ the potential function value (13.6). Prove that

$$\frac{1}{2} C(f) \le \Phi(f) \le C(f)$$

for every flow f.

Exercise 13.5 In a *weighted* atomic selfish routing network, each agent i has a positive weight w_i and chooses a single o_i-d_i path on which to route all of her traffic. Consider the network shown in Figure 13.3, and suppose there are two agents with weights 1 and 2, both with the origin vertex o and the destination vertex d. Each edge is labeled with its cost function, which is a function of the total amount of traffic routed on the edge. For example, if agents 1 and 2 choose the paths $o \to v \to w \to d$ and $o \to w \to d$, then they incur costs of 48 and 74 per-unit of traffic, respectively.

Prove that there is no (pure) equilibrium flow in this network.

Exercise 13.6 Consider a weighted atomic selfish routing network (Exercise 13.5) where each edge has an affine cost function. Use the potential function

$$\Phi(f) = \sum_{e \in E} \left(c_e(f_e) f_e + \sum_{i \in S_e} c_e(w_i) w_i \right),$$

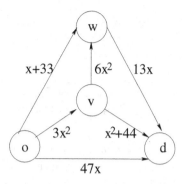

Figure 13.3: Exercise 13.5. A weighted atomic selfish routing network with no equilibrium.

where S_e denotes the set of agents that use edge e in the flow f, to prove that there is at least one (pure) equilibrium flow.

Problems

Problem 13.1 *(H)* Recall the class of cost-minimization games introduced in Problem 12.3, where each agent $i = 1, 2, \ldots, k$ has a positive weight w_i and chooses one of m identical machines to minimize her load. We again consider the objective of minimizing the makespan, defined as the maximum load of a machine. Prove that, as k and m tend to infinity, the worst-case POA of mixed Nash equilibria (13.3) in such games is not upper bounded by any constant.

Problem 13.2 This problem and the next two problems develop further theory about potential games (Section 13.3). Recall that a *potential function* is defined on the outcomes of a cost-minimization game and satisfies

$$\Phi(s_i', \mathbf{s}_{-i}) - \Phi(\mathbf{s}) = C_i(s_i', \mathbf{s}_{-i}) - C_i(\mathbf{s})$$

for every outcome $\mathbf{s}$, agent i, and deviation s_i' by i.

(a) Prove that if a cost-minimization game admits two potential functions Φ_1 and Φ_2, then there is a constant $b \in \mathbb{R}$ such that $\Phi_1(\mathbf{s}) = \Phi_2(\mathbf{s}) + b$ for every outcome $\mathbf{s}$ of the game.

(b) Prove that a cost-minimization game is a potential game if and only if for every two outcomes $\mathbf{s}^1$ and $\mathbf{s}^2$ that differ in the strategies of exactly two agents i and j,

$$\left[C_i(s_i^2, \mathbf{s}_{-i}^1) - C_i(\mathbf{s}^1)\right] + \left[C_j(\mathbf{s}^2) - C_j(s_i^2, \mathbf{s}_{-i}^1)\right] = \left[C_j(s_j^2, \mathbf{s}_{-j}^1) - C_j(\mathbf{s}^1)\right] + \left[C_i(\mathbf{s}^2) - C_i(s_j^2, \mathbf{s}_{-j}^1)\right].$$

Problem 13.3 *(H)* A *team game* is a cost-minimization game in which all agents have the same cost function: $C_1(\mathbf{s}) = \cdots = C_k(\mathbf{s})$ for every outcome $\mathbf{s}$. In a *dummy game*, the cost of every agent i is independent of her strategy: $C_i(s_i, \mathbf{s}_{-i}) = C_i(s_i', \mathbf{s}_{-i})$ for every $\mathbf{s}_{-i}$ and every $s_i, s_i' \in S_i$.

Prove that a cost-minimization game with agent cost functions $C_1, \ldots, C_k$ is a potential game if and only if

$$C_i(\mathbf{s}) = C_i^t(\mathbf{s}) + C_i^d(\mathbf{s})$$

for every i and $\mathbf{s}$, where $C_1^t, \ldots, C_k^t$ is a team game and $C_1^d, \ldots, C_k^d$ is a dummy game.

Problem 13.4 Section 13.2.3 defines congestion games and notes that every such game is a potential game, even when cost functions need not be nondecreasing. This problem proves the converse, that every potential game is a congestion game in disguise. Call two games $\mathcal{G}_1$ and $\mathcal{G}_2$ *isomorphic* if: (1) they have the same number k of agents; (2) for each agent i, there is a bijection f_i from the strategies S_i of i in $\mathcal{G}_1$ to the strategies T_i of i in $\mathcal{G}_2$; and (3) these bijections preserve costs, so that $C_i^1(s_1, \ldots, s_k) = C_i^2(f_1(s_1), \ldots, f_k(s_k))$ for every agent i and outcome $s_1, \ldots, s_k$ of $\mathcal{G}_1$. (Here C^1 and C^2 denote agents' cost functions in $\mathcal{G}_1$ and $\mathcal{G}_2$, respectively.)

(a) *(H)* Prove that every team game, as defined in the previous problem, is isomorphic to a congestion game.

(b) *(H)* Prove that every dummy game, as defined in the previous problem, is isomorphic to a congestion game.

(c) Prove that every potential game is isomorphic to a congestion game.

Lecture 14

Robust Price-of-Anarchy Bounds in Smooth Games

The preceding lecture introduced several relaxations of the pure Nash equilibrium concept. The benefit of enlarging the set of equilibria is increased plausibility and computational tractability. The drawback is that price-of-anarchy bounds, which concern the worst equilibrium of a game, can only degrade as the set of equilibria grows. This lecture introduces "smooth games," in which POA bounds for PNE extend without degradation to several relaxed equilibrium concepts, including coarse correlated equilibria.

Section 14.1 outlines a four-step recipe for proving POA bounds for PNE, inspired by our results for atomic selfish routing networks. Section 14.2 introduces a class of location games and uses the four-step recipe to prove a good POA bound for the PNE of such games. Section 14.3 defines smooth games, and Section 14.4 proves that POA bounds in such games extend to several relaxations of PNE.

*14.1 A Recipe for POA Bounds

Theorem 12.3 shows that the POA in every atomic selfish routing network with affine cost functions is at most $\frac{5}{2}$. To review, the proof has the following high-level steps.

1. Given an arbitrary PNE **s**, the equilibrium hypothesis is invoked once per agent i with the hypothetical deviation s_i^*, where **s*** is an optimal outcome, to derive the inequality $C_i(\mathbf{s}) \leq C_i(s_i^*, \mathbf{s}_{-i})$ for each i. Importantly, the deviations **s*** are independent of the choice of the PNE **s**. This is the only time that the PNE hypothesis is invoked in the entire proof.

2. The k inequalities that bound individuals' equilibrium costs are summed over the agents. The left-hand side of the resulting

187

inequality (12.9) is the cost of the PNE $\mathbf{s}$; the right-hand side is a strange entangled function of $\mathbf{s}$ and $\mathbf{s}^*$.

3. The hardest step is to relate the entangled term $\sum_{i=1}^{k} C_i(s_i^*, \mathbf{s}_{-i})$ generated by the previous step to the only two quantities that we care about, the costs of $\mathbf{s}$ and $\mathbf{s}^*$. Specifically, inequality (12.10) proves an upper bound of $\frac{5}{3} \sum_{i=1}^{k} C_i(\mathbf{s}^*) + \frac{1}{3} \sum_{i=1}^{k} C_i(\mathbf{s})$. This step is just algebra, and is agnostic to our choices of $\mathbf{s}$ and $\mathbf{s}^*$ as a PNE and an optimal outcome, respectively.

4. The final step is to solve for the POA. Subtracting $\frac{1}{3} \sum_{i=1}^{k} C_i(\mathbf{s})$ from both sides and multiplying through by $\frac{3}{2}$ proves that the POA is at most $\frac{5}{2}$.

This proof is canonical, in that POA proofs for many other classes of games follow the same four-step recipe. The main point of this lecture is that this recipe generates "robust" POA bounds that apply to all of the equilibrium concepts defined in Lecture 13.

*14.2 A Location Game

Before proceeding to the general theory, it is helpful to have another concrete example under our belt.

14.2.1 The Model

Consider a *location game* with the following ingredients:

- A set L of possible locations. These could represent servers capable of hosting a Web cache, gentrifying neighborhoods ready for an artisanal chocolate shop, and so on.

- A set of k agents. Each agent i chooses one location from a set $L_i \subseteq L$ from which to provide a service. All agents provide the same service, and differ only in where they are located. There is no limit on the number of markets that an agent can provide service to.

- A set M of markets. Each market $j \in M$ has a value v_j that is known to all agents. This is the market's maximum willingness-to-pay for receiving the service.

- For each location $\ell \in L$ and market $j \in M$, there is a cost $c_{\ell j}$ of serving j from ℓ. This could represent physical distance, the degree of incompatibility between two technologies, and so on.

Given a location choice by each agent, each agent tries to capture as many markets as possible, at the highest prices possible. To define the payoffs precisely, we start with an example. Figure 14.1 shows a location game with $L = \{\ell_1, \ell_2, \ell_3\}$ and $M = \{m_1, m_2\}$. There are two agents, with $L_1 = \{\ell_1, \ell_2\}$ and $L_2 = \{\ell_2, \ell_3\}$. Both markets have value 3. The cost between location ℓ_2 and either market is 2. Locations ℓ_1 and ℓ_3 have cost 1 to markets m_1 and m_2, respectively, and infinite cost to the other market.

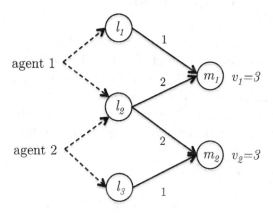

Figure 14.1: A location game with two agents (1 and 2), three locations ($L = \{\ell_1, \ell_2, \ell_3\}$), and two markets ($M = \{m_1, m_2\}$).

Continuing the example, suppose the first agent chooses location ℓ_1 and the second agent chooses location ℓ_3. Then, each agent has a monopoly in the market that they entered. The only thing restricting the price charged is the maximum willingness-to-pay of each market. Thus, each agent can charge 3 for her service to her market. Since the cost of service is 1 in both cases, both agents have a payoff of $3 - 1 = 2$.

Alternatively, suppose the first agent switches to location ℓ_2, while the second agent remains at location ℓ_3. Agent 1 still has a monopoly in market m_1, and thus can still charge 3. Her service cost has jumped to 2, however, so her payoff from that market has dropped to 1. In market m_2, agent 2 can no longer charge a price of 3 without consequence—at any price strictly bigger than 2, agent 1 can profitably undercut the price and take the market. Thus, agent 2 will charge the highest price she can without losing the market to the competition, which is 2. Since her cost of serving the market is 1, agent 2's payoff is $2 - 1 = 1$.

In general, in a strategy profile $\mathbf{s}$ of a location game in which T is the set of chosen locations and agent i chooses $\ell \in T$, agent i's payoff from a market $j \in M$ is

$$\pi_{ij}(\mathbf{s}) = \begin{cases} 0 & \text{if } c_{\ell j} \geq v_j \text{ or } \ell \text{ is not the closest} \\ & \text{location of } T \text{ to } j \\ d_j^{(2)}(\mathbf{s}) - c_{\ell j} & \text{otherwise,} \end{cases} \qquad (14.1)$$

where $d_j^{(2)}(\mathbf{s})$ is the highest price that agent i can get away with, namely the minimum of v_j and the second-smallest cost between a location of T and j. The definition in (14.1) assumes that each market is served by the potential provider with the lowest service cost, at the highest competitive price. The payoff $\pi_{ij}(\mathbf{s})$ is thus the "competitive advantage" that i has over the other agents for market j, up to a cap of v_j minus the service cost.

Agent i's total payoff is then

$$\pi_i(\mathbf{s}) = \sum_{j \in M} \pi_{ij}(\mathbf{s}).$$

Location games are examples of payoff-maximization games (Remark 13.1).

The objective function in a location game is to maximize the social welfare, which for a strategy profile $\mathbf{s}$ is defined as

$$W(\mathbf{s}) = \sum_{j \in M} (v_j - d_j(\mathbf{s})), \qquad (14.2)$$

where $d_j(\mathbf{s})$ is the minimum of v_j and the smallest cost between a chosen location and j. The definition (14.2) assumes that each market j is served by the chosen location with the smallest cost of serving j, or not at all if this cost is at least v_j.

The welfare $W(\mathbf{s})$ depends on the strategy profile $\mathbf{s}$ only through the set of locations chosen by some agent in $\mathbf{s}$. The definition (14.2) makes sense more generally for any subset of chosen locations T, and we sometimes write $W(T)$ for this quantity.

Every location game has at least one PNE (Exercise 14.1). We next work toward a proof that every PNE of every location game has social welfare at least 50% times the maximum possible.[1]

Theorem 14.1 (POA Bound for Location Games) *The POA of every location game is at least $\frac{1}{2}$.*

The bound of $\frac{1}{2}$ is tight in the worst case (Exercise 14.2).

14.2.2   Properties of Location Games

We next identify three properties possessed by every location game. Our proof of Theorem 14.1 relies only on these properties.

(P1) For every strategy profile $\mathbf{s}$, the sum $\sum_{i=1}^{k} \pi_i(\mathbf{s})$ of agents' payoffs is at most the social welfare $W(\mathbf{s})$.

This property follows from the facts that each market $j \in M$ contributes $v_j - d_j(\mathbf{s})$ to the social welfare and $d_j^{(2)}(\mathbf{s}) - d_j(\mathbf{s})$ to the payoff of the closest location, and that $d_j^{(2)}(\mathbf{s}) \leq v_j$ by definition.

(P2) For every strategy profile $\mathbf{s}$, $\pi_i(\mathbf{s}) = W(\mathbf{s}) - W(\mathbf{s}_{-i})$. That is, an agent's payoff is exactly the extra welfare created by the presence of her location.

To see this property, write the contribution of a market j to $W(\mathbf{s}) - W(\mathbf{s}_{-i})$ as $\min\{v_j, d_j(\mathbf{s}_{-i})\} - \min\{v_j, d_j(\mathbf{s})\}$. When the upper bound v_j is not binding, this is the extent to which the closest chosen location to j is closer in $\mathbf{s}$ than in $\mathbf{s}_{-i}$. This quantity is zero unless agent i's location is the closest to j in $\mathbf{s}$, in which case it is

$$\min\{v_j, d_j^{(2)}(\mathbf{s})\} - \min\{v_j, d_j(\mathbf{s})\}. \tag{14.3}$$

Either way, this is precisely market j's contribution $\pi_{ij}(\mathbf{s})$ to agent i's payoff in $\mathbf{s}$. Summing over all $j \in M$ proves the property.

---

[1] With a maximization objective, the POA is always at most 1, the closer to 1 the better.

(P3) The social welfare W is *monotone* and *submodular* as a function of the set of chosen locations. Monotonicity just means that $W(T_1) \leq W(T_2)$ whenever $T_1 \subseteq T_2 \subseteq L$; this property is evident from (14.2). Submodularity is a set-theoretic version of diminishing returns, defined formally as

$$W(T_2 \cup \{\ell\}) - W(T_2) \leq W(T_1 \cup \{\ell\}) - W(T_1) \qquad (14.4)$$

for every location $\ell \in L$ and subsets $T_1 \subseteq T_2 \subseteq L$ of locations (Figure 14.2). This property follows from our expression (14.3) for the welfare increase caused by one new location ℓ; Exercise 14.3 asks you to provide the details.

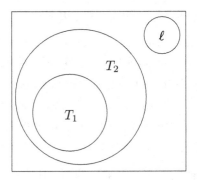

Figure 14.2: Definition of submodularity. Adding ℓ to the bigger set T_2 yields a smaller increase in social welfare than adding ℓ to the smaller set T_1.

14.2.3   Proof of Theorem 14.1

We follow the four-step recipe in Section 14.1. Let $\mathbf{s}$ denote an arbitrary PNE and $\mathbf{s}^*$ a social welfare-maximizing outcome. In the first step, we invoke the PNE hypothesis once per agent, with the outcome $\mathbf{s}^*$ providing hypothetical deviations. That is, since $\mathbf{s}$ is a PNE,

$$\pi_i(\mathbf{s}) \geq \pi_i(s_i^*, \mathbf{s}_{-i}) \qquad (14.5)$$

for every agent i. This is the only step of the proof that uses the assumption that $\mathbf{s}$ is a PNE.

The second step is to sum (14.5) over all of the agents, yielding

$$W(\mathbf{s}) \geq \sum_{i=1}^{k} \pi_i(\mathbf{s}) \geq \sum_{i=1}^{k} \pi_i(s_i^*, \mathbf{s}_{-i}), \qquad (14.6)$$

where the first inequality is property (P1) of location games.

The third step is to disentangle the final term of (14.6) and relate it to the only two quantities that we care about, $W(\mathbf{s})$ and $W(\mathbf{s}^*)$. By property (P2) of location games, we have

$$\sum_{i=1}^{k} \pi_i(s_i^*, \mathbf{s}_{-i}) = \sum_{i=1}^{k} [W(s_i^*, \mathbf{s}_{-i}) - W(\mathbf{s}_{-i})]. \qquad (14.7)$$

To massage the right-hand side into a telescoping sum, we add the extra locations $s_1^*, \ldots, s_{i-1}^*$ to the ith term.[2] By submodularity of W (property (P3)), we have

$$W(s_i^*, \mathbf{s}_{-i}) - W(\mathbf{s}_{-i}) \geq W(s_1^*, \ldots, s_i^*, \mathbf{s}) - W(s_1^*, \ldots, s_{i-1}^*, \mathbf{s})$$

for each $i = 1, 2, \ldots, k$. Thus, the right-hand side of (14.7) can be bounded below by

$$\sum_{i=1}^{k} \left[W(s_1^*, \ldots, s_i^*, \mathbf{s}) - W(s_1^*, \ldots, s_{i-1}^*, \mathbf{s}) \right],$$

which simplifies to

$$W(s_1^*, \ldots, s_k^*, s_1, \ldots, s_k) - W(\mathbf{s}) \geq W(\mathbf{s}^*) - W(\mathbf{s}),$$

where the inequality follows from the monotonicity of W (property (P3)). Summarizing, we have

$$\sum_{i=1}^{k} \pi_i(s_i^*, \mathbf{s}_{-i}) \geq W(\mathbf{s}^*) - W(\mathbf{s}), \qquad (14.8)$$

completing the third step of the proof.

---

[2]Some of the locations in $\mathbf{s}$ and $\mathbf{s}^*$ may coincide, but this does not affect the proof.

The fourth and final step is to solve for the POA. Inequalities (14.6) and (14.8) imply that

$$W(\mathbf{s}) \geq W(\mathbf{s}^*) - W(\mathbf{s}),$$

and so

$$\frac{W(\mathbf{s})}{W(\mathbf{s}^*)} \geq \frac{1}{2}$$

and the POA is at least $\frac{1}{2}$. This completes the proof of Theorem 14.1.

*14.3 Smooth Games

The following definition is an abstract version of the third "disentanglement" step in the proofs of the POA bounds for atomic selfish routing games (Theorem 12.3) and location games (Theorem 14.1). The goal is not generalization for its own sake; POA bounds established via this condition are automatically robust in several senses.

Definition 14.2 (Smooth Games)

(a) A cost-minimization game is (λ, μ)-*smooth* if

$$\sum_{i=1}^{k} C_i(s_i^*, \mathbf{s}_{-i}) \leq \lambda \cdot \text{cost}(\mathbf{s}^*) + \mu \cdot \text{cost}(\mathbf{s}) \qquad (14.9)$$

for all strategy profiles $\mathbf{s}, \mathbf{s}^*$. Here $\text{cost}(\cdot)$ is an objective function that satisfies $\text{cost}(\mathbf{s}) \leq \sum_{i=1}^{k} C_i(\mathbf{s})$ for every strategy profile $\mathbf{s}$.

(b) A payoff-maximization game is (λ, μ)-*smooth* if

$$\sum_{i=1}^{k} \pi_i(s_i^*, \mathbf{s}_{-i}) \geq \lambda \cdot W(\mathbf{s}^*) - \mu \cdot W(\mathbf{s}) \qquad (14.10)$$

for all strategy profiles $\mathbf{s}, \mathbf{s}^*$. Here $W(\cdot)$ is an objective function that satisfies $W(\mathbf{s}) \geq \sum_{i=1}^{k} \pi_i(\mathbf{s})$ for every strategy profile $\mathbf{s}$.

Every game is (λ, μ)-smooth for suitable choices of λ and μ, but good POA bounds require that neither λ nor μ is too large (see Section 14.4).

The smoothness condition controls the effect of a set of "one-dimensional perturbations" of an outcome, as a function of both the initial outcome $\mathbf{s}$ and the perturbations $\mathbf{s}^*$. Intuitively, in a (λ, μ)-smooth game with small values of λ and μ, the externality imposed by one agent on the others is bounded.

Atomic selfish routing networks are $(\frac{5}{3}, \frac{1}{3})$-smooth cost-minimization games. This follows from our proof that the right-hand side of (12.6) is bounded above by the right-hand side of (12.10), and the choice of the objective function (11.3) as $\mathrm{cost}(\mathbf{s}) = \sum_{i=1}^{k} C_i(\mathbf{s})$. Location games are $(1, 1)$-smooth payoff-maximization games, as witnessed by property (P1) of Section 14.2.2 and inequality (14.8).[3]

Remark 14.3 (Smoothness with Respect to a Profile)
A game is (λ, μ)-*smooth with respect to the strategy profile* $\mathbf{s}^*$ if the inequality (14.9) or (14.10) holds for the specific strategy profile $\mathbf{s}^*$ and all strategy profiles $\mathbf{s}$. All known consequences of Definition 14.2, including those in Section 14.4, only require smoothness with respect to some optimal outcome $\mathbf{s}^*$. See Problems 14.1–14.3 for applications of this relaxed condition.

*14.4   Robust POA Bounds in Smooth Games

This section shows that POA bounds for smooth games apply to several relaxations of PNE. In general, the POA of an equilibrium concept is defined as the ratio (13.3), with the "MNE" in the numerator replaced by the present concept.

14.4.1   POA Bounds for PNE

In a (λ, μ)-smooth cost-minimization game with $\mu < 1$, every PNE $\mathbf{s}$ has cost at most $\frac{\lambda}{1-\mu}$ times that of an optimal outcome $\mathbf{s}^*$. To see this, use the assumption that the objective function satisfies $\mathrm{cost}(\mathbf{s}) \leq$

---

[3]When we proved the "disentanglement" inequalities for atomic selfish routing and location games, we had in mind the case where $\mathbf{s}$ and $\mathbf{s}^*$ are a PNE and an optimal outcome, respectively. Our proofs do not use these facts, however, and apply more generally to all pairs of strategy profiles.

$\sum_{i=1}^{k} C_i(\mathbf{s})$, the PNE condition (once per agent), and the smoothness assumption to derive

$$\text{cost}(\mathbf{s}) \leq \sum_{i=1}^{k} C_i(\mathbf{s})$$

$$\leq \sum_{i=1}^{k} C_i(s_i^*, \mathbf{s}_{-i})$$

$$\leq \lambda \cdot \text{cost}(\mathbf{s}^*) + \mu \cdot \text{cost}(\mathbf{s}).$$

Rearranging terms establishes the bound of $\frac{\lambda}{1-\mu}$.

Similarly, every PNE of a (λ, μ)-smooth payoff-maximization game has objective function value at least $\frac{\lambda}{1+\mu}$ times that of an optimal outcome. These observations generalize our POA bounds of $\frac{5}{2}$ and $\frac{1}{2}$ for atomic selfish routing networks with affine cost functions and location games, respectively.

14.4.2   POA Bounds for CCE

We next describe the first sense in which the POA bound of $\frac{\lambda}{1-\mu}$ or $\frac{\lambda}{1+\mu}$ for a (λ, μ)-smooth game is robust: it applies to all coarse correlated equilibria (CCE) of the game (Definition 13.5).

Theorem 14.4 (POA of CCE in Smooth Games) *In   every (λ, μ)-smooth cost-minimization game with $\mu < 1$, the POA of CCE is at most $\frac{\lambda}{1-\mu}$.*

That is, the exact same POA bound that we derived in in the previous section for PNE holds more generally for all CCE. CCE are therefore a "sweet spot" equilibrium concept in smooth games—permissive enough to be highly tractable (see Lecture 17), yet stringent enough to allow good worst-case bounds.

Given the definitions, we can prove Theorem 14.4 just by following our nose.

Proof of Theorem 14.4: Consider a (λ, μ)-smooth cost-minimization game, a coarse correlated equilibrium σ, and an optimal outcome $\mathbf{s}^*$.

We can write

$$\mathbf{E}_{\mathbf{s}\sim\sigma}[\mathrm{cost}(\mathbf{s})] \;\leq\; \mathbf{E}_{\mathbf{s}\sim\sigma}\left[\sum_{i=1}^{k} C_i(\mathbf{s})\right] \tag{14.11}$$

$$= \sum_{i=1}^{k} \mathbf{E}_{\mathbf{s}\sim\sigma}[C_i(\mathbf{s})] \tag{14.12}$$

$$\leq \sum_{i=1}^{k} \mathbf{E}_{\mathbf{s}\sim\sigma}[C_i(s_i^*, \mathbf{s}_{-i})] \tag{14.13}$$

$$= \mathbf{E}_{\mathbf{s}\sim\sigma}\left[\sum_{i=1}^{k} C_i(s_i^*, \mathbf{s}_{-i})\right] \tag{14.14}$$

$$\leq \mathbf{E}_{\mathbf{s}\sim\sigma}[\lambda \cdot \mathrm{cost}(\mathbf{s}^*) + \mu \cdot \mathrm{cost}(\mathbf{s})] \tag{14.15}$$

$$= \lambda \cdot \mathrm{cost}(\mathbf{s}^*) + \mu \cdot \mathbf{E}_{\mathbf{s}\sim\sigma}[\mathrm{cost}(\mathbf{s})], \tag{14.16}$$

where inequality (14.11) follows from the assumption on the objective function, equations (14.12), (14.14), and (14.16) follow from linearity of expectation, inequality (14.13) follows from the definition (13.5) of a coarse correlated equilibrium (applied once per agent i, with the hypothetical deviation s_i^*), and inequality (14.15) follows from (λ, μ)-smoothness. Rearranging terms completes the proof. ∎

Similarly, in (λ, μ)-smooth payoff-maximization games, the POA bound of $\frac{\lambda}{1+\mu}$ applies to all CCE (Exercise 14.4).

Our POA bounds of $\frac{5}{2}$ and $\frac{1}{2}$ for atomic selfish routing games (Theorem 12.3) and location games (Theorem 14.1) may initially seem specific to PNE, but since the proofs establish the stronger smoothness condition (Definition 14.2), Theorem 14.4 implies that they hold for all CCE.

14.4.3   POA Bounds for Approximate PNE

Smooth games have a number of other nice properties, as well. For example, the POA bound of $\frac{\lambda}{1-\mu}$ or $\frac{\lambda}{1+\mu}$ for a (λ, μ)-smooth game applies automatically to approximate equilibria, with the POA bound degrading gracefully as a function of the approximation parameter.

Definition 14.5 (ϵ-Pure Nash Equilibrium) For $\epsilon \geq 0$, an outcome $\mathbf{s}$ of a cost-minimization game is an ϵ-*pure Nash equilibrium* *(ε-PNE)* if, for every agent i and deviation $s'_i \in S_i$,

$$C_i(\mathbf{s}) \leq (1 + \epsilon) \cdot C_i(s'_i, \mathbf{s}_{-i}). \qquad (14.17)$$

This is, in an ϵ-PNE, no agent can decrease her cost by more than a $1 + \epsilon$ factor via a unilateral deviation. The following guarantee holds (Exercise 14.5).

Theorem 14.6 (POA of ϵ-PNE in Smooth Games) *In every* (λ, μ)-*smooth cost-minimization game with $\mu < 1$, for every $\epsilon < \frac{1}{\mu} - 1$, the POA of ϵ-PNE is at most*

$$\frac{(1 + \epsilon)\lambda}{1 - \mu(1 + \epsilon)}.$$

Similar results hold for (λ, μ)-smooth payoff-maximization games, and for approximate versions of other equilibrium concepts.

For example, in atomic selfish routing networks with affine cost functions, which are $(\frac{5}{3}, \frac{1}{3})$-smooth, the POA of ϵ-PNE with $\epsilon < 2$ is at most $\frac{5 + 5\epsilon}{2 - \epsilon}$.

The Upshot

☆ A four-step recipe for proving POA bounds is: (1) invoke the equilibrium condition once per agent, using an optimal outcome to define hypothetical deviations, to bound agents' equilibrium costs; (2) add up the resulting inequalities to bound the total equilibrium cost; (3) relate this entangled bound back to the equilibrium and optimal costs; (4) solve for the POA.

☆ The POA bound for atomic selfish routing networks with affine cost functions follows from this four-step recipe.

☆ In a location game where agents choose locations from which to provide a service and compete for several markets, this four-step recipe proves that the POA is at least $\frac{1}{2}$.

☆ The definition of a smooth game is an abstract

version of the third "disentanglement" step in this recipe.

☆ The POA bound implied by the smoothness condition extends to all coarse correlated equilibria.

☆ The POA bound implied by the smoothness condition extends to all approximate equilibria, with the POA bound degrading gracefully as a function of the approximation parameter.

Notes

The definition of location games and Theorem 14.1 are due to Vetta (2002). The importance of POA bounds that apply beyond Nash equilibria is articulated in Mirrokni and Vetta (2004). The POA of CCE is first studied in Blum et al. (2008). Definition 14.2 and Theorems 14.4 and 14.6 are from Roughgarden (2015). The term "smooth" is meant to succinctly suggest an analogy between Definition 14.2 and a Lipschitz-type condition. Problems 14.1–14.3 are from Hoeksma and Uetz (2011), Caragiannis et al. (2015), and Christodoulou et al. (2008), respectively. For more on the POA in (non-DSIC) auctions and mechanisms, see the survey by Roughgarden et al. (2016).

Exercises

Exercise 14.1 *(H)* Prove that every location game is a potential game (Section 13.3) and hence has at least one PNE.

Exercise 14.2 Prove that Theorem 14.1 is tight, in that there is a location game in which the POA of PNE is $\frac{1}{2}$.

Exercise 14.3 Prove that the social welfare function of a location game is a submodular function of the set of chosen locations.

Exercise 14.4 Prove that the POA of CCE of a (λ, μ)-smooth payoff-maximization game is at least $\frac{\lambda}{1+\mu}$.

Exercise 14.5 *(H)* Prove Theorem 14.6.

Problems

Problem 14.1 This problem studies a scenario with k agents, where agent j has a processing time p_j. There are m identical machines. Each agent chooses a machine, and the agents on each machine are processed serially from shortest to longest. (You can assume that the p_j's are distinct.) For example, if agents with processing times 1, 3, and 5 are scheduled on a common machine, then they will complete at times 1, 4, and 9, respectively. The following questions concern the cost-minimization game in which agents choose machines to minimize their completion times, and the objective function of minimizing the sum $\sum_{j=1}^{k} C_j$ of the agents' completion times.

(a) Define the *rank* R_j of agent j in a schedule as the number of agents on j's machine with processing time at least p_j, including j itself. For example, if agents with processing times 1, 3, and 5 are scheduled on a common machine, then they have ranks 3, 2, and 1, respectively.

Prove that the objective function value $\sum_{j=1}^{k} C_j$ of an outcome can also be written as $\sum_{j=1}^{k} p_j R_j$.

(b) Prove that the following algorithm produces an optimal outcome: (1) sort the agents from largest to smallest; (2) for $j = 1, 2, \ldots, k$, assign the jth agent in this ordering to machine $j \bmod m$ (where machine 0 means machine m).

(c) *(H)* Prove that in every such scheduling game, the POA of CCE is at most 2.

Problem 14.2 The Generalized Second Price sponsored search auction described in Problem 3.1 induces a payoff-maximization game, where bidder i strives to maximize her utility $\alpha_{j(i)}(v_i - p_{j(i)})$, where v_i is her value-per-click, $j(i)$ is her assigned slot, and $p_{j(i)}$ and $\alpha_{j(i)}$

are the price-per-click and click-through rate of this slot. (If i is not assigned a slot, then $\alpha_{j(i)} = p_{j(i)} = 0$.)

(a) Assume that each bidder can bid any nonnegative number. Show that even with one slot and two bidders, the POA of PNE can be 0.

(b) *(H)* Now assume that each bidder i always bids a number between 0 and v_i. Prove that the POA of CCE is at least $\frac{1}{4}$.

Problem 14.3 This problem concerns combinatorial auctions (Example 7.2) where each bidder i has a unit-demand valuation v_i (Exercise 7.5). This means that there are values $v_{i1}, \ldots, v_{im}$ such that $v_i(S) = \max_{j \in S} v_{ij}$ for every subset S of items.

Consider a payoff-maximization game in which each bidder i submits one bid b_{ij} for each item j and each item is sold separately using a second-price single-item auction. Similarly to Problem 14.2(b), assume that each bid b_{ij} lies between 0 and v_{ij}. The utility of a bidder is her value for the items won less her total payment. For example, if bidder i has values v_{i1} and v_{i2} for two items, and wins both items when the second-highest bids are p_1 and p_2, then her utility is $\max\{v_{i1}, v_{i2}\} - (p_1 + p_2)$.

(a) *(H)* Prove that the POA of PNE in such a game can be at most $\frac{1}{2}$.

(b) *(H)* Prove that the POA of CCE in every such game is at least $\frac{1}{2}$.

Lecture 15

Best-Case and Strong Nash Equilibria

This lecture has two purposes. The first is to introduce a simple model of network formation that resembles atomic selfish routing games but has positive externalities, meaning that an agent prefers to share the edges of her path with as many other agents as possible. Such games generally have multiple PNE with wildly varying costs. The second purpose of the lecture is to explain two approaches for confining attention to a subset of "reasonable" PNE. Ideally, better worst-case approximation bounds should hold for such a subset than for all PNE, and there should also be a plausible narrative as to why PNE in the subset are more worthy of study than the others.

Section 15.1 defines network cost-sharing games and considers two important examples. Section 15.2 proves an approximation bound for the best-case PNE of a network cost-sharing game. Sections 15.3 and 15.4 prove a bound on the POA of strong Nash equilibria, the subset of PNE for which no coalition of agents has a beneficial deviation.

15.1 Network Cost-Sharing Games

15.1.1 Externalities

The network formation model introduced next is a concrete example of a game with positive externalities. The *externality* caused by an agent in a game is the difference between her individual objective function value and her contribution to the social objective function value. The models studied in previous lectures have *negative* externalities, meaning that agents do not fully account for the harm that they cause. In a routing game, for example, an agent does not take into account the additional cost her presence creates for the other agents using the edges in her path.

There are also important applications that exhibit *positive* externalities. You usually join a campus organization or a social network to derive personal benefit from it, but your presence also enriches the experience of other people in the same group. As an agent, you're generally bummed to see new agents show up in a game with negative externalities, and excited for the windfalls of new agents in a game with positive externalities.

15.1.2   The Model

A *network cost-sharing game* takes place in a graph $G = (V, E)$, which can be directed or undirected, and each edge $e \in E$ carries a fixed cost $\gamma_e \geq 0$. There are k agents. Agent i has an origin vertex $o_i \in V$ and a destination vertex $d_i \in V$, and her strategy set is the set of o_i-d_i paths of the graph. Outcomes of the game correspond to path vectors $\mathbf{P} = (P_1, \ldots, P_k)$, with the semantics that the subnetwork $(V, \cup_{i=1}^{k} P_i)$ gets formed.

We think of γ_e as the cost of building the edge e, for example of laying down high-speed Internet fiber to a neighborhood. This cost is independent of the number of agents that use the edge. Agents' costs are defined edge-by-edge, as in routing games (Lectures 11–12). If multiple agents use an edge e in their chosen paths, then they are jointly responsible for the edge's fixed cost γ_e, and we assume that they split it equally. In the language of cost-minimization games (Lecture 13), the cost $C_i(\mathbf{P})$ of agent i in the outcome $\mathbf{P}$ is

$$C_i(\mathbf{P}) = \sum_{e \in P_i} \frac{\gamma_e}{f_e}, \tag{15.1}$$

where $f_e = |\{j \: : \: e \in P_j\}|$ denotes the number of agents that choose a path that includes e. The objective function is to minimize the total cost of the formed network:

$$\text{cost}(\mathbf{P}) = \sum_{e \in E \, : \, f_e \geq 1} \gamma_e. \tag{15.2}$$

Analogous to the objective function (11.3) and (11.4) in routing games, the function (15.2) can equally well be written as the sum $\sum_{i=1}^{k} C_i(\mathbf{P})$ of the agents' costs.

15.1.3   Example: VHS or Betamax

Let's build our intuition for network cost-sharing games through a couple of examples. The first example demonstrates how tragic miscoordination can occur in games with positive externalities.

Consider the simple network in Figure 15.1, with k agents with a common origin o and destination d. One interpretation of this example is as a choice between two competing technologies. For example, back in the 1980s, there were two new technologies enabling home movie rentals. Betamax was lauded by technology geeks as the better one, and thus corresponds to the cheaper edge in Figure 15.1. VHS was the other technology, and it grabbed a larger market share early on. Coordinating on a single technology proved the primary driver in consumers' decisions—having the better technology is little consolation for being unable to rent anything from your corner store—and Betamax was eventually driven to extinction.

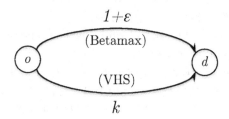

Figure 15.1: VHS or Betamax. The POA in a network cost-sharing game can be as large as the number k of agents. The parameter $\epsilon > 0$ can be arbitrarily small.

The optimal outcome in the network in Figure 15.1 is for all agents to pick the upper edge, for a total cost of $1 + \epsilon$. This is also a PNE (Definition 13.2). Unfortunately, there is a second PNE, in which all agents pick the lower edge. Since the cost of k is split equally, each agent pays 1. If an agent deviated unilaterally to the upper edge, she would pay the full cost $1 + \epsilon$ of that edge and thus suffer a higher cost. This example shows that the POA in network cost-sharing games can be as high as k, the number of agents. Exercise 15.1 proves a matching upper bound.

The VHS-or-Betamax example is exasperating. We proposed a reasonable network model capturing positive externalities, and the POA—which has helped us reason about several models already—is distracted by an extreme equilibrium and yields no useful information. What if we focus only on the "nice" equilibria? We'll return to this question after considering another important example.

15.1.4   Example: Opting Out

Consider the network cost-sharing game shown in Figure 15.2. The k agents have distinct origins $o_1, \ldots, o_k$ but a common destination d. They have the option of meeting at the rendezvous point v and continuing together to d, incurring a joint cost of $1 + \epsilon$. Each agent can also "opt out," meaning take the direct o_i-d path solo. Agent i incurs a cost of $1/i$ for her opt-out strategy.

The optimal outcome is clear: if all agents travel through the rendezvous point, the cost is $1 + \epsilon$. Unfortunately, this is not a PNE: agent k can pay slightly less by switching to her opt-out strategy, which is a dominant strategy for her. Given that agent k does not use the rendezvous in a PNE, agent $k - 1$ does not either; she would have to pay at least $(1 + \epsilon)/(k - 1)$ with agent k absent, and her opt-out strategy is cheaper. Iterating this argument, there is no PNE in which any agent travels through v. Meanwhile, the outcome in which all agents opt out is a PNE.[1] The cost of this unique PNE is the kth harmonic number $\sum_{i=1}^{k} \frac{1}{i}$. This number lies between $\ln k$ and $\ln k + 1$, and we denote it by $\mathcal{H}_k$.

The POA in the opt-out example approaches $\mathcal{H}_k$ as ϵ tends to 0. Unlike the VHS-or-Betamax example, this inefficiency is not the result of multiple or unreasonable equilibria.

15.2   The Price of Stability

The two examples in the previous section limit our ambitions: we cannot hope to prove anything interesting about worst-case PNE of network cost-sharing games, and even when there is a unique PNE, it can cost $\mathcal{H}_k$ times that of an optimal outcome. This section proves the following guarantee on the *best* PNE of a network cost-sharing game.

---

[1]This argument is an example of the iterated removal of strictly dominated strategies. When a unique outcome survives this procedure, it is the unique PNE of the game.

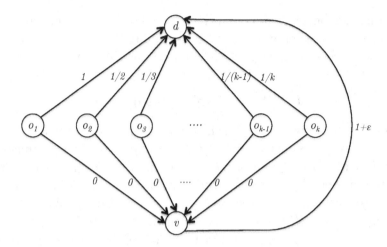

Figure 15.2: Opting out. There can be a unique PNE with cost $\mathcal{H}_k$ times that of an optimal outcome. The parameter $\epsilon > 0$ can be arbitrarily small.

Theorem 15.1 (Price of Stability) *In every network cost-sharing game with k agents, there exists a PNE with cost at most $\mathcal{H}_k$ times that of an optimal outcome.*

The theorem asserts in particular that every network cost-sharing game possesses at least one PNE. The opt-out example shows that the factor of $\mathcal{H}_k$ in Theorem 15.1 cannot be replaced by anything smaller.

The *price of stability* is the "optimistic" version of the POA, defined as the ratio

$$\frac{\text{cost of best equilibrium}}{\text{cost of optimal outcome}}.$$

Thus Theorem 15.1 states that the price of stability is at most $\mathcal{H}_k$ in every network cost-sharing game.

Proof of Theorem 15.1: Network cost-sharing games have the same form as atomic selfish routing games (Section 12.4), with each agent i picking an o_i-d_i path in a network. Moreover, an agent's cost (15.1) is the sum of the costs of the edges in her path, and each edge cost depends only on the number of agents using it. The "cost function" of an edge e can be thought of as $c_e(f_e) = \gamma_e/f_e$, where f_e is the number of agents using the edge.

Adapting the potential function (13.7) from the proof of Theorem 13.6 to network cost-sharing games yields

$$\Phi(\mathbf{P}) = \sum_{e \in E} \sum_{i=1}^{f_e} \frac{\gamma_e}{i} = \sum_{e \in E} \gamma_e \sum_{i=1}^{f_e} \frac{1}{i}. \qquad (15.3)$$

As in that proof, the outcome that minimizes this function Φ is a PNE.[2] For instance, in the VHS-or-Betamax example, the low-cost PNE minimizes (15.3) while the high-cost PNE does not. While the minimizer of the potential function need not be the best PNE (Problem 15.1), we next prove that its cost is at most $\mathcal{H}_k$ times that of an optimal outcome.

The key observation is that the potential function (15.3), whose numerical value we don't care about per se, approximates well the objective function (15.2) that we do care about. Precisely, since

$$\gamma_e \leq \gamma_e \sum_{i=1}^{f_e} \frac{1}{i} \leq \gamma_e \cdot \mathcal{H}_k$$

for every edge e with $f_e \geq 1$, we can sum over such edges to derive

$$\mathrm{cost}(\mathbf{P}) \leq \Phi(\mathbf{P}) \leq \mathcal{H}_k \cdot \mathrm{cost}(\mathbf{P}) \qquad (15.4)$$

for every outcome $\mathbf{P}$. The inequalities (15.4) state that PNE are inadvertently trying to minimize an approximately correct function Φ, so it makes sense that one PNE should approximately minimize the correct objective function.

To finish the proof, let $\mathbf{P}$ denote a PNE minimizing the potential function (15.3) and $\mathbf{P}^*$ an optimal outcome. We have

$$
\begin{aligned}
\mathrm{cost}(\mathbf{P}) \ &\leq \ \Phi(\mathbf{P}) \\
&\leq \ \Phi(\mathbf{P}^*) \\
&\leq \ \mathcal{H}_k \cdot \mathrm{cost}(\mathbf{P}^*),
\end{aligned}
$$

where the first and last inequalities follow from (15.4) and the middle inequality follows from the choice of $\mathbf{P}$ as a minimizer of Φ. ∎

---

[2]Network cost-sharing games have decreasing per-agent cost functions, reflecting the positive externalities and contrasting with routing games. The proof of Theorem 13.6 holds for any edge cost functions, decreasing or otherwise.

How should we interpret Theorem 15.1? A bound on the price of stability, which only ensures that one equilibrium is approximately optimal, provides a significantly weaker guarantee than a bound on the POA. The price of stability is relevant for games where there is a third party who can propose an initial outcome—default behavior for the agents. It's easy to find examples in real life where an institution or society effectively proposes one equilibrium out of many, even just in choosing which side of the road everybody drives on. For a computer science example, consider the problem of choosing the default values of user-defined parameters of software or a network protocol. One sensible approach is to set default parameters so that users are not motivated to change them and, subject to this, to optimize performance. The price of stability quantifies the necessary degradation in the objective function value caused by the restriction to equilibrium outcomes.

The proof of Theorem 15.1 implies that every minimizer of the potential function (15.3) has cost at most $\mathcal{H}_k$ times that of an optimal outcome. There are plausible narratives for why such PNE are more relevant than arbitrary PNE; see the Notes for details. This gives a second interpretation of Theorem 15.1 that makes no reference to a third party and instead rests on the belief that potential function minimizers are in some sense the most important of the PNE.

15.3   The POA of Strong Nash Equilibria

This section gives an alternative approach to eluding the bad PNE of the VHS-or-Betamax example and proving meaningful bounds on the inefficiency of equilibria in network cost-sharing games. We once again argue about all (i.e., worst-case) equilibria, but first restrict attention to a well-motivated subset of PNE.[3]

In general, when studying the inefficiency of equilibria in a class of games, one should zoom out (i.e., enlarge the set of equilibria) as much as possible subject to the existence of meaningful POA bounds. In games with negative externalities, such as routing and location games, we zoomed all the way out to the set of coarse correlated equilibria (Lecture 14). The POA of PNE is reasonably close to 1 in

---

[3]When one equilibrium concept is only more stringent than another, the former is called an *equilibrium refinement* of the latter.

these games, so we focused on extending our worst-case bounds to ever-larger sets of equilibria. In network cost-sharing games, where worst-case PNE can be highly suboptimal, we need to zoom in to recover interesting POA bounds (Figure 15.3).

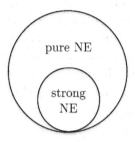

Figure 15.3: Strong Nash equilibria are a special case of pure Nash equilibria.

Recall the VHS or Betamax example (Section 15.1.3). The high-cost outcome is a PNE because an agent that deviates unilaterally would pay the full cost $1 + \epsilon$ of the upper edge. What if a coalition of *two* agents deviated jointly to the upper edge? Each deviating agent would then pay only $\approx \frac{1}{2}$, so this would be a profitable deviation for both of them. We conclude that the high-cost PNE does not persist when coalitional deviations are allowed.

Definition 15.2 (Strong Nash Equilibrium) Let **s** be an outcome of a cost-minimization game.

(a) Strategies $\mathbf{s}'_A \in \prod_{i \in A} S_i$ are a *beneficial deviation* for a subset A of agents if

$$C_i(\mathbf{s}'_A, \mathbf{s}_{-A}) \leq C_i(\mathbf{s})$$

for every agent $i \in A$, with the inequality holding strictly for at least one agent of A.

(b) The outcome **s** is a *strong Nash equilibrium* if there is no coalition of agents with a beneficial deviation.

Every strong Nash equilibrium is a PNE, as beneficial deviations for singleton coalitions correspond to improving unilateral deviations. It is plausible that strong Nash equilibria are more likely to occur than other PNE.

To get a better feel for strong Nash equilibria, let's return to
our two examples. As noted above, the high-cost PNE of the VHS
or Betamax example is not a strong Nash equilibrium. The low-cost
PNE is a strong Nash equilibrium. More generally, since the coalition
of the entire agent set is allowed, intuition might suggest that strong
Nash equilibria are always optimal outcomes. This is the case when
all agents share the same origin and destination (Exercise 15.3), but
not in general. In the opt-out example (Section 15.1.4), the same
argument that proves that the all-opt-out outcome is the unique PNE
also proves that it is a strong Nash equilibrium. This strong Nash
equilibrium has cost arbitrarily close to $\mathcal{H}_k$ times that of an optimal
outcome. Our next result states that no worse example is possible.

Theorem 15.3 (The POA of Strong Nash Equilibria) *In every network cost-sharing game with k agents, every strong Nash equilibrium has cost at most $\mathcal{H}_k$ times that of an optimal outcome.*

The guarantee in Theorem 15.3 differs from that in Theorem 15.1
in two ways. On the positive side, the guarantee holds for *every*
strong Nash equilibrium, as opposed to just *one* PNE. Were it true
that every network cost-sharing game has at least one strong Nash
equilibrium, Theorem 15.3 would be a strictly stronger statement
than Theorem 15.1. Unfortunately, a strong Nash equilibrium may
or may not exist in a network cost-sharing game (see Figure 15.4 and
Exercise 15.4), and so Theorems 15.1 and 15.3 offer incomparable
guarantees.

*15.4 Proof of Theorem 15.3

The proof of Theorem 15.3 bears some resemblance to our previous
POA analyses, but it has a couple of extra ideas. One nice feature
is that the proof uses the potential function (15.3) in an interesting
way. Our POA analyses of selfish routing and location games did not
make use of their potential functions.

Fix a network cost-sharing game and a strong Nash equilibrium **P**.
The usual first step in a POA analysis is to invoke the equilibrium
hypothesis once per agent to generate upper bounds on agents' equilibrium costs. To use the strong Nash equilibrium assumption in the
strongest-possible way, the natural place to start is with the most

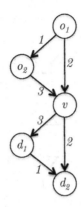

Figure 15.4: A network cost-sharing game with no strong Nash equilibrium.

powerful coalition $A_k = \{1, 2, \ldots, k\}$ of all k agents. Why doesn't this coalition collectively switch to the optimal outcome $\mathbf{P}^*$? It must be that for some agent i, $C_i(\mathbf{P}) \leq C_i(\mathbf{P}^*)$.[4] Rename the agents so that this is agent k.

We want an upper bound on the equilibrium cost of *every* agent, not just that of agent k. To ensure that we get an upper bound for a new agent, we next invoke the strong Nash equilibrium hypothesis for the coalition $A_{k-1} = \{1, 2, \ldots, k-1\}$ that excludes agent k. Why don't these $k - 1$ agents collectively deviate to $\mathbf{P}^*_{A_{k-1}}$? There must be an agent $i \in \{1, 2, \ldots, k - 1\}$ with $C_i(\mathbf{P}) \leq C_i(\mathbf{P}^*_{A_{k-1}}, P_k)$. We rename the agents of A_{k-1} so that this is true for agent $k - 1$ and continue.

By iterating this argument, we obtain a renaming of the agents as $\{1, 2, \ldots, k\}$ such that, for every i,

$$C_i(\mathbf{P}) \leq C_i(\mathbf{P}^*_{A_i}, \mathbf{P}_{-A_i}),   \tag{15.5}$$

where $A_i = \{1, 2, \ldots, i\}$. Now that we have an upper bound on the equilibrium cost of every agent, we can sum (15.5) over the agents to

---

[4]This inequality is strict if at least one other agent is better off, but we don't need this stronger statement.

obtain

$$
\begin{aligned}
\mathrm{cost}(\mathbf{P}) \;&=\; \sum_{i=1}^{k} C_i(\mathbf{P}) \\
&\leq\; \sum_{i=1}^{k} C_i(\mathbf{P}^*_{A_i}, \mathbf{P}_{-A_i}) \tag{15.6} \\
&\leq\; \sum_{i=1}^{k} C_i(\mathbf{P}^*_{A_i}). \tag{15.7}
\end{aligned}
$$

Inequality (15.6) is immediate from (15.5). Inequality (15.7) follows from the fact that network cost-sharing games have positive externalities; removing agents only decreases the number of agents using each edge and hence only increases the cost share of each remaining agent on each edge. The purpose of the inequality (15.7) is to simplify our upper bound on the equilibrium cost to the point that it becomes a telescoping sum.

Next we use the potential function Φ defined in (15.3). Letting f_e^i denote the number of agents of A_i that use a path in $\mathbf{P}^*$ that includes edge e, we have

$$
C_i(\mathbf{P}^*_{A_i}) = \sum_{e \in P_i^*} \frac{\gamma_e}{f_e^i} = \Phi(\mathbf{P}^*_{A_i}) - \Phi(\mathbf{P}^*_{A_{i-1}}), \tag{15.8}
$$

with the second equation following from the definition of Φ.

Combining (15.7) with (15.8), we obtain

$$
\begin{aligned}
\mathrm{cost}(\mathbf{P}) \;&\leq\; \sum_{i=1}^{k} \left[\Phi(\mathbf{P}^*_{A_i}) - \Phi(\mathbf{P}^*_{A_{i-1}}) \right] \\
&=\; \Phi(\mathbf{P}^*) \\
&\leq\; \mathcal{H}_k \cdot \mathrm{cost}(\mathbf{P}^*), \tag{15.9}
\end{aligned}
$$

where inequality (15.9) follows from our earlier observation (15.4) that the potential function Φ can only overestimate the cost of an outcome by an $\mathcal{H}_k$ factor. This completes the proof of Theorem 15.3.

The Upshot

☆ In a network cost-sharing game, each agent picks a path from her origin to her destination, and the fixed cost of each edge used is split equally among its users.

☆ Different PNE of a network cost-sharing game can have wildly different costs, and the POA can be as large as the number k of agents. These facts motivate approximation bounds that apply only to a subset of PNE.

☆ The price of stability of a game is the ratio between the lowest cost of an equilibrium and the cost of an optimal outcome.

☆ The worst-case price of stability of network cost-sharing games is $\mathcal{H}_k = \sum_{i=1}^{k} \frac{1}{i} \approx \ln k$.

☆ A strong Nash equilibrium is an outcome such that no coalition of agents has a collective deviation that benefits at least one agent and harms no agent of the coalition.

☆ Every strong Nash equilibrium of a network-cost sharing game has cost at most $\mathcal{H}_k$ times that of an optimal outcome.

☆ Strong Nash equilibria are not guaranteed to exist in network cost-sharing games.

Notes

Network cost-sharing games and Theorem 15.1 are from Anshelevich et al. (2008a). The VHS or Betamax example is from Anshelevich et al. (2008b). Many other models of network formation have been proposed and studied; see Jackson (2008) for a textbook treatment. It is an open question to analyze the worst-case price of stability in undirected network cost-sharing games; see Bilò et al. (2016) for the latest progress. Experimental evidence that potential function minimizers are more commonly played than other PNE is given in Chen and Chen (2011); related theoretical results appear in Blume (1993) and Asadpour and Saberi (2009). The strong Nash equilibrium concept is due to Aumann (1959), and Andelman et al. (2009) propose studying the price of anarchy of strong Nash equilibria. Theorem 15.3, the example in Figure 15.4, and Problem 15.2 are from Epstein et al. (2009).

Exercises

Exercise 15.1 Prove that in every network cost-sharing game, the POA of PNE is at most k, the number of agents.

Exercise 15.2 If we modify the opt-out example (Section 15.1.4) so that all of the edges are undirected, and each agent i can choose an o_i-d path that traverses edges in either direction, what is the price of stability in the resulting network cost-sharing game?

Exercise 15.3 Prove that in every network cost-sharing game in which all agents have a common origin vertex and a common destination vertex, there is a one-to-one correspondence between strong Nash equilibria and minimum-cost outcomes. (Thus, in such games, strong Nash equilibria always exist and the POA of such equilibria is 1.)

Exercise 15.4 Prove that the network cost-sharing game shown in Figure 15.4 has no strong Nash equilibrium.

Exercise 15.5 Extend the model of network cost-sharing games by allowing each edge e to have a cost $\gamma_e(x)$ that depends on the number x of agents that use it. The joint cost $\gamma_e(x)$ is again split equally between the x users of the edge. Assume that each function γ_e is *concave*, meaning that

$$\gamma_e(i+1) - \gamma_e(i) \le \gamma_e(i) - \gamma_e(i-1)$$

for each $i = 1, 2, \ldots, k-1$. Extend Theorems 15.1 and 15.3 to this more general model.

Exercise 15.6 *(H)* Continuing the previous exercise, suppose $\gamma_e(x) = a_e x^p$ for every edge e, where each $a_e > 0$ is a positive constant and the common exponent p lies in $(0, 1]$. For this special case, improve the upper bounds of $\mathcal{H}_k$ in Theorems 15.1 and 15.3 to $\frac{1}{p}$, independent of the number of agents k.

Problems

Problem 15.1   (a) Exhibit a network cost-sharing game in which the minimizer of the potential function (15.3) is not the lowest-cost PNE.

(b) Exhibit a network cost-sharing game with at least one strong Nash equilibrium in which the minimizer of the potential function is not a strong Nash equilibrium.

Problem 15.2 Suppose we weaken the definition of a strong Nash equilibrium (Definition 15.2) by requiring only that no coalition of at most ℓ agents has a beneficial deviation, where $\ell \in \{1, 2, \ldots, k\}$ is a parameter. Pure Nash equilibria and strong Nash equilibria correspond to the $\ell = 1$ and $\ell = k$ cases, respectively. What is the worst-case POA of ℓ-strong Nash equilibria in network cost-sharing games, as a function of ℓ and k? Prove the best upper and lower bounds that you can.

Problem 15.3 *(H)* Prove that in every atomic selfish routing network (Section 12.4) with edge cost functions that are polynomials with nonnegative coefficients and degree at most p, the price of stability is at most $p + 1$.

Best-Response Dynamics

This lecture segues into the third part of the course, where we ask: Do we expect strategic agents to reach an equilibrium? If so, which learning algorithms quickly converge to an equilibrium? Reasoning about these questions requires specifying *dynamics*, which describe how agents act when not at equilibrium. We consider dynamics where each agent's behavior is governed by an algorithm that attempts to, in some sense, learn the best response to how the other agents are acting. Ideally, we seek results that hold for multiple simple and natural learning algorithms. Then, even though agents may not literally follow such an algorithm, we can still have some confidence that our conclusions are robust and not an artifact of the particular choice of dynamics. This lecture focuses on variations of "best-response dynamics," while the next two lectures study dynamics based on regret-minimization.

Section 16.1 defines best-response dynamics and proves convergence in potential games. Sections 16.2 and 16.3 introduce ϵ-best-response dynamics and prove that several variants of it converge quickly in atomic selfish routing games where all agents have a common origin and destination. Section 16.4 proves that, in the (λ, μ)-smooth games defined in Lecture 14, several variants of best-response dynamics quickly reach outcomes with objective function value almost as good as at an equilibrium.

16.1 Best-Response Dynamics in Potential Games

Best-response dynamics is a straightforward procedure by which agents search for a pure Nash equilibrium (PNE) of a game (Definition 13.2), using successive unilateral deviations.

Best-Response Dynamics

While the current outcome **s** is not a PNE:
  pick an arbitrary agent i and an arbitrary
  beneficial deviation s'_i for agent i, and update
  the outcome to $(s'_i, \mathbf{s}_{-i})$

There might be many options for the deviating agent i and for the beneficial deviation s'_i. We leave both unspecified for the moment, specializing these choices later as needed.[1] We always allow the initial outcome to be arbitrary.

Best-response dynamics can be visualized as a walk in a graph, with vertices corresponding to strategy profiles, and outgoing edges corresponding to beneficial deviations (Figure 16.1). The PNE are precisely the vertices of this graph that have no outgoing edges. Best-response dynamics can only halt at a PNE, so it cycles in any game without one. It can also cycle in games that have a PNE (Exercise 16.1).

Best-response dynamics is a perfect fit for potential games (Section 13.3). Recall that a potential game admits a real-valued function Φ with the property that, for every unilateral deviation by some agent, the change in the potential function value equals the change in the deviator's cost (13.9). Routing games (Section 12.4), location games (Section 14.2), and network cost-sharing games (Section 15.2) are all potential games.

Theorem 13.7 notes that every potential game has at least one PNE, since the potential function minimizer is one. Best-response dynamics offers a more constructive proof of this fact.

Proposition 16.1 (Convergence of Best-Response Dynamics)
In a potential game, from an arbitrary initial outcome, best-response dynamics converges to a PNE.

Proof: In every iteration of best-response dynamics, the deviator's cost strictly decreases. By (13.9), the potential function strictly decreases. Thus, no cycles are possible. Since the game is finite by

---

[1]This procedure is sometimes called "better-response dynamics," with the term "best-response dynamics" reserved for the version in which s'_i is chosen to minimize i's cost, given the strategies $\mathbf{s}_{-i}$ of the other agents.

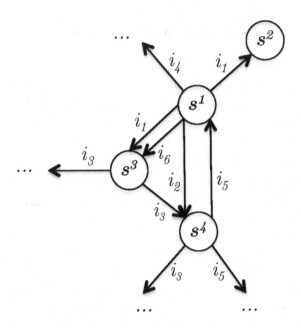

Figure 16.1: Best-response dynamics can be viewed as a walk in a graph. There is one vertex for each strategy profile. There is one edge for each beneficial unilateral deviation, labeled with the name of the deviating agent. PNE correspond to vertices with no outgoing edges, such as $\mathbf{s}^2$.

assumption, best-response dynamics eventually halts, necessarily at a PNE. ∎

Translated to the graph in Figure 16.1, Proposition 16.1 asserts that every walk in a directed acyclic graph eventually stops at a vertex with no outgoing edges.

Proposition 16.1 shows that there is a natural procedure by which agents can reach a PNE of a potential game. How fast does this happen? One strong notion of "fast convergence" is convergence to a PNE in a reasonably small number of iterations. This occurs when, for example, the potential function Φ takes on only a small number of distinct values (Exercise 16.2). In general, best-response dynamics can decrease the potential function very slowly and require an exponential (in the number of agents k) number of iterations to converge (Lecture 19). This fact motivates the relaxed definitions of convergence studied in the rest of this lecture.

16.2   Approximate PNE in Selfish Routing Games

Our second notion of "fast convergence" settles for an approximate PNE.

Definition 16.2 (ϵ-Pure Nash Equilibrium) For $\epsilon \in [0, 1]$, an outcome **s** of a cost-minimization game is an ϵ-*pure Nash equilibrium* (*ϵ-PNE*) if, for every agent i and deviation $s_i' \in S_i$,

$$C_i(s_i', \mathbf{s}_{-i}) \geq (1 - \epsilon) \cdot C_i(\mathbf{s}). \tag{16.1}$$

Definition 16.2 is the same as Definition 14.5, reparametrized for convenience. An ϵ-PNE in the sense of Definition 16.2 corresponds to a $\frac{\epsilon}{1-\epsilon}$-PNE under Definition 14.5.

We next study ϵ-*best-response dynamics*, in which we only permit moves that yield significant improvements.

ϵ-Best-Response Dynamics

While the current outcome **s** is not an ϵ-PNE:
  pick an arbitrary agent i who has an ϵ-*move*—a
  deviation s_i' with $C_i(s_i', \mathbf{s}_{-i}) < (1 - \epsilon)C_i(\mathbf{s})$—and
  an arbitrary such move for the agent, and
  update the outcome to $(s_i', \mathbf{s}_{-i})$

ϵ-best-response dynamics can only halt at an ϵ-PNE, and it eventually converges in every potential game.

Our next result identifies a subclass of atomic selfish routing games (Section 12.4) in which a specialized variant of ϵ-best response dynamics converges quickly, meaning in a number of iterations that is bounded above by a polynomial function of all of the relevant parameters.[2]

---

[2]The number of outcomes of a game with k agents is exponential in k, so any polynomial bound on the number of iterations required is significant.

ε-Best-Response Dynamics (Maximum-Gain)

While the current outcome $\mathbf{s}$ is not an ε-PNE:
among all agents with an ε-move, let i denote an
agent who can obtain the largest cost decrease

$$C_i(\mathbf{s}) - \min_{\hat{s}_i \in S_i} C_i(\hat{s}_i, \mathbf{s}_{-i}),$$

and s_i' a best response to $\mathbf{s}_{-i}$
update the outcome to $(s_i', \mathbf{s}_{-i})$

Theorem 16.3 (Convergence to an ε-PNE) *Consider an atomic selfish routing game where:*

1. *All agents have a common origin vertex and a common destination vertex.*

2. *For $\alpha \geq 1$, the cost function c_e of each edge e satisfies the α-bounded jump condition, meaning $c_e(x+1) \in [c_e(x), \alpha \cdot c_e(x)]$ for every edge e and positive integer x.*

Then, the maximum-gain variant of ε-best-response dynamics converges to an ε-PNE in at most $\frac{k\alpha}{\epsilon} \ln \frac{\Phi(\mathbf{s}^0)}{\Phi_{\min}}$ iterations, where $\mathbf{s}_0$ is the initial outcome and $\Phi_{\min} = \min_{\mathbf{s}} \Phi(\mathbf{s})$.

Analogs of Theorem 16.3 continue to hold for many different variants of ε-best-response dynamics (Problem 16.2); the only essential requirement is that every agent is given the opportunity to move sufficiently often. Even if we don't literally believe that agents will follow one of these variants of ε-best-response dynamics, the fact that simple and natural learning procedures converge quickly to approximate PNE in these games provides compelling justification for their study. Unfortunately, if either hypothesis of Theorem 16.3 is dropped, then all variants of ε-best-response dynamics can take an exponential (in k) number of iterations to converge (see the Notes).

*16.3   Proof of Theorem 16.3

The plan for proving Theorem 16.3 is to strengthen quantitatively the proof of Proposition 16.1 and show that every iteration of maximum-gain ϵ-best-response dynamics decreases the potential function by a lot. We need two lemmas. The first one guarantees the existence of an agent with a high cost; if this agent is chosen to move in an iteration, then the potential function decreases significantly. The issue is that some other agent might move instead. The second lemma, which is the one that needs the two hypotheses in Theorem 16.3, proves that the agent chosen to move has cost within an α factor of that of any other agent. This is good enough for fast convergence.

Lemma 16.4 *In every outcome* $\mathbf{s}$, *there is an agent* i *with* $C_i(\mathbf{s}) \geq \Phi(\mathbf{s})/k$.

Proof: In atomic selfish routing games, which have nondecreasing edge cost functions, the potential function can only underestimate the cost of an outcome. To see this, recall the definitions of the potential function (13.7) and objective function (11.3)–(11.4) of an atomic selfish routing game, and derive

$$\Phi(\mathbf{s}) = \sum_{e \in E} \sum_{i=1}^{f_e} c_e(i) \leq \sum_{e \in E} f_e \cdot c_e(f_e) = \sum_{i=1}^{k} C_i(\mathbf{s}) \qquad (16.2)$$

for every outcome $\mathbf{s}$, where f_e denotes the number of agents that choose in $\mathbf{s}$ a path including edge e. The inequality follows from the fact that cost functions are nondecreasing.

Since some agent must have cost at least as large as the average, we have

$$\max_{i=1}^{k} C_i(\mathbf{s}) \geq \frac{\sum_{i=1}^{k} C_i(\mathbf{s})}{k} \geq \frac{\Phi(\mathbf{s})}{k}$$

for every outcome $\mathbf{s}$, as claimed. ■

The next lemma relates the cost of the deviating agent in maximum-gain ϵ-best-response dynamics to those of the other agents.

Lemma 16.5 *Suppose agent* i *is chosen by maximum-gain* ϵ-best-*response dynamics to move in the outcome* $\mathbf{s}$, *and takes the* ϵ-move s'_i. *Then*

$$C_i(\mathbf{s}) - C_i(s'_i, \mathbf{s}_{-i}) \geq \frac{\epsilon}{\alpha} C_j(\mathbf{s}) \qquad (16.3)$$

for every other agent j.

Proof: Fix the agent j. If j has an ϵ-move s_j' in $\mathbf{s}$, which by definition would decrease agent j's cost by at least $\epsilon C_j(\mathbf{s})$, then

$$C_i(\mathbf{s}) - C_i(s_i', \mathbf{s}_{-i}) \geq C_j(\mathbf{s}) - C_j(s_j', \mathbf{s}_{-j}) \geq \epsilon C_j(\mathbf{s}).$$

The first inequality holds because i was chosen over j in maximum-game ϵ-best-response dynamics.

The trickier case is when the agent j has no ϵ-move available. We use here that all agents have the same set of available strategies. If s_i' is such a great deviation for agent i, why isn't it for agent j as well? That is, how can it be that

$$C_i(s_i', \mathbf{s}_{-i}) \leq (1 - \epsilon)C_i(\mathbf{s}) \tag{16.4}$$

while

$$C_j(s_i', \mathbf{s}_{-j}) \geq (1 - \epsilon)C_j(\mathbf{s})? \tag{16.5}$$

A key observation is that the outcomes $(s_i', \mathbf{s}_{-i})$ and $(s_i', \mathbf{s}_{-j})$ have at least $k - 1$ strategies in common. The strategy s_i' is used by i in the former outcome and by j in the latter outcome, and the $k - 2$ agents other than i and j use the same strategies in both outcomes. Since the two outcomes differ in only one chosen strategy, for every edge e of the network, the number of agents using e differs by at most one in the two outcomes. By the α-bounded jump hypothesis in Theorem 16.3, the cost of every edge differs by at most a factor of α in the two outcomes. In particular, the cost of agent j after deviating unilaterally to s_i' is at most α times that of agent i after the same unilateral deviation:

$$C_j(s_i', \mathbf{s}_{-j}) \leq \alpha \cdot C_i(s_i', \mathbf{s}_{-i}). \tag{16.6}$$

The inequalities (16.4)–(16.6) imply that $C_j(\mathbf{s}) \leq \alpha \cdot C_i(\mathbf{s})$. Combining this with (16.4) yields

$$C_i(\mathbf{s}) - C_i(s_i', \mathbf{s}_{-i}) \geq \epsilon \cdot C_i(\mathbf{s}) \geq \frac{\epsilon}{\alpha} \cdot C_j(\mathbf{s}),$$

as required. ■

Lemma 16.4 guarantees that there is always an agent whose ϵ-move would rapidly decrease the potential function. Lemma 16.5

extends this conclusion to the agent who actually moves in maximum-gain ϵ-best-response dynamics. The bound on the number of iterations required for convergence now follows straightforwardly.

Proof of Theorem 16.3: In an iteration of maximum-gain ϵ-best-response dynamics where agent i makes an ϵ-move to the strategy s'_i,

$$\Phi(\mathbf{s}) - \Phi(s'_i, \mathbf{s}_{-i}) \;=\; C_i(\mathbf{s}) - C_i(s'_i, \mathbf{s}_{-i}) \tag{16.7}$$

$$\geq \;\frac{\epsilon}{\alpha} \cdot \max_{j=1}^{k} C_j(\mathbf{s}) \tag{16.8}$$

$$\geq \;\frac{\epsilon}{\alpha k} \cdot \Phi(\mathbf{s}), \tag{16.9}$$

where equation (16.7) follows from the defining property (13.9) of a potential function, and inequalities (16.8) and (16.9) follow from Lemmas 16.5 and 16.4, respectively.

The derivation (16.7)–(16.9) shows that every iteration of maximum-gain ϵ-best-response dynamics decreases the potential function by at least a factor of $(1 - \frac{\epsilon}{\alpha k})$. Thus, every $\frac{k\alpha}{\epsilon}$ iterations decrease the potential function by at least a factor of $e = 2.718\ldots$.[3] Since the potential function begins with the value $\Phi(\mathbf{s}^0)$ and cannot drop lower than $\Phi_{\min}$, maximum-gain ϵ-best-response dynamics converges in at most $\frac{k\alpha}{\epsilon} \ln \frac{\Phi(\mathbf{s}^0)}{\Phi_{\min}}$ iterations. ∎

*16.4   Low-Cost Outcomes in Smooth Potential Games

This section explores our final notion of "fast convergence": quickly reaching outcomes with objective function value *as good as if* agents had already converged to an approximate PNE. This guarantee does not imply convergence to an approximate PNE, but it is still quite compelling. When the primary reason for an equilibrium analysis is a price-of-anarchy bound, this weaker guarantee is a costless surrogate for convergence to an approximate equilibrium.

Weakening our notion of fast convergence enables positive results with significantly wider reach. The next result applies to all potential games that are (λ, μ)-smooth in the sense of Definition 14.2, including

---

[3]To see this, use that $(1 - x)^{1/x} \leq (e^{-x})^{1/x} = 1/e$ for $x \neq 0$.

all atomic selfish routing games (Section 12.4) and location games (Section 14.2). It uses the following variant of best-response dynamics, which is the analog of the variant of ϵ-best-response dynamics used in Theorem 16.3.

Best-Response Dynamics (Maximum-Gain)

While the current outcome $\mathbf{s}$ is not a PNE:

among all agents with a beneficial deviation, let i
denote an agent who can obtain the largest cost
decrease

$$C_i(\mathbf{s}) - \min_{\hat{s}_i \in S_i} C_i(\hat{s}_i, \mathbf{s}_{-i}),$$

and s_i' a best response to $\mathbf{s}_{-i}$
update the outcome to $(s_i', \mathbf{s}_{-i})$

We state the theorem for cost-minimization games; an analogous result holds for (λ, μ)-smooth payoff-maximization games (Remark 13.1).

Theorem 16.6 (Convergence to Low-Cost Outcomes)
Consider a (λ, μ)-smooth cost-minimization game with $\mu < 1$ that has a positive potential function Φ that satisfies $\Phi(\mathbf{s}) \leq \mathrm{cost}(\mathbf{s})$ for every outcome $\mathbf{s}$. Let $\mathbf{s}^0, \ldots, \mathbf{s}^T$ be a sequence of outcomes generated by maximum-gain best-response dynamics, $\mathbf{s}^*$ a minimum-cost outcome, and $\eta \in (0, 1)$ a parameter. Then all but at most

$$\frac{k}{\eta(1 - \mu)} \ln \frac{\Phi(\mathbf{s}^0)}{\Phi_{\min}}$$

outcomes $\mathbf{s}^t$ satisfy

$$\mathrm{cost}(\mathbf{s}^t) \leq \left(\frac{\lambda}{(1 - \mu)(1 - \eta)} \right) \cdot \mathrm{cost}(\mathbf{s}^*), \qquad (16.10)$$

where $\Phi_{\min} = \min_{\mathbf{s}} \Phi(\mathbf{s})$ and k is the number of agents.

Recall that in a (λ, μ)-smooth cost-minimization game, every PNE has cost at most $\cdot\frac{\lambda}{1-\mu}$ times the minimum possible (Section 14.4).

Thus Theorem 16.6 states that for all but a small number of outcomes in the sequence, the cost is almost as low as if best-response dynamics had already converged to a PNE.

Proof of Theorem 16.6: Fix $\eta \in (0,1)$. The plan is to show that if $\mathbf{s}^t$ is a *bad state*, meaning one that fails to obey the guarantee in (16.10), then the next iteration of maximum-gain best-response dynamics decreases the potential function significantly. This yields the desired bound on the number of bad states.

For an outcome $\mathbf{s}^t$, define $\delta_i(\mathbf{s}^t) = C_i(\mathbf{s}^t) - C_i(s_i^*, \mathbf{s}_{-i}^t)$ as the cost decrease that agent i would experience by switching her strategy to s_i^*, and $\Delta(\mathbf{s}^t) = \sum_{i=1}^{k} \delta_i(\mathbf{s}^t)$. The value $\delta_i(\mathbf{s}^t)$ is nonpositive when $\mathbf{s}^t$ is a PNE, but in general it can be positive or negative. Using this notation and the defining property (14.9) of a (λ, μ)-smooth cost-minimization game, we can derive

$$\mathrm{cost}(\mathbf{s}^t) \le \sum_{i=1}^{k} C_i(\mathbf{s}^t)$$

$$= \sum_{i=1}^{k} \left[C_i(s_i^*, \mathbf{s}_{-i}^t) + \delta_i(\mathbf{s}^t) \right]$$

$$\le \lambda \cdot \mathrm{cost}(\mathbf{s}^*) + \mu \cdot \mathrm{cost}(\mathbf{s}^t) + \sum_{i=1}^{k} \delta_i(\mathbf{s}^t),$$

and hence

$$\mathrm{cost}(\mathbf{s}^t) \le \frac{\lambda}{1-\mu} \cdot \mathrm{cost}(\mathbf{s}^*) + \frac{1}{1-\mu} \Delta(\mathbf{s}^t). \qquad (16.11)$$

This inequality implies that an outcome can be bad only when the amount $\Delta(\mathbf{s}^t)$ that agents have to gain by unilateral deviations to $\mathbf{s}^*$ is large.

In a bad state $\mathbf{s}^t$, using inequality (16.11) and the assumption that $\Phi(\mathbf{s}) \le \mathrm{cost}(\mathbf{s})$ for all outcomes $\mathbf{s}$,

$$\Delta(\mathbf{s}^t) \ge \eta(1-\mu)\,\mathrm{cost}(\mathbf{s}^t) \ge \eta(1-\mu)\Phi(\mathbf{s}^t). \qquad (16.12)$$

If an agent i switches her strategy to a best response in the outcome $\mathbf{s}^t$, then her cost decreases by at least $\delta_i(\mathbf{s}^t)$. (It could decrease by more, if her best response s_i' is better than s_i^*.) Inequality (16.12) implies that, in a bad state $\mathbf{s}^t$, the cost of the agent chosen by maximum-gain best-response dynamics decreases by at least $\frac{\eta(1-\mu)}{k}\Phi(\mathbf{s}^t)$. Since Φ is a potential function and satisfies (13.9),

$$\Phi(\mathbf{s}^{t+1}) \le \Phi(\mathbf{s}^t) - \max_{i=1}^{k} \delta_i(\mathbf{s}^t) \le \left(1 - \frac{\eta(1-\mu)}{k}\right) \cdot \Phi(\mathbf{s}^t)$$

whenever $\mathbf{s}^t$ is a bad state. This inequality, together with the fact that Φ can only decrease in each iteration of best-response dynamics, implies that the potential function decreases by a factor of at least $e = 2.718\ldots$ for every sequence of $\frac{k}{\eta(1-\mu)}$ bad states. This yields the desired upper bound of $\frac{k}{\eta(1-\mu)} \ln \frac{\Phi(\mathbf{s}^0)}{\Phi_{min}}$ on the total number of bad states. ∎

The Upshot

☆ In each iteration of best-response dynamics, one agent unilaterally deviates to a better strategy.

☆ Best-response dynamics converges, necessarily to a PNE, in every potential game.

☆ Several variants of ϵ-best-response dynamics, where only moves that yield significant improvements are permitted, converge quickly to an approximate PNE in atomic selfish routing games where all agents have the same origin and destination.

☆ In (λ, μ)-smooth games, several variants of best-response dynamics quickly reach outcomes with objective function value almost as good as a PNE.

Notes

Proposition 16.1 and Exercises 16.3–16.4 are from Monderer and Shapley (1996). Theorem 16.3 and Problem 16.2

are due to Chien and Sinclair (2011). Skopalik and Vöcking (2008) show that, if either hypothesis of Theorem 16.3 is dropped, then ϵ-best-response dynamics can require an exponential number of iterations to converge, no matter how the deviating agent and deviation are chosen in each iteration. Approximation bounds for outcome sequences generated by best-response dynamics are first considered in Mirrokni and Vetta (2004). Theorem 16.6 is from Roughgarden (2015), inspired by results of Awerbuch et al. (2008). Problems 16.1 and 16.3 are from Even-Dar et al. (2007) and Milchtaich (1996), respectively.

Exercises

Exercise 16.1 *(H)* Exhibit a game with a PNE and an initial outcome from which best-response dynamics cycles forever.

Exercise 16.2 Consider an atomic selfish routing game (Section 12.4) with m edges and cost functions taking values in $\{1, 2, 3, \ldots, H\}$. Prove that best-response dynamics converges to a PNE in at most mH iterations.

Exercise 16.3 A *generalized ordinal potential game* is a cost-minimization game for which there exists a *generalized ordinal potential function* Ψ such that $\Psi(s_i', \mathbf{s}_{-i}) < \Psi(\mathbf{s})$ whenever $C_i(s_i', \mathbf{s}_{-i}) < C_i(\mathbf{s})$ for some outcome $\mathbf{s}$, agent i, and deviation s_i'. Extend Proposition 16.1 to generalized ordinal potential games.

Exercise 16.4 *(H)* Prove the converse of Exercise 16.3: if best-response dynamics always converges to a PNE, for every choice of initial outcome and beneficial unilateral deviation at each iteration, then the game admits a generalized ordinal potential function.

Problems

Problem 16.1 Recall the class of cost-minimization games introduced in Problem 12.3, where each agent $i = 1, 2, \ldots, k$ has a positive weight w_i and chooses one of m identical machines to minimize her load. Consider the following restriction of best-response dynamics:

Maximum-Weight Best-Response Dynamics

While the current outcome **s** is not a PNE:
among all agents with a beneficial deviation, let i
denote an agent with the largest weight w_i and
s_i' a best response to $\mathbf{s}_{-i}$
update the outcome to $(s_i', \mathbf{s}_{-i})$

Prove that MaxWeight best-response dynamics converges to a PNE in at most k iterations.

Problem 16.2 *(H)* This problem considers another variant of ϵ-best-response dynamics.

**ϵ-Best-Response Dynamics
(Maximum-Relative-Gain)**

While the current outcome **s** is not an ϵ-PNE:
among all agents with an ϵ-move, let i denote an
agent who can obtain the largest relative cost
decrease

$$\frac{C_i(\mathbf{s}) - \min_{\hat{s}_i \in S_i} C_i(\hat{s}_i, \mathbf{s}_{-i})}{C_i(\mathbf{s})}$$

and s_i' a best response to $\mathbf{s}_{-i}$
update the outcome to $(s_i', \mathbf{s}_{-i})$

Prove that the iteration bound in Theorem 16.3 applies also to the maximum-relative-gain variant of ϵ-best-response dynamics.

Problem 16.3 This problem considers a variant of the cost-minimization games in Problem 16.1 where every agent has weight 1 but agents can have different individual cost functions. Formally, each agent i incurs a cost $c_j^i(\ell)$ on machine j if she is among ℓ agents using j. Assume that for each fixed i and j, $c_j^i(\ell)$ is nondecreasing in ℓ.

(a) Prove that if there are only two machines, then best-response dynamics converges to a PNE.

(b) *(H)* Prove that if there are three machines, then best-response dynamics need not converge.

(c) *(H)* Prove that, no matter how many machines there are, a PNE always exists.

Lecture 17

No-Regret Dynamics

This lecture studies a second fundamental class of dynamics, *no-regret dynamics*. While best-response dynamics can only converge to a pure Nash equilibrium and is most relevant for potential games, no-regret dynamics converges to the set of coarse correlated equilibria in arbitrary finite games.

Section 17.1 considers a single decision maker playing a game online against an adversary, and defines no-regret algorithms.[1] Section 17.2 presents the multiplicative weights algorithm, and Section 17.3 proves that it is a no-regret algorithm. Section 17.4 defines no-regret dynamics in multi-agent games, and proves that it converges to the set of coarse correlated equilibria.

17.1 Online Decision Making

17.1.1 The Model

Consider a set A of $n \geq 2$ actions and a time horizon $T \geq 1$, both known in advance to a decision maker. For example, A could represent different investment strategies, or different driving routes between home and work. When we return to multi-agent games (Section 17.4), the action set will be the strategy set of a single agent, with the consequence of each action determined by the strategies chosen by all of the other agents.

We consider the following setup.[2]

---

[1] In this context, "online" means that the protagonist must make a sequence of decisions without knowledge of the future.

[2] For extensions to costs in an interval $[-c_{\max}, c_{\max}]$, see Exercise 17.1.

> ## Online Decision Making
>
> At each time step $t = 1, 2, \ldots, T$:
>
> a decision maker picks a probability distribution p^t over her actions A
>
> an adversary picks a cost vector $c^t : A \to [-1, 1]$
>
> an action a^t is chosen according to the distribution p^t, and the decision maker incurs cost $c^t(a^t)$
>
> the decision maker learns c^t, the entire cost vector[3]

An *online decision-making algorithm* specifies for each t the probability distribution p^t, as a function of the cost vectors $c^1, \ldots, c^{t-1}$ and realized actions $a^1, \ldots, a^{t-1}$ of the first $t - 1$ time steps. An *adversary* for such an algorithm $\mathcal{A}$ specifies for each t the cost vector c^t, as a function of the probability distributions $p^1, \ldots, p^t$ used by $\mathcal{A}$ on the first t days and the realized actions $a^1, \ldots, a^{t-1}$ of the first $t - 1$ days. We evaluate the performance of an online decision-making algorithm by its expected cost (over the realized actions) with respect to a worst-case adversary. Negative costs are allowed, and can be used to model payoffs.

17.1.2   Definitions and Examples

We seek a "good" online decision-making algorithm. But the setup seems a bit unfair, no? The adversary is allowed to choose each cost function c^t *after* the decision maker has committed to her probability distribution p^t. With such asymmetry, what kind of guarantee can we hope for? This section gives three examples that establish limitations on what is possible.

The first example shows that there is no hope of achieving cost close to that of the best action sequence in hindsight. This benchmark $\sum_{t=1}^{T} \min_{a \in A} c^t(a)$ is just too strong.

---

[3]The guarantees presented in this lecture carry over, with somewhat worse bounds and more complex algorithms, to the *bandit model* in which the decision maker only learns the cost of her chosen action.

Example 17.1 (Comparing to the Best Action Sequence)
Suppose $A = \{1, 2\}$ and fix an arbitrary online decision-making algorithm. Each day t, the adversary chooses the cost vector c^t as follows: if the algorithm chooses a distribution p^t for which the probability on action 1 is at least $\frac{1}{2}$, then c^t is set to the vector $(1, 0)$. Otherwise, the adversary sets c^t equal to $(0, 1)$. This adversary forces the expected cost of the algorithm to be at least $\frac{T}{2}$ while ensuring that the cost of the best action sequence in hindsight is 0.

Example 17.1 motivates the following important definitions. Rather than comparing the expected cost of an algorithm to that of the best action *sequence* in hindsight, we compare it to the cost incurred by the best *fixed action* in hindsight. That is, we change our benchmark from $\sum_{t=1}^{T} \min_{a \in A} c^t(a)$ to $\min_{a \in A} \sum_{t=1}^{T} c^t(a)$.

Definition 17.2 (Regret) Fix cost vectors $c^1, \ldots, c^T$. The *regret* of the action sequence $a^1, \ldots, a^T$ is

$$\frac{1}{T} \left[\sum_{t=1}^{T} c^t(a^t) - \min_{a \in A} \sum_{t=1}^{T} c^t(a) \right]. \tag{17.1}$$

The quantity in (17.1) is sometimes called *external* regret.[4] Lecture 18 discusses swap regret, a more stringent notion.

Definition 17.3 (No-Regret Algorithm) An online decision-making algorithm $\mathcal{A}$ has *no regret* if for every $\epsilon > 0$ there exists a sufficiently large time horizon $T = T(\epsilon)$ such that, for every adversary for $\mathcal{A}$, in expectation over the action realizations, the regret (17.1) is at most ϵ.

In Definition 17.3, we think of the number n of actions as fixed, and the time horizon T tending to infinity.[5]

This lecture adopts the no-regret guarantee of Definition 17.3 as the holy grail in the design of online decision-making algorithms. The

---

[4]This quantity can be negative, but it is positive for worst-case adversaries (Example 17.5).

[5]Strictly speaking, Definition 17.3 concerns a *family* of online decision-making algorithms, one for each value of T (with the action set A fixed). See Remark 17.8 and Exercise 17.2 for extensions to the scenario where T is not known to the decision maker a priori.

first reason is that this goal can be achieved by simple and natural learning algorithms (Section 17.2). The second reason is that the goal is nontrivial: as the following examples make clear, some ingenuity is required to achieve it. The third reason is that, when we pass to multi-agent games in Section 17.4, the no-regret guarantee translates directly to the coarse correlated equilibrium conditions (Definition 13.5).

One natural online decision-making algorithm is *follow-the-leader (FTL)*, which at time step t chooses the action a with minimum cumulative cost $\sum_{u=1}^{t-1} c^u(a)$ so far. The next example shows that FTL is not a no-regret algorithm, and more generally rules out any deterministic no-regret algorithm.

Example 17.4 (Randomization Is Necessary for No Regret)
Fix a deterministic online decision-making algorithm. At each time step t, the algorithm commits to a single action a^t. The obvious strategy for the adversary is to set the cost of action a^t to 1, and the cost of every other action to 0. Then, the cost of the algorithm is T while the cost of the best action in hindsight is at most $\frac{T}{n}$. Even when there are only 2 actions, for arbitrarily large T, the worst-case regret of the algorithm is at least $\frac{1}{2}$.

For randomized algorithms, the next example limits the rate at which regret can vanish as the time horizon T grows.

Example 17.5 ($\sqrt{(\ln n)/T}$ Lower Bound on Regret) Suppose there are $n = 2$ actions, and that we choose each cost vector c^t independently and equally likely to be $(1,0)$ or $(0,1)$. No matter how smart or dumb an online decision-making algorithm is, with respect to this random choice of cost vectors, its expected cost at each time step is exactly $\frac{1}{2}$ and its expected cumulative cost is $\frac{T}{2}$. The expected cumulative cost of the best fixed action in hindsight is only $\frac{T}{2} - b\sqrt{T}$, where b is some constant independent of T. This follows from the fact that if a fair coin is flipped T times, then the expected number of heads is $\frac{T}{2}$ and the standard deviation is $\frac{1}{2}\sqrt{T}$.

Fix an online decision-making algorithm $\mathcal{A}$. A random choice of cost vectors causes $\mathcal{A}$ to experience expected regret at least $b/\sqrt{T}$, where the expectation is over both the random choice of cost vectors and the action realizations. At least one choice of cost vectors induces an adversary that causes $\mathcal{A}$ to have expected regret at least $b/\sqrt{T}$, where the expectation is over the action realizations.

A similar argument shows that, with n actions, the expected regret of an online decision-making algorithm cannot vanish faster than $b\sqrt{(\ln n)/T}$, where $b > 0$ is some constant independent of n and T (Problem 17.1).

17.2 The Multiplicative Weights Algorithm

The most important result in this lecture is that *no-regret algorithms exist*. Lecture 18 shows that this fact alone has some amazing consequences. Even better, there are simple and natural such algorithms. While not a literal description of human behavior, the guiding principles behind such algorithms are recognizable from the way many people learn and make decisions. Finally, the algorithm discussed next has optimal worst-case expected regret, matching the lower bound in Example 17.5 up to constant factors.

Theorem 17.6 (No-Regret Algorithms Exist) *For every set A of n actions and time horizon $T \geq 4\ln n$, there is an online decision-making algorithm that, for every adversary, has expected regret at most $2\sqrt{(\ln n)/T}$.*

An immediate corollary is that the number of time steps needed to drive the expected regret down to a small constant is only logarithmic in the number of actions.

Corollary 17.7 (Logarithmic Number of Steps Suffice) *For every $\epsilon \in (0, 1]$, set A of n actions and time horizon $T \geq (4\ln n)/\epsilon^2$, there is an online decision-making algorithm that, for every adversary, has expected regret at most ϵ.*

The guarantees of Theorem 17.6 and Corollary 17.7 are achieved in particular by the *multiplicative weights (MW)* algorithm.[6] Its design follows two guiding principles.

---

[6]Variants of this algorithm have been rediscovered many times; see the Notes.

No-Regret Algorithm Design Principles

1. Past performance of actions should guide which action is chosen at each time step, with the probability of choosing an action decreasing in its cumulative cost.

2. The probability of choosing a poorly performing action should decrease at an exponential rate.

The first principle is essential for obtaining a no-regret algorithm, and the second for optimal regret bounds.

The MW algorithm maintains a weight, intuitively a "credibility," for each action. At each time step the algorithm chooses an action with probability proportional to its current weight.

Multiplicative Weights (MW) Algorithm

initialize $w^1(a) = 1$ for every $a \in A$

for each time step $t = 1, 2, \ldots, T$ **do**

use the distribution $p^t = w^t / \Gamma^t$ over actions, where $\Gamma^t = \sum_{a \in A} w^t(a)$ is the sum of the weights

given the cost vector c^t, for every action $a \in A$ use the formula $w^{t+1}(a) = w^t(a) \cdot (1 - \eta c^t(a))$ to update its weight

---

For example, if all costs are either -1, 0, or 1, then the weight of each action a either stays the same (if $c^t(a) = 0$) or gets multiplied by $1 - \eta$ (if $c^t(a) = 1$) or $1 + \eta$ (if $c^t(a) = -1$). The parameter η, which is sometimes called the "learning rate," lies between 0 and $\frac{1}{2}$, and is chosen at the end of the proof of Theorem 17.6 as a function of n and T. When η is close to 0, the distributions p^t stay close to the uniform distribution. Thus small values of η encourage exploration. As η tends to 1, the distributions p^t increasingly favor the actions with the smallest cumulative cost so far. Thus large values of η encourage exploitation, and the parameter provides a knob for interpolating between these two extremes. The MW algorithm is simple to implement, as the only requirement is to maintain a weight for each action.

*17.3 Proof of Theorem 17.6

17.3.1 Adaptive vs. Oblivious Adversaries

In the definition of an adversary for an online decision-making algorithm (Section 17.1), the cost vector c^t can depend on what happened in the first $t - 1$ time steps. Such adversaries are called *adaptive*. An *oblivious adversary* for an algorithm specifies the entire sequence $c^1, \ldots, c^T$ of cost vectors in advance, before any actions are realized.

To prove Theorem 17.6 for the MW algorithm, we only need to consider oblivious adversaries. The reason is that the behavior of the MW algorithm is independent of the realized actions, with each distribution p^t chosen by the algorithm a deterministic function of $c^1, \ldots, c^{t-1}$. Thus, to maximize the expected regret of the MW algorithm, there is no reason for an adversary to condition its cost vectors on previously realized actions. Similarly, there is no need for an adversary for the MW algorithm to condition a cost vector c^t explicitly on the distributions $p^1, \ldots, p^t$, since these distributions are uniquely determined by the adversary's previous cost vectors $c^1, \ldots, c^{t-1}$.

17.3.2 The Analysis

Fix a set A of n actions and a time horizon $T \geq 4 \ln n$. Fix an oblivious adversary, or equivalently a sequence $c^1, \ldots, c^T$ of cost vectors. This fixes the corresponding sequence $p^1, \ldots, p^T$ of probability distributions used by the MW algorithm. Recall that $\Gamma^t = \sum_{a \in A} w^t(a)$ denotes the sum of the actions' weights in the MW algorithm at the beginning of time step t. The proof plan is to relate the only two quantities that we care about, the expected cost of the MW algorithm and the cost of the best fixed action, to the intermediate quantity Γ^{T+1}.

The first step, and the step that is special to the MW algorithm, shows that the sum of the weights Γ^t evolves together with the expected cost incurred by the algorithm. Letting ν^t denote the expected cost of the MW algorithm at time step t, we have

$$\nu^t = \sum_{a \in A} p^t(a) \cdot c^t(a) = \sum_{a \in A} \frac{w^t(a)}{\Gamma^t} \cdot c^t(a). \qquad (17.2)$$

We want to upper bound the sum of the ν^t's.

To understand Γ^{t+1} as a function of Γ^t and the expected cost (17.2), we derive

$$
\begin{aligned}
\Gamma^{t+1} &= \sum_{a \in A} w^{t+1}(a) \\
&= \sum_{a \in A} w^t(a) \cdot (1 - \eta c^t(a)) \\
&= \Gamma^t (1 - \eta \nu^t).
\end{aligned}
\tag{17.3}
$$

For convenience, we'll bound this quantity from above, using the fact that $1 + x \le e^x$ for all real-valued x (Figure 17.1). Then,

$$
\Gamma^{t+1} \le \Gamma^t \cdot e^{-\eta \nu^t}
$$

for each t and hence

$$
\Gamma^{T+1} \le \underbrace{\Gamma^1}_{=n} \prod_{t=1}^{T} e^{-\eta \nu^t} = n \cdot e^{-\eta \sum_{t=1}^{T} \nu^t}.
\tag{17.4}
$$

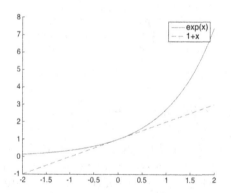

Figure 17.1: The inequality $1 + x \le e^x$ holds for all real-valued x.

The second step is to show that if there is a good fixed action, then the weight of this action single-handedly shows that the final value Γ^{T+1} is pretty big. This implies that the algorithm can only incur large cost if all fixed actions are bad.

Formally, let OPT denote the cumulative cost $\sum_{t=1}^{T} c^t(a^*)$ of the best fixed action a^* for the cost vector sequence. Then, since weights are always nonnegative,

$$\Gamma^{T+1} \geq w^{T+1}(a^*)$$

$$= \underbrace{w^1(a^*)}_{=1} \prod_{t=1}^{T} (1 - \eta c^t(a^*)). \tag{17.5}$$

It is again convenient to approximate $1+x$ by an exponential function, this time from below. Figure 17.1 indicates that the two functions are close to each other for x near 0. This can be made precise through the Taylor expansion

$$\ln(1 - x) = -x - \frac{x^2}{2} - \frac{x^3}{3} - \frac{x^4}{4} - \cdots .$$

Provided $|x| \leq \frac{1}{2}$, we can obtain a lower bound of $-x - x^2$ on $\ln(1-x)$ by throwing out all terms of the expansion except the first two, and doubling the second term to compensate. Hence, $1 - x \geq e^{-x-x^2}$ for $|x| \leq \frac{1}{2}$.

Since $\eta \leq \frac{1}{2}$ and $|c^t(a^*)| \leq 1$ for every t, we can combine this lower bound with (17.5) to obtain

$$\Gamma^{T+1} \geq \prod_{t=1}^{T} e^{-\eta c^t(a^*) - \eta^2 c^t(a^*)^2}$$

$$\geq e^{-\eta OPT - \eta^2 T}, \tag{17.6}$$

where in (17.6) we're just using the crude estimate $c^t(a^*)^2 \leq 1$ for all t.

Through (17.4) and (17.6), we've connected the cumulative expected cost $\sum_{t=1}^{T} \nu^t$ of the MW algorithm with the cumulative cost OPT of the best fixed action via the intermediate quantity Γ^{T+1}:

$$n \cdot e^{-\eta \sum_{t=1}^{T} \nu^t} \geq \Gamma^{T+1} \geq e^{-\eta OPT - \eta^2 T}.$$

Taking the natural logarithm of both sides and dividing through by $-\eta$ yields

$$\sum_{t=1}^{T} \nu^t \leq OPT + \eta T + \frac{\ln n}{\eta}. \tag{17.7}$$

Finally, we set the free parameter η. There are two error terms in (17.7), the first one corresponding to inaccurate learning (higher for larger η), the second corresponding to learning overhead (higher for smaller η). To equalize the two terms, we choose $\eta = \sqrt{(\ln n)/T}$. As $T \geq 4\ln n$, $\eta \leq \frac{1}{2}$, as required. The cumulative expected cost of the MW algorithm is then at most $2\sqrt{T\ln n}$ more than the cumulative cost of the best fixed action. This completes the proof of Theorem 17.6.

Remark 17.8 (Unknown Time Horizons) The choice of η in the proof above assumes advance knowledge of the time horizon T. Minor modifications extend the multiplicative weights algorithm and its regret guarantee to the case where T is not known a priori, with the "2" in Theorem 17.6 replaced by a modestly larger factor (Exercise 17.2).

17.4   No Regret and Coarse Correlated Equilibria

We now move from single-agent to multi-agent settings and study *no-regret dynamics* in finite games.

17.4.1   No-Regret Dynamics

We describe no-regret dynamics using the language of cost-minimization games (Section 13.1.1). There is an obvious analog for payoff-maximization games, with payoffs acting as negative costs.

No-Regret Dynamics

At each time step $t = 1, 2, \ldots, T$:

    each agent i independently chooses a mixed strategy p_i^t using a no-regret algorithm, with actions corresponding to pure strategies

    each agent i receives a cost vector c_i^t, where $c_i^t(s_i)$ is the expected cost of the pure strategy s_i given the mixed strategies chosen by the other agents:

$$c_i^t(s_i) = \mathbf{E}_{\mathbf{s}_{-i}^t \sim \sigma_{-i}^t}\left[C_i(s_i, \mathbf{s}_{-i}^t) \right],$$

where σ_{-i}^t is the product distribution $\prod_{j \neq i} p_j^t$

For example, if every agent uses the MW algorithm, then in each iteration each agent simply updates the weight of each of her pure strategies. In this case, if every agent has at most n strategies and costs lie in $[-c_{max}, c_{max}]$, then only $(4c_{max}^2 \ln n)/\epsilon^2$ iterations of no-regret dynamics are required before every agent has expected regret at most ϵ (Theorem 17.6 and Exercise 17.1).

17.4.2   Convergence to Coarse Correlated Equilibria

The next result is simple but important: the time-averaged history of joint play under no-regret dynamics converges to the set of coarse correlated equilibria, the biggest set in our hierarchy of equilibrium concepts (Definition 13.5). This forges a fundamental connection between a static equilibrium concept and the outcomes generated by natural learning dynamics.

Proposition 17.9 (No-Regret Dynamics Converges to CCE)
Suppose that after T iterations of no-regret dynamics, each agent $i = 1, 2, \ldots, k$ of a cost-minimization game has expected regret at most ϵ. Let $\sigma^t = \prod_{i=1}^k p_i^t$ denote the outcome distribution at iteration t and $\sigma = \frac{1}{T} \sum_{t=1}^T \sigma^t$ the time-averaged history of these distributions. Then σ is an approximate coarse correlated equilibrium, in the sense that

$$\mathbf{E}_{\mathbf{s} \sim \sigma}[C_i(\mathbf{s})] \leq \mathbf{E}_{\mathbf{s} \sim \sigma}[C_i(s_i', \mathbf{s}_{-i})] + \epsilon \qquad (17.8)$$

for every agent i and unilateral deviation s_i'.

Proof: By the definition of σ, for every agent i,

$$\mathbf{E}_{\mathbf{s} \sim \sigma}[C_i(\mathbf{s})] = \frac{1}{T} \sum_{t=1}^T \mathbf{E}_{\mathbf{s} \sim \sigma^t}[C_i(\mathbf{s})] \qquad (17.9)$$

and

$$\mathbf{E}_{\mathbf{s} \sim \sigma}[C_i(s_i', \mathbf{s}_{-i})] = \frac{1}{T} \sum_{t=1}^T \mathbf{E}_{\mathbf{s} \sim \sigma^t}[C_i(s_i', \mathbf{s}_{-i})] . \qquad (17.10)$$

The right-hand sides of (17.9) and (17.10) are the time-averaged expected costs of agent i when playing according to her no-regret algorithm and when playing the fixed action s_i' every iteration, respectively. Since every agent has regret at most ϵ, the former is at most ϵ

more than the latter. This verifies the approximate coarse correlated equilibrium conditions (17.8). ∎

Proposition 17.9 gives a sense in which the coarse correlated equilibrium concept is particularly computationally tractable, and hence a relatively plausible prediction of agent behavior.

17.4.3   Final Remarks

The conventional interpretation of coarse correlated and correlated equilibria involves a third party who samples an outcome from the equilibrium distribution (Section 13.1). Proposition 17.9 demonstrates how such correlation arises endogenously when independent agents play the same game repeatedly. The correlation stems from the shared history of joint play.

The notion of approximate equilibrium in Proposition 17.9 concerns additive error, while Definitions 14.5 and 16.2 use relative error. These choices are primarily for technical convenience.

An alternative form of no-regret dynamics samples an outcome $\mathbf{s}^t$ according to the distribution $\sigma^t = \prod_{i=1}^{k} p_i^t$ at each iteration t, with agent i receiving the cost vector c_i^t with $c_i^t(s_i) = C_i(s_i, \mathbf{s}_{-i}^t)$ for each strategy $s_i \in S_i$. An analog of Proposition 17.9 holds for the uniform distribution σ over the multi-set $\{\mathbf{s}^1, \dots, \mathbf{s}^T\}$ of sampled outcomes, with the statement and the proof modified to accommodate sampling error. In these alternative dynamics, it is essential that agents use algorithms that have no regret with respect to adaptive adversaries (Section 17.3.1).

Lecture 14 shows that price-of-anarchy bounds for (λ, μ)-smooth games (Definition 14.2) hold for all coarse correlated equilibria (Theorem 14.4) and degrade gracefully for approximate equilibria (Theorem 14.6). Thus, Proposition 17.9 suggests that such bounds should apply also to the time-averaged expected objective function value of an outcome sequence generated by no-regret dynamics. This is indeed the case (Exercise 17.3).

Corollary 17.10 (POA Bounds for No-Regret Dynamics)
Suppose that after T iterations of no-regret dynamics, each of the k agents of a (λ, μ)-smooth cost-minimization game has expected regret at most ϵ. If $\sigma^t = \prod_{i=1}^{k} p_i^t$ denotes the outcome distribution at

iteration t and $\mathbf{s}^*$ an optimal outcome, then

$$\frac{1}{T} \sum_{t=1}^{T} \mathbf{E}_{\mathbf{s} \sim \sigma^t}[\text{cost}(\mathbf{s})] \leq \frac{\lambda}{1 - \mu} \text{cost}(\mathbf{s}^*) + \frac{k\epsilon}{1 - \mu}.$$

As $\epsilon \to 0$, this guarantee converges to $\frac{\lambda}{1-\mu}$, the standard price-of-anarchy bound for smooth games (Section 14.4).

The Upshot

☆ In each time step of an online decision-making problem, an algorithm chooses a probability distribution over actions and then an adversary reveals the cost of each action.

☆ The regret of an action sequence is the difference between the time-averaged costs of the sequence and of the best fixed action in hindsight.

☆ A no-regret algorithm guarantees expected regret tending to 0 as the time horizon tends to infinity.

☆ The multiplicative weights algorithm is a simple no-regret algorithm with optimal worst-case expected regret.

☆ In every iteration of no-regret dynamics, each agent independently chooses a mixed strategy using a no-regret algorithm.

☆ The time-averaged history of joint play in no-regret dynamics converges to the set of coarse correlated equilibria.

☆ Price-of-anarchy bounds in smooth games apply to the time-averaged expected objective function value of an outcome sequence generated by no-regret dynamics.

Notes

The versions of the multiplicative weights algorithm and Theorem 17.6 described here are from Cesa-Bianchi et al. (2007). Many variants and extensions, including to the bandit model where the decision maker only learns the cost of the chosen action at each time step, are discussed by Cesa-Bianchi and Lugosi (2006) and Blum and Mansour (2007b). These sources, together with Foster and Vohra (1999) and Arora et al. (2012), also cover the history of online decision-making problems, no-regret algorithms, and important precursors to the multiplicative weights algorithm such as "randomized weighted majority" and "hedge." Key references include Blackwell (1956), Hannan (1957), Littlestone and Warmuth (1994), and Freund and Schapire (1997). Proposition 17.9 is already implicit in Hannan (1957). Problems 17.2 and 17.4 are from Littlestone (1988) and Kalai and Vempala (2005), respectively.

Exercises

Exercise 17.1 *(H)* Extend Corollary 17.7 to online decision-making problems where actions' costs lie in $[-c_{\max}, c_{\max}]$ rather than $[-1, 1]$, losing a factor of $c_{\max}^2$ in the number of time steps. You can assume that the value $c_{\max}$ is known in advance.

Exercise 17.2 *(H)* The multiplicative weights algorithm requires advance knowledge of the time horizon T to set the parameter η. Modify the algorithm so that it does not need to know T a priori. Your algorithm should have expected regret at most $b\sqrt{(\ln n)/T}$ for all sufficiently large T and for every adversary, where $b > 0$ is a constant independent of n and T.

Exercise 17.3 *(H)* Prove Corollary 17.10.

Exercise 17.4 Proposition 17.9 proves that the time-averaged joint distribution $\frac{1}{T}\sum_{t=1}^{T}\sigma^t$ generated by no-regret dynamics is an approximate coarse correlated equilibrium, but it says nothing about the outcome distribution σ^t in a given iteration t. Prove that such a distribution σ^t is an approximate coarse correlated equilibrium if and only if it is an approximate Nash equilibrium (with the same additive error term).

Problems

Problem 17.1 Consider an online decision-making problem with n actions. Prove that the worst-case expected regret of an online decision-making algorithm cannot vanish faster than $b\sqrt{(\ln n)/T}$, where $b > 0$ is some constant independent of n and T.

Problem 17.2 This problem considers a variant of the online decision-making problem. There are n "experts," where n is a power of 2.

Combining Expert Advice

At each time step $t = 1, 2, \dots, T$:

    each expert offers a prediction of the realization of a binary event (e.g., whether a stock will go up or down)

    a decision maker picks a probability distribution p^t over the possible realizations 0 and 1 of the event

    the actual realization $r^t \in \{0, 1\}$ of the event is revealed

    a 0 or 1 is chosen according to the distribution p^t, and a *mistake* occurs whenever it is different from r^t

---

You are promised that there is at least one omniscient expert who makes a correct prediction at every time step.

(a) *(H)* A deterministic algorithm always assigns all of the probability mass in p^t to one of 0 or 1. Prove that the minimum worst-case number of mistakes that a deterministic algorithm can make is precisely $\log_2 n$.

(b) Prove that for every randomized algorithm, there is a sequence of expert predictions and event realizations such that the expected number of mistakes made by the algorithm is at least $\frac{1}{2} \log_2 n$.

(c) *(H)* Prove that there is a randomized algorithm such that, for every sequence of expert predictions and event realizations, the expected number of mistakes is at most $b \log_2 n$, where $b < 1$ is a constant independent of n. How small can you take b?

Problem 17.3 *(H)* Consider a k-agent cost-minimization game in which no agent i incurs equal cost $C_i(\mathbf{s})$ in two different outcomes. Prove the following converse to Proposition 17.9: for every coarse correlated equilibrium σ of the game, there exist choices of no-regret algorithms $\mathcal{A}_1, \ldots, \mathcal{A}_k$ for the agents so that the time-averaged history of the corresponding no-regret dynamics converges to σ as the number of iterations T tends to infinity.

Problem 17.4 Example 17.4 shows that the follow-the-leader (FTL) algorithm, and more generally every deterministic algorithm, fails to have no regret. This problem outlines a randomized variant of FTL, the *follow-the-perturbed-leader (FTPL)* algorithm, with worst-case expected regret comparable to that of the multiplicative weights algorithm. We define each probability distribution p^t over actions implicitly through a randomized subroutine.

Follow-the-Perturbed-Leader (FTPL) Algorithm

for each action $a \in A$ **do**
    independently sample a geometric random
    variable with parameter η,[7] denoted by X_a
for each time step $t = 1, 2, \ldots, T$ **do**
    choose the action a that minimizes the perturbed
    cumulative cost $-2X_a + \sum_{u=1}^{t-1} c^u(a)$ so far

---

[7]Equivalently, when repeatedly flipping a coin that comes up "heads" with probability η, count the number of flips up to and including the first "heads."

Fix an oblivious adversary, meaning a sequence $c^1, \ldots, c^T$ of cost vectors. For convenience, assume that, at every time step t, there is no pair of actions whose (unperturbed) cumulative costs-so-far differ by an integer.

(a) *(H)* Prove that, at each time step $t = 1, 2, \ldots, T$, with probability at least $1 - \eta$, the smallest perturbed cumulative cost of an action prior to t is more than 2 less than the second-smallest such perturbed cost.

(b) *(H)* As a thought experiment, consider the (unimplementable) algorithm that, at each time step t, picks the action that minimizes the perturbed cumulative cost $-2X_a + \sum_{u=1}^{t} c^u(a)$, *taking into account the current cost vector.* Prove that the regret of this algorithm is at most $\max_{a \in A} X_a$.

(c) Prove that $\mathbf{E}[\max_{a \in A} X_a] \leq b\eta^{-1} \ln n$, where n is the number of actions and $b > 0$ is a constant independent of η and n.

(d) *(H)* Prove that, for a suitable choice of η, the worst-case expected regret of the FTPL algorithm is at most $b\sqrt{(\ln n)/T}$, where $b > 0$ is a constant independent of n and T.

(e) *(H)* How would you modify the FTPL algorithm and its analysis to achieve the same regret guarantee with respect to adaptive adversaries?

Lecture 18

Swap Regret and the Minimax Theorem

Lecture 17 proves that the coarse correlated equilibrium concept is tractable in a satisfying sense: there are simple and computationally efficient learning procedures that converge quickly to the set of coarse correlated equilibria in every finite game. What can we say if we zoom in to one of the smaller sets in our hierarchy of equilibrium concepts (Figure 13.1)? Sections 18.1 and 18.2 present a second and more stringent notion of regret, and use it to prove that the correlated equilibrium concept is tractable in a similar sense. Sections 18.3 and 18.4 zoom in further to the mixed Nash equilibrium concept, and prove its tractability in the special case of two-player zero-sum games.

18.1 Swap Regret and Correlated Equilibria

This lecture works with the definition of a correlated equilibrium given in Exercise 13.3, which is equivalent to Definition 13.4.

Definition 18.1 (Correlated Equilibrium) A distribution σ on the set $S_1 \times \cdots \times S_k$ of outcomes of a cost-minimization game is a *correlated equilibrium* if for every agent $i \in \{1, 2, \ldots, k\}$ and swapping function $\delta : S_i \to S_i$,

$$\mathbf{E}_{\mathbf{s} \sim \sigma}[C_i(\mathbf{s})] \leq \mathbf{E}_{\mathbf{s} \sim \sigma}[C_i(\delta(s_i), \mathbf{s}_{-i})].$$

Every correlated equilibrium is a coarse correlated equilibrium, and the converse does not generally hold (Section 13.1.6).

Is there an analog of no-regret dynamics (Section 17.4) that converges to the set of correlated equilibria in the sense of Proposition 17.9? For an affirmative answer, the key is to define the appropriate more stringent notion of regret, which compares the cost of an online decision-making algorithm to that of the best swapping function in hindsight. This is a stronger benchmark than the best fixed action in hindsight, since fixed actions correspond to the special case of constant swapping functions.

Recall the model of online decision-making problems introduced in Section 17.1. At each time step $t = 1, 2, \ldots, T$, a decision maker commits to a distribution p^t over her n actions A, then an adversary chooses a cost function $c^t : A \to [-1, 1]$, and finally an action a^t is chosen according to p^t, resulting in cost $c^t(a^t)$ to the decision maker.

Definition 18.2 (Swap Regret) Fix cost vectors $c^1, \ldots, c^T$. The *swap regret* of the action sequence $a^1, \ldots, a^T$ is

$$\frac{1}{T} \left[\sum_{t=1}^{T} c^t(a^t) - \min_{\delta: A \to A} \sum_{t=1}^{T} c^t(\delta(a^t)) \right], \tag{18.1}$$

where the minimum ranges over all swapping functions δ.[1]

Definition 18.3 (No-Swap-Regret Algorithm) An online decision-making algorithm $\mathcal{A}$ has *no swap regret* if for every $\epsilon > 0$ there exists a sufficiently large time horizon $T = T(\epsilon)$ such that, for every adversary for $\mathcal{A}$, the expected swap regret is at most ϵ.

As with Definition 17.3, we think of the number n of actions as fixed and the time horizon T tending to infinity, and we allow $\mathcal{A}$ to depend on T.

In every time step t of *no-swap-regret dynamics*, every agent i independently chooses a mixed strategy p_i^t using a no-swap-regret algorithm. Cost vectors are defined as in no-regret dynamics, with $c_i^t(s_i)$ the expected cost of the pure strategy $s_i \in S_i$, given that every other agent j plays the mixed strategy p_j^t. The connection between correlated equilibria and no-swap-regret dynamics is the same as that between coarse correlated equilibria and no-(external-)regret dynamics.

---

[1] *Internal regret* is a closely related notion, and is defined using the best single swap from one action to another in hindsight, rather than the best swapping function. The swap and internal regret of an action sequence differ by at most a factor of n.

Proposition 18.4 (No-Swap-Regret Dynamics and CE)

Suppose that after T iterations of no-swap-regret dynamics, each agent $i = 1, 2, \ldots, k$ of a cost-minimization game has expected swap regret at most ϵ. Let $\sigma^t = \prod_{i=1}^{k} p_i^t$ denote the outcome distribution at iteration t and $\sigma = \frac{1}{T} \sum_{t=1}^{T} \sigma^t$ the time-averaged history of these distributions. Then σ is an approximate correlated equilibrium, in the sense that

$$\mathbf{E}_{\mathbf{s} \sim \sigma}[C_i(\mathbf{s})] \leq \mathbf{E}_{\mathbf{s} \sim \sigma}[C_i(\delta(s_i), \mathbf{s}_{-i})] + \epsilon$$

for every agent i and swapping function $\delta : S_i \to S_i$.

Definitions 18.2–18.3 and Proposition 18.4 are all fine and good, but do any no-swap-regret algorithms exist? The next result is a "black-box reduction" from the problem of designing a no-swap-regret algorithm to that of designing a no-external-regret algorithm.

Theorem 18.5 (Black-Box Reduction) *If there is a no-external-regret algorithm, then there is a no-swap-regret algorithm.*

Combining Theorems 17.6 and 18.5, we conclude that no-swap-regret algorithms exist. For example, plugging the multiplicative weights algorithm (Section 17.2) into this reduction yields a no-swap-regret algorithm that is also computationally efficient. We conclude that correlated equilibria are tractable in the same strong sense as coarse correlated equilibria.

*18.2   Proof of Theorem 18.5

The reduction is very natural, one that you'd hope would work. It requires one clever trick at the end of the proof.

Fix a set $A = \{1, 2, \ldots, n\}$ of actions. Let $M_1, \ldots, M_n$ denote n different no-(external)-regret algorithms, such as n instantiations of the multiplicative weights algorithm. Each of these algorithms is poised to produce probability distributions over the actions A and receive cost vectors as feedback. Roughly, we can think of algorithm M_j as responsible for protecting against profitable deviations from action j to other actions. Assume for simplicity that, as with the multiplicative weights algorithm, the probability distribution produced by each algorithm M_j at a time step t depends only on the cost vectors $c^1, \ldots, c^{t-1}$ of previous time steps, and not on the realized actions $a^1, \ldots, a^{t-1}$. This assumption lets us restrict attention to oblivious adversaries (Section 17.3.1), or equivalently to cost vector sequences $c^1, \ldots, c^T$ that are fixed a priori.

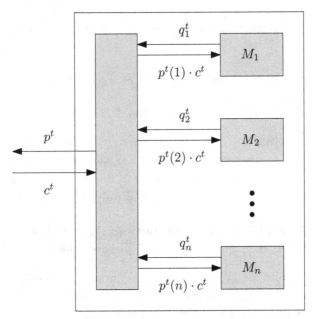

Figure 18.1: Black-box reduction from swap-regret-minimization to external-regret-minimization.

The following "master algorithm" M coordinates $M_1, \ldots, M_n$; see also Figure 18.1.

The Master Algorithm

for each time step $t = 1, 2, \ldots, T$ **do**
    receive distributions $q_1^t, \ldots, q_n^t$ over the actions A
    from the algorithms $M_1, \ldots, M_n$
    compute and output a consensus distribution p^t
    receive a cost vector c^t from the adversary
    give each algorithm M_j the cost vector $p^t(j) \cdot c^t$

We discuss how to compute the consensus distribution p^t from the distributions $q_1^t, \ldots, q_n^t$ at the end of the proof; this is the clever trick in the reduction. At the end of a time step, the true cost vector c^t is parceled out to the no-regret algorithms, scaled according to the current relevance (i.e., $p^t(j)$) of the algorithm.

We hope to piggyback on the no-external-regret guarantee provided by each algorithm M_j and conclude a no-swap-regret guarantee for the master algorithm M. Let's take stock of what we've got and what we want, parameterized by the consensus distributions $p^1, \ldots, p^T$.

Fix a cost vector sequence $c^1, \ldots, c^T$. The time-averaged expected cost of the master algorithm is

$$\frac{1}{T} \sum_{t=1}^{T} \sum_{i=1}^{n} p^t(i) \cdot c^t(i). \tag{18.2}$$

The time-averaged expected cost under a fixed swapping function $\delta : A \to A$ is

$$\frac{1}{T} \sum_{t=1}^{T} \sum_{i=1}^{n} p^t(i) \cdot c^t(\delta(i)). \tag{18.3}$$

Our goal is to prove that (18.2) is at most (18.3), plus a term that goes to 0 as T tends to infinity, for every swapping function δ.

Adopt the perspective of an algorithm M_j. This algorithm believes that actions are being chosen according to its recommended distributions $q_j^1, \ldots, q_j^T$ and that the true cost vectors are $p^1(j) \cdot c^1, \ldots, p^T(j) \cdot c^T$. Thus, algorithm M_j perceives its time-averaged expected cost as

$$\frac{1}{T} \sum_{t=1}^{T} \sum_{i=1}^{n} q_j^t(i) \left(p^t(j) c^t(i) \right). \tag{18.4}$$

Since M_j is a no-regret algorithm, its perceived cost (18.4) is, up to a term R_j that tends to 0 as T tends to infinity, at most that of every fixed action $k \in A$. That is, the quantity (18.4) is bounded above by

$$\frac{1}{T} \sum_{t=1}^{T} p^t(j) c^t(k) + R_j. \tag{18.5}$$

Now fix a swapping function δ. Summing the inequality between (18.4) and (18.5) over all $j = 1, 2, \ldots, n$, with k instantiated as $\delta(j)$

in (18.5), proves that

$$\frac{1}{T}\sum_{t=1}^{T}\sum_{i=1}^{n}\sum_{j=1}^{n} q_j^t(i)p^t(j)c^t(i) \tag{18.6}$$

is at most

$$\frac{1}{T}\sum_{t=1}^{T}\sum_{j=1}^{n} p^t(j)c^t(\delta(j)) + \sum_{j=1}^{n} R_j. \tag{18.7}$$

The expression (18.7) is equivalent to (18.3), up to a term $\sum_{j=1}^{n} R_j$ that goes to 0 as T goes to infinity. Indeed, we chose the splitting of the cost vector c^t among the no-external-regret algorithms $M_1, \ldots, M_n$ to guarantee this property.

We complete the reduction by showing how to choose the consensus distributions $p^1, \ldots, p^T$ so that (18.2) and (18.6) coincide. For each $t = 1, 2, \ldots, T$, we show how to choose the consensus distribution p^t so that, for each $i \in A$,

$$p^t(i) = \sum_{j=1}^{n} q_j^t(i)p^t(j). \tag{18.8}$$

The left- and right-hand sides of (18.8) are the coefficients of $c^t(i)$ in (18.2) and in (18.6), respectively.

The key trick in the reduction is to recognize the equations (18.8) as those defining the stationary distribution of a Markov chain. Precisely, given distributions $q_1^t, \ldots, q_n^t$ from the algorithms $M_1, \ldots, M_n$ at time step t, form the following Markov chain (Figure 18.2): the set of states is $A = \{1, 2, \ldots, n\}$, and for every $i, j \in A$, the transition probability from j to i is $q_j^t(i)$. That is, the distribution q_j^t specifies the transition probabilities out of state j. A probability distribution p^t satisfies (18.8) if and only if it is a stationary distribution of this Markov chain. At least one such distribution exists, and one can be computed efficiently using an eigenvector computation (see the Notes). This completes the proof of Theorem 18.5.

Remark 18.6 (Interpretation of Consensus Distributions)
The choice of the consensus distribution p^t given the no-regret algorithms' suggestions $q_1^t, \ldots, q_n^t$ follows from the proof approach, but it also has a natural interpretation as the limit of an iterative

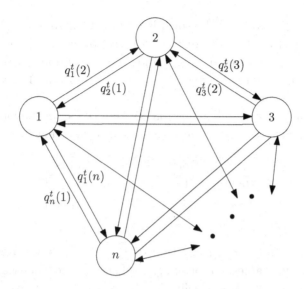

Figure 18.2: Markov chain used to compute consensus distributions.

decision-making process. Consider asking some algorithm M_{j_1} for a recommended strategy. It gives a recommendation j_2 drawn from its distribution $q_{j_1}^t$. Then ask algorithm M_{j_2} for a recommendation j_3, which it draws from its distribution $q_{j_2}^t$, and so on. This random process is effectively trying to converge to a stationary distribution p^t of the Markov chain defined in the proof of Theorem 18.5.

18.3   The Minimax Theorem for Zero-Sum Games

The rest of this lecture restricts attention to games with two agents. As per convention, we call each agent a *player*, and use the payoff-maximization formalism of games (Remark 13.1).

18.3.1   Two-Player Zero-Sum Games

A two-player game is *zero-sum* if, in every outcome, the payoff of each player is the negative of the other. These are games of pure competition, with one player's gain the other player's loss. A two-player zero-sum game can be specified by a single matrix $\mathbf{A}$, with the two strategy sets corresponding to the rows and columns. The entry

a_{ij} specifies the payoff of the row player in the outcome (i, j) and the negative payoff of the column player in this outcome. Thus, the row and column players prefer bigger and smaller numbers, respectively. We can assume that all payoffs lie between -1 and 1, scaling the payoffs if necessary.

For example, the following matrix describes the payoffs in the Rock-Paper-Scissors game (Section 1.3) in our current language.

	Rock	Paper	Scissors
Rock	0	-1	1
Paper	1	0	-1
Scissors	-1	1	0

Pure Nash equilibria (Definition 13.2) generally don't exist in two-player zero-sum games, so the analysis of such games focuses squarely on mixed Nash equilibria (Definition 13.3), with each player randomizing independently according to a mixed strategy. We use $\mathbf{x}$ and $\mathbf{y}$ to denote mixed strategies over the rows and columns, respectively.

When payoffs are given by an $m \times n$ matrix $\mathbf{A}$, the row strategy is $\mathbf{x}$, and the column strategy is $\mathbf{y}$, we can write the expected payoff of the row player as

$$\sum_{i=1}^{m} \sum_{j=1}^{n} x_i \cdot y_j \cdot a_{ij} = \mathbf{x}^\top \mathbf{A} \mathbf{y}.^2$$

The column player's expected payoff is the negative of this. Thus, the mixed Nash equilibria are precisely the pairs $(\hat{\mathbf{x}}, \hat{\mathbf{y}})$ such that

$$\hat{\mathbf{x}}^\top \mathbf{A} \hat{\mathbf{y}} \geq \mathbf{x}^\top \mathbf{A} \hat{\mathbf{y}} \qquad \text{for all mixed strategies } \mathbf{x} \text{ over rows}$$

and

$$\hat{\mathbf{x}}^\top \mathbf{A} \hat{\mathbf{y}} \leq \hat{\mathbf{x}}^\top \mathbf{A} \mathbf{y} \qquad \text{for all mixed strategies } \mathbf{y} \text{ over columns.}$$

18.3.2   The Minimax Theorem

In a two-player zero-sum game, would you prefer to commit to a mixed strategy before or after the other player commits to hers? Intuitively, there is only a first-mover disadvantage, since the second

---

[2]The symbol "⊤" denotes vector or matrix transpose.

player can adapt to the first player's strategy. The Minimax theorem is the amazing statement that *it doesn't matter.*

Theorem 18.7 (Minimax Theorem) *For every two-player zero-sum game* $\mathbf{A}$,

$$\max_{\mathbf{x}} \left(\min_{\mathbf{y}} \mathbf{x}^\top \mathbf{A} \mathbf{y} \right) = \min_{\mathbf{y}} \left(\max_{\mathbf{x}} \mathbf{x}^\top \mathbf{A} \mathbf{y} \right). \qquad (18.9)$$

On the left-hand side of (18.9), the row player moves first and the column player second. The column player plays optimally given the strategy chosen by the row player, and the row player plays optimally anticipating the column player's response. On the right-hand side of (18.9), the roles of the two players are reversed. The Minimax theorem asserts that, under optimal play, the expected payoff of each player is the same in the two scenarios. The quantity (18.9) is called the *value* of the game $\mathbf{A}$.

The Minimax theorem is equivalent to the statement that every two-player zero-sum game has at least one mixed Nash equilibrium (Exercise 18.3). It also implies the following "mix and match" property (Exercise 18.4): if $(\mathbf{x}^1, \mathbf{y}^1)$ and $(\mathbf{x}^2, \mathbf{y}^2)$ are mixed Nash equilibria of the same two-player zero-sum game, then so are $(\mathbf{x}^1, \mathbf{y}^2)$ and $(\mathbf{x}^2, \mathbf{y}^1)$.

*18.4   Proof of Theorem 18.7

In a two-player zero-sum game, it's only worse to go first: if $\hat{\mathbf{x}}$ is an optimal mixed strategy for the row player when she plays first, she always has the option of playing $\hat{\mathbf{x}}$ when she plays second. Thus the left-hand side of (18.9) is at most the right-hand side. We turn our attention to the reverse inequality.

Fix a two-player zero-sum game $\mathbf{A}$ with payoffs in $[-1, 1]$ and a parameter $\epsilon \in (0, 1]$. Suppose we run no-regret dynamics (Section 17.4) for enough iterations T that both players have expected (external) regret at most ϵ. For example, if both players use the multiplicative weights algorithm, then $T = (4 \ln(\max\{m, n\}))/\epsilon^2$ iterations are enough, where m and n are the dimensions of $\mathbf{A}$ (Corollary 17.7).[3]

---

[3]In Lecture 17, the multiplicative weights algorithm and its guarantee are stated for cost-minimization problems. Viewing payoffs as negative costs, they carry over immediately to the present setting.

Let $\mathbf{p}^1, \ldots, \mathbf{p}^T$ and $\mathbf{q}^1, \ldots, \mathbf{q}^T$ be the mixed strategies played by the row and column players, respectively, as advised by their no-regret algorithms. The payoff vector revealed to each no-regret algorithm after iteration t is the expected payoff of each strategy, given the mixed strategy played by the other player in iteration t. This translates to the payoff vectors $\mathbf{Aq}^t$ and $(\mathbf{p}^t)^\top \mathbf{A}$ for the row and column player, respectively.

Let

$$\hat{\mathbf{x}} = \frac{1}{T} \sum_{t=1}^{T} \mathbf{p}^t$$

be the time-averaged mixed strategy of the row player,

$$\hat{\mathbf{y}} = \frac{1}{T} \sum_{t=1}^{T} \mathbf{q}^t$$

the time-averaged mixed strategy of the column player, and

$$v = \frac{1}{T} \sum_{t=1}^{T} (\mathbf{p}^t)^\top \mathbf{A} \mathbf{q}^t$$

the time-averaged expected payoff of the row player.

Adopt the row player's perspective. Since her expected regret is at most ϵ, for every vector e_i corresponding to a fixed pure strategy i, we have

$$e_i^\top \mathbf{A}\hat{\mathbf{y}} = \frac{1}{T} \sum_{t=1}^{T} e_i^\top \mathbf{A} \mathbf{q}^t \leq \frac{1}{T} \sum_{t=1}^{T} (\mathbf{p}^t)^\top \mathbf{A} \mathbf{q}^t + \epsilon = v + \epsilon. \qquad (18.10)$$

Since an arbitrary mixed strategy $\mathbf{x}$ over the rows is just a probability distribution over the e_i's, inequality (18.10) and linearity imply that

$$\mathbf{x}^\top \mathbf{A}\hat{\mathbf{y}} \leq v + \epsilon \qquad (18.11)$$

for every mixed strategy $\mathbf{x}$.

A symmetric argument from the column player's perspective, using that her expected regret is also at most ϵ, shows that

$$\hat{\mathbf{x}}^\top \mathbf{A}\mathbf{y} \geq v - \epsilon \qquad (18.12)$$

for every mixed strategy $\mathbf{y}$ over the columns. Thus

$$
\max_{\mathbf{x}} \left(\min_{\mathbf{y}} \mathbf{x}^\top \mathbf{A} \mathbf{y} \right) \geq \min_{\mathbf{y}} \hat{\mathbf{x}}^\top \mathbf{A} \mathbf{y}
$$

$$
\geq v - \epsilon \tag{18.13}
$$

$$
\geq \max_{\mathbf{x}} \mathbf{x}^\top \mathbf{A} \hat{\mathbf{y}} - 2\epsilon \tag{18.14}
$$

$$
\geq \min_{\mathbf{y}} \left(\max_{\mathbf{x}} \mathbf{x}^\top \mathbf{A} \mathbf{y} \right) - 2\epsilon,
$$

where (18.13) and (18.14) follow from (18.12) and (18.11), respectively. Taking the limit as $\epsilon \to 0$ (and $T \to \infty$) completes the proof of the Minimax theorem.

The Upshot

☆ The swap regret of an action sequence is the difference between the time-averaged costs of the sequence and of the best swapping function in hindsight.

☆ A no-swap-regret algorithm guarantees expected swap regret tending to 0 as the time horizon tends to infinity.

☆ There is a black-box reduction from the problem of no-swap-regret algorithm design to that of no-(external)-regret algorithm design.

☆ The time-averaged history of joint play in no-swap-regret dynamics converges to the set of correlated equilibria.

☆ A two-player game is zero-sum if, in every outcome, the payoff of each player is the negative of the other.

☆ The Minimax theorem states that, under optimal play in a two-player zero-sum game, the expected payoff of a player is the same whether she commits to a mixed strategy before or after the other player.

Notes

The close connection between no-swap-regret algorithms and correlated equilibria is developed in Foster and Vohra (1997) and Hart and Mas-Colell (2000). Theorem 18.5 is due to Blum and Mansour (2007a). Background on Markov chains is in Karlin and Taylor (1975), for example. The first proof of the Minimax theorem (Theorem 18.7) is due to von Neumann (1928). von Neumann and Morgenstern (1944), inspired by Ville (1938), give a more elementary proof. Dantzig (1951), Gale et al. (1951), and Adler (2013) make explicit the close connection between the Minimax theorem and linear programming duality, following the original suggestion of von Neumann (see Dantzig (1982)). Our proof of the Minimax theorem, using no-regret algorithms, follows Freund and Schapire (1999); a similar result is implicit in Hannan (1957). Cai et al. (2016) investigate generalizations of the Minimax theorem to wider classes of games. Problems 18.2 and Problem 18.3 are from Freund and Schapire (1999) and Gilboa and Zemel (1989), respectively.

Exercises

Exercise 18.1 *(H)* Prove that, for arbitrarily large T, the swap regret of an action sequence of length T can exceed its external regret by at least T.

Exercise 18.2 In the black-box reduction in Theorem 18.5, suppose we take each of the no-regret algorithms $M_1, \ldots, M_n$ to be the multiplicative weights algorithm (Section 17.2), where n denotes the number of actions. What is the swap regret of the resulting master algorithm, as a function of n and T?

Exercise 18.3 Let $\mathbf{A}$ denote the matrix of row player payoffs of a two-player zero-sum game. Prove that a pair $\hat{\mathbf{x}}, \hat{\mathbf{y}}$ of mixed strategies forms a mixed Nash equilibrium of the game if and only if it is a *minimax pair*, meaning

$$\hat{\mathbf{x}} \in \text{argmax}_{\mathbf{x}} \left(\min_{\mathbf{y}} \mathbf{x}^\top \mathbf{A} \mathbf{y} \right)$$

and

$$\hat{\mathbf{y}} \in \text{argmin}_{\mathbf{y}} \left(\max_{\mathbf{x}} \mathbf{x}^\top \mathbf{A} \mathbf{y} \right).$$

Exercise 18.4 *(H)* Prove that if $(\mathbf{x}_1, \mathbf{y}_1)$ and $(\mathbf{x}_2, \mathbf{y}_2)$ are mixed Nash equilibria of a two-player zero-sum game, then so are $(\mathbf{x}_1, \mathbf{y}_2)$ and $(\mathbf{x}_2, \mathbf{y}_1)$.

Exercise 18.5 A two-player game is *constant-sum* if there is a constant a such that, in every outcome, the sum of the players' payoffs equals a. Does the Minimax theorem (Theorem 18.7) hold in all constant-sum games?

Exercise 18.6 *(H)* Call a game with three players *zero-sum* if, in every outcome, the payoffs of the three players sum to zero. Prove that, in a natural sense, three-player zero-sum games include arbitrary two-player games as a special case.

Problems

Problem 18.1 *(H)* Exhibit a (non-zero-sum) two-player game in which the time-averaged history of joint play generated by no-regret dynamics need not converge to a mixed Nash equilibrium.

Problem 18.2 Fix a two-player zero-sum game $\mathbf{A}$ with payoffs in $[-1, 1]$ and a parameter $\epsilon \in (0, 1]$. Suppose that, at each time step $t = 1, 2 \ldots, T$, the row player moves first and uses the multiplicative weights algorithm to choose a mixed strategy $\mathbf{p}^t$, and the column moves second and chooses a best response $\mathbf{q}^t$ to $\mathbf{p}^t$. Assume that $T \geq (4 \ln m)/\epsilon^2$, where m is the number of rows of $\mathbf{A}$.

(a) Adopt the row player's perspective to prove that the time-averaged expected payoff $\frac{1}{T} \sum_{t=1}^{T} (\mathbf{p}^t)^\top \mathbf{A} \mathbf{q}^t$ of the row player is at least

$$\min_{\mathbf{y}} \left(\max_{\mathbf{x}} \mathbf{x}^\top \mathbf{A} \mathbf{y} \right) - \epsilon.$$

(b) Adopt the column player's perspective to prove that the time-averaged expected payoff of the row player is at most

$$\max_{\mathbf{x}} \left(\min_{\mathbf{y}} \mathbf{x}^\top \mathbf{A} \mathbf{y} \right).$$

(c) Use (a) and (b) to give an alternative proof of Theorem 18.7.

Problem 18.3 This problem and the next assume familiarity with linear programming, and show that all of our computationally tractable equilibrium concepts can be characterized by linear programs.

Consider a cost-minimization game with k agents that each have at most m strategies. We can view a probability distribution over the outcomes O of the game as a point $\mathbf{z} \in \mathbb{R}^O$ for which $z_\mathbf{s} \geq 0$ for every outcome $\mathbf{s}$ and $\sum_{\mathbf{s} \in O} z_\mathbf{s} = 1$.

(a) *(H)* Exhibit a system of at most km additional inequalities, each linear in $\mathbf{z}$, such that the coarse correlated equilibria of the game are precisely the distributions that satisfy all of the inequalities.

(b) Exhibit a system of at most km^2 additional inequalities, each linear in $\mathbf{z}$, such that the correlated equilibria of the game are precisely the distributions that satisfy all of the inequalities.

Problem 18.4 *(H)* Prove that the mixed Nash equilibria of a two-player zero-sum game can be characterized as the optimal solutions to a pair of linear programs.

Pure Nash Equilibria and $\mathcal{PLS}$-Completeness

The final two lectures study the limitations of learning dynamics and computationally efficient algorithms for converging to and computing equilibria, and develop analogs of $\mathcal{NP}$-completeness that are tailored to equilibrium computation problems. After setting the stage by reviewing our positive results and motivating the use of computational complexity theory (Section 19.1), this lecture develops the theory of $\mathcal{PLS}$-completeness (Section 19.2) and applies it to give evidence that computing a pure Nash equilibrium of a congestion game is an intractable problem (Section 19.3).

This lecture and the next assume basic familiarity with polynomial-time algorithms and $\mathcal{NP}$-completeness (see the Notes for references).

19.1 When Are Equilibrium Concepts Tractable?

19.1.1 Recap of Tractability Results

Lectures 16–18 prove four satisfying equilibrium tractability results, stating that simple and natural dynamics converge quickly to an approximate equilibrium. See also Figure 19.1. These results support the predictive power of these equilibrium concepts.

Four Tractability Results

1. (Corollary 17.7 and Proposition 17.9) In every game, the time-averaged history of joint play of no-regret dynamics converges quickly to an approximate coarse correlated equilibrium (CCE).

2. (Proposition 18.4 and Theorem 18.5) In every game, the time-averaged history of joint play of no-swap-

---

> regret dynamics converges quickly to an approximate
> correlated equilibrium (CE).
>
> 3. (Corollary 17.7 and Theorem 18.7) In every two-
>   player zero-sum game, the time-averaged history of
>   joint play of no-regret dynamics converges quickly to
>   an approximate mixed Nash equilibrium (MNE).
>
> 4. (Theorem 16.3) In every atomic routing game where
>   all agents share the same origin and destination, many
>   variants of ϵ-best-response dynamics converge quickly
>   to an approximate pure Nash equilibrium (PNE).

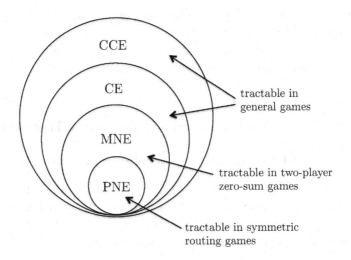

Figure 19.1: Tractability results for the hierarchy of equilibrium concepts. "Tractable" means that simple and natural dynamics converge quickly to an approximate equilibrium, and also that there are polynomial-time algorithms for computing an exact equilibrium.

Can we prove stronger tractability results? For example, can simple dynamics converge quickly to approximate MNE in general two-player games, or to approximate PNE in general atomic selfish routing games?

19.1.2   Dynamics vs. Algorithms

With an eye toward intractability results, we weaken our standing notion of tractability from

> Are there simple and natural dynamics that converge quickly to a given equilibrium concept in a given class of games?

to

> Is there an algorithm that computes quickly a given equilibrium concept in a given class of games?

Technically, by "quickly" we mean that the number of iterations required for convergence or the number of elementary operations required for computation is bounded by a polynomial function of the number of parameters needed to specify all of the agents' cost or payoff functions.[1]   For instance, kn^k parameters are required to define all of the costs or payoffs of an arbitrary game with k agents with n strategies each (k payoffs per outcome). Special classes of games often have compact descriptions with much fewer than kn^k parameters. For example, in an atomic selfish routing game with k agents and m edges, mk parameters suffice to specify fully the agents' cost functions (the cost $c_e(i)$ of each edge e for each $i \in \{1, 2, \ldots, k\}$).

One particular type of algorithm for computing an approximate equilibrium is to simulate a choice of dynamics until it (approximately) converges. Provided each iteration of the dynamics can be simulated in polynomial time and that the dynamics requires only a polynomial number of iterations to converge, the induced algorithm runs in polynomial time. This is the case for the four tractability results reviewed in Section 19.1.1, provided no-regret and no-swap-regret dynamics are implemented using a computationally efficient subroutine like the multiplicative weights algorithm. We conclude that the second goal is weaker than the first, and hence impossibility results for it are only stronger.

In all four of the settings mentioned in Section 19.1.1, there are also polynomial-time algorithms for computing an exact equilibrium that are not based on any natural dynamics (Problems 18.3, 18.4,

---

[1]To be fully rigorous, we should also keep track of the number of bits required to describe these costs or payoffs. We omit further discussion of this issue.

and 19.1). These exact algorithms seem far removed from any reasonable model of how agents learn in strategic environments.

19.1.3 Toward Intractability Results

There is no simple learning procedure that is known to converge quickly to approximate MNE in general two-player games or to approximate PNE in general atomic selfish routing games. There are not even any known polynomial-time algorithms for computing such equilibria. Do we merely need a new and clever idea, or are such results impossible? How might we prove limitations on equilibrium tractability?

These questions are in the wheelhouse of computational complexity theory. Why is it so easy to come up with polynomial-time algorithms for the minimum-spanning tree problem and so difficult to come up with one for the traveling salesman problem? Could it be that no efficient algorithm for the latter problem exists? If so, how can we prove it? If we can't prove it, how can we nevertheless amass evidence of computational intractability? These questions are addressed by the theory of $\mathcal{NP}$-completeness. This lecture and the next assume basic knowledge of this theory and describe analogs of $\mathcal{NP}$-completeness for equilibrium computation problems.

19.2 Local Search Problems

This section is a detour into a branch of complexity theory designed to reason about local search problems. The resulting theory is perfectly suited to provide evidence of the inherent intractability of computing a PNE of an atomic selfish routing game. Briefly, the connection is that computing a PNE of such a game is equivalent to computing a local minimum of the potential function defined in (13.7).

19.2.1 Canonical Example: The Maximum Cut Problem

A canonical problem through which to study local search is the *maximum cut* problem. The input is an undirected graph $G = (V, E)$ with a nonnegative weight $w_e \geq 0$ for each edge $e \in E$. Feasible solutions correspond to *cuts* $(X, \overline{X})$, where $(X, \overline{X})$ is a partition of V into two sets. The objective is to maximize the total weight of the cut edges, meaning the edges with one endpoint in each of X and $\overline{X}$.[2] The maximum cut problem is $\mathcal{NP}$-hard, so assuming that $\mathcal{P} \neq \mathcal{NP}$, there is no polynomial-time algorithm that solves it.

Local search is a natural heuristic that is useful for many $\mathcal{NP}$-hard problems, including the maximum cut problem. The algorithm is very simple.

Local Search for Maximum Cut

initialize with an arbitrary cut $(X, \overline{X})$
while there is an improving local move **do**
   take an arbitrary such move

By a *local move*, we mean moving a single vertex v from one side of the cut to the other. For example, when moving a vertex v from X to $\overline{X}$, the increase in objective function value is

$$\underbrace{\sum_{u \in X \,:\, (u,v) \in E} w_{uv}}_{\text{newly cut}} - \underbrace{\sum_{u \in \overline{X} \,:\, (u,v) \in E} w_{uv}}_{\text{newly uncut}}. \qquad (19.1)$$

If the difference in (19.1) is positive, then this is an *improving* local move. Local search stops at a solution with no improving local move, a *local optimum*. A local optimum need not be a global optimum (Figure 19.2).

We can visualize local search as a walk in a directed graph H (Figure 19.3). For a maximum cut instance with input graph G, vertices of H correspond to cuts of G. Each directed edge of H represents an improving local move from one cut to another. There can be no cycle of such moves, so H is a directed acyclic graph. Vertices with no outgoing edges—*sink vertices* of the graph H—correspond to the local optima. Local search repeatedly follows outgoing edges of H until it reaches a sink vertex.

Since there are only more local optima than global optima, they are only easier to find. For example, consider the special case of maximum cut instances in which every edge has weight 1. Computing

---

[2]Graph cuts are usually defined with the additional restriction that both sides are nonempty. Permitting empty cuts as feasible solutions does not change the maximum cut problem.

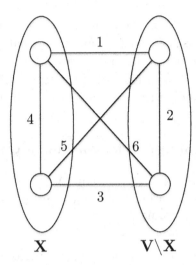

$$\mathbf{X} \qquad\qquad \mathbf{V \backslash X}$$

Figure 19.2: A local maximum of a maximum cut instance that is not a global maximum. The cut $(X, V \setminus X)$ has objective function value 15, and every local move results in a cut with smaller objective function value. The maximum cut value is 17.

a global maximum remains an $\mathcal{NP}$-hard problem, but computing a local maximum is easy. Because the objective function in this case can only take on values in the set $\{0, 1, 2, \ldots, |E|\}$, local search stops (at a local maximum) within at most $|E|$ iterations.

There is no known polynomial-time algorithm, based on local search or otherwise, for computing a local optimum of a maximum cut instance with arbitrary nonnegative edge weights. How might we amass evidence that no such algorithm exists?

The strongest negative result would be an "unconditional" one, meaning a proof with no unproven assumptions that there is no polynomial-time algorithm for the problem. No one knows how to prove unconditional results like this, and such a result would separate $\mathcal{P}$ from $\mathcal{NP}$. The natural next goal is to prove that the problem is $\mathcal{NP}$-hard, and therefore admits a polynomial-time algorithm only if $\mathcal{P} = \mathcal{NP}$. Lecture 20 explains why this is also too strong a negative result to shoot for. Instead, we develop an analog of $\mathcal{NP}$-completeness tailored to local search problems. As a by-product, we also obtain strong unconditional lower bounds on the worst-case number of iterations required by local search to reach a local optimum.

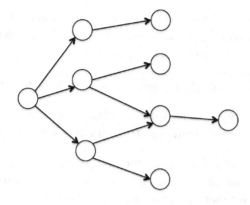

improving objective function value - - - - - - - - - - - - - ➤

Figure 19.3:   Local search can be visualized as a walk in a directed acyclic graph. Vertices correspond to feasible solutions, edges to improving local moves, and sink vertices to local minima.

19.2.2 $\mathcal{PLS}$: Abstract Local Search Problems

This section and the next make precise the idea that the problem of computing a local optimum of a maximum cut instance is *as hard as any other local search problem*. This statement is in the spirit of an $\mathcal{NP}$-completeness result, which establishes that a problem is as hard as any problem with efficiently verifiable solutions. For such "hardest" local search problems, we don't expect any clever, problem-dependent algorithms that always improve significantly over local search. This parallels the idea that for $\mathcal{NP}$-complete problems, we don't expect any algorithms that always improve significantly over brute-force search.

What could we mean by "any other local search problem?" For an analogy, recall that an $\mathcal{NP}$ problem is defined by a polynomial-time verifier of alleged solutions to a given instance, like truth assignments to the variables of a logical formula or potential Hamiltonian cycles of a graph. In some sense, an efficient verifier of purported solutions is the minimal ingredient necessary to execute brute-force search through all possible solutions, and $\mathcal{NP}$ is the class of problems that admit such a brute-force search procedure. So what are the minimal ingredients necessary to run local search?

An abstract local search problem can be a maximization or a minimization problem. One is specified by three algorithms, each running in time polynomial in the input size.

Ingredients of an Abstract Local Search Problem

1. The first polynomial-time algorithm takes as input an instance and outputs an arbitrary feasible solution.

2. The second polynomial-time algorithm takes as input an instance and a feasible solution, and returns the objective function value of the solution.

3. The third polynomial-time algorithm takes as input an instance and a feasible solution and either reports "locally optimal" or produces a solution with better objective function value.[3]

For example, in the maximum cut problem, the first algorithm can just output an arbitrary cut. The second algorithm computes the total weight of the edges crossing the given cut. The third algorithm checks all $|V|$ local moves. If none are improving, it outputs "locally optimal"; otherwise, it takes some improving local move and outputs the resulting cut.

Every abstract local search problem admits a local search procedure that uses the given three algorithms as subroutines in the obvious way. Given an instance, the generic local search procedure uses the first algorithm to obtain an initial solution, and iteratively applies the third algorithm until a local optima solution is reached.[4]

---

[3]We're glossing over some details. For example, all algorithms should check if the given input is a legitimate encoding of an instance. There is also some canonical interpretation when an algorithm misbehaves, by running too long or outputting something invalid. For example, we can interpret the output of the third algorithm as "locally optimal" unless it outputs a feasible solution better than the previous one, as verified by the second algorithm, within a specified polynomial number of steps. These details guarantee that a generic local search procedure, which uses these three algorithms only as "black boxes," eventually stops with a local optimum.

[4]The purpose of the second algorithm is to keep the third algorithm honest, and ensure that each solution produced does indeed have better objective function value than the previous one. If the third algorithm fails to produce an improved solution, the generic procedure can interpret its output as "locally optimal."

Since the objective function values of the candidate solutions strictly improve until a local optima solution is found, and since there is only a finite number of feasible solutions, this procedure eventually stops.[5] As in the maximum cut problem, this local search procedure can be visualized as a walk in a directed acyclic graph (Figure 19.3)—the first algorithm identifies the starting vertex, and the third algorithm the sequence of outgoing edges. Because the number of feasible solutions can be exponential in the input size, this local search procedure could require more than a polynomial number of iterations to complete.

The goal in an abstract local search problem is to compute a local optimum, or equivalently to find a sink vertex of the corresponding directed acyclic graph. This can be done by running the generic local search procedure, but any correct algorithm for computing a local optimum is also allowed. The complexity class $\mathcal{PLS}$ is, by definition, the set of all such abstract local search problems.[6] Most if not all of the local search problems that you've ever seen can be cast as problems in $\mathcal{PLS}$.

19.2.3 $\mathcal{PLS}$-Completeness

Our goal is to prove that the problem of computing a local optimum of a maximum cut instance is as hard as any other local search problem. Having formalized "any other search problem," we now formalize the phrase "as hard as." This is done using polynomial-time reductions, as in the theory of $\mathcal{NP}$-completeness.

Formally, a *reduction* from a problem $L_1 \in \mathcal{PLS}$ to a problem $L_2 \in \mathcal{PLS}$ consists of two polynomial-time algorithms with the following properties.

A $\mathcal{PLS}$ Reduction

1. Algorithm $\mathcal{A}_1$ maps every instance $x \in L_1$ to an instance $\mathcal{A}_1(x) \in L_2$.

2. Algorithm $\mathcal{A}_2$ maps every local optimum of $\mathcal{A}_1(x)$ to a local optimum of x.

---

[5]The three algorithms run in polynomial time, which implicitly forces feasible solutions to have polynomial description length. Hence, there are at most exponentially many feasible solutions.

[6]The letters in $\mathcal{PLS}$ stand for "polynomial local search."

The definition of a reduction ensures that if we can solve the problem L_2 in polynomial time then, by combining the solution with algorithms $\mathcal{A}_1$ and $\mathcal{A}_2$, we can also solve the problem L_1 in polynomial time (Figure 19.4).

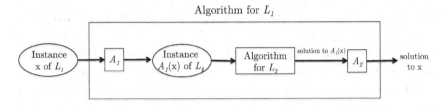

Figure 19.4: A reduction from L_1 to L_2 transfers solvability from $\mathcal{PLS}$ problem L_2 to $\mathcal{PLS}$ problem L_1.

Definition 19.1 ($\mathcal{PLS}$-Complete Problem) A problem L is $\mathcal{PLS}$-*complete* if $L \in \mathcal{PLS}$ and every problem in $\mathcal{PLS}$ reduces to it.

By definition, there is a polynomial-time algorithm for solving a $\mathcal{PLS}$-complete problem if and only if every $\mathcal{PLS}$ problem can be solved in polynomial time.[7]

A $\mathcal{PLS}$-complete problem is a *single* local search problem that simultaneously encodes *every* local search problem. If we didn't already have the remarkable theory of $\mathcal{NP}$-completeness to guide us, we might not believe that a $\mathcal{PLS}$-complete problem could exist. But just like $\mathcal{NP}$-complete problems, $\mathcal{PLS}$-complete problems *do* exist. Even more remarkably, many natural and practically relevant problems are $\mathcal{PLS}$-complete, including the maximum cut problem.

Theorem 19.2 (Maximum Cut is $\mathcal{PLS}$-Complete) *Computing a local maximum of a maximum cut instance with general nonnegative edge weights is a $\mathcal{PLS}$-complete problem.*

The proof of Theorem 19.2 is difficult and outside the scope of this book (see the Notes).

---

[7]Most researchers believe that $\mathcal{PLS}$-complete problems cannot be solved in polynomial time, though confidence is not quite as strong as for the $\mathcal{P} \neq \mathcal{NP}$ conjecture.

We already mentioned the conditional result that, unless every $\mathcal{PLS}$ problem can be solved in polynomial time, there is no polynomial-time algorithm, based on local search or otherwise, for any $\mathcal{PLS}$-complete problem. Independent of whether or not all $\mathcal{PLS}$ problems can be solved in polynomial time, the proof of Theorem 19.2 implies that the specific algorithm of local search requires exponential time in the worst case.

Theorem 19.3 (Lower Bounds for Local Search) *Computing a local maximum of a maximum cut instance with general nonnegative edge weights using local search can require an exponential (in $|V|$) number of iterations, no matter how an improving local move is chosen in each iteration.*

19.3   Computing a PNE of a Congestion Game

19.3.1   Computing a PNE as a $\mathcal{PLS}$ Problem

Section 13.2.3 introduces *congestion games* as a natural generalization of atomic selfish routing games in which strategies are arbitrary subsets of a ground set, rather than paths in a graph. Thus a congestion game is described by a set E of resources (previously, the edges), an explicitly described strategy set $S_i \subseteq 2^E$ for each agent $i = 1, 2, \ldots, k$ (previously, the o_i-d_i paths), and the possible costs $c_e(1), \ldots, c_e(k)$ for each resource $e \in E$. The cost $C_i(\mathbf{s})$ of an agent in an outcome $\mathbf{s}$ remains the sum $\sum_{e \in s_i} c_e(n_e(\mathbf{s}))$ of the costs of the resources she uses, where $n_e(\mathbf{s})$ denotes the number of agents in the outcome $\mathbf{s}$ that use a strategy that includes the resource e.

All of our major results for atomic selfish routing games (Theorems 12.3, 13.6 and 16.3) hold more generally, with exactly the same proofs, for the analogous classes of congestion games. In particular, every congestion game is a potential game (Section 13.3) with the potential function

$$\Phi(\mathbf{s}) = \sum_{e \in E} \sum_{i=1}^{n_e(\mathbf{s})} c_e(i) \tag{19.2}$$

satisfying

$$\Phi(s_i', \mathbf{s}_{-i}) - \Phi(\mathbf{s}) = C_i(s_i', \mathbf{s}_{-i}) - C_i(\mathbf{s}) \tag{19.3}$$

for every outcome **s**, agent i, and unilateral deviation s_i' by i.

We claim that the problem of computing a PNE of a congestion game is a $\mathcal{PLS}$ problem. This follows from the correspondence between best-response dynamics (Section 16.1) in a congestion game and local search with respect to the potential function (19.2). Proving the claim formally involves describing the three polynomial-time algorithms that define a $\mathcal{PLS}$ problem. The first algorithm takes as input a congestion game, described via agents' strategy sets and the resource cost functions, and returns an arbitrary outcome, such as the one in which each agent chooses her first strategy. The second algorithm takes a congestion game and an outcome **s**, and returns the value of the potential function (19.2). The third algorithm checks whether or not the given outcome is a PNE, by considering each unilateral deviation of each agent.[8] If so, it reports "locally optimal"; if not, it executes an iteration of best-response dynamics and returns the resulting outcome, which by (19.3) has a smaller potential function value.

19.3.2   Computing a PNE is a $\mathcal{PLS}$-Complete Problem

Computing a PNE of a congestion game is as hard as every other local search problem.[9]

Theorem 19.4 (Computing a PNE is $\mathcal{PLS}$-Complete) *The problem of computing a PNE of a congestion game is $\mathcal{PLS}$-complete.*

Proof: Since reductions are transitive, we only need to exhibit a reduction from some $\mathcal{PLS}$-complete problem to the problem of computing a PNE of a congestion game. We give a reduction from the problem of computing a local maximum of a maximum cut instance, which is $\mathcal{PLS}$-complete (Theorem 19.2).

The first polynomial-time algorithm $\mathcal{A}_1$ of the reduction is given as input a graph $G = (V, E)$ with nonnegative edge weights $\{w_e\}_{e \in E}$. The algorithm constructs the following congestion game.

---

[8]Because the strategy set of each agent is given explicitly as part of the input, this algorithm runs in time polynomial in the length of the game's description.

[9]Changing the goal to computing all PNE or a PNE that meets additional criteria can only result in a harder problem (e.g., Exercise 19.3). Intractability results are most compelling for the easier problem of computing an arbitrary PNE.

1. Agents correspond to the vertices V.

2. There are two resources for each edge $e \in E$, r_e and $\bar{r}_e$.

3. Agent v has two strategies, each comprising $|\delta(v)|$ resources, where $\delta(v)$ is the set of edges incident to v in G: $\{r_e\}_{e \in \delta(v)}$ and $\{\bar{r}_e\}_{e \in \delta(v)}$.

4. A resource r_e or $\bar{r}_e$ with $e = (u, v)$ can only be used by the agents corresponding to u and v. The cost of such a resource is 0 if used by only one agent, and w_e if used by two agents.

This construction can be carried out in polynomial time.

The key point is that the PNE of this congestion game are in one-to-one correspondence with the local optima of the given maximum cut problem. We prove this using a bijection between the $2^{|V|}$ outcomes of this congestion game and cuts of the graph G, where the cut $(X, \overline{X})$ corresponds to the outcome in which every agent corresponding to $v \in X$ (respectively, $v \in \overline{X}$) chooses her strategy that contains resources of the form r_e (respectively, $\bar{r}_e$).

This bijection maps cuts $(X, \overline{X})$ of G with weight $w(X, \overline{X})$ to outcomes with potential function value (19.2) equal to $W - w(X, \overline{X})$, where $W = \sum_{e \in E} w_e$ denotes the sum of the edges' weights. To see this, fix a cut $(X, \overline{X})$. For an edge e cut by $(X, \overline{X})$, each resource r_e and $\bar{r}_e$ is used by only one agent and hence contributes 0 to (19.2). For an edge e not cut by $(X, \overline{X})$, two agents use one of $r_e, \bar{r}_e$ and none use the other. These two resources contribute w_e and 0 to (19.2) in this case. We conclude that the potential function value of the corresponding outcome is the total weight of the edges not cut by $(X, \overline{X})$, or $W - w(X, \overline{X})$.

Cuts of G with larger weight thus correspond to outcomes with smaller potential function value, so locally maximum cuts of G are in one-to-one correspondence with the local minima of the potential function. By (19.3), the local minima of the potential function are in one-to-one correspondence with the PNE of the congestion game.

The second algorithm $\mathcal{A}_2$ of the reduction simply translates a PNE of the congestion game constructed by $\mathcal{A}_1$ to the corresponding locally maximum cut of G. ∎

The reduction in the proof of Theorem 19.4 establishes a one-to-one correspondence between improving moves in a maximum cut instance and beneficial unilateral deviations in the constructed congestion game. Thus, the unconditional lower bound on the number of iterations required for local search to converge in the maximum cut problem (Theorem 19.3) translates to a lower bound on the number of iterations required by best-response dynamics to converge in a congestion game.

Corollary 19.5 (Lower Bound for Best-Response Dynamics)
Computing a PNE of a k-agent congestion game using best-response dynamics can require an exponential (in k) number of iterations, no matter how a beneficial unilateral deviation is chosen in each iteration.

Lower bounds like Corollary 19.5 are often much easier to prove via reductions than from scratch.

19.3.3   Symmetric Congestion Games

We conclude this lecture with another reduction that extends Theorem 19.4 and Corollary 19.5 to the special case of *symmetric* congestion games, where every agent has the same set of strategies. Such games generalize atomic selfish routing games in which all agents have a common origin vertex and a common destination vertex.[10]

Theorem 19.6 ($\mathcal{PLS}$-Completeness in Symmetric Games)
The problem of computing a PNE of a symmetric congestion game is $\mathcal{PLS}$-complete.

As with Corollary 19.5, the proof of Theorem 19.6 implies unconditional lower bounds on the number of iterations required for convergence in best-response dynamics (Exercise 19.4).

Corollary 19.7 (Lower Bound for Best-Response Dynamics)
Computing a PNE of a k-agent symmetric congestion game using best-response dynamics can require an exponential (in k) number of iterations, no matter how a beneficial unilateral deviation is chosen in each iteration.

---

[10]The problem of computing a PNE of a symmetric atomic selfish routing game can be solved in polynomial time (Problem 19.1), so it is probably not $\mathcal{PLS}$-complete.

Why don't Theorem 19.6 and Corollary 19.7 contradict Theorem 16.3, which states that ϵ-best-response dynamics converges quickly in symmetric congestion games? The reason is that ϵ-best-response dynamics only converges to an approximate PNE, while Theorem 19.6 asserts the intractability of computing an exact PNE.[11] Thus, Theorem 19.6 and Corollary 19.7 provide an interesting separation between the tractability of exact and approximate PNE, and between the convergence properties of best-response and ϵ-best-response dynamics, in symmetric congestion games.

Proof of Theorem 19.6: We reduce the problem of computing a PNE of a general congestion game, which is $\mathcal{PLS}$-complete (Theorem 19.4), to that of computing a PNE of a symmetric congestion game. Given a general congestion game with resources E and k agents with arbitrary strategy sets $S_1, \ldots, S_k$, the first polynomial-time algorithm $\mathcal{A}_1$ of the reduction constructs a "symmetrized" version. The agent set remains the same. The new resource set is $E \cup \{r_1, \ldots, r_k\}$. Resources of E retain their cost functions. The cost function of each new resource r_i is defined to be zero if used by only one agent, and extremely large if used by two or more. Each strategy of S_i is supplemented by the resource r_i, and any agent can use any one of these augmented strategies. That is, the common strategy set of all agents is $\{s_i \cup \{r_i\} : i \in \{1, 2, \ldots, k\}, s_i \in S_i\}$. We can think of an agent choosing a strategy containing resource r_i as adopting the identity of agent i in the original game. The key insight is that at a PNE of the constructed symmetric game, each agent adopts the identity of exactly one agent of the original game. This is due to the large penalty incurred by two agents that choose strategies that share one of the new resources. The algorithm $\mathcal{A}_2$ can easily map such a PNE to a PNE of the original congestion game, completing the reduction. ∎

The Upshot

☆ Simple and natural dynamics converge quickly to approximate CCE and approximate CE in arbitrary games, to approximate MNE in two-

---

[11] Our proof of Theorem 19.6 also violates the α-bounded jump assumption made in Theorem 16.3, but the proof can be modified to respect this condition.

player zero-sum games, and to approximate PNE in symmetric congestion games.

☆ Designing an algorithm that computes an (approximate) equilibrium quickly is a weaker goal than proving fast convergence of simple dynamics.

☆ $\mathcal{PLS}$ is the class of abstract local search problems, and it includes the problems of computing a locally maximum graph cut and of computing a PNE of a congestion game.

☆ A problem is $\mathcal{PLS}$-complete if every problem in $\mathcal{PLS}$ reduces to it.

☆ There is a polynomial-time algorithm for a $\mathcal{PLS}$-complete problem if and only if every $\mathcal{PLS}$ problem can be solved in polynomial time. Most experts believe that $\mathcal{PLS}$-complete problems cannot be solved in polynomial time.

☆ Computing a PNE of a congestion game is a $\mathcal{PLS}$-complete problem, even in the special case of symmetric congestion games.

☆ Best-response dynamics can require an exponential number of iterations to converge to a PNE in a congestion game, even in the special case of a symmetric congestion game.

Notes

Garey and Johnson (1979) is an accessible introduction to the theory of $\mathcal{NP}$-completeness; see also Roughgarden (2010b) for examples germane to algorithmic game theory. The definition of the complexity class $\mathcal{PLS}$ is due to Johnson et al. (1988), who also provided several examples of $\mathcal{PLS}$-complete problems and proved unconditional lower bounds on the worst-case number of iterations required by local search to compute a local optimum in these problems. Theorems 19.2 and 19.3 are proved in Schäffer and Yannakakis (1991). All of the results in Section 19.3, and also Problem 19.1(a), are from Fabrikant et al. (2004). Problem 19.1(b) is from Fotakis (2010). Fabrikant et al. (2004) also show that computing a PNE of an atomic selfish routing game with multiple origins and destinations is a $\mathcal{PLS}$-complete problem. Skopalik and Vöcking (2008) show that, in general atomic selfish routing games, Theorem 19.4 and Corollary 19.5 hold even for the problem of computing an ϵ-PNE and for ϵ-best-response dynamics, respectively. The problem of computing an exact or approximate correlated equilibrium in time polynomial in the number of agents (cf., Exercises 19.1–19.2) is addressed by Papadimitriou and Roughgarden (2008) and Jiang and Leyton-Brown (2015) for compactly represented games like congestion games, and by Hart and Nisan (2013) for general games.

Exercises

Exercise 19.1 Assume for this exercise that an optimal solution to a linear program, if one exists, can be computed in time polynomial in the size of the linear program's description. Use this fact and Problem 18.3 to give an algorithm for computing the correlated equilibrium of a general cost-minimization game with the minimum expected sum of agents' costs. Your algorithm should run in time polynomial in the description length of the game.

Exercise 19.2 *(H)* Does Exercise 19.1 imply that a correlated equilibrium of a congestion game can be computed in time polynomial in the game's description?

Exercise 19.3 *(H)* Prove that the following problem is $\mathcal{NP}$-complete: given a description of a general congestion game and a real-valued target τ, decide whether or not the game has a PNE with cost at most τ.

Exercise 19.4 Explain why the reduction in the proof of Theorem 19.6 implies Corollary 19.7.

Exercise 19.5 Given a general atomic selfish routing game with origins $o_1, \ldots, o_k$ and destinations $d_1, \ldots, d_k$, construct a symmetric such game by adding new origin and destination vertices o and d, and new directed edges $(o, o_1), \ldots, (o, o_k)$ and $(d_1, d), \ldots, (d_k, d)$, each with a cost function that is zero with one agent and extremely large with two or more agents.

Why doesn't this idea lead to a reduction, analogous to that in the proof of Theorem 19.6, from the problem of computing a PNE of a general atomic selfish routing game to that of computing a PNE of a symmetric such game?

Problems

Problem 19.1 This problem considers atomic selfish routing networks with a common origin vertex o and a common destination vertex d.

(a) *(H)* Prove that a PNE can be computed in time polynomial in the description length of the game. As usual, assume that each edge cost function is nondecreasing.

(b) *(H)* Suppose the network is just a collection of parallel edges from o to d, with no other vertices. Prove a converse to Theorem 13.6: every equilibrium flow minimizes the potential function (13.6).

(c) Show by example that (b) does not hold in general networks with a common origin vertex and a common destination vertex.

Mixed Nash Equilibria and $\mathcal{PPAD}$-Completeness

This lecture continues our study of the limitations of learning dynamics and polynomial-time algorithms for converging to and computing equilibria, with a focus on mixed Nash equilibria (MNE). The theory of $\mathcal{PPAD}$-completeness, which resembles that of $\mathcal{PLS}$-completeness except for certain details, provides evidence that the problem of computing a MNE of a general two-player game is computationally intractable. This suggests that the positive results in Lecture 18 for two-player zero-sum games cannot be extended to a significantly larger class of games.

Section 20.1 formally defines the problem of computing a MNE of a bimatrix game. Section 20.2 explains why $\mathcal{NP}$-completeness is not the right intractability notion for the problem, or for the $\mathcal{PLS}$ problems studied in Lecture 19. Section 20.3 formally defines the complexity class $\mathcal{PPAD}$, the class for which computing a MNE is a complete problem. Section 20.4 describes a canonical $\mathcal{PPAD}$ problem inspired by Sperner's lemma, while Section 20.5 explains why computing a MNE of a bimatrix game is a $\mathcal{PPAD}$ problem. Section 20.6 discusses the ramifications of the $\mathcal{PPAD}$-completeness of this problem.

20.1 Computing a MNE of a Bimatrix Game

A two-player game that is not necessarily zero-sum is called a *bimatrix* game. A bimatrix game can be specified by two $m \times n$ payoff matrices $\mathbf{A}$ and $\mathbf{B}$, one for the row player, one for the column player. In zero-sum games, $\mathbf{B} = -\mathbf{A}$. We consider the problem of computing a mixed Nash equilibrium (MNE) of a bimatrix game, or equivalently mixed strategies $\hat{\mathbf{x}}$ and $\hat{\mathbf{y}}$ over the rows and columns such that

$$\hat{\mathbf{x}}^\top \mathbf{A} \hat{\mathbf{y}} \geq \mathbf{x}^\top \mathbf{A} \hat{\mathbf{y}} \tag{20.1}$$

for all row mixed strategies $\mathbf{x}$ and

$$\hat{\mathbf{x}}^\top \mathbf{B}\hat{\mathbf{y}} \geq \hat{\mathbf{x}}^\top \mathbf{B}\mathbf{y} \tag{20.2}$$

for all column mixed strategies $\mathbf{y}$.

There is no known polynomial-time algorithm for computing a MNE of a bimatrix game, despite significant effort by many experts. This lecture develops the appropriate complexity theory for arguing that the problem may be inherently intractable. The goal is to prove that the problem is complete for a suitable complexity class. But which class? Before providing the solution in Section 20.3, Section 20.2 explains why plain old $\mathcal{NP}$-completeness is not the right intractability notion for equilibrium computation problems.

20.2 Total $\mathcal{NP}$ Search Problems ($\mathcal{TFNP}$)

20.2.1 $\mathcal{NP}$ Search Problems ($\mathcal{FNP}$)

An $\mathcal{NP}$ problem is defined by a polynomial-time verifier of alleged solutions to a given instance, and the inputs accepted by the verifier are called the *witnesses* for the instance. $\mathcal{NP}$ problems are traditionally defined as decision problems, where the correct answer to an instance is either "yes" or "no," depending on whether or not the instance has at least one witness.

Equilibrium computation problems are not decision problems, as the output should be a bona fide equilibrium. To address this typechecking error, we work with the complexity class $\mathcal{FNP}$, which stands for "functional $\mathcal{NP}$." $\mathcal{FNP}$ problems are just like $\mathcal{NP}$ problems except that, for "yes" instances, a witness must be produced. These are also called *search* problems.

An algorithm for a $\mathcal{FNP}$ problem takes as input an instance of an $\mathcal{NP}$ problem, like an encoding of a logical formula or an undirected graph. The responsibility of the algorithm is to output a witness for the instance, like a satisfying truth assignment or a Hamiltonian cycle, provided one exists. If no witnesses exist for the instance, then the algorithm should output "no." $\mathcal{FP}$ denotes the subclass of $\mathcal{FNP}$ problems that can be solved by a polynomial-time algorithm.

A reduction from one search problem L_1 to another one L_2 is defined as in Section 19.2.3 via two polynomial-time algorithms, the first algorithm $\mathcal{A}_1$ mapping instances x of L_1 to instances $\mathcal{A}_1(x)$ of

L_2, the second algorithm $\mathcal{A}_2$ mapping witnesses of $\mathcal{A}_1(x)$ to witnesses of x (and "no" to "no").[1]

The class $\mathcal{PLS}$ of local search problems, defined in Section 19.2, is a subset of $\mathcal{FNP}$. The witnesses of an instance of a $\mathcal{PLS}$ problem are its local optima, and the third algorithm in the $\mathcal{PLS}$ problem description acts as an efficient verifier of witnesses. In fact, the third algorithm of a $\mathcal{PLS}$ problem does considerably more than is asked of an $\mathcal{NP}$ verifier. When this algorithm is given a solution that is not locally optimal, it does not merely say "no," and instead offers an alternative solution with superior objective function value.

The problem of computing a MNE of a bimatrix game also belongs to $\mathcal{FNP}$. This assertion boils down to an efficient solution to the problem of checking whether or not given mixed strategies $\hat{\mathbf{x}}$ and $\hat{\mathbf{y}}$ of a given bimatrix game $(\mathbf{A}, \mathbf{B})$ constitute a MNE. While the equilibrium conditions (20.1) and (20.2) reference an infinite number of mixed strategies, it is enough to check only the pure-strategy deviations (cf., Exercise 13.1), and this can be done in polynomial time.[2]

20.2.2 $\mathcal{NP}$ Search Problems with Guaranteed Witnesses

Could computing a MNE of a bimatrix game be $\mathcal{FNP}$-complete? Being as hard as every problem in $\mathcal{FNP}$ would constitute strong evidence of intractability. Intriguingly, $\mathcal{FNP}$-completeness would have astonishing consequences.

Theorem 20.1 (Computing a MNE Not $\mathcal{FNP}$-Complete)
The problem of computing a MNE of a bimatrix game is not $\mathcal{FNP}$-complete unless $\mathcal{NP} = co\mathcal{NP}$.

While $\mathcal{NP} = co\mathcal{NP}$ doesn't immediately imply that $\mathcal{P} = \mathcal{NP}$, experts regard it as an equally unlikely state of affairs. For example, if $\mathcal{NP} = co\mathcal{NP}$, then the $co\mathcal{NP}$-complete unsatisfiability problem has short and efficiently verifiable proofs of membership. Convincing someone that a formula in propositional logic is satisfiable is easy

---

[1]Intuition for the class $\mathcal{NP}$ works fine for $\mathcal{FNP}$. For example, the proofs showing that the decision version of the satisfiability problem (SAT) is $\mathcal{NP}$-complete also show that the functional version of SAT is $\mathcal{FNP}$-complete.
[2]To be completely rigorous, we also need to argue that there is a MNE whose description length (in bits) is polynomial in that of $\mathbf{A}$ and $\mathbf{B}$ (Exercise 20.1).

enough—just exhibit a satisfying truth assignment. But how would you quickly convince someone that none of the exponentially many truth assignments satisfy a formula? Most researchers believe that there is no way to do it, or equivalently that $\mathcal{NP} \neq co\mathcal{NP}$. If this is indeed the case, then Theorem 20.1 implies that the problem of computing a MNE of a bimatrix game is not $\mathcal{FNP}$-complete.

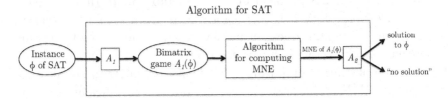

Figure 20.1: A reduction from the functional SAT problem to the problem of computing a MNE of a bimatrix game. Such a reduction would yield a polynomial-time verifier for the unsatisfiability problem.

Proof of Theorem 20.1: The proof is short but a bit of a mind-bender. Suppose there is a reduction, in the same sense of the $\mathcal{PLS}$ reductions described in Section 19.2.3, from the functional SAT problem to the problem of computing a MNE of a bimatrix game. By definition, the reduction comprises two algorithms:

1. A polynomial-time algorithm $\mathcal{A}_1$ that maps every SAT formula ϕ to a bimatrix game $\mathcal{A}_1(\phi)$.

2. A polynomial-time algorithm $\mathcal{A}_2$ that maps every MNE $(\hat{\mathbf{x}}, \hat{\mathbf{y}})$ of a game $\mathcal{A}_1(\phi)$ to a satisfying assignment $\mathcal{A}_2(\hat{\mathbf{x}}, \hat{\mathbf{y}})$ of ϕ, if one exists, and to the string "no" otherwise.

See also Figure 20.1.

We claim that the existence of these algorithms $\mathcal{A}_1$ and $\mathcal{A}_2$ imply that $\mathcal{NP} = co\mathcal{NP}$. In proof, consider an unsatisfiable SAT formula ϕ, and an arbitrary MNE $(\hat{\mathbf{x}}, \hat{\mathbf{y}})$ of the game $\mathcal{A}_1(\phi)$.[3] We claim that $(\hat{\mathbf{x}}, \hat{\mathbf{y}})$ is a short, efficiently verifiable proof of the unsatisfiability of ϕ, implying that $\mathcal{NP} = co\mathcal{NP}$. Given an alleged certificate $(\hat{\mathbf{x}}, \hat{\mathbf{y}})$ that ϕ is unsatisfiable, the verifier performs two checks: (1) compute the

---

[3]Crucially, $\mathcal{A}_1(\phi)$ has at least one MNE (Theorem 20.5), including one whose description length is polynomial in that of the game (Exercise 20.1).

game $\mathcal{A}_1(\phi)$ using algorithm $\mathcal{A}_1$ and verify that $(\hat{\mathbf{x}}, \hat{\mathbf{y}})$ is a MNE of $\mathcal{A}_1(\phi)$; (2) use the algorithm $\mathcal{A}_2$ to verify that $\mathcal{A}_2(\hat{\mathbf{x}}, \hat{\mathbf{y}})$ is the string "no." This verifier runs in time polynomial in the description lengths of ϕ and $(\hat{\mathbf{x}}, \hat{\mathbf{y}})$. If $(\hat{\mathbf{x}}, \hat{\mathbf{y}})$ passes both of these tests, then correctness of the algorithms $\mathcal{A}_1$ and $\mathcal{A}_2$ implies that ϕ is unsatisfiable. ∎

What's really going on in the proof of Theorem 20.1 is a mismatch between a $\mathcal{FNP}$-complete problem like the functional version of SAT, where an instance may or may not have a witness, and a problem like computing a MNE, where every instance has at least one witness. While the correct answer to a SAT instance might well be "no," a correct answer to an instance of MNE computation is always a MNE.

The subset of $\mathcal{FNP}$ problems for which every instance has at least one witness is called $\mathcal{TFNP}$, for "total functional $\mathcal{NP}$." The proof of Theorem 20.1 shows more generally that if *any* $\mathcal{TFNP}$ problem is $\mathcal{FNP}$-complete, then $\mathcal{NP} = co\mathcal{NP}$. In particular, since every instance of a $\mathcal{PLS}$ problem has at least one witness—local search has to stop somewhere, necessarily at a local optimum—$\mathcal{PLS}$ is a subset of $\mathcal{TFNP}$. Hence no $\mathcal{PLS}$ problem, such as computing a PNE of a congestion game, can be $\mathcal{FNP}$-complete unless $\mathcal{NP} = co\mathcal{NP}$.

Theorem 20.2 ($\mathcal{PLS}$ Problems Not $\mathcal{FNP}$-Complete)
No $\mathcal{PLS}$ problem is $\mathcal{FNP}$-complete, unless $\mathcal{NP} = co\mathcal{NP}$.

Theorem 20.2 justifies the development in Lecture 19 of $\mathcal{PLS}$-completeness, a weaker analog of $\mathcal{FNP}$-completeness tailored for local search problems.

20.2.3   Syntactic vs. Semantic Complexity Classes

Membership in $\mathcal{TFNP}$ precludes proving that computing a MNE of a bimatrix game is $\mathcal{FNP}$-complete (unless $\mathcal{NP} = co\mathcal{NP}$). The sensible refined goal is to prove that the problem is $\mathcal{TFNP}$-complete, and hence as hard as any other problem in $\mathcal{TFNP}$.

Unfortunately, $\mathcal{TFNP}$-completeness is also too ambitious a goal. The reason is that $\mathcal{TFNP}$ does not seem to have complete problems. To explain, think about the complexity classes that *are* known to have complete problems—$\mathcal{NP}$ of course, and also classes like $\mathcal{P}$ and $\mathcal{PSPACE}$. What do these complexity classes have in common? They are "syntactic," meaning that membership can be characterized via acceptance by some concrete computational model, such as polynomial-time or polynomial-space deterministic or nondeterministic Turing machines. In this sense, there is a generic reason for membership in these complexity classes.

Syntactically defined complexity classes always have a "generic" complete problem, where the input is a description of a problem in terms of the accepting machine and an instance of the problem, and the goal is to solve the given instance of the given problem. For example, the generic $\mathcal{NP}$-complete problem takes as input a description of a verifier, a polynomial time bound, and an encoding of an instance, and the goal is to decide whether or not there is a witness, meaning a string that causes the given verifier to accept the given instance in at most the given number of steps.

$\mathcal{TFNP}$ has no obvious generic reason for membership, and as such is called a "semantic" class.[4] For example, the problem of computing a MNE of a bimatrix game belongs to $\mathcal{TFNP}$ because of the topological arguments that guarantee the existence of a MNE (see Section 20.5). Another problem in $\mathcal{TFNP}$ is factoring: given a positive integer, output its factorization. Here, membership in $\mathcal{TFNP}$ has a number-theoretic explanation. Can the guaranteed existence of a MNE of a game and of a factorization of an integer be regarded as separate instantiations of some "generic" $\mathcal{TFNP}$ argument? No one knows the answer.

20.2.4 Where We're Going

Section 20.3 defines a subclass of $\mathcal{TFNP}$, known as $\mathcal{PPAD}$, that characterizes the computational complexity of computing a MNE of a bimatrix game. Figure 20.2 summarizes the conjectured relationships between $\mathcal{PPAD}$ and the other complexity classes discussed.

The definition of $\mathcal{PPAD}$ is technical and may seem unnatural, but it is justified by the following result.

Theorem 20.3 (Computing a MNE Is $\mathcal{PPAD}$-Complete)
Computing a MNE of a bimatrix game is a $\mathcal{PPAD}$-complete problem.

The known proofs of Theorem 20.3 are much too long and complex to describe here (see the Notes). The remainder of this lecture focuses

---

[4]There are many other interesting examples, such as $\mathcal{NP} \cap co\mathcal{NP}$ (Exercise 20.2).

Complexity Class	Informal Definition
$\mathcal{FP}$	Polynomial-time solvable search problems
$\mathcal{FNP}$	Polynomial-time verifiable witnesses
$\mathcal{TFNP}$	Witnesses guaranteed to exist
$\mathcal{PLS}$	Solvable by local search
$\mathcal{PPAD}$	Solvable by directed path-following

(a) Recap of complexity classes

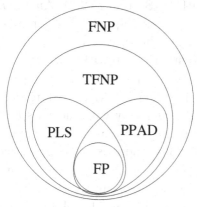

(b) Suspected relationships

Figure 20.2:　Summary of complexity classes. The inclusions $\mathcal{PLS} \cup \mathcal{PPAD} \subseteq \mathcal{TFNP} \subseteq \mathcal{FNP}$ follow from the definitions. Every problem in $\mathcal{FP}$ can be viewed as a degenerate type of $\mathcal{PLS}$ or $\mathcal{PPAD}$ problem by treating the transcript of a correct computation as a legitimate (and efficiently verifiable) witness.

on the definition of and intuition behind the complexity class $\mathcal{PPAD}$, and explains why computing a MNE of a bimatrix game is a $\mathcal{PPAD}$ problem.

*20.3　$\mathcal{PPAD}$: A Syntactic Subclass of $\mathcal{TFNP}$

Our goal is to provide evidence of the computational intractability of the problem of computing a MNE of a bimatrix game by proving that it is complete for a suitable complexity class $\mathcal{C}$, where $\mathcal{C}$ is plausibly a strict superset of $\mathcal{FP}$. Section 20.2 argues that $\mathcal{C}$ needs to be a subset of $\mathcal{TFNP}$ that also has complete problems. Roughly equivalently, the class $\mathcal{C}$ should have a "syntactic" definition, in the form of a generic reason for membership in $\mathcal{TFNP}$.

We already know one example of a subclass of $\mathcal{TFNP}$ that appears larger than $\mathcal{FP}$ and also admits complete problems, namely $\mathcal{PLS}$ (Section 19.2). For example, computing a local optimum of a maximum cut instance is a $\mathcal{PLS}$-complete problem that is not known to be polynomial-time solvable. The definition of $\mathcal{PLS}$ is syntactic in that every $\mathcal{PLS}$ problem is specified by the descriptions of three algorithms (Section 19.2.2). Among $\mathcal{PLS}$ problems, the common reason for membership in $\mathcal{TFNP}$ is that the generic local search procedure, using the three given algorithms as "black boxes," is guaranteed to eventually stop with a witness (a local optimum).

The right complexity class for studying the computation of MNE in bimatrix games is called $\mathcal{PPAD}$.[5] Before defining the class formally, we describe it by analogy with the class $\mathcal{PLS}$, which is similar in spirit but different in the details. The connection to computing MNE is far from obvious, and it is taken up in Section 20.5.

Recall that we can view a local search problem as one of searching a directed acyclic graph for a sink vertex (Figure 19.3). Vertices of this graph correspond to feasible solutions, such as outcomes in a congestion game, and the number of vertices can be exponential in the description length of the instance. Every $\mathcal{PLS}$ problem can be solved by a generic local search procedure that corresponds to following outgoing edges until a sink vertex is reached.

$\mathcal{PPAD}$ problems, like $\mathcal{PLS}$ problems, are those solvable by a particular generic path-following procedure. Every $\mathcal{PPAD}$ problem can be thought of as a directed graph (Figure 20.3), where the vertices again correspond to "solutions" and directed edges to "moves." The essential difference between $\mathcal{PLS}$ and $\mathcal{PPAD}$ is that the graph corresponding to a $\mathcal{PLS}$ problem is directed acyclic, while the graph corresponding to a $\mathcal{PPAD}$ problem is directed with all in- and out-degrees at most 1. Also, by definition, the graph corresponding to a $\mathcal{PPAD}$ problem has a canonical *source* vertex, meaning a vertex with no incoming edges. Traversing outgoing edges starting from the canonical source vertex cannot produce a cycle, since every vertex has in-degree at most 1 and the canonical source vertex has no incoming edges. We conclude that there is a sink vertex reachable from the

---

[5]The letters in $\mathcal{PPAD}$ stand for "polynomial parity argument, directed version."

canonical source vertex. Unlike a $\mathcal{PLS}$ problem, there is no objective function, and a $\mathcal{PPAD}$ directed graph can possess cycles. The witnesses of a $\mathcal{PPAD}$ problem are, by definition, all of the solutions that correspond to a sink vertex or to a source vertex other than the canonical one.

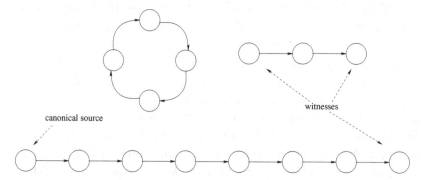

Figure 20.3: A $\mathcal{PPAD}$ problem corresponds to a directed graph with all in- and out-degrees at most 1.

Formally, as with $\mathcal{PLS}$, the class $\mathcal{PPAD}$ is defined syntactically as the problems that can be specified by three algorithms.

Ingredients of a $\mathcal{PPAD}$ Problem

1. The first polynomial-time algorithm takes as input an instance and outputs two distinct solutions, corresponding to the canonical source vertex and its successor.

2. The second polynomial-time algorithm takes as input an instance and a solution x other than the canonical source vertex and its successor, and either returns another solution y, the *predecessor* of x, or declares "no predecessor."

3. The third polynomial-time algorithm takes as input an instance and a solution x other than the canonical source vertex, and either returns another solution y, the *successor* of x, or declares "no successor."

These three algorithms implicitly define a directed graph. The vertices correspond to the possible solutions. There is a directed edge

(x, y) if and only if the second algorithm outputs x as the predecessor of y and the third algorithm agrees that y is the successor of x. There is also a directed edge from the canonical source vertex to its successor, as defined by the first algorithm; this ensures that the canonical source vertex is not also a sink vertex. Every vertex of the graph has in- and out-degree at most 1. The witnesses are all of the solutions that correspond to vertices with in-degree or out-degree 0, other than the canonical source vertex.[6]

Every $\mathcal{PPAD}$ problem has at least one witness, and a witness can be computed by a generic path-following procedure that uses the given three algorithms as "black boxes." This procedure effectively traverses outgoing edges, beginning at the canonical source vertex, until a sink vertex (a witness) is reached.[7] In this sense, the problems in $\mathcal{PPAD}$ have a generic reason for membership in $\mathcal{TFNP}$.

What do $\mathcal{PPAD}$ problems have to do with computing MNE, or anything else for that matter? To get a feel for this complexity class, we next discuss a canonical example of a $\mathcal{PPAD}$ problem.

*20.4   A Canonical $\mathcal{PPAD}$ Problem: Sperner's Lemma

This section presents a computational problem that is clearly well matched with the $\mathcal{PPAD}$ complexity class. Section 20.5 describes its relevance to computing a MNE of a bimatrix game.

Consider a subdivided triangle in the plane (Figure 20.4). A *legal coloring* of its vertices colors the top corner vertex red, the left corner vertex green, and the right corner vertex blue. A vertex on the boundary must have one of the two colors of the endpoints of its side. Internal vertices are allowed to possess any of the three colors. A small triangle is *trichromatic* if all three colors are represented at its vertices.

Sperner's lemma asserts that for every legal coloring, there is at least one trichromatic triangle.[8]

---

[6] As in the definition of a $\mathcal{PLS}$ problem, there is some canonical interpretation when an algorithm misbehaves. For example, the output of the third algorithm is interpreted as "no successor" if it does not stop within a specified polynomial number of steps, and also if it outputs the canonical source vertex or its successor.

[7] The purpose of the second algorithm is to keep the third algorithm honest, and ensure that the latter never creates an in-degree larger than 1.

[8] The same result and proof extend by induction to higher dimensions. Every

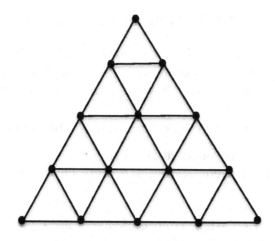

Figure 20.4: A subdivided triangle in the plane.

Theorem 20.4 (Sperner's Lemma) *For every legal coloring of a subdivided triangle, there is an odd number of trichromatic triangles.*

Proof: The proof is constructive. Define an undirected graph G that has one vertex corresponding to each small triangle, plus a source vertex that corresponds to the region outside the big triangle. The graph G has one edge for each pair of small triangles that share a side with one red and one green endpoint. Every trichromatic small triangle corresponds to a degree-one vertex of G. Every small triangle with one green and two red corners or two green and one red corners corresponds to a vertex with degree two in G. The source vertex of G has degree equal to the number of red-green segments on the left side of the big triangle, which is an odd number. Because every undirected graph has an even number of vertices with odd degree, there is an odd number of trichromatic triangles. ∎

The proof of Sperner's lemma shows that following a path from a canonical source vertex in a suitable graph leads to a trichromatic triangle. Thus, computing a trichromatic triangle of a legally colored subdivided triangle is a $\mathcal{PPAD}$ problem.[9]

---

subdivided simplex in $\mathbb{R}^n$ with vertices legally colored with $n + 1$ colors has an odd number of panchromatic subsimplices, with a different color at each vertex.

[9]We're glossing over some details. The graph of a $\mathcal{PPAD}$ problem is directed,

*20.5 MNE and $\mathcal{PPAD}$

What does computing a MNE have to do with $\mathcal{PPAD}$, the subclass of $\mathcal{FNP}$ problems that are solvable by a particular generic path-following procedure? There are two fundamental connections.

20.5.1 Sperner's Lemma and Nash's Theorem

Sperner's lemma (Theorem 20.4) turns out to be the combinatorial heart of Nash's theorem, stating that every finite game has at least one MNE.

Theorem 20.5 (Nash's Theorem) *Every finite game has at least one mixed Nash equilibrium.*

The reduction of Nash's theorem to Sperner's lemma has two parts. The first part is to use Sperner's lemma to prove Brouwer's fixed-point theorem. The latter theorem states that every continuous function f that maps a convex compact subset C of $\mathbb{R}^n$ to itself has at least one fixed point, meaning a point $x \in C$ with $f(x) = x$.[10]

Consider the special case where C is a simplex in $\mathbb{R}^2$. Let $f : C \to C$ be continuous. Subdivide C into small triangles as in Figure 20.4. Color a triangle corner x green if $f(x)$ is farther from the left corner of C than x; red if $f(x)$ is farther from the top corner of C than x; and blue if x is farther from the right corner of C than x. If two of these conditions apply to x, either corresponding color can be used. (If none of them apply, x is a fixed point and there's nothing left to prove.) This results in a legal coloring of the subdivision. By Sperner's lemma, there is at least one trichromatic triangle, representing a triangle whose corners are pulled in different directions by f. Taking a sequence of finer and finer subdivisions, we get a sequence of ever-smaller trichromatic triangles. Because C is compact, the centers of these triangles contain a subsequence that

---

while the graph G defined in the proof of Theorem 20.4 is undirected. There is, however, a canonical way to direct the edges of the graph G. Also, the canonical source vertex of a $\mathcal{PPAD}$ problem has out-degree 1, while the source of the graph G has degree $2k - 1$ for some positive integer k. This can be rectified by splitting the source vertex of G into k vertices, a source vertex with out-degree 1 and $k - 1$ vertices with in- and out-degree 1.

[10] So after stirring a cup of coffee, there is some point in the coffee that ends up exactly where it started!

converges to a point x^* in C. Because f is continuous, in the limit, $f(x^*)$ is at least as far from each of the three corners of C as x^*. This means that x^* is a fixed point of f.[11]

To sketch how Nash's theorem (Theorem 20.5) reduces to Brouwer's fixed-point theorem, consider a k-agent game with strategy sets $S_1, \ldots, S_k$ and payoff functions $\pi_1, \ldots, \pi_k$. The relevant convex compact set is $C = \Delta_1 \times \cdots \times \Delta_k$, where Δ_i is the simplex representing the mixed strategies over S_i. We want to define a continuous function $f : C \to C$, from mixed strategy profiles to mixed strategy profiles, such that the fixed points of f are the MNE of this game. We define f separately for each component $f_i : C \to \Delta_i$. A natural idea is to set f_i to be a best response of agent i to the mixed strategy profiles of the other agents. This does not lead to a continuous, or even well defined, function. We instead use a "regularized" version of this idea, defining

$$f_i(x_i, \mathbf{x}_{-i}) = \operatorname*{argmax}_{x_i' \in \Delta_i} g_i(x_i', \mathbf{x}), \qquad (20.3)$$

where

$$g_i(x_i', \mathbf{x}) = \underbrace{\operatorname*{\mathbf{E}}_{s_i \sim x_i', \mathbf{s}_{-i} \sim \mathbf{x}_{-i}} [\pi_i(\mathbf{s})]}_{\text{linear in } x_i'} - \underbrace{\|x_i' - x_i\|_2^2}_{\text{strictly convex}}. \qquad (20.4)$$

The first term of the function g_i encourages a best response while the second "penalty term" discourages big changes to i's mixed strategy. Because the function g_i is strictly concave in x_i', f_i is well defined. The function $f = (f_1, \ldots, f_k)$ is continuous (Exercise 20.5). By definition, every MNE of the given game is a fixed point of f. For the converse, suppose that $\mathbf{x}$ is not a MNE, with agent i able to increase her expected payoff by deviating unilaterally from x_i to x_i'. A simple computation shows that, for sufficiently small $\epsilon > 0$,

---

[11]Here's the idea for extending Brouwer's fixed-point theorem to all convex compact subsets of $\mathbb{R}^n$. First, since Sperner's lemma extends to higher dimensions, the same argument shows that Brouwer's fixed-point theorem holds for simplices in any number of dimensions. Second, radial projection shows that every pair C_1, C_2 of convex compact subsets of equal dimension are homeomorphic, meaning there is a bijection $h : C_1 \to C_2$ with h and h^{-1} continuous. Homeomorphisms preserve fixed-point theorems (Exercise 20.4).

$g_i((1 - \epsilon)x_i + \epsilon x'_i, \mathbf{x}) > g_i(x_i, \mathbf{x})$, and hence $\mathbf{x}$ is not a fixed point of f (Exercise 20.6).

This proof of Nash's theorem translates the path-following algorithm for computing a panchromatic subsimplex of a legally colored subdivided simplex to a path-following algorithm for computing an approximate MNE of a finite game. This establishes membership of this problem in $\mathcal{PPAD}$.

20.5.2   The Lemke-Howson Algorithm

There is also a second way to prove that computing a MNE of a bimatrix game is a $\mathcal{PPAD}$ problem, via the Lemke-Howson algorithm. Describing this algorithm is outside the scope of this book, but the essential point is that the Lemke-Howson algorithm reduces computing a MNE of a bimatrix game to a path-following problem, much in the way that the simplex algorithm reduces computing an optimal solution of a linear program to following a path of improving edges along the boundary of the feasible region. The biggest difference between the Lemke-Howson algorithm and the simplex method is that the former is not guided by an objective function. All known proofs of its inevitable convergence use parity arguments akin to the one in the proof of Sperner's lemma. These convergence proofs show that the problem of computing a MNE of a bimatrix game lies in $\mathcal{PPAD}$.

20.5.3   Final Remarks

The two connections between $\mathcal{PPAD}$ and computing a MNE are incomparable. The Lemke-Howson algorithm applies only to games with two players, but it shows that the problem of computing an *exact* MNE of a bimatrix game belongs to $\mathcal{PPAD}$. The path-following algorithm derived from Sperner's lemma applies to games with any fixed finite number of players, but only shows that the problem of computing an *approximate* MNE is in $\mathcal{PPAD}$.[12]

In any case, we conclude that our motivating problem of computing a MNE of a bimatrix game is a $\mathcal{PPAD}$ problem. Theorem 20.3 shows the complementary result that the problem is as hard as every

---

[12] In fact, with 3 or more players, the problem of computing an exact MNE of a game appears to be strictly harder than any problem in $\mathcal{PPAD}$ (see the Notes).

other problem that can be solved by a generic path-following procedure in a directed graph with a canonical source vertex and all in- and out-degrees at most 1. This shows that $\mathcal{PPAD}$ is, at last, the right complexity class for building evidence that the problem is computationally intractable.

For example, Theorem 20.3 implies that the problem of computing an approximate fixed point of a finitely represented continuous function, a $\mathcal{PPAD}$ problem, reduces to the problem of computing a MNE. This effectively reverses the reduction outlined in Section 20.5.1.

20.6   Discussion

One interpretation of Theorem 20.3, which is somewhat controversial, is that the seeming intractability of the Nash equilibrium concept renders it unsuitable for general-purpose behavioral prediction. If no polynomial-time algorithm can compute a MNE of a game, then we don't expect a bunch of strategic players to find one quickly, either.

Intractability is not necessarily first on the list of the Nash equilibrium's issues. For example, its non-uniqueness already limits its predictive power in many settings. But the novel computational intractability critique in Theorem 20.3 is one that theoretical computer science is particularly well suited to contribute.

If we don't analyze the Nash equilibria of a game, then what should we analyze? Theorem 20.3 suggests shining a brighter spotlight on computationally tractable classes of games and equilibrium concepts. For example, our convergence guarantees for no-regret dynamics motivate identifying properties that hold for all correlated or coarse correlated equilibria of a game.

How hard are $\mathcal{PPAD}$ problems, anyways? This basic question is not well understood. In the absence of an unconditional proof about whether or not $\mathcal{PPAD}$ problems are polynomial-time solvable, it is important to relate the assumption that $\mathcal{PPAD} \not\subseteq \mathcal{FP}$ to other complexity assumptions stronger than $\mathcal{P} \neq \mathcal{NP}$. For example, can we base the computational intractability of $\mathcal{PPAD}$ problems on cryptographic assumptions like the existence of one-way functions?

The Upshot

★ There is no known polynomial-time algorithm for computing a MNE of a bimatrix game, despite significant effort by many experts.

★ $\mathcal{TFNP}$ is the subclass of $\mathcal{NP}$ search problems $(\mathcal{FNP})$ for which the existence of a witness is guaranteed. Examples include all $\mathcal{PLS}$ problems and computing a MNE of a bimatrix game.

★ No $\mathcal{TFNP}$ problem can be $\mathcal{FNP}$-complete, unless $\mathcal{NP} = co\mathcal{NP}$.

★ $\mathcal{TFNP}$ does not seem to contain complete problems.

★ $\mathcal{PPAD}$ is the subclass of $\mathcal{TFNP}$ where a witness can always be computed by a generic path-following procedure in a directed graph with a source vertex and all in- and out-degrees at most 1.

★ The problem of computing a MNE of a bimatrix game is $\mathcal{PPAD}$-complete.

Notes

The definition of $\mathcal{TFNP}$ and Theorem 20.1 are due to Megiddo and Papadimitriou (1991). Theorem 20.2 is from Johnson et al. (1988). The complexity class $\mathcal{PPAD}$, as well as several other syntactically defined subclasses of $\mathcal{TFNP}$, is defined by Papadimitriou (1994). Daskalakis et al. (2009a) develop most of the machinery in the proof of Theorem 20.3 and prove that computing an approximate MNE of a three-player game is $\mathcal{PPAD}$-complete. The result stated for bimatrix games (Theorem 20.3) is due to Chen and Deng; see Chen et al. (2009). For overviews of this proof in order of increasing levels of detail, see Roughgarden (2010b),

Papadimitriou (2007), and Daskalakis et al. (2009b). Sperner's lemma (Theorem 20.4) is from Sperner (1928). Our proof of Nash's theorem (Theorem 20.5) follows Geanakoplos (2003) and is a variant of the one in Nash (1951). The Lemke-Howson algorithm is from Lemke and Howson (1964); see von Stengel (2002) for a thorough exposition. Etessami and Yannakakis (2010) show that the problem of exact MNE computation in games with more than two players is complete for a complexity class $\mathcal{FIXP}$ that appears to be strictly larger than $\mathcal{PPAD}$. Bitansky et al. (2015) and Rosen et al. (2016) discuss the prospects of basing the intractability of $\mathcal{PPAD}$-complete problems on cryptographic assumptions.

Problem 20.2, which shows that an approximate MNE of a bimatrix game can be computed in quasipolynomial time, is due to Lipton et al. (2003).[13] Such an approximate MNE need not be close to any exact MNE. Rubinstein (2016) proves that, under plausible complexity assumptions, there is no significantly faster algorithm for computing an approximate MNE. Problem 20.3 is derived from Brown and von Neumann (1950) and Gale et al. (1950).

Exercises

Exercise 20.1 *(H)* Assume for this exercise that every system of linear equations $\mathbf{Cx} = \mathbf{d}$ that has a solution has at least one solution with description length (in bits) polynomial in that of $\mathbf{C}$ and $\mathbf{d}$.

Prove that every bimatrix game $(\mathbf{A}, \mathbf{B})$ has a MNE with description length polynomial in that of the payoff matrices $\mathbf{A}$ and $\mathbf{B}$.

Exercise 20.2 *(H)* Consider the following problem: given descriptions of a nondeterministic algorithm $\mathcal{A}_1$ (for accepting "yes" instances) and a co-nondeterministic algorithm $\mathcal{A}_2$ (for accepting "no" instances), a polynomial time bound, and an encoding of an instance, find a witness that causes one of $\mathcal{A}_1, \mathcal{A}_2$ to accept the given instance in the prescribed number of time steps.

Why isn't this a generic complete problem for $\mathcal{NP} \cap co\mathcal{NP}$, in the sense of Section 20.2.3?

---

[13]The approximation in this result is additive. Daskalakis (2013) proves that for multiplicative approximation, as in Definitions 14.5 and 16.2, the problem of computing an approximate MNE of a bimatrix game is $\mathcal{PPAD}$-complete, and hence unlikely to admit a quasipolynomial-time algorithm.

Exercise 20.3 This exercise demonstrates the necessity of all of the hypotheses of Brouwer's fixed-point theorem, even in a single dimension.

(a) Exhibit a (discontinuous) function f from a compact interval to itself that has no fixed point.

(b) Exhibit a continuous function f from the union of two compact intervals to itself that has no fixed point.

(c) Exhibit a continuous function f from a bounded open interval to itself that has no fixed point.

Exercise 20.4 Suppose C_1 and C_2 are subsets of $\mathbb{R}^n$ that are *homeomorphic*, meaning that there is a bijection $h : C_1 \to C_2$ such that both h and h^{-1} are continuous. Prove that if every continuous function from C_1 to itself has a fixed point, then every continuous function from C_2 to itself has a fixed point.

Exercise 20.5 Prove that the function defined in (20.3)–(20.4) is continuous.

Exercise 20.6 In the mixed strategy profile $\mathbf{x}$, suppose that agent i can increase her expected payoff by deviating unilaterally from x_i to x_i'. Prove that $g_i((1 - \epsilon)x_i + \epsilon x_i', \mathbf{x}) > g_i(x_i, \mathbf{x})$ for all sufficiently small $\epsilon > 0$, where g_i is the function defined in (20.4).

Problems

Problem 20.1 *(H)* Assume for this problem that there is a polynomial-time algorithm that determines whether or not a system of linear equations has a solution, and computes a solution if one exists. Use such an algorithm as a subroutine to compute a MNE of a bimatrix game in time bounded above by $2^n \cdot p(n)$ for some polynomial p, where n is the combined number of rows and columns.

Problem 20.2 Let $(\mathbf{A}, \mathbf{B})$ be a bimatrix game in which each player has at most n strategies and all payoffs lie in $[0, 1]$. An *ϵ-approximate* *mixed Nash equilibrium (ε-MNE)* is a pair $(\hat{\mathbf{x}}, \hat{\mathbf{y}})$ of mixed strategies over the rows and columns such that

$$\hat{\mathbf{x}}^\top \mathbf{A}\hat{\mathbf{y}} \geq \mathbf{x}^\top \mathbf{A}\hat{\mathbf{y}} - \epsilon$$

for all row mixed strategies $\mathbf{x}$ and

$$\hat{\mathbf{x}}^\top \mathbf{B}\hat{\mathbf{y}} \geq \hat{\mathbf{x}}^\top \mathbf{B}\mathbf{y} - \epsilon$$

for all column mixed strategies $\mathbf{y}$.

(a) *(H)* Fix $\epsilon \in (0,1)$, let $(\mathbf{x}^*, \mathbf{y}^*)$ be a MNE of $(\mathbf{A}, \mathbf{B})$, and define $K = (b\ln n)/\epsilon^2$, where $b > 0$ is a sufficiently large constant, independent of n and ϵ. Let $(r_1, c_1), \ldots, (r_K, c_K)$ denote K outcomes sampled independently from the product distribution defined by $(\mathbf{x}^*, \mathbf{y}^*)$. Let $\hat{\mathbf{x}}$ and $\hat{\mathbf{y}}$ denote the corresponding marginal empirical distributions. For example, the component $\hat{x}_i$ is defined as the fraction of outcomes (r_ℓ, c_ℓ) for which r_ℓ is the row i. Prove that, with high probability over the choice of $(r_1, c_1), \ldots, (r_K, c_K)$, $(\hat{\mathbf{x}}, \hat{\mathbf{y}})$ is an ϵ-MNE.

(b) *(H)* Give an algorithm for computing an ϵ-MNE of a bimatrix game that runs in time at most $n^{2K} \cdot p(n)$ for some polynomial p, where K is defined as in (a).[14]

(c) Extend your algorithm and analysis to compute an ϵ-MNE with expected total payoff close to that of the maximum expected payoff achieved by any exact MNE. Your running time bound should remain the same.

Problem 20.3 A bimatrix game $(\mathbf{A}, \mathbf{B})$ is *symmetric* if both players have the same strategy set and $\mathbf{B} = \mathbf{A}^\top$. Examples include Rock-Paper-Scissors (Section 18.3.1) and the traffic light game (Section 13.1.4). Nash's theorem and the Lemke-Howson algorithm can both be adapted to show that every symmetric game has a *symmetric* MNE $(\hat{\mathbf{x}}, \hat{\mathbf{y}})$, in which both players employ the same mixed strategy (i.e., $\hat{\mathbf{x}} = \hat{\mathbf{y}}$).

---

[14]A running time bound of the form $n^{b\ln^a n}$ for constants a and b is called *quasipolynomial.* Such a bound is bigger than every polynomial but smaller than every exponential function.

(a) *(H)* Give a reduction, in the sense of Section 19.2.3, from the problem of computing a MNE of a general bimatrix game to that of computing a symmetric MNE of a symmetric bimatrix game.

(b) Give a reduction from the problem of computing a MNE of a general bimatrix game to that of computing *any* MNE of a symmetric bimatrix game.

(c) *(H)* Give a reduction from the problem of computing a MNE of a general bimatrix game to that of the problem of computing an *asymmetric* MNE of a symmetric bimatrix game, or reporting "no solution" if there are no asymmetric MNE.

The Top 10 List

1. *The second-price single-item auction.* Our first example of an "ideal" auction, which is dominant-strategy incentive compatible (DSIC), welfare maximizing, and computationally efficient (Theorem 2.4). Single-item auctions already show how small design changes, such as a first-price vs. a second-price payment rule, can have major ramifications for participant behavior.

2. *Myerson's lemma.* For single-parameter problems, DSIC mechanism design reduces to monotone allocation rule design (Theorem 3.7). Applications include ideal sponsored search auctions (Section 3.5), polynomial-time approximately optimal knapsack auctions (Theorem 4.2), and the reduction of expected revenue maximization with respect to a valuation distribution to expected virtual welfare maximization (Theorem 5.4).

3. *The Bulow-Klemperer theorem.* In a single-item auction, adding an extra bidder is as good as knowing the underlying distribution and running an optimal auction (Theorem 6.5). This result, along with the prophet inequality (Theorem 6.1), is an important clue that simple and prior-independent auctions can be almost as good as optimal ones.

4. *The VCG mechanism.* Charging participants their externalities yields a DSIC welfare-maximizing mechanism, even in very general settings (Theorem 7.3). The VCG mechanism is impractical in many real-world applications, including wireless spectrum auctions (Lecture 8), which motivates simpler and indirect auction formats like simultaneous ascending auctions (Section 8.3).

5. *Mechanism design without money.* Many of the most elegant and widely deployed mechanisms do not use payments. Exam-

ples include the Top Trading Cycle mechanism (Theorems 9.7
and 9.8), mechanisms for kidney exchange (Theorem 10.1), and
the Gale-Shapley stable matching mechanism (Theorems 10.5,
10.7, and 10.8).

6. *Selfish routing.* Worst-case selfish routing networks are always
   simple, with Pigou-like networks maximizing the price of anarchy (POA) (Theorems 11.1 and 11.2). The POA of selfish
   routing is therefore large only when cost functions are highly
   nonlinear, corroborating empirical evidence that network over-
   provisioning leads to good network performance (Section 12.1).

7. *Robust POA Bounds.* All of the proofs of POA bounds in these
   lectures are smoothness arguments (Definition 14.2). As such,
   they apply to relatively permissive and tractable equilibrium
   concepts like coarse correlated equilibria (Theorem 14.4).

8. *Potential games.* In many classes of games, including routing, location, and network cost-sharing games, players are inadvertently striving to optimize a potential function. Every
   potential game has at least one pure Nash equilibrium (Theorem 13.7) and best-response dynamics always converges (Proposition 16.1). Potential functions are also useful for proving POA-
   type bounds (Theorems 15.1 and 15.3).

9. *No-regret algorithms.* No-regret algorithms exist, including simple ones with optimal regret bounds, like the multiplicative
   weights algorithm (Theorem 17.6). If each agent of a repeatedly played game uses a no-regret or no-swap-regret algorithm
   to choose her mixed strategies, then the time-averaged history
   of joint play converges to the sets of coarse correlated equilibria
   (Proposition 17.9) or correlated equilibria (Proposition 18.4), respectively. These two equilibrium concepts are computationally
   tractable, as are mixed Nash equilibria in two-player zero-sum
   games (Theorem 18.7).

10. *Complexity of equilibrium computation.* Computing a Nash
    equilibrium appears computationally intractable in general.
    $\mathcal{PLS}$-completeness (Section 19.2) and $\mathcal{PPAD}$-completeness
    (Section 20.3) are analogs of $\mathcal{NP}$-completeness tailored to pro-
    vide evidence of intractability for pure and mixed equilibrium
    computation problems, respectively (Theorems 19.4 and 20.3).

Hints to Selected Exercises and Problems

Problem 2.1(c): Shoot for $c = \frac{1}{4}$. Use the first half of the bidders to get calibrated.

Problem 3.1(b): Adopt bidder i's perspective and "target" slot j.

Problem 3.1(d): First prove that, in a locally envy-free bid profile, the bidders must be sorted in nonincreasing order of values-per-click.

Problem 3.1(e): Use (3.8). What bids would yield these payments in a GSP auction? Use part (d) to argue that these bids form an equilibrium.

Problem 3.2(b): This boils down to checking that the payment rule of the Revenue Target Auction satisfies Myerson's payment formula.

Exercise 4.7: For example, what do auction houses such as Christie's and Sotheby's use?

Problem 4.2(b): If S^* is the optimal solution (with item values $\mathbf{v}$), and S is the computed solution (optimal for item values $\tilde{\mathbf{v}}$), then $\sum_{i \in S} v_i \geq m \sum_{i \in S} \tilde{v}_i \geq m \sum_{i \in S^*} \tilde{v}_i \geq \sum_{i \in S^*}(v_i - m)$.

Problem 4.2(e): Try many different values of m and use part (c). Under what conditions does taking the better of two monotone allocation rules yield another monotone allocation rule?

Problem 4.3(a): Reduce from the problem of computing the largest independent set of a graph (see, e.g., Garey and Johnson (1979)).

Problem 4.3(c): When the greedy algorithm makes a mistake by selecting some bidder, how many other bidders can it "block"?

Exercise 5.6: The distribution has infinite expectation, violating the assumptions of Section 5.1.3.

Problem 5.2: Use Problem 5.1(c).

Problem 5.3(c): First extend part (a), with $b_i(v_i)$ set to the expected value of the second-highest valuation, conditioned on the event that v_i is the highest valuation.

Exercise 6.1(b): Two bidders with valuations drawn from different uniform distributions suffice.

Exercise 6.2: Define t such that $\Pr[\pi_i > t$ for all $i] \leq \frac{1}{2} \leq \Pr[\pi_i \geq t$ for all $i]$. Show that at least one of the two corresponding strategies—either taking the first prize with value at least t, or the first with value exceeding t—satisfies the requirement.

Exercise 6.4: Use the Bulow-Klemperer theorem. Use Theorem 5.2 to bound the amount by which the optimal expected revenue can decrease when one bidder is removed.

Problem 6.1(a): Take $n = 2$.

Problem 6.2(b): Use downward-closure to reason about the outcome selected by $\mathcal{M}^*$.

Problem 6.2(c): Use part (a).

Problem 6.3(b): Given posted prices $p_1, \ldots, p_n$, consider a single-item auction that applies a reserve price of p_i to each bidder i and then awards the item to the remaining bidder (if any) with the largest value of $v_i - p_i$.

Problem 6.3(c): Identify posted prices $p_1, \ldots, p_n$ as in the proof of Theorem 6.4.[15] Show that only less expected revenue is earned by the single-item auction that applies a reserve price of p_i to each bidder i and then awards the item to the remaining bidder (if any) with the smallest value of p_i. Use the prophet inequality (Theorem 6.1 and Remark 6.2) to lower bound the expected virtual welfare, and hence expected revenue, of this auction.

Problem 6.4(b): Instantiate Theorem 6.5 with $n = 1$ to deduce that, with one bidder and one item, the expected revenue earned

---

[15]Warning: as a non-single-parameter setting, you cannot assume that expected revenue equals expected virtual welfare (cf., Theorem 5.2).

by a posted price p drawn randomly from F is at least half that by a monopoly price p^* for F. Use regularity to argue that, for every $t \geq 0$, this guarantee continues to hold for the prices $\max\{p, t\}$ and $\max\{p^*, t\}$. How much expected revenue does a bidder $i \neq j$ contribute to the optimal and given mechanisms?

Exercise 7.5: Use the fact that a maximum-weight matching of a bipartite graph can be computed in polynomial time.

Problem 7.1(b): Sum up the VCG payments (7.2) and simplify to obtain a multiple of the left-hand side of (7.4) and bid-independent terms.

Problem 7.3(b): Use subadditivity.

Problem 7.3(c): Use Problem 7.2. Exercise 7.5 is also relevant.

Exercise 8.1: First show that the sum of bidders' utilities (at prices $\mathbf{p}$) is maximized, then cancel out the price terms.

Exercise 8.2: Use the same example that illustrates the exposure problem.

Problem 8.3: For the reader familiar with linear programming duality, the allocation corresponds to a maximum-weight bipartite matching, the prices to an optimal dual solution, and the equilibrium conditions to complementary slackness conditions. Alternatively, use the payments of the VCG mechanism to define the item prices, and the structure of optimal matchings to verify the equilibrium conditions.

Exercise 9.3: Construct an example where one bidder can delay reporting a demand decrease to cause a different bidder to pay extra, resulting in lower prices for future items.

Exercise 9.4(c): Consider the realistic setting in which each B_i/v_i is modestly large but still far smaller than m.

Problem 9.1(b): First prove that, for every such deterministic DSIC auction, there is a simple probability distribution over valuation profiles such that the expected social welfare of the auction is at most c/n times the expected highest valuation. Explain why this implies the desired lower bound for both deterministic and randomized auctions.

Problem 9.3(c): Generalize the mechanism in (b) in two different ways. The less obvious way is to supplement the reported peaks with additional "dummy peaks."

Exercise 10.1: Adding back an edge of $E_i \setminus F_i$ either has no effect on which vertices before i get matched, or else guarantees that i is matched.

Exercise 10.6: If a hospital w prefers its match v in the applicant-optimal stable matching to its match v' in some other stable matching M', then (v, w) form a blocking pair for M'.

Problem 10.1: First consider a misreport that differs from the true preference list only in the order of two consecutive hospitals. Use induction to extend to arbitrary misreports.

Exercise 11.1: Prove that there is no loss of generality restricting to Pigou-like networks with $a = r = 1$. The POA in such networks is decreasing in b.

Exercise 11.2: Proceed by direct computation, or alternatively show how to replace the concave cost functions of a network by affine cost functions so that the POA can only increase.

Exercise 11.3(c): Transform a network with polynomial cost functions into one with the same POA and monomial cost functions.

Exercise 11.4(a): Starting from a Pigou-like example, simulate the edge with constant cost function $c(x) = \beta$ by many parallel edges, each with a cost function c satisfying $c(0) = \beta$.

Exercise 11.4(b): Let $\overline{C}$ denote the set of all nonnegative scalar multiples of cost functions in C. Apply part (a) to $\overline{C}$ and simulate scalar multiples using paths of multiple edges.

Problem 11.2(b): Braess's paradox.

Problem 11.2(c): This is a relatively straightforward consequence of Theorem 11.2 and Exercise 11.1.

Problem 11.3(b): Add two edges to a network with six vertices.

Exercise 12.2(c): Follow the proof of Theorem 11.2. In (11.10), invoke the β-over-provisioned assumption to justify using α_β in place of $\alpha(\mathcal{C})$.

Exercise 12.6: Check all cases where y and z are both small. What happens as y or z grows large?

Problem 12.1: Prove that, with an affine cost function, the inequality (12.4) holds even with an extra factor of $\frac{1}{4}$ on the right-hand side.

Problem 12.3(a): Two useful lower bounds on the minimum-possible makespan are $\max_{i=1}^{k} w_i$ and $\sum_{i=1}^{k} w_i/m$.

Exercise 13.4: Proceed edge-by-edge.

Problem 13.1: Consider the special case of $k = m$ and $w_i = 1$ for all agents i. Invoke well-known properties of occupancy (i.e., "balls into bins") problems that are discussed in standard texts like Mitzenmacher and Upfal (2005) and Motwani and Raghavan (1996).

Problem 13.3: For the "only if" direction, set $C_1^t, \ldots, C_k^t$ equal to the potential function.

Problem 13.4(a): The resources E correspond to the outcomes of the team game. Map each strategy s_i of agent i in the team game to the subset of E corresponding to outcomes where i chooses s_i. The cost of each resource is zero except when used by all of the agents.

Problem 13.4(b): The resources E correspond to choices of an agent i and strategies $\mathbf{s}_{-i}$ of the others. Map each strategy s_i of agent i in the dummy game to the set of resources of the form $\mathbf{s}_{-i}$ or $\mathbf{s}_{-j}$ with i playing a strategy other than s_i. The cost of each resource is zero except when used by a single agent. (Such cost functions may be decreasing, as permitted in congestion games.)

Exercise 14.1: Use property (P2).

Exercise 14.5: Follow the derivation in Section 14.4.1.

Problem 14.1(c): Prove that every such game is $(2,0)$-smooth with respect to the optimal outcome in (b) (see Remark 14.3).

Problem 14.2(b): Prove that every such game is $(\frac{1}{2}, 1)$-smooth with respect to the optimal outcome in which each bidder bids half her value.

Problem 14.3(a): Consider two bidders and two items, with $v_{11} = v_{22} = 2$ and $v_{12} = v_{21} = 1$.

Problem 14.3(b): Fix an optimal outcome in which each bidder i receives at most one item $j(i)$. Prove that every such game is $(1,1)$-smooth with respect to the optimal outcome in which each bidder i bids $v_{ij(i)}$ on item $j(i)$ and zero on all other items.

Exercise 15.6: Prove a stronger version of (15.4).

Problem 15.3: Generalize Exercise 13.4 and proceed as in the proof of Theorem 15.1.

Exercise 16.1: Two agents with three strategies each suffice.

Exercise 16.4: Create a directed graph as in Figure 16.1 and topologically sort the vertices.

Problem 16.2: Reprove Lemma 16.5, again using that agent i was chosen over j and that agent j has the option of deviating to s'_i.

Problem 16.3(b): Three agents suffice.

Problem 16.3(c): Proceed by induction on the number of agents. After adding a new agent to an inductively defined PNE, show that best-response dynamics converges to a PNE in at most k iterations.

Exercise 17.1: Reduce the problem to the special case of costs in $[-1, 1]$.

Exercise 17.2: Restart the algorithm with a new "guess" for T each time it reaches a time step t that is a power of 2.

Exercise 17.3: Use a time-averaged version of (16.11).

Problem 17.2(a): For the upper bound, follow the advice of the majority of the remaining potentially omniscient experts.

Problem 17.2(c): Follow the advice of one of the remaining potentially omniscient experts, chosen uniformly at random.

Problem 17.3: Pre-program σ into the algorithms $\mathcal{A}_1, \ldots, \mathcal{A}_k$. To make sure that each $\mathcal{A}_i$ is a no-regret algorithm, switch to the multiplicative weights algorithm if some other agent j fails to use the agreed-upon algorithm $\mathcal{A}_j$.

Problem 17.4(a): Sample the X_a's gradually by flipping coins only as needed, pausing once the action a^* with smallest perturbed cumulative cost is identified. Resuming, only X_{a^*} is not yet fully determined. What can you say if the next coin flip comes up "tails?"

Problem 17.4(b): Consider first the special case where $X_a = 0$ for all a. Iteratively transform the action sequence that always selects the best action in hindsight to the sequence chosen by the proposed algorithm. Work backward from time T, showing that the cost only decreases with each step of the transformation.

Problem 17.4(d): By (a), at each time step, the FTPL algorithm chooses the same action as the algorithm in (b) except with probability η.

Problem 17.4(e): Use a new perturbation at each time step.

Exercise 18.1: Look to Rock-Paper-Scissors for inspiration.

Exercise 18.4: Use Exercise 18.3.

Exercise 18.6: Given an arbitrary two-player game, add a "dummy player" to make it zero-sum.

Problem 18.1: Two agents with two strategies each suffice.

Problem 18.3(a): Each inequality has the form $\sum_{\mathbf{s} \in O} z_{\mathbf{s}} \cdot C_i(\mathbf{s}) \le \sum_{\mathbf{s} \in O} z_{\mathbf{s}} \cdot C_i(s_i', \mathbf{s}_{-i})$ for an agent i and a strategy $s_i' \in S_i$.

Problem 18.4: Use Exercise 18.3 and characterize the minimax pairs instead. To compute a strategy for the row player, solve for a mixed strategy $\mathbf{x}$ and the largest real number ζ such that, for every pure (and hence mixed) strategy that the column player might play, the row player's expected payoff when playing $\mathbf{x}$ is at least ζ.

Exercise 19.2: No. Describing a congestion game with k agents and m edges requires only km parameters, while the linear program in Problem 18.3 has size exponential in k.

Exercise 19.3: Use the reduction in the proof of Theorem 19.4.

Problem 19.1(a): Reduce the problem of computing a global minimizer of the potential function (13.6) to the minimum-cost flow problem (see, e.g., Cook et al. (1998)).

Problem 19.1(b): Proceed directly or use the fact that minimum-cost flows are characterized by the nonexistence of improving cycles in the "residual graph."

Exercise 20.1: Consider some MNE of $(\mathbf{A}, \mathbf{B})$, and suppose the row and column players place positive probability only on the rows R and columns C, respectively. Solve a system of linear equations to recover the probabilities of a MNE where the row and column players randomize only over R and C, respectively.

Exercise 20.2: Given only the descriptions of $\mathcal{A}_1$ and $\mathcal{A}_2$, how can you be sure there is always such a witness? If there isn't one, how do you solve the problem in $\mathcal{NP} \cap co\mathcal{NP}$?

Problem 20.1: Use the solution to Exercise 20.1.

Problem 20.2(a): Use Chernoff-Hoeffding bounds, as presented in standard texts like Mitzenmacher and Upfal (2005) and Motwani and Raghavan (1996), to prove that that the expected payoff of every pure strategy is almost the same in $(\mathbf{x}^*, \mathbf{y}^*)$ and in $(\hat{\mathbf{x}}, \hat{\mathbf{y}})$.

Problem 20.2(b): Adapt the solution to Problem 20.1. How many components of $\hat{\mathbf{x}}$ and $\hat{\mathbf{y}}$ are nonzero?

Problem 20.3(a): Given a bimatrix game $(\mathbf{A}, \mathbf{B})$, have the players play twice in parallel, once in either role. That is, after translating the payoffs, use the payoff matrix $\begin{pmatrix} \mathbf{0} & \mathbf{A} \\ \mathbf{B}^\top & \mathbf{0} \end{pmatrix}$ and its transpose.

Problem 20.3(c): Prove that the symmetric games generated by the reduction in (a) are guaranteed to possess asymmetric MNE.

Bibliography

Abdulkadiroğlu, A. and Sönmez, T. (1999). House allocation with existing tenants. *Journal of Economic Theory*, 88(2):233–260. (Cited on page 142.)

Adler, I. (2013). The equivalence of linear programs and zero-sum games. *International Journal of Game Theory*, 42(1):165–177. (Cited on page 258.)

Aggarwal, G., Goel, A., and Motwani, R. (2006). Truthful auctions for pricing search keywords. In *Proceedings of the 7th ACM Conference on Electronic Commerce (EC)*, pages 1–7. (Cited on page 35.)

Alaei, S., Hartline, J. D., Niazadeh, R., Pountourakis, E., and Yuan, Y. (2015). Optimal auctions vs. anonymous pricing. In *Proceedings of the 56th Annual Symposium on Foundations of Computer Science (FOCS)*, pages 1446–1463. (Cited on page 83.)

Aland, S., Dumrauf, D., Gairing, M., Monien, B., and Schoppmann, F. (2011). Exact price of anarchy for polynomial congestion games. *SIAM Journal on Computing*, 40(5):1211–1233. (Cited on page 169.)

Andelman, N., Feldman, M., and Mansour, Y. (2009). Strong price of anarchy. *Games and Economic Behavior*, 65(2):289–317. (Cited on page 214.)

Anshelevich, E., Dasgupta, A., Kleinberg, J., Tardos, É., Wexler, T., and Roughgarden, T. (2008a). The price of stability for network design with fair cost allocation. *SIAM Journal on Computing*, 38(4):1602–1623. (Cited on page 213.)

Anshelevich, E., Dasgupta, A., Tardos, É., and Wexler, T. (2008b). Near-optimal network design with selfish agents. *Theory of Computing*, 4(1):77–109. (Cited on page 213.)

Archer, A. F. and Tardos, É. (2001). Truthful mechanisms for one-parameter agents. In *Proceedings of the 42nd Annual Symposium on Foundations of Computer Science (FOCS)*, pages 482–491. (Cited on page 49.)

Arora, S., Hazan, E., and Kale, S. (2012). The multiplicative weights update method: a meta-algorithm and applications. *Theory of Computing*, 8(1):121–164. (Cited on page 243.)

Asadpour, A. and Saberi, A. (2009). On the inefficiency ratio of stable equilibria in congestion games. In *Proceedings of the 5th International Workshop on Internet and Network Economics (WINE)*, pages 545–552. (Cited on page 214.)

Ashlagi, I., Fischer, F. A., Kash, I. A., and Procaccia, A. D. (2015). Mix and match: A strategyproof mechanism for multi-hospital kidney exchange. *Games and Economic Behavior*, 91:284–296. (Cited on page 143.)

Aumann, R. J. (1959). Acceptable points in general cooperative *n*-person games. In Luce, R. D. and Tucker, A. W., editors, *Contributions to the Theory of Games*, volume 4, pages 287–324. Princeton University Press. (Cited on page 214.)

Aumann, R. J. (1974). Subjectivity and correlation in randomized strategies. *Journal of Mathematical Economics*, 1(1):67–96. (Cited on page 183.)

Ausubel, L. M. (2004). An efficient ascending-bid auction for multiple objects. *American Economic Review*, 94(5):1452–1475. (Cited on page 123.)

Ausubel, L. M. and Milgrom, P. (2002). Ascending auctions with package bidding. *Frontiers of Theoretical Economics*, 1(1):1–42. (Cited on page 110.)

Ausubel, L. M. and Milgrom, P. (2006). The lovely but lonely Vickrey auction. In Cramton, P., Shoham, Y., and Steinberg, R., editors, *Combinatorial Auctions*, chapter 1, pages 57–95. MIT Press. (Cited on page 93.)

Awerbuch, B., Azar, Y., Epstein, A., Mirrokni, V. S., and Skopalik, A. (2008). Fast convergence to nearly optimal solutions in potential games. In *Proceedings of the 9th ACM Conference on Electronic Commerce (EC)*, pages 264–273. (Cited on page 227.)

Awerbuch, B., Azar, Y., and Epstein, L. (2013). The price of routing unsplittable flow. *SIAM Journal on Computing*, 42(1):160–177. (Cited on page 169.)

Awerbuch, B., Azar, Y., Richter, Y., and Tsur, D. (2006). Tradeoffs in worst-case equilibria. *Theoretical Computer Science*, 361(2–3):200–209. (Cited on page 169.)

Azar, P., Daskalakis, C., Micali, S., and Weinberg, S. M. (2013). Optimal and efficient parametric auctions. In *Proceedings of the 24th Annual ACM-SIAM Symposium on Discrete Algorithms (SODA)*, pages 596–604. (Cited on page 70.)

Beckmann, M. J., McGuire, C. B., and Winsten, C. B. (1956). *Studies in the Economics of Transportation*. Yale University Press. (Cited on pages 156 and 183.)

Bertsekas, D. P. and Gallager, R. G. (1987). *Data Networks*. Prentice-Hall. Second Edition, 1991. (Cited on page 169.)

Bhawalkar, K., Gairing, M., and Roughgarden, T. (2014). Weighted congestion games: Price of anarchy, universal worst-case examples, and tightness. *ACM Transactions on Economics and Computation*, 2(4):14. (Cited on page 169.)

Bilò, V., Flammini, M., and Moscardelli, L. (2016). The price of stability for undirected broadcast network design with fair cost allocation is constant. *Games and Economic Behavior*. To appear. (Cited on page 214.)

Bitansky, N., Paneth, O., and Rosen, A. (2015). On the cryptographic hardness of finding a Nash equilibrium. In *Proceedings of the 56th Annual Symposium on Foundations of Computer Science (FOCS)*, pages 1480–1498. (Cited on page 295.)

Blackwell, D. (1956). Controlled random walks. In Noordhoff, E. P., editor, *Proceedings of the International Congress of Mathematicians 1954*, volume 3, pages 336–338. North-Holland. (Cited on page 243.)

Blum, A., Hajiaghayi, M. T., Ligett, K., and Roth, A. (2008). Regret minimization and the price of total anarchy. In *Proceedings of the 39th Annual ACM Symposium on Theory of Computing (STOC)*, pages 373–382. (Cited on page 199.)

Blum, A. and Mansour, Y. (2007a). From external to internal regret. *Journal of Machine Learning Research*, 8:1307–1324. (Cited on page 258.)

Blum, A. and Mansour, Y. (2007b). Learning, regret minimization, and equilibria. In Nisan, N., Roughgarden, T., Tardos, É., and Vazirani, V., editors, *Algorithmic Game Theory*, chapter 4, pages 79–101. Cambridge University Press. (Cited on page 243.)

Blume, L. (1993). The statistical mechanics of strategic interaction. *Games and Economic Behavior*, 5(3):387–424. (Cited on page 214.)

Blumrosen, L. and Nisan, N. (2007). Combinatorial auctions. In Nisan, N., Roughgarden, T., Tardos, É., and Vazirani, V., editors, *Algorithmic Game Theory*, chapter 11, pages 267–299. Cambridge University Press. (Cited on page 93.)

Börgers, T. (2015). *An Introduction to the Theory of Mechanism Design*. Oxford University Press. (Cited on page 20.)

Braess, D. (1968). Über ein Paradoxon aus der Verkehrsplanung. *Unternehmensforschung*, 12(1):258–268. (Cited on pages 9 and 156.)

Brandt, F., Conitzer, V., Endriss, U., Lang, J., and Procaccia, A. D., editors (2016). *Handbook of Computational Social Choice*. Cambridge University Press. (Cited on page xi.)

Briest, P., Krysta, P., and Vöcking, B. (2005). Approximation techniques for utilitarian mechanism design. In *Proceedings of the 36th Annual ACM Symposium on Theory of Computing (STOC)*, pages 39–48. (Cited on page 50.)

Brown, J. W. and von Neumann, J. (1950). Solutions of games by differential equations. In Kuhn, H. W. and Tucker, A. W., editors, *Contributions to the Theory of Games*, volume 1, pages 73–79. Princeton University Press. (Cited on page 295.)

Bulow, J. and Klemperer, P. (1996). Auctions versus negotiations. *American Economic Review*, 86(1):180–194. (Cited on page 83.)

Bulow, J. and Roberts, J. (1989). The simple economics of optimal auctions. *Journal of Political Economy*, 97(5):1060–1090. (Cited on page 70.)

Cai, Y., Candogan, O., Daskalakis, C., and Papadimitriou, C. H. (2016). Zero-sum polymatrix games: A generalization of minmax. *Mathematics of Operations Research*, 41(2):648–655. (Cited on page 258.)

Caragiannis, I., Kaklamanis, C., Kanellopoulos, P., Kyropoulou, M., Lucier, B., Paes Leme, R., and Tardos, É. (2015). On the efficiency of equilibria in generalized second price auctions. *Journal of Economic Theory*, 156:343–388. (Cited on page 199.)

Cesa-Bianchi, N. and Lugosi, G. (2006). *Prediction, Learning, and Games*. Cambridge University Press. (Cited on page 243.)

Cesa-Bianchi, N., Mansour, Y., and Stolz, G. (2007). Improved second-order bounds for prediction with expert advice. *Machine Learning*, 66(2–3):321–352. (Cited on page 243.)

Chakrabarty, D. (2004). Improved bicriteria results for the selfish routing problem. Unpublished manuscript. (Cited on page 169.)

Chawla, S., Hartline, J. D., and Kleinberg, R. D. (2007). Algorithmic pricing via virtual valuations. In *Proceedings of the 8th ACM Conference on Electronic Commerce (EC)*, pages 243–251. (Cited on page 83.)

Chawla, S., Hartline, J. D., Malec, D., and Sivan, B. (2010). Multi-parameter mechanism design and sequential posted pricing. In *Proceedings of the 41st Annual ACM Symposium on Theory of Computing (STOC)*, pages 311–320. (Cited on page 83.)

Chekuri, C. and Gamzu, I. (2009). Truthful mechanisms via greedy iterative packing. In *Proceedings of the 12th International Workshop on Approximation Algorithms for Combinatorial Optimization Problems (APPROX)*, pages 56–69. (Cited on page 50.)

Chen, R. and Chen, Y. (2011). The potential of social identity for equilibrium selection. *American Economic Review*, 101(6):2562–2589. (Cited on page 214.)

Chen, X., Deng, X., and Teng, S.-H. (2009). Settling the complexity of computing two-player Nash equilibria. *Journal of the ACM*, 56(3):14. (Cited on page 294.)

Chien, S. and Sinclair, A. (2011). Convergence to approximate Nash equilibria in congestion games. *Games and Economic Behavior*, 71(2):315–327. (Cited on page 227.)

Christodoulou, G. and Koutsoupias, E. (2005a). On the price of anarchy and stability of correlated equilibria of linear congestion games. In *Proceedings of the 13th Annual European Symposium on Algorithms (ESA)*, pages 59–70. (Cited on page 169.)

Christodoulou, G. and Koutsoupias, E. (2005b). The price of anarchy of finite congestion games. In *Proceedings of the 36th Annual ACM Symposium on Theory of Computing (STOC)*, pages 67–73. (Cited on page 169.)

Christodoulou, G., Kovács, A., and Schapira, M. (2008). Bayesian combinatorial auctions. In *Proceedings of the 35th International Colloquium on Automata, Languages and Programming (ICALP)*, pages 820–832. (Cited on page 199.)

Clarke, E. H. (1971). Multipart pricing of public goods. *Public Choice*, 11(1):17–33. (Cited on page 93.)

Cohen, J. E. and Horowitz, P. (1991). Paradoxical behaviour of mechanical and electrical networks. *Nature*, 352(8):699–701. (Cited on page 9.)

Cominetti, R., Correa, J. R., and Stier Moses, N. E. (2009). The impact of oligopolistic competition in networks. *Operations Research*, 57(6):1421–1437. (Cited on page 169.)

Cook, W. J., Cunningham, W. H., Pulleyblank, W. R., and Schrijver, A. (1998). *Combinatorial Optimization*. Wiley. (Cited on pages 156 and 308.)

Correa, J. R., Schulz, A. S., and Stier Moses, N. E. (2004). Selfish routing in capacitated networks. *Mathematics of Operations Research*, 29(4):961–976. (Cited on page 156.)

Cramton, P. (2006). Simultaneous ascending auctions. In Cramton, P., Shoham, Y., and Steinberg, R., editors, *Combinatorial Auctions*, chapter 4, pages 99–114. MIT Press. (Cited on page 110.)

Cramton, P. and Schwartz, J. (2000). Collusive bidding: Lessons from the FCC spectrum auctions. *Journal of Regulatory Economics*, 17(3):229–252. (Cited on page 110.)

Cramton, P., Shoham, Y., and Steinberg, R., editors (2006). *Combinatorial Auctions*. MIT Press. (Cited on page 110.)

Crémer, J. and McLean, R. P. (1985). Optimal selling strategies under uncertainty for a discriminating monopolist when demands are interdependent. *Econometrica*, 53(2):345–361. (Cited on page 69.)

Dantzig, G. B. (1951). A proof of the equivalence of the programming problem and the game problem. In Koopmans, T. C., editor, *Activity Analysis of Production and Allocation*, Cowles Commission Monograph No. 13, chapter XX, pages 330–335. Wiley. (Cited on page 258.)

Dantzig, G. B. (1982). Reminiscences about the origins of linear programming. *Operations Research Letters*, 1(2):43–48. (Cited on page 258.)

Daskalakis, C. (2013). On the complexity of approximating a Nash equilibrium. *ACM Transactions on Algorithms*, 9(3):23. (Cited on page 295.)

Daskalakis, C., Goldberg, P. W., and Papadimitriou, C. H. (2009a). The complexity of computing a Nash equilibrium. *SIAM Journal on Computing*, 39(1):195–259. (Cited on page 294.)

Daskalakis, C., Goldberg, P. W., and Papadimitriou, C. H. (2009b). The complexity of computing a Nash equilibrium. *Communications of the ACM*, 52(2):89–97. (Cited on page 295.)

Devanur, N. R., Ha, B. Q., and Hartline, J. D. (2013). Prior-free auctions for budgeted agents. In *Proceedings of the 14th ACM Conference on Electronic Commerce (EC)*, pages 287–304. (Cited on page 123.)

Dhangwatnotai, P., Roughgarden, T., and Yan, Q. (2015). Revenue maximization with a single sample. *Games and Economic Behavior*, 91:318–333. (Cited on page 83.)

Diamantaras, D., Cardamone, E. I., Campbell, K. A., Deacle, S., and Delgado, L. A. (2009). *A Toolbox for Economic Design*. Palgrave Macmillan. (Cited on page 20.)

Dobzinski, S., Lavi, R., and Nisan, N. (2012). Multi-unit auctions with budget limits. *Games and Economic Behavior*, 74(2):486–503. (Cited on pages 123 and 124.)

Dobzinski, S., Nisan, N., and Schapira, M. (2010). Approximation algorithms for combinatorial auctions with complement-free bidders. *Mathematics of Operations Research*, 35(1):1–13. (Cited on page 93.)

Dobzinski, S. and Paes Leme, R. (2014). Efficiency guarantees in auctions with budgets. In *Proceedings of the 41st International Colloquium on Automata, Languages and Programming (ICALP)*, pages 392–404. (Cited on page 124.)

Dubins, L. E. and Freedman, D. A. (1981). Machiavelli and the Gale-Shapley algorithm. *American Mathematical Monthly*, 88(7):485–494. (Cited on page 143.)

Dynkin, E. B. (1963). The optimum choice of the instant for stopping a Markov process. *Soviet Mathematics Doklady*, 4:627–629. (Cited on page 20.)

Edelman, B., Ostrovsky, M., and Schwarz, M. (2007). Internet advertising and the Generalized Second-Price Auction: Selling billions of dollars worth of keywords. *American Economic Review*, 97(1):242–259. (Cited on pages 20 and 35.)

Epstein, A., Feldman, M., and Mansour, Y. (2009). Strong equilibrium in cost sharing connection games. *Games and Economic Behavior*, 67(1):51–68. (Cited on page 214.)

Etessami, K. and Yannakakis, M. (2010). On the complexity of Nash equilibria and other fixed points. *SIAM Journal on Computing*, 39(6):2531–2597. (Cited on page 295.)

Even-Dar, E., Kesselman, A., and Mansour, Y. (2007). Convergence time to Nash equilibrium in load balancing. *ACM Transactions on Algorithms*, 3(3):32. (Cited on page 227.)

Fabrikant, A., Papadimitriou, C. H., and Talwar, K. (2004). The complexity of pure Nash equilibria. In *Proceedings of the 35th Annual ACM Symposium on Theory of Computing (STOC)*, pages 604–612. (Cited on page 277.)

Facchini, G., van Megan, F., Borm, P., and Tijs, S. (1997). Congestion models and weighted Bayesian potential games. *Theory and Decision*, 42(2):193–206. (Cited on page 183.)

Federal Communications Commission (2015). Procedures for competitive bidding in auction 1000, including initial clearing target determination, qualifying to bid, and bidding in auctions 1001 (reverse) and 1002 (forward). Public notice FCC 15-78. (Cited on page 110.)

Foster, D. P. and Vohra, R. (1997). Calibrated learning and correlated equilibrium. *Games and Economic Behavior*, 21(1–2):40–55. (Cited on page 258.)

Foster, D. P. and Vohra, R. (1999). Regret in the on-line decision problem. *Games and Economic Behavior*, 29(1–2):7–35. (Cited on page 243.)

Fotakis, D. (2010). Congestion games with linearly independent paths: Convergence time and price of anarchy. *Theory of Computing Systems*, 47(1):113–136. (Cited on page 277.)

Fotakis, D., Kontogiannis, S. C., and Spirakis, P. G. (2005). Selfish unsplittable flows. *Theoretical Computer Science*, 348(2–3):226–239. (Cited on page 183.)

Fréchette, A., Newman, N., and Leyton-Brown, K. (2016). Solving the station repacking problem. In *Proceedings of the 30th AAAI Conference on Artificial Intelligence (AAAI)*. (Cited on page 110.)

Freund, Y. and Schapire, R. E. (1997). A decision-theoretic generalization of on-line learning and an application to boosting. *Journal of Computer and System Sciences*, 55(1):119–139. (Cited on page 243.)

Freund, Y. and Schapire, R. E. (1999). Adaptive game playing using multiplicative weights. *Games and Economic Behavior*, 29(1–2):79–103. (Cited on page 258.)

Gale, D., Kuhn, H. W., and Tucker, A. W. (1950). On symmetric games. In Kuhn, H. W. and Tucker, A. W., editors, *Contributions to the Theory of Games*, volume 1, pages 81–87. Princeton University Press. (Cited on page 295.)

Gale, D., Kuhn, H. W., and Tucker, A. W. (1951). Linear programming and the theory of games. In Koopmans, T. C., editor, *Activity Analysis of Production and Allocation*, Cowles Commission Monograph No. 13, chapter XIX, pages 317–329. Wiley. (Cited on page 258.)

Gale, D. and Shapley, L. S. (1962). College admissions and the stability of marriage. *American Mathematical Monthly*, 69(1):9–15. (Cited on page 143.)

Gale, D. and Sotomayor, M. (1985). Ms. Machiavelli and the stable matching problem. *American Mathematical Monthly*, 92(4):261–268. (Cited on page 143.)

Garey, M. R. and Johnson, D. S. (1979). *Computers and Intractability: A Guide to the Theory of NP-Completeness*. Freeman. (Cited on pages 50, 276, and 301.)

Geanakoplos, J. (2003). Nash and Walras equilibrium via Brouwer. *Economic Theory*, 21(2/3):585–603. (Cited on page 295.)

Gibbard, A. (1973). Manipulation of voting schemes: A general result. *Econometrica*, 41(4):587–601. (Cited on page 50.)

Gilboa, I. and Zemel, E. (1989). Nash and correlated equilibria: Some complexity considerations. *Games and Economic Behavior*, 1(1):80–93. (Cited on page 258.)

Goemans, M. X., Mirrokni, V. S., and Vetta, A. (2005). Sink equilibria and convergence. In *Proceedings of the 46th Annual Symposium on Foundations of Computer Science (FOCS)*, pages 142–151. (Cited on page 183.)

Goeree, J. K. and Holt, C. A. (2010). Hierarchical package bidding: A paper & pencil combinatorial auction. *Games and Economic Behavior*, 70(1):146–169. (Cited on page 110.)

Goldberg, A. V., Hartline, J. D., Karlin, A., Saks, M., and Wright, A. (2006). Competitive auctions. *Games and Economic Behavior*, 55(2):242–269. (Cited on pages 35 and 83.)

Groves, T. (1973). Incentives in teams. *Econometrica*, 41(4):617–631. (Cited on page 93.)

Hajiaghayi, M. T., Kleinberg, R. D., and Parkes, D. C. (2004). Adaptive limited-supply online auctions. In *Proceedings of the 5th ACM Conference on Electronic Commerce (EC)*, pages 71–80. (Cited on page 20.)

Hannan, J. (1957). Approximation to Bayes risk in repeated play. In Dresher, M., Tucker, A. W., and Wolfe, P., editors, *Contributions to the Theory of Games*, volume 3, pages 97–139. Princeton University Press. (Cited on pages 183, 243, and 258.)

Harks, T. (2011). Stackelberg strategies and collusion in network games with splittable flow. *Theory of Computing Systems*, 48(4):781–802. (Cited on page 169.)

Harstad, R. M. (2000). Dominant strategy adoption and bidders' experience with pricing rules. *Experimental Economics*, 3(3):261–280. (Cited on page 110.)

Hart, S. and Mas-Colell, A. (2000). A simple adaptive procedure leading to correlated equilibrium. *Econometrica*, 68(5):1127–1150. (Cited on page 258.)

Hart, S. and Nisan, N. (2013). The query complexity of correlated equilibria. Working paper. (Cited on page 277.)

Hartline, J. D. (2016). Mechanism design and approximation. Book in preparation. (Cited on pages xi, 69, and 83.)

Hartline, J. D. and Kleinberg, R. D. (2012). Badminton and the science of rule making. *The Huffington Post.* (Cited on page 9.)

Hartline, J. D. and Roughgarden, T. (2009). Simple versus optimal mechanisms. In *Proceedings of the 10th ACM Conference on Electronic Commerce (EC)*, pages 225–234. (Cited on page 83.)

Hoeksma, R. and Uetz, M. (2011). The price of anarchy for min-sum related machine scheduling. In *Proceedings of the 9th International Workshop on Approximation and Online Algorithms (WAOA)*, pages 261–273. (Cited on page 199.)

Holmstrom, B. (1977). *On Incentives and Control in Organizations.* PhD thesis, Stanford University. (Cited on page 93.)

Hurwicz, L. (1972). On informationally decentralized systems. In McGuire, C. B. and Radner, R., editors, *Decision and Organization*, pages 297–336. University of Minnesota Press. (Cited on page 20.)

Ibarra, O. H. and Kim, C. E. (1975). Fast approximation algorithms for the knapsack and sum of subset problems. *Journal of the ACM*, 22(4):463–468. (Cited on page 50.)

Jackson, M. O. (2008). *Social and Economic Networks.* Princeton University Press. (Cited on page 213.)

Jiang, A. X. and Leyton-Brown, K. (2015). Polynomial-time computation of exact correlated equilibrium in compact games. *Games and Economic Behavior*, 91:347–359. (Cited on page 277.)

Johnson, D. S., Papadimitriou, C. H., and Yannakakis, M. (1988). How easy is local search? *Journal of Computer and System Sciences*, 37(1):79–100. (Cited on pages 276 and 294.)

Kalai, A. and Vempala, S. (2005). Efficient algorithms for online decision problems. *Journal of Computer and System Sciences*, 71(3):291–307. (Cited on page 243.)

Karlin, S. and Taylor, H. (1975). *A First Course in Stochastic Processes*. Academic Press, second edition. (Cited on page 258.)

Kirkegaard, R. (2006). A short proof of the Bulow-Klemperer auctions vs. negotiations result. *Economic Theory*, 28(2):449–452. (Cited on page 83.)

Klemperer, P. (2004). *Auctions: Theory and Practice*. Princeton University Press. (Cited on page 110.)

Koutsoupias, E. and Papadimitriou, C. H. (1999). Worst-case equilibria. In *Proceedings of the 16th Annual Symposium on Theoretical Aspects of Computer Science (STACS)*, volume 1563 of *Lecture Notes in Computer Science*, pages 404–413. (Cited on pages 9, 169, and 183.)

Krishna, V. (2010). *Auction Theory*. Academic Press, second edition. (Cited on pages 20 and 70.)

Lehmann, D., O'Callaghan, L. I., and Shoham, Y. (2002). Truth revelation in approximately efficient combinatorial auctions. *Journal of the ACM*, 49(5):577–602. (Cited on pages 49 and 50.)

Lemke, C. E. and Howson, Jr., J. T. (1964). Equilibrium points of bimatrix games. *SIAM Journal*, 12(2):413–423. (Cited on page 295.)

Lipton, R. J., Markakis, E., and Mehta, A. (2003). Playing large games using simple strategies. In *Proceedings of the 4th ACM Conference on Electronic Commerce (EC)*, pages 36–41. (Cited on page 295.)

Littlestone, N. (1988). Learning quickly when irrelevant attributes abound: A new linear-threshold algorithm. *Machine Learning*, 2(4):285–318. (Cited on page 243.)

Littlestone, N. and Warmuth, M. K. (1994). The weighted majority algorithm. *Information and Computation*, 108(2):212–261. (Cited on page 243.)

Mas-Colell, A., Whinston, M. D., and Green, J. R. (1995). *Microeconomic Theory*. Oxford University Press. (Cited on page 20.)

McVitie, D. G. and Wilson, L. B. (1971). The stable marriage problem. *Communications of the ACM*, 14(7):486–490. (Cited on page 143.)

Megiddo, N. and Papadimitriou, C. H. (1991). On total functions, existence theorems and computational complexity. *Theoretical Computer Science*, 81(2):317–324. (Cited on page 294.)

Milchtaich, I. (1996). Congestion games with player-specific payoff functions. *Games and Economic Behavior*, 13(1):111–124. (Cited on page 227.)

Milgrom, P. (2004). *Putting Auction Theory to Work*. Cambridge University Press. (Cited on page 110.)

Milgrom, P. and Segal, I. (2015a). Deferred-acceptance auctions and radio spectrum reallocation. Working paper. (Cited on page 110.)

Milgrom, P. and Segal, I. (2015b). Designing the US Incentive Auction. Working paper. (Cited on page 110.)

Mirrokni, V. S. and Vetta, A. (2004). Convergence issues in competitive games. In *Proceedings of the 7th International Workshop on Approximation Algorithms for Combinatorial Optimization Problems (APPROX)*, pages 183–194. (Cited on pages 199 and 227.)

Mitzenmacher, M. and Upfal, E. (2005). *Probability and Computing: Randomized Algorithms and Probabilistic Analysis*. Cambridge University Press. (Cited on pages 305 and 308.)

Monderer, D. and Shapley, L. S. (1996). Potential games. *Games and Economic Behavior*, 14(1):124–143. (Cited on pages 183 and 226.)

Motwani, R. and Raghavan, P. (1996). *Randomized Algorithms*. Cambridge University Press. (Cited on pages 305 and 308.)

Moulin, H. (1980). On strategy-proofness and single peakedness. *Public Choice*, 35(4):437–455. (Cited on page 124.)

Moulin, H. and Shenker, S. (2001). Strategyproof sharing of submodular costs: Budget balance versus efficiency. *Economic Theory*, 18(3):511–533. (Cited on page 35.)

Moulin, H. and Vial, J. P. (1978). Strategically zero-sum games: The class of games whose completely mixed equilibria cannot be improved upon. *International Journal of Game Theory*, 7(3–4):201–221. (Cited on page 183.)

Mu'Alem, A. and Nisan, N. (2008). Truthful approximation mechanisms for restricted combinatorial auctions. *Games and Economic Behavior*, 64(2):612–631. (Cited on page 50.)

Myerson, R. (1981). Optimal auction design. *Mathematics of Operations Research*, 6(1):58–73. (Cited on pages 35 and 69.)

Nash, Jr., J. F. (1950). Equilibrium points in N-person games. *Proceedings of the National Academy of Sciences*, 36(1):48–49. (Cited on pages 9 and 183.)

Nash, Jr., J. F. (1951). Non-cooperative games. *Annals of Mathematics*, 54(2):286–295. (Cited on page 295.)

Nisan, N. (2015). Algorithmic mechanism design: Through the lens of multi-unit auctions. In Young, H. P. and Zamir, S., editors, *Handbook of Game Theory*, volume 4, chapter 9, pages 477–515. North-Holland. (Cited on page 49.)

Nisan, N. and Ronen, A. (2001). Algorithmic mechanism design. *Games and Economic Behavior*, 35(1–2):166–196. (Cited on page 49.)

Nisan, N., Roughgarden, T., Tardos, É., and Vazirani, V., editors (2007). *Algorithmic Game Theory*. Cambridge University Press. (Cited on page xi.)

Nobel Prize Committee (2007). Scientific background on the Sveriges Riksbank Prize in Economic Sciences in Memory of Alfred Nobel: Mechanism Design Theory. Prize Citation. (Cited on page 20.)

Olifer, N. and Olifer, V. (2005). *Computer Networks: Principles, Technologies and Protocols for Network Design*. Wiley. (Cited on page 169.)

Ostrovsky, M. and Schwarz, M. (2009). Reserve prices in Internet advertising auctions: A field experiment. Working paper. (Cited on page 70.)

Papadimitriou, C. H. (1994). On the complexity of the parity argument and other inefficient proofs of existence. *Journal of Computer and System Sciences*, 48(3):498–532. (Cited on page 294.)

Papadimitriou, C. H. (2007). The complexity of finding Nash equilibria. In Nisan, N., Roughgarden, T., Tardos, É., and Vazirani, V., editors, *Algorithmic Game Theory*, chapter 2, pages 29–51. Cambridge University Press. (Cited on page 295.)

Papadimitriou, C. H. and Roughgarden, T. (2008). Computing correlated equilibria in multi-player games. *Journal of the ACM*, 55(3):14. (Cited on page 277.)

Parkes, D. C. and Seuken, S. (2016). Economics and computation. Book in preparation. (Cited on page xi.)

Pigou, A. C. (1920). *The Economics of Welfare*. Macmillan. (Cited on page 156.)

Rabin, M. O. (1957). Effective computability of winning strategies. In Dresher, M., Tucker, A. W., and Wolfe, P., editors, *Contributions to the Theory of Games*, volume 3, pages 147–157. Princeton University Press. (Cited on page 9.)

Rassenti, S. J., Smith, V. L., and Bulfin, R. L. (1982). A combinatorial auction mechanism for airport time slot allocation. *Bell Journal of Economics*, 13(2):402–417. (Cited on page 110.)

Rochet, J. C. (1987). A necessary and sufficient condition for rationalizability in a quasi-linear context. *Journal of Mathematical Economics*, 16(2):191–200. (Cited on page 93.)

Rosen, A., Segev, G., and Shahaf, I. (2016). Can PPAD hardness be based on standard cryptographic assumptions? Working paper. (Cited on page 295.)

Rosenthal, R. W. (1973). A class of games possessing pure-strategy Nash equilibria. *International Journal of Game Theory*, 2(1):65–67. (Cited on pages 169 and 183.)

Roth, A. E. (1982a). The economics of matching: Stability and incentives. *Mathematics of Operations Research*, 7(4):617–628. (Cited on page 143.)

Roth, A. E. (1982b). Incentive compatibility in a market with indivisible goods. *Economics Letters*, 9(2):127–132. (Cited on page 124.)

Roth, A. E. (1984). The evolution of the labor market for medical interns and residents: A case study in game theory. *Journal of Political Economy*, 92(6):991–1016. (Cited on page 143.)

Roth, A. E. and Peranson, E. (1999). The redesign of the matching market for American physicians: Some engineering aspects of economic design. *American Economic Review*, 89(4):748–780. (Cited on page 143.)

Roth, A. E. and Postlewaite, A. (1977). Weak versus strong domination in a market with indivisible goods. *Journal of Mathematical Economics*, 4(2):131–137. (Cited on page 124.)

Roth, A. E., Sönmez, T., and Ünver, M. U. (2004). Kidney exchange. *Quarterly Journal of Economics*, 119(2):457–488. (Cited on page 142.)

Roth, A. E., Sönmez, T., and Ünver, M. U. (2005). Pairwise kidney exchange. *Journal of Economic Theory*, 125(2):151–188. (Cited on page 143.)

Roth, A. E., Sönmez, T., and Ünver, M. U. (2007). Efficient kidney exchange: Coincidence of wants in markets with compatibility-based preferences. *American Economic Review*, 97(3):828–851. (Cited on page 143.)

Rothkopf, M., Teisberg, T., and Kahn, E. (1990). Why are Vickrey auctions rare? *Journal of Political Economy*, 98(1):94–109. (Cited on page 93.)

Roughgarden, T. (2003). The price of anarchy is independent of the network topology. *Journal of Computer and System Sciences*, 67(2):341–364. (Cited on page 156.)

Roughgarden, T. (2005). *Selfish Routing and the Price of Anarchy*. MIT Press. (Cited on page 156.)

Roughgarden, T. (2006). On the severity of Braess's Paradox: Designing networks for selfish users is hard. *Journal of Computer and System Sciences*, 72(5):922–953. (Cited on pages 9 and 156.)

Roughgarden, T. (2010a). Algorithmic game theory. *Communications of the ACM*, 53(7):78–86. (Cited on page 169.)

Roughgarden, T. (2010b). Computing equilibria: A computational complexity perspective. *Economic Theory*, 42(1):193–236. (Cited on pages 276 and 294.)

Roughgarden, T. (2015). Intrinsic robustness of the price of anarchy. *Journal of the ACM*, 62(5):32. (Cited on pages 169, 199, and 227.)

Roughgarden, T. and Schoppmann, F. (2015). Local smoothness and the price of anarchy in splittable congestion games. *Journal of Economic Theory*, 156:317–342. (Cited on page 169.)

Roughgarden, T. and Sundararajan, M. (2007). Is efficiency expensive? In *Proceedings of the 3rd Workshop on Sponsored Search*. (Cited on page 83.)

Roughgarden, T., Syrgkanis, V., and Tardos, É.. (2016). The price of anarchy in auctions. Working paper. (Cited on page 199.)

Roughgarden, T. and Tardos, É. (2002). How bad is selfish routing? *Journal of the ACM*, 49(2):236–259. (Cited on pages 156 and 169.)

Rubinstein, A. (2016). Settling the complexity of computing approximate two-player Nash equilibria. Working paper. (Cited on page 295.)

Sack, K. (2012). 60 lives, 30 kidneys, all linked. *New York Times*. February 18. (Cited on page 143.)

Samuel-Cahn, E. (1984). Comparison of threshold stop rules and maximum for independent nonnegative random variables. *Annals of Probability*, 12(4):1213–1216. (Cited on page 83.)

Schäffer, A. A. and Yannakakis, M. (1991). Simple local search problems that are hard to solve. *SIAM Journal on Computing*, 20(1):56–87. (Cited on page 277.)

Shapley, L. and Scarf, H. (1974). On cores and indivisibility. *Journal of Mathematical Economics*, 1(1):23–37. (Cited on page 124.)

Shapley, L. S. and Shubik, M. (1971). The assignment game I: The core. *International Journal of Game Theory*, 1(1):111–130. (Cited on page 110.)

Sheffi, Y. (1985). *Urban Transportation Networks: Equilibrium Analysis with Mathematical Programming Methods.* Prentice-Hall. (Cited on page 156.)

Shoham, Y. and Leyton-Brown, K. (2009). *Multiagent Systems: Algorithmic, Game-Theoretic, and Logical Foundations.* Cambridge University Press. (Cited on page xi.)

Skopalik, A. and Vöcking, B. (2008). Inapproximability of pure Nash equilibria. In *Proceedings of the 39th Annual ACM Symposium on Theory of Computing (STOC)*, pages 355–364. (Cited on pages 227 and 277.)

Smith, A. (1776). *An Inquiry into the Nature and Causes of the Wealth of Nations.* Methuen. (Cited on page 9.)

Sperner, E. (1928). Neuer Beweis für die Invarianz der Dimensionszahl und des Gebietes. *Abhandlungen aus dem Mathematischen Seminar der Universität Hamburg*, 6(1):265–272. (Cited on page 295.)

Varian, H. R. (2007). Position auctions. *International Journal of Industrial Organization*, 25(6):1163–1178. (Cited on pages 20 and 35.)

Vazirani, V. V. (2001). *Approximation Algorithms.* Springer. (Cited on page 50.)

Vetta, A. (2002). Nash equilibria in competitive societies, with applications to facility location, traffic routing and auctions. In *Proceedings of the 43rd Annual Symposium on Foundations of Computer Science (FOCS)*, pages 416–425. (Cited on page 199.)

Vickrey, W. (1961). Counterspeculation, auctions, and competitive sealed tenders. *Journal of Finance*, 16(1):8–37. (Cited on pages 20, 70, and 93.)

Ville, J. (1938). Sur la theorie générale des jeux ou intervient l'habileté des joueurs. Fascicule 2 in Volume 4 of É. Borel, *Traité du Calcul des probabilités et de ses applications*, pages 105–113. Gauthier-Villars. (Cited on page 258.)

Vohra, R. V. (2011). *Mechanism Design: A Linear Programming Approach.* Cambridge University Press. (Cited on page 93.)

Vojnović, M. (2016). *Contest Theory.* Cambridge University Press. (Cited on page xi.)

von Neumann, J. (1928). Zur Theorie der Gesellschaftsspiele. *Mathematische Annalen*, 100:295–320. (Cited on page 258.)

von Neumann, J. and Morgenstern, O. (1944). *Theory of Games and Economic Behavior.* Princeton University Press. (Cited on page 258.)

von Stengel, B. (2002). Computing equilibria for two-person games. In Aumann, R. J. and Hart, S., editors, *Handbook of Game Theory with Economic Applications*, volume 3, chapter 45, pages 1723–1759. North-Holland. (Cited on page 295.)

Voorneveld, M., Borm, P., van Megen, F., Tijs, S., and Facchini, G. (1999). Congestion games and potentials reconsidered. *International Game Theory Review*, 1(3–4):283–299. (Cited on page 183.)

Wardrop, J. G. (1952). Some theoretical aspects of road traffic research. In *Proceedings of the Institute of Civil Engineers, Pt. II*, volume 1, pages 325–378. (Cited on page 156.)

Williamson, D. P. and Shmoys, D. B. (2010). *The Design of Approximation Algorithms.* Cambridge University Press. (Cited on page 50.)

Index

Printed in the United States
by Bookmasters

Printed in the United States
By Bookmasters